WITHDRAWN

M000221063

722

Download Forms on Nolo.com

You can download the forms in this book at:

 www.nolo.com/back-of-book/LBEV.html

We'll also post updates whenever there's an important change to the law affecting this book—as well as articles and other related materials.

More Resources
from Nolo.com

Legal Forms, Books, & Software

Hundreds of do-it-yourself products—all written in plain English, approved, and updated by our in-house legal editors.

Legal Articles

Get informed with thousands of free articles on everyday legal topics. Our articles are accurate, up to date, and reader friendly.

Find a Lawyer

Want to talk to a lawyer? Use Nolo to find a lawyer who can help you with your case.

NOLO
LAW for ALL

19th Edition

The California Landlord's Law Book:
Evictions

Attorney Nils Rosenquest

NINETEENTH EDITION	JUNE 2022
Editor	JANET PORTMAN
Cover & Book Design	SUSAN PUTNEY
Proofreading	SUSAN CARLSON GREENE
Index	THÉRÈSE SHERE
Printing	SHERIDAN

ISSN: 2163-0291 (print)

ISSN: 2326-0173 (online)

ISBN: 978-1-4133-2866-0 (pbk)

ISBN: 978-1-4133-2867-7 (ebook)

This book covers only United States law, unless it specifically states otherwise.

Please note

Plain-English legal information can help you solve many of your own legal problems. But this text is not a substitute for personalized advice from a knowledgeable lawyer. If you want the help of a trained professional—and we'll always point out situations in which we think that's a good idea—consult an attorney licensed to practice in your state.

About the Author

Attorney Nils Rosenquest (www.rosenquest.com) has practiced housing, landlord-tenant, real estate, and business law for more than 35 years on behalf of individual landlords and tenants, small businesses, and community organizations. A graduate of Dartmouth College and UC Hastings College of the Law, Rosenquest has been involved in San Francisco's legal "housing wars" from the inception of rent control through its many revisions. He has tried landlord-tenant and related cases in counties throughout Northern California, including the United States District Court and the United States Bankruptcy Court. He also serves as a neutral mediator in real estate and landlord-tenant matters. AV rated by Martindale-Hubbell, he practices in all state and federal courts in California as well as the Ninth Circuit United States Court of Appeals. He is also admitted to the United States Court of Claims and the United States Tax Court. In addition to helping private individuals and companies in housing and real estate matters, he represents nonprofit subsidized housing developers and nonprofit live-work communities. Apart from practicing law, he serves on the board of directors for a San Francisco community development organization, volunteers at the San Francisco Superior Court in two departments, and teaches legal continuing education classes from time to time.

Table of Contents

Appendix

Index

The California Landlord's Evictions Companion

Sometimes even the most sincere and professional attempts at conscientious landlording fail, and you have to consider evicting a tenant. This do-it-yourself eviction manual for California landlords shows you, step by step, how to file and conduct an uncontested eviction lawsuit against a residential tenant. It includes all the forms you need, along with clear instructions, on how to prepare a three-day notice for tenants who are late with rent and other types of notices, and how to file the necessary forms in court to win possession of your rental property (and a court judgment for unpaid rent or other money the tenant owes you).

This book also explains what's involved when the tenant contests the eviction, including advice on how to settle (and when it makes sense to do so), the different legal challenges a tenant may make to your eviction lawsuit (and how to respond), and how to collect a money judgment if you win your eviction case. It also includes useful advice on how to deal with evicting a tenant who has filed for bankruptcy, or tenants (but not prior owners) who are occupying property you have purchased at a foreclosure sale.

The goal of this book is to take you step by step through the whole eviction process. Most of the tasks you can do yourself, but we are quick to point out situations when an attorney's help will be useful or necessary.

COVID-19

In March, 2020, COVID-19 spread widely in California. The pandemic temporarily changed many rules—shutting down the court system and suspending nearly all evictions and civil actions in California. Local governments, public health orders, and the state legislature provided different versions of rent relief, and they changed the time limits for payment of rent, the means to enforce payment, just cause to terminate leases, and even the rules to enforce rental agreements.

As we go to press, many of these laws continue to affect rent payments, enforceability of rent and rental debt, and evictions.

In this book, we attempt to flag the changed laws that are in effect as of our publication date. However, particularly with respect to evictions, the laws are in flux and change remains the order of the day in many communities. If the state or municipalities extend those temporary rules or provide new procedures, we will explain the changes on this book's companion page on Nolo.com to keep you up to date (see "Get Updates, Forms, and More at This Book's Companion Page on Nolo.com," below).

Who Should Not Use This Book

Do not use this book, or its forms, if you want to evict a hotel guest, or if any of the following scenarios describes your situation.

You want to evict a tenant in a mobile home. Different rules often apply. Read the California Department of Housing and Community Development publication, *2017 Mobilehome Residency Law*, for details on applicable rules and exceptions when normal eviction procedures must be used. (To access a downloadable PDF file for this brochure, go to the department website at www.hcd.ca.gov and type the publication name, as just noted, in the search box on the home page.)

You have bought the property at a foreclosure sale and need to evict the former owner, who has not moved out. If you now want to get rid of the former owner-occupant, you must use a special unlawful detainer complaint, unlike the forms contained in this book. You'll need to see a lawyer. (If you have purchased occupied rental property at a foreclosure sale and have inherited tenants, see Chapter 11, "Eviction of Tenants in Rental Property Purchased at Foreclosure," for advice on this situation.)

The California Landlord's Law Book: Rights & Responsibilities
—Another Useful Guide for California Landlords

This book is a companion volume to Nolo's *The California Landlord's Law Book: Rights & Responsibilities*, by Nils Rosenquest and Janet Portman. *Rights & Responsibilities* discusses the legal rules of renting residential real property, with an eye toward avoiding legal problems and fostering good tenant relations. It provides crucial information on the substance of landlord-tenant law that you almost certainly will need to know to defend yourself if the tenant contests your unlawful detainer lawsuit, including:

- issues relevant to preparing and serving a Three-Day Notice for Nonpayment of Rent (covered in Chapter 2 of this book), including how to deduct amounts, such as late fees or the cost of repairing damage, from the security deposit; how to change the rent due date; and how to account for "last month's rent"

- detailed information on antidiscrimination and illegal retaliation rules and tenant rights (such as reasonable notice of entry to make repairs), which you'll need to know when evicting a tenant with a 30- or 60-day notice (topic of Chapter 3)
- how leases and rental agreements end (relevant to Chapter 5),
- statewide and local eviction just cause limitations on termination of tenancies, and
- legal and illegal lease clauses; the differences among cotenants, subtenants, and assignees; notice requirements for increasing rent; the landlord's responsibility to provide safe housing; what you can legally do with a tenant's abandoned property; and many more crucially important areas of landlord-tenant law.

You own commercial property and want to evict a tenant for nonpayment of rent or other lease violations. Commercial landlords should not use this book. Here's why:

- Many commercial leases require tenants to pay for common-area maintenance, prorated property taxes, and utility charges, in addition to a set monthly sum. Because the exact rent amount is often not clear, a special termination notice (not supplied in this book) should be used.
- Many commercial leases provide for special types of notice periods and ways to serve notices, which are different from the ones specified in this book.
- Because commercial leases often run for five or ten years, and may have options

to renew, they can be quite valuable to tenants. Commercial tenants are much more likely than residential tenants to contest an eviction—and judges are less likely to order an eviction for minor lease violations.

In short, with all these possible complications, we suggest seeing an attorney to handle an eviction of a commercial tenant. To find a lawyer experienced in landlord-tenant law in your area, check out Nolo's "Find a Lawyer" directory at www.nolo.com. (Also see "Attorneys and Eviction Services" in Chapter 1 for more on the subject.)

We will also update the rent control chart with important changes or additions (we don't include temporary measures or ordinances, however). You can get to the live version of the chart from the companion page, at the URL noted above.

Evictions in California: An Overview

This book covers all the rules, procedures, and forms you need to evict a tenant in California, in most cases. Before getting into the details, it's important to have a clear road map of the eviction process. That's the purpose of this chapter.

The Landlord's Role in Evictions

Strictly speaking, the word "evict" refers to the process of a sheriff or marshal ordering a tenant to get out or be forcibly removed. It is illegal for you to try to physically evict a tenant yourself. The sheriff or marshal will only evict a tenant pursuant to a court order known in California as an "unlawful detainer judgment." To get such a judgment, you must bring an eviction lawsuit, called an "unlawful detainer action," against the tenant.

The linchpin of an unlawful detainer suit is proper termination of the tenancy; you can't get a judgment without it. This usually means giving your tenant adequate written notice, in a specified way. The law sets out very detailed requirements for a landlord who wants to end a tenancy. If you don't meet them exactly, you will lose your suit even if your tenant has bounced rent checks repeatedly, violated the lease, or disturbed the neighbors.

Eviction Forms and Procedures

There are specific forms and procedures for each step of the eviction process, including:

- termination forms for ending a tenancy, such as a Three-Day Notice to Pay Rent or Quit, or a notice to cure another type of breach or quit (the exact form and procedures vary depending on the reason for the termination), or a notice to terminate for nuisance
- unlawful detainer forms for filing an eviction lawsuit, such as a summons and a complaint (the documents that actually initiate your lawsuit)

- forms for taking a default judgment in an uncontested eviction, such as a Request for Entry of Default and Writ of Possession (paperwork sent to the court that asks for possession of the property and for money the tenant owes you)
- forms for contested evictions, such as a Request/Counter-Request to Set Case for Trial and a Stipulation for Entry of Judgment, both used when a tenant has filed a response to your unlawful detainer complaint
- forms for obtaining your money judgment, such as a Declaration in Support of Default Judgment, and the judgment, and
- forms for collecting your money judgment, such as the Writ of Execution; and related forms, such as Application for Earnings Withholding Order (wage garnishment).

This book includes over 30 forms. We clearly explain which forms you need for different situations, and how and when to prepare and serve each form. At the start of each chapter, we've included a checklist of the different steps, timelines, and forms you need to prepare for a particular type of eviction, whether for nonpayment of rent or violation of a lease term. And we provide details on how rent control rules enter the mix.

It might seem overwhelming, but keep in mind that most landlords will primarily be concerned with evicting a tenant for nonpayment of rent, and that in many situations, the tenant will leave without contesting the eviction. In these cases, you might only need a few of the forms included here. But we've got you covered when it comes to a tenant's contesting a termination or filing for bankruptcy.

Types of Forms in This Book

This book includes both official California court forms, published by the Judicial Council, and Nolo forms prepared by this book's attorney author. We also include a few official forms that are specific to evictions in Los Angeles,

San Francisco, Palo Alto, and Oakland. All the 30-plus forms in this book are legally accurate as of the date this book went to press (early 2022).

We've provided downloadable versions of all forms on the Nolo website (see the appendix for advice on accessing the forms and the link to this book's companion page on the Nolo site). In addition to being available on the Nolo website, current Judicial Council forms are available for free at www.courts.ca.gov/forms.htm.

To find a specific Judicial Council form on the Council website, click the category you wish to use, such as "Eviction," then click the form or forms you wish to use. The Judicial Council forms will have the words Judicial Council of California in the bottom left, the effective date of the form, and a statement on whether the form is mandatory or optional. It will also have a form number in the upper right; for example, the Judgment—Unlawful Detainer is Judicial Council Form UD-110. Always use the most current form.

How to Fill in the Forms in This Book

We provide detailed instructions on how to fill in each form in the relevant chapters. Also, the appendix explains how to download the forms from the Nolo website. In addition, if you download a form from the Judicial Council site, you'll find useful information there on filling out one of the official court forms (see www.courts.ca.gov/selfhelp-howtofill.htm).

Many of you will prefer to download the relevant forms and complete them online, then print them. If you're old fashioned and prefer to use a typewriter, you may type in the required information on any of the forms in this book. Courts are also required to accept forms that are filled in by hand.

The Importance of Attention to Detail

Because an eviction judgment means tenants won't have a roof over their heads (and their families' heads), judges are very demanding of the landlord.

The forms must be filled in just right and delivered ("served") on the tenant properly, and you must adhere to strict timelines. When landlords don't follow these rules, they often find themselves out of court and having to start over.

In addition, new state and local laws go beyond the basic law that permitted termination of periodic tenancies at the will of the landlord, and now require the landlord to show a "just cause" for eviction. Nonpayment of rent remains a straightforward ground for eviction (with some modifications from COVID relief), but there are few others as clear.

Why do we emphasize the negatives of evicting a tenant? Because we want you to understand at the outset that even if you properly bring and conduct an unlawful detainer action, you are not assured of winning and having the tenant evicted if the tenant decides to file a defense. In other words, despite the merits of your position, you may face a judge who will hold you to every technicality and bend over backwards to sustain the tenant's position. A tenant can raise many substantive, as well as procedural, objections to an unlawful detainer suit. Essentially, any breach by you of any duty imposed on landlords by state or local law can be used by your tenant as a defense to your action.

Paying the Tenant to Leave May Be Cheaper Than Doing an Eviction

Before you proceed with an unlawful detainer lawsuit, consider that paying the tenant a few hundred dollars to leave right away might be cheaper in the long run. Even if you win in court, the time you spend in litigation usually approximates more lost rent.

For example, paying a tenant $750 or more to leave right away (with payment made only as the tenant leaves and hands you the keys) will be cheaper than spending several hundred dollars to file suit and going without rent for four to nine weeks while the tenant contests the lawsuit and stays.

Unless you thoroughly know your legal rights and duties as a landlord before you go to court, and unless you dot every "i" and cross every "t," you may end up on the losing side of an eviction. Our advice: Especially if the tenant contests your lawsuit, be meticulous in your preparation.

Landlords in a Squeeze Play

As if the procedural rules weren't difficult enough to understand and apply, the big-picture rules on evictions have changed to favor tenants. New state and local laws go beyond the basic law that used to permit terminating periodic tenancies at the will of the landlord. Now you must have a "just cause" for eviction. Nonpayment of rent remains a straightforward ground for eviction (with some modifications from COVID relief), but there are few others as clear.

TIP

Note of sanity. Between 80% and 90% of all unlawful detainer actions are won by landlords. Either the tenants fail to contest them, or they lack a real defense but need time to move. So the odds favor relatively smooth sailing in your unlawful detainer action.

Proceed With Caution When Evicting a Tenant

The moment relations between you and one of your tenants begins to sour, you will be wise to remember a cardinal truth. Any activity by you that might be construed by your tenants as illegal, threatening, humiliating, abusive, or invasive of their privacy can give rise to a lawsuit against you

for big bucks. So, although the unlawful detainer procedure can be tedious, it's important to understand that it is the only game in town.

Shortcuts such as threats, intimidation, utility shutoffs, or attempts to physically remove a tenant, are illegal and dangerous. If you resort to them, you may well find yourself on the wrong end of a lawsuit for such personal injuries as trespass, assault, battery, slander and libel, intentional infliction of emotional distress, harassment, and wrongful eviction—or even criminal charges.

To avoid liability, we recommend that you do the following:

- Avoid all unnecessary one-on-one personal contact with the tenant during the eviction process unless it occurs in a structured setting.
- Keep your written communications to the point and as neutral as you can, even if you are boiling inside. Remember, any manifestations of anger on your part can come back to haunt you legally somewhere down the line.
- Treat tenants like they have a right to remain on the premises, even though that is not your position.

Until the day the sheriff or marshal shows up with a writ of possession, the tenants' home is legally their castle, and you may come to regret any actions on your part that don't recognize that fact.

How This Book Will Help You Do an Eviction

Here's an overview of how this book is organized and what you need to know each step of the way. The whole eviction process typically takes from two to three months (although the COVID pandemic has extended those times in many counties).

Legal Grounds for Eviction

Chapters 2 through 5 explain the legal grounds for eviction under the following circumstances:

- The tenant has failed to leave or pay the rent due within three days of having received from you a written Three-Day Notice to Pay Rent or Quit (Chapter 2).
- A month-to-month tenant has failed to leave within the time allowed after having received from you a written notice giving 30 days, or 60 days if the tenant rented for a year or more, or 90 days (certain government-subsidized tenancies). (Chapter 3.)
- The tenant has failed to leave or to comply with a provision of your lease or rental agreement within three days after having received your written three-day notice to correct the violation or quit (Chapter 4).
- The tenant has sublet the property contrary to the lease or rental agreement (which specifies that a breach is grounds for termination), has caused or allowed a nuisance or serious damage to the property, or has used the property for an illegal purpose, and has failed to leave within three days of having received from you an unconditional three-day notice to vacate (Chapter 4).
- A tenant whose fixed-term lease has expired and has not been renewed has failed to leave (Chapter 5).
- A month-to-month tenant has failed to leave within the stated time after having given *you* a written 30-day or 60-day notice terminating the tenancy (Chapter 5).

Court Procedures for Evictions

After the tenancy is terminated (in almost all cases, by a three-day or other notice), most of the procedures in unlawful detainer lawsuits are the same no matter which reason your suit is based on. Thus, after you read either Chapter 2, 3, 4, or 5, depending on the way you're terminating the tenancy, go next to the chapters that explain the court procedures. These begin with Chapter 6 on filing a complaint to begin your unlawful detainer lawsuit.

If Your Tenant Doesn't Contest the Eviction

If your tenant doesn't contest the lawsuit within five days after being served with a copy of your complaint, you will go next to Chapter 7 on getting an eviction judgment by default.

If Your Tenant Contests the Eviction

If the tenant does contest your unlawful detainer suit, you will proceed directly to Chapter 8, which tells you how to handle contested actions and when the services of a lawyer are advisable.

Bankruptcy and Foreclosure Issues

Chapter 10 discusses your option when a tenant files for bankruptcy, and Chapter 11 covers eviction of tenants in rental property you purchased at a foreclosure sale.

Collecting a Money Judgment and COVID Debt

Chapter 9, on collecting your money judgment, will be your last stop after you win the lawsuit or you need to collect "COVID debt" (rent that came due between March 2020 and September 2021).

If you live in a city with a rent control ordinance, you will be referred to the "Tenant Protections Chart for California," on Nolo.com, for more detailed information on your locality's ordinance.

rent or quit (after checking the current Los Angeles rent control ordinance to see if there are any special requirements you should know about).

Roy neither pays the rent nor moves in three days. You then turn to Chapter 6, which tells you how to begin an unlawful detainer suit by filing a complaint with the court and serving a copy of the complaint and a summons on the tenant. You are entitled to a default judgment when the other side does not do the things necessary to contest a case. Roy does not respond to your complaint in five court days, and Chapter 6 steers you to Chapter 7 on how to get a default judgment. After you successfully use Chapter 7 to take default judgments both for possession of the premises and the money Roy owes you, your final step is to turn to Chapter 9 for advice on how to collect the money.

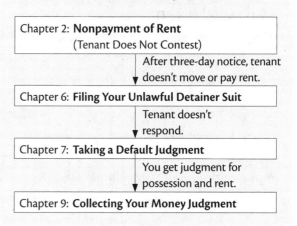

Eviction for Nonpayment

Chapter 2: **Nonpayment of Rent** (Tenant Does Not Contest)

After three-day notice, tenant doesn't move or pay rent.

Chapter 6: **Filing Your Unlawful Detainer Suit**

Tenant doesn't respond.

Chapter 7: **Taking a Default Judgment**

You get judgment for possession and rent.

Chapter 9: **Collecting Your Money Judgment**

Here are two examples of common pathways through this book:

EXAMPLE 1: A tenant in your Los Angeles apartment building, Roy, doesn't pay the rent when it's due on the first of the month. A few days pass, and you decide he's probably never going to pay it. You turn to Chapter 2 on nonpayment of rent. Following the instructions, you serve Roy with a three-day notice to pay

EXAMPLE 2: You decide that you want to move a new tenant into the house you rent out in Sacramento. The current tenant, Maria, occupies the house under a month-to-month rental agreement. She pays her rent on time, and you've never had any serious problems with her, but you would rather have your friend Jim live there. You turn to Chapter 3 and follow the instructions to prepare and serve a notice terminating Maria's tenancy—a 60-day notice because she's lived there more than a year. Maria doesn't leave after her 60 days are up, so you go to Chapter 6 for instructions on how to file your unlawful detainer suit. After you serve her with the summons and complaint, Maria files a written response with the court. You then go to Chapter 8 to read about contested lawsuits.

Eviction With 30-Day or 60-Day Notice (Tenant Contests)

Chapter 3: **Terminating a Tenancy With a 30-Day or 60-Day Notice**

↓ After notice, tenant doesn't move.

Chapter 6: **Filing Your Unlawful Detainer Suit**

↓ Tenant doesn't move.

Chapter 8: **Contested Cases**

Statewide Rent Control: The Tenant Protection Act of 2019

Starting in 2020, some form of eviction or rent control governed most residential tenancies of one year or more. The Tenant Protection Act of 2019 ("TPA") extended a rent "cap" (which affects rent increases but not initial base rents) and eviction control to the entire state where rent control did not already exist. In 2019, about 47 cities and counties had some form of strict rent control and eviction protection.

Local strict rent control laws already on the books remained unaffected by the new legislation, and tenants covered by those existing laws will generally enjoy greater protections than the new state law provides. The law is written so that when a local ordinance also applies, the landlord must follow the rule that gives the most protection to the tenant.

For the purpose of evictions, Civil Code Section 1946.2 implements "just cause" limitations. They prohibit termination of a tenant who has lived in the unit for at least 12 months unless the landlord has a "just cause." The just causes include both tenant at-fault behavior (such as repeated late rent) and no-fault reasons (like owner move-ins).

Some properties and landlords are exempt from just cause restrictions. These are:

- Owner-occupied single family dwellings, subject to some limitations described below.
- A duplex in which the owner occupies one of the units as the owner's principal place of residence, from the beginning of the tenancy.
- Tenancies where none of the tenants have resided in the unit for twelve months or more. (The law does not provide any tenant protection for short-term occupancies of less than one year).
- Units that are "separately alienable from title" (that's a standalone property that can be sold on its own), but only if the owner is an individual and not a corporation or Real Estate Investment Trust (REIT).
- Owner-occupied shared housing with common bathroom or kitchen facilities for use by the tenants; or owner-occupied properties with no more than two in-law units.

Just Cause Termination Protections

Civil Code Section 1946.2 limits the reasons for terminating tenancies where all tenants have occupied the unit continuously for 12 months. When the tenants have changed over time, just cause protections attach when at least one of the tenants has occupied the unit for 24 months or more.

The main "at fault" causes do not differ from the termination reasons set out in the standard lease in Nolo's books. Tenants must still pay the

Rent Regulation in California

The following cities and counties have some form of rent regulation, which can include rent control, just cause eviction protection, required mediation following a rent increase, or some other form of regulation. Check the full Tenant Protections Chart for California on Nolo.com for specifics.

City or County	Rent Control	Just Cause Eviction Protection	Mediation/ Arbitration	Other
Alameda	X	X		2
Alameda County		X	X	
Berkeley	X	X		1, 4, 5
Beverly Hills	X	X		4
Burbank		X		4
Camarillo			X	
Campbell			X	
City of Commerce	X	X		
Concord			X	
East Palo Alto	X	X		5
Emeryville		X		4
Fremont			X	
Fresno			X	3
Gardena			X	4
Glendale		X		4
Hayward	X	X		
Los Angeles	X	X		4
Los Angeles (county)	X	X		4
Los Gatos			X	
Marin County		X	X	5
Maywood		X		4
Menlo Park				2
Mountain View	X	X		4
Oakland	X	X		1, 4
Palm Springs	X	X		
Palo Alto			X	2, 4
Pasadena				4
Redwood City				2, 4
Richmond	X	X		4
San Diego		X		5
San Francisco	X	X	X	1, 3, 4, 5
San Jose	X	X		1, 2, 4
San Leandro			X	
Santa Ana	X	X		4
Santa Barbara			X	4
Santa Cruz		X		4
Santa Monica	X	X		1, 4, 5
Thousand Oaks	X	X		
Union City			X	
West Hollywood	X	X		4
Westlake Village	X			

[1] Buyout agreement regulations   [3] Paid legal representation for tenants   [5] Source of income discrimination prohibited
[2] Required minimum lease term   [4] Relocation fee in certain circumstances

rent, uphold their obligations under the lease, and not cause problems for the landlord or neighbors.

The causes listed in the new law include:

- nonpayment of rent
- an uncured or incurable material breach of the lease after a written notice to correct the breach
- maintaining or committing a nuisance or waste
- criminal activity on the property or threats of harm to the landlord or agents
- assigning or subletting in violation of the lease
- refusal to allow a lawful entry under Civil Code § 1954
- failing to move out after giving the landlord a notice to terminate under C.C.P. § 1161
- using the unit for an unlawful purpose (illegal activity like drug dealing, or zoning code violations like operating a non-permitted business)
- for resident managers and maintenance or cleaning staff, failing to move out after the landlord has terminated the tenant's employment, agency, or license, and
- refusing to sign a new lease that is similar to the old lease.

Landlords can also terminate the lease for certain "no-fault" reasons (when the tenant has done nothing wrong), but must compensate the tenant for relocation expenses equal to one month's rent. No–fault termination causes include:

- an owner's or relative's intent to occupy the unit, provided that the lease contains a notice of that possibility
- the landlord's planned withdrawal of the unit from the rental market
- notice from the government to vacate based on the need to address a violation of health or safety or other codes; or any other court or administrative order that requires vacating the unit, and

- the planned demolition or substantial remodeling of the unit (substantial remodeling does not include cosmetic upgrades).

The TPA also affects notice requirements. Any termination notice must include a statement of the cause that forms the basis for termination, as well as the tenant's rights to relocation assistance.

For an in-depth analysis of the TPA, see *The California Landlord's Law Book: Rights and Responsibilities*, Chapter 4.

Evictions in Cities with Rent Control and Others

In addition to the TPA, local ordinances in many California cities address evictions—specifying under what circumstances you may proceed, and how to proceed. Most of these cities also have rent control ordinances, but not all, as you'll see below.

Cities With Rent Control

Local rent control laws affect evictions in two important ways: First, many (but not all) rent control ordinances and regulations impose important restrictions or additional procedural requirements on evictions. For example, the ordinances of many cities require a landlord to have a "just cause" (good reason) to evict a tenant, even for rental units that are exempt from rent control. Local ordinances commonly require tenancy termination notices and complaints to contain statements not required by state law.

Second, any violation of any provision of a rent control law might provide a tenant with a defense to your eviction lawsuit. Even a failure to register your rental units with the local rent board, if that is required under the ordinance, might provide a tenant with a successful defense against an eviction suit. As noted in the Companion section earlier, check the chart, Tenant Protections Chart for California, to see the requirements that state law or each rent control city imposes on eviction lawsuits—such as any applicable registration requirements or extra information required in three-day or other termination notices or in the eviction complaint itself.

In most cases, you can edit the forms in our book to comply with your rent control ordinance requirement for extra information, but if you have any questions, consult with an attorney experienced in rent control in your community.

No two cities' rent control ordinances are identical. Within the space of one book, we can write instructions and forms for use only by the majority of California landlords. We cannot include additional sets that are tailor-made for use in all of the cities that have rent regulations and impose additional requirements when it comes to filling out forms.

Your rent control ordinance might affect almost every step in your eviction proceeding. If you do not conform your notices and court filings to your ordinance's requirements, it's very likely that your case will be tossed out or lost, perhaps after you've spent considerable time and effort.

We cannot say this strongly enough: **Read your rent control ordinance before you begin an unlawful detainer proceeding and before you use any of the forms in this book.** Most rent control authorities maintain a web page with descriptions of the law, forms, and other information. You should always check the websites for the rent control authority in your area and look for updates. Yesterday's rules become yesterday's news very quickly; and cities without just cause can impose these requirements with very little notice or fanfare.

Just Cause Protection Without Rent Control

Three cities without rent control—San Diego, Glendale, and Maywood—also restrict evictions. During the pandemic, additional cities created emergency measures to restrict evictions. These cities' rules do not affect the procedure for evicting with a three-day notice based on nonpayment of non-COVID classified rent or another breach, or commission of waste or nuisance. They do affect evictions based on 30-day or 60-day terminations of month-to-month tenancies. (See "Checklist for 30- or 60-Day Notice Eviction" in Chapter 3.)

Reading Your Rent Control Ordinance

The rent control chart that you can access via a link on this book's companion page (www.nolo.com/back-of-book/LBEV.html) summarizes the major features of California's local rent control laws. We recommend you check an ordinance itself and always make sure it hasn't changed since this chart was printed. Here are a few hints about reading and understanding rent control ordinances.

Almost all rent control ordinances begin with a statement of purpose, followed by definitions of terms used in them. If such terms as "rental unit" and "landlord" aren't defined specifically enough to tell you who and what is covered by the ordinance, another section dealing with applicability of the ordinance usually follows. After that, the ordinance usually sets out the structure and rules of the rent board and will say whether landlords must register their properties with the board. Your ordinance probably then has a section entitled something like "Annual Increases" or "General Rent Ceiling."

Following the rent sections should be a section on "Individual Adjustments" or "Hardship Adjustments," which tells landlords how to get an increase over and above any general across-the-board increase. Finally, any requirement that landlords show "just cause" for eviction should be found under a section entitled "Just (or Good) Cause for Eviction." It will contain a list of the permissible reasons for eviction, along with any extra requirements for eviction notices.

Before beginning an eviction, be sure you have complied with your rent control ordinance. Check for:

- **Registration requirements.** If the landlord is required to register the unit with the rent board but didn't, you may be able to win an eviction lawsuit.
- **Rent increase restrictions.** Read the individual adjustments section to see if the landlord must apply to the rent board for increases over a certain amount. If so, make sure any rent increases were properly applied for and legal.
- **Special notice requirements.** Check both the general and individual rent adjustment sections, as well as any regulations adopted by the rent board, for special notice requirements for rent increase notices.
- **Just cause requirements.** This is crucial; if applicable, a landlord can evict only for one of the permissible reasons, and must comply with any additional notice requirements. If a landlord wants to evict tenants in order to demolish the building or simply go out of business, the landlord may do so under the Ellis Act (Gov't. Code §§ 7060–7060.7), even if this reason isn't listed in the ordinance.

CAUTION

The rules might change due to declared states of emergency or the enactment of temporary measures.

- **Declared states of emergency.** In response to a disaster, the Governor or local officials can declare a state of emergency, prohibiting price gouging on basic goods and services—including rent.
- **Temporary ordinances.** Cities and counties may enact temporary ordinances that expire unless later made permanent. Our chart does not include temporary ordinances. To check for temporary ordinances, contact your city or county.

A Reason for Which You Must Evict: Drug Dealing

In cases of drug dealing, it's not a question of whether or not it's permissible to evict a tenant—it's imperative to do so. In fact, a landlord who fails to evict a tenant who deals illegal drugs on the property can face lawsuits from other tenants, neighbors, and local authorities. Many landlords have been held liable for tens of thousands of dollars in damages for failing to evict a drug-dealing tenant. A landlord can also face loss of the property.

When it's a month-to-month tenancy, terminate the tenancy with a 30-day notice (or 60-day notice if the tenant has stayed a year or more—see Chapter 3) as soon as you suspect illegal drug activity by the tenant or any members of the tenant's family. (If the tenant has a fixed-term lease, you will have to follow the procedures in Chapter 4.) Evictions for drug dealing may be a little more difficult with "just cause eviction" provisions in the applicable rent control laws; even so, landlords faced with a drug-dealing tenant should do everything they can to evict, and should begin gathering evidence against the drug dealer—including getting tenants and neighbors to keep records of heavy traffic at odd hours in and out of the suspected tenant's home and installing security cameras in common areas.

Evicting Roommates

This book was written with the small property owner in mind, such as an owner of a modest apartment complex or a single-family rental.

However, some of our readers have used this book to evict a roommate.

If you want to use this book to evict a roommate, you must be the original tenant (or the one who has signed a lease or rental agreement with the landlord), and the roommate you want to evict must be your "subtenant." A subtenant is usually someone who is renting part of your place from you and paying rent to you instead of your landlord. In this relationship, you are the "landlord" and your roommate is your "tenant."

A tenant can't evict a roommate if both parties are "cotenants." You are cotenants if you and your roommate both signed the lease or rental agreement, or you each pay rent directly to the landlord.

> EXAMPLE 1: Marlena Mastertenant rents a two-bedroom house from Oscar Owner for $1,600 a month. Marlena rents one of the bedrooms (plus half the common areas such as kitchen, bathroom, and hallways) to Susie Subtenant for $700 a month. Marlena is the tenant and Susie is the subtenant. Marlena can use the procedures in this book to evict Susie if Susie doesn't pay her rent. In the unlawful detainer complaint (see "Preparing the Complaint," Item 4, in Chapter 6), Marlena should list herself as "lessee/sublessor" or "master tenant."

> EXAMPLE 2: Tom Tenant and Tami Tenant (brother and sister) jointly rent a two-bedroom apartment from Louise Landlord. They moved in at the same time and both of them signed the lease. They are both Louise's tenants. Because neither Tom nor Tami are each other's subtenant, they cannot use this book to evict one or the other.

If you have any questions about legal relationships with roommates, see *The California Landlord's Law Book: Rights & Responsibilities*, by Nils Rosenquest and Janet Portman (Nolo).

TIP

The legal relationship between roommates is often unclear. For example, if one tenant moved in first, is the second occupant a subtenant because she negotiated with and rented from the first tenant, or a cotenant because she claims to have a separate verbal understanding with the owner regarding rent? If in doubt, see a lawyer before using this book to evict a roommate you claim is your subtenant.

Evicting a Resident Manager

When you fire resident managers, or when they quit, you will often want them to move out of your property, particularly if they occupy a special manager's unit or if the firing or quitting has generated (or resulted from) ill will. Eviction lawsuits against former managers can be extremely complicated. This is especially true if you have a management agreement that requires good cause for termination of employment or a certain period of notice. Such lawsuits can also be complicated where you have used a single combined management/rental agreement or if local rent control laws impose special requirements. While all rent control cities do allow eviction of fired managers, some cities impose restrictions on it.

This section outlines some of the basic issues involved in evicting a resident manager. We do not, and cannot, provide you complete advice on how to evict a resident manager. In many cases, you will need an experienced attorney who specializes in landlord-tenant law to evict a former manager, particularly if the ex-manager questions whether the firing was legally effective or proper. (See "Attorneys and Eviction Services," below, for more on the subject.)

Separate Management and Rental Agreements

To evict a tenant-manager with whom you signed separate management and month-to-month rental agreements (which allows you to terminate the employment at any time), you will have to give a normal 30-day written termination notice, or a 60-day notice if the tenant-manager stayed for a year or more, subject in either case to any just cause eviction requirements in rent control cities. (See Chapter 3.) If the tenant has a separate fixed-term lease, you cannot terminate the tenancy until the lease expires.

Evicting a Lodger

A lodger, or roomer, is someone who rents a room in a house that you own and live in. The rules for evicting a lodger are covered by California Civil Code § 1946.5 and Penal Code §§ 602.3 and 837 and apply only if you rent to one lodger. In addition, you must have overall control of the dwelling unit and have retained a right of access to areas occupied by the lodger.

If you have two or more lodgers, you must use the unlawful detainer procedures described in this book. The following material applies only if you rent to one lodger.

If your lodger is a month-to-month tenant and you want to terminate the tenancy, you can serve the lodger with a 30-day notice, as explained in Chapter 3. You may also use a shortcut (not available to landlords serving nonlodger tenants) and send the notice by certified or registered mail, restricted delivery, with a return receipt requested.

A lodger who doesn't leave at the end of the notice period is guilty of an infraction. Technically, this entitles you to do a citizen's arrest, which means that you can eject the lodger using reasonable, but not deadly, force. However, we strongly advise against this tactic, and instead suggest calling local law enforcement to handle the situation. Have a copy of your dated termination notice available. Be aware that many local police do not know the procedures for evicting lodgers or might not want to get involved, fearing potential liability for improperly ousting someone who later claims he or she was, in fact, a tenant. The police may insist that you go through the normal unlawful detainer lawsuit process—which will result in a court order authorizing the police or sheriff to evict the lodger. If the lodger has stayed for a year or more and the police won't evict on your 30-day notice, you will have to start all over with a 60-day notice according to a different law, Civ. Code § 1946.1. Check with your chief of police to find out how this issue is handled.

If you need to evict "for cause"—that is, for failing to pay the rent or violation of the rental agreement— you can serve your lodger with a three-day notice, but if the lodger doesn't leave, you will have to go through an unlawful detainer lawsuit as explained in this book. You cannot hand your copy of the three-day notice to the local police and ask them to remove the lodger. For this reason, you might want to use the less complicated route of the 30-day notice, in hopes that, if the lodger refuses to budge, local law enforcement will enforce your termination notice.

Finally, if your lodger has a lease, you cannot evict unless he or she has failed to pay the rent, violated a term of the lease, or engaged in illegal activity. In these situations, you will need to use a 30-day or 60-day notice. If the lodger fails to vacate, you must file an unlawful detainer lawsuit in order to get the lodger out.

Single Management/Rental Agreement

What happens to the tenancy when you fire a manager (or the manager quits) depends on the kind of agreement you and the manager had.

When the Manager Occupied a Special Manager's Unit

If your manager occupies a specially constructed manager's unit (such as one with a reception area or built-in desk) that must be used by the manager, or receives an apartment rent-free as part or all of the compensation, your ability to evict the ex-manager depends on:

- the terms of the management/rental agreement, and
- local rent control provisions.

If the agreement says nothing about a tenancy continuing if the manager quits or is fired, terminating the employment also terminates the occupancy. You can insist that the ex-manager leave right away, without serving any three-day or other termination notice, and can file an eviction lawsuit the next day if the ex-manager refuses to leave. (See C.C.P. § 1161 (1) and *Lombardo v. Santa Monica Y.M.C.A.* (1985) 169 Cal.App.3d 529, 541.) (See the "Checklist for Uncontested 'No-Notice' Eviction" in Chapter 5.)

The just cause eviction provisions of any applicable rent control law, however, might still require a separate notice or otherwise restrict your ability to evict a fired manager.

Evicting a terminated employee, particularly in a rent control city, falls into the most difficult type of eviction category, and in rent control cities you should engage a qualified attorney. Succeeding at trial often depends upon the manager's occupancy classification. Is the manager a "tenant" or a "licensee"? A licensee has only the right to occupy an apartment, and does not have the same rights as tenants to exclusive possession or rent control protection.

Licensee status avoids most tenancy problems, but also has limitations. Among other things, the employer cannot charge any rent or fee for use of the apartment to a licensee. You need the assistance of a qualified attorney to draft the license agreement and the employment agreement.

A manager's status as a licensee worked to the advantage of the employer/landlord in the following case, which arose in a rent control city. In *Chan v. Antepenko* (1988) 203 Cal.App.3d Supp 21, 25-26, the court permitted the eviction of the manager where the manager was required to live in the apartment rent free as a term of employment. The court decided the manager was not technically a "tenant" under the rent control ordinance, but a licensee occupying the apartment with the permission of the owner. This kept the manager's occupancy from falling under rent control.

Landlords must be very careful when dealing with managers who are arguably licensees. As you have seen, it's to the landlord's advantage to establish and maintain the manager's status as a licensee.

But watch out: Sending a rent notice to the manager asking for payment of rent after the termination can convert the manager from a pure licensee to a rent-controlled tenant. The notice creates a new tenancy, giving tenant rights to the terminated manager. (*Karz v. Meecham* (1981) 120 Cal.App.3d Supp 1.)

When the Manager Didn't Occupy a Manager's Unit

If the manager was simply compensated by a rent reduction, and you did not make a separate employment agreement, there may be confusion as to whether the rent can be "increased" after you've fired the manager.

If an ex-manager refuses to pay the full rent, you will have to serve a Three-Day Notice to Pay Rent or Quit, demanding the unpaid rent. If the fired manager still won't pay, you'll have to follow up with an eviction lawsuit. (See Chapter 2.)

Attorneys and Eviction Services

While you can do most evictions yourself, in a few circumstances you may want to consult an attorney who specializes in landlord-tenant law:

- The property you own is too far from where you live. Because you must file an eviction lawsuit where the property is located, the time and travel involved in representing yourself may be great.
- Your tenant is already represented by a lawyer, even before you proceed with an eviction.
- Your property is under Section 8 or is subject to rent control and local ordinances governing evictions.
- The tenant you are evicting is an ex-manager whom you have fired.
- Your tenant contests the eviction in court. (See Chapter 8 for more details on hiring an attorney in contested cases.)
- Your tenant files for bankruptcy or you purchased the rental property at foreclosure. (See Chapter 10 and Chapter 11.)

Hiring an Attorney to Handle or Assist With an Eviction

Finding a good, reasonably priced lawyer expert in residential evictions is not always an easy task. If you just pick a name out of an online listing, you may find someone who charges too much or who's not qualified to deal with your particular problem. The best way to find a suitable attorney is through a trusted person who has had a satisfactory experience with one. Your best referral sources are other landlords in your area. If you talk to a few landlords, or check with your local landlords' association, you'll likely come away with several leads on good lawyers experienced in landlord-tenant law and evictions.

 RESOURCE

Find a lawyer at www.nolo.com/lawyers. You can also check at Nolo's Lawyer Directory, which offers comprehensive profiles of lawyers who advertise, including each one's expertise (such as landlord-tenant law), education, and fees. Lawyers also indicate whether they are willing to review documents or coach clients who are doing their own legal work. California permits attorneys to accept partial or "limited scope" representation for limited tasks, such as drafting an agreement, reviewing pleadings, or representing the landlord at a settlement conference but not a trial (or, representing the client at trial but not at a settlement conference). (The Notice of Limited Scope Representation is contained in the official Judicial Council Form MC-950.)

You can also submit information about your legal issue to several local attorneys who handle landlord-tenant issues, and then pick the lawyer you'd like to work with. (For advice on hiring and working with lawyers, including what to ask a prospective attorney, see www.nolo.com/lawyers/tips.html.)

How you pay your lawyer depends on the type of legal services you need and the amount of legal work you have. The lawyer might charge an hourly rate to represent you in a contested eviction case, or a flat fee to represent you in court for a routine eviction for nonpayment of rent. In any case, always ask for a written fee agreement, explaining all fees (including work by legal assistants and court filing fees) and how costs will be billed and paid. A written agreement will help prevent disputes about legal fees and clarify the relationship you expect to have with the attorney and the services the lawyer will provide. Some agreements state how each of you can end the agreement and explain how you expect to work together, such as decisions the lawyer can make alone and those that require your approval.

Using an Eviction Service

Filing and following through with an eviction lawsuit involves filling out a number of legal forms. And once the forms are filed with the court, they must be served on the tenant. You can do it yourself, using all the forms and instructions in this book, or you can hire a lawyer. There is also a third route: getting help with the paperwork, filing, and service from an eviction service run by nonlawyers, known as "legal typing services," "independent paralegals," or "unlawful detainer assistants."

For a flat fee that is usually much lower than what lawyers charge, nonlawyer eviction services take the basic information from you, provide the appropriate eviction forms, and fill them out according to your instructions. This normally involves filling in your eviction papers so they'll be accepted by the court, arranging for filing, and then serving the papers on the tenant.

Eviction services cannot give legal advice about the requirements of your case and can't represent you in court—only you or your lawyers can present your case in court. Most eviction services handle only routine cases, and they are not helpful in more complex eviction cases or where the tenant contests the eviction in court.

Eviction services must be registered as "unlawful detainer assistants" with the county in which they operate, and must also be bonded or insured. (Bus. & Prof. Code §§ 6400-6415.)

In addition, all court papers filed by an "unlawful detainer assistant" must indicate that person's name, address, and county registration number.

To find an eviction service, check with a local landlords' association or look online or in the yellow pages under "eviction services" or "paralegals." Be sure the eviction service is reputable and experienced, as well as reasonably priced. If the service isn't registered, don't use it. Ask for references and check them.

Eviction for Nonpayment of Rent

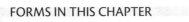 FORMS IN THIS CHAPTER

Chapter 2 includes instructions for and a sample of the Three-Day Notice to Pay Rent or Quit, and the Nolo website includes a downloadable copy of this form. (See the appendix for the link to the forms in this book and other information on using the forms.)

This chapter also includes a Checklist for Uncontested Three-Day Notice Eviction (Nonpayment of Rent), which outlines the steps involved in evicting a tenant for nonpayment of rent and the earliest times you can do each step.

Approximately nine out of ten unlawful detainer lawsuits result from the tenant's failure to pay rent when due. Although you don't want to sue your tenants every time they're a day late with the rent, obviously it's unwise to let a tenant get very far behind. You have to use your own best judgment to decide how long to wait, but if you want to collect all back rent in one court action, you must act within one year after rent becomes due—though surely, few landlords would wait that long. (C.C.P. § 1161(2).)

Once you've decided that your tenants either can't or won't pay the rent within a reasonable time (or move out), you should evict them as fast as possible. The only legal way to do this requires an "unlawful detainer" lawsuit. This chapter shows you how to do this step by step.

Overview of the Process

Before you can file an unlawful detainer lawsuit against a tenant, the law requires that you terminate the tenancy. To properly terminate a tenancy for nonpayment of rent, you must give the tenant three days' written notice using a form called a Three-Day Notice to Pay Rent or Quit. This is normally referred to as a three-day notice, and these rules apply to all unpaid rents that came due as of October 1, 2021 or later. Special rules apply to Covid-19 rental debt, which are rents due from March 1, 2020, through September 30, 2021.

If, within three days after you properly serve the tenant with this notice (you don't count the first day), the tenant offers you the entire rent demanded, the termination does not occur and the tenant can legally stay. If, however, the tenant neither pays nor moves by the end of the notice period, you can begin your lawsuit.

You do not have to accept a partial payment or a payment offered after the end of the notice period. If you do accept the rent, you no longer have the right to evict the tenant based on the three-day notice.

EXAMPLE: Tara's lease requires her to pay $1,200 rent to her landlord, Lenny, on the first day of each month in advance. Tara fails to pay November's rent on November 1. By November 9, it's evident to Lenny that Tara has no intention of paying the rent, so he serves her with a Three-Day Notice to Pay Rent or Quit following the instructions set out below. The day the notice is given doesn't count, and Tara has three business days, starting on the 10th, to pay. Tara doesn't pay the rent on the 10th, 11th, or 12th. However, because the 12th is a Saturday, Tara is not legally required to pay until the close of the next business day, which is November 15 (because November 13 is a Sunday and the 14th is a holiday—Veteran's Day). In other words, Lenny cannot bring his lawsuit until November 16.

How to Count the Days for a Three-Day Notice

The amount of time that a three-day notice gives the tenant (to pay or move out) depends on what day of the week you serve the notice and whether you're up against any weekends or court holidays. The notice period is three *business* days, not three calendar days. For example, during a nonholiday week, if you serve a notice on Thursday, the first day will be Friday and the second day will be Monday (because you've excluded Saturday and Sunday). The third day will be Tuesday. If the tenant hasn't paid or moved out, you can't file your eviction lawsuit until Wednesday. The three-day notice becomes a five-day notice in this example. And if the Monday in the example happens to be a holiday, such as Labor Day, the second day will be Tuesday, the third will be Wednesday, and you can't file until Thursday. (See C.C.P. §1161(2).)

Checklist for Uncontested Three-Day Notice Eviction (Nonpayment of Rent)	
Step	**Earliest Time to Do It**
☐ 1. Prepare and serve the three-day notice on the tenant.	Any time when the rent is past due.
☐ 2. Prepare the summons (or summonses, if there is more than one tenant) and complaint and make copies. (Chapter 6)	Any day after the rent is due, and a three-day notice has expired—for example, on or after the second of the month when the rent is due on the first. (If rent due date falls on Saturday, Sunday, or holiday, it's due the next business day.)
☐ 3. File the complaint at the courthouse and have the summons(es) issued. (Chapter 6)	After expiration of the three-day notice. If the third day after service falls on a Saturday, Sunday, or holiday, the second business day after that third day.
☐ 4. Have the sheriff, the marshal, a registered process server, or a friend serve the summons and complaint. (Chapter 6)	As soon as possible after filing the complaint and having the summons(es) issued.
☐ 5. Prepare Request for Entry of Default, Judgment, Declaration, and Writ of Possession. (Chapter 7)	While you're waiting for five-day (or 15-day, if complaint not personally served) response time to pass.
☐ 6. Call the court to find out whether or not tenant(s) has filed written response.	Just before closing on the fifth court day after service of summons, or early on the sixth day. (Do not count holidays that fall on weekdays, however. Also, if fifth court day after service falls on weekend, or holiday, count the first business day after that as the fifth day.)
☐ 7. Mail copy of Request for Entry of Default to tenant(s), file original at courthouse. Also file Declaration and Proof of Service, and have clerk issue Judgment and Writ for Possession for the property. (Chapter 7)	Sixth day after service of summons and complaint. (Again, count first business day after fifth day that falls on weekend or holiday.)
☐ 8. Prepare letter of instruction for, and give writ and copies to, sheriff, or marshal. (Chapter 7)	As soon as possible after above step. Sheriff or marshal won't evict for at least five days after posting notice.
☐ 9. Change locks after tenant vacates.	As soon as possible.
For Money Judgment	
☐ 10. Prepare Request for Entry of Default, Judgment, and, if allowed by local rule, Declaration in Support of default judgment (or a declaration in lieu of testimony). (Chapter 7)	As soon as possible after property is vacant.
☐ 11. Mail Request for Entry of Default copy to tenant, file request at courthouse. If a declaration in lieu of testimony is allowed, file that too, and give clerk judgment and writ forms for money part of judgment. If testimony required, ask clerk for default hearing. (Chapter 7)	As soon as possible after above.
☐ 12. If testimony required, attend default hearing before judge, testify, and turn in your judgment form for entry of money judgment. (Chapter 7)	When scheduled by court clerk.
☐ 13. Apply security deposit to cleaning and repair of property, and to any rent not accounted for in judgment, then apply balance to judgment amount. Notify tenant in writing of deductions, keeping a copy. Refund any balance remaining. If deposit does not cover entire judgment, collect balance of judgment. (Chapter 9)	As soon as possible after default hearing. Deposit must be accounted for within three weeks of when the tenants vacate.

Due to crowded court calendars, court procedures, and other factors, very few eviction cases will finish in a month or less. Far more likely, an uncontested case will take five to six weeks, and a contested case nine weeks or more. Several factors account for the wait. In particular, many courts make trial assignments on only one day of each week, and unlawful detainer cases compete for courtrooms with other cases. While unlawful detainer cases have the second highest trial priority (after criminal cases), crowded dockets still cause delays in busy areas. In addition, the COVID pandemic created an additional backlog of civil cases. The time required to accomplish normal court procedures and even the volume of the sheriff's civil load can cause delays of a week or more before the sheriff can perform an eviction.

 CAUTION

Be sure the tenant knows the details on how and where rent is to be paid. Before you prepare your three-day notice for nonpayment of rent, make sure you have previously complied with the requirement of Civil Code §§ 1962 and 1962.5, to notify the tenant of the name and street address of the owner or manager responsible for collection of rent, how rent is to be paid, and who is available for service of notices; you can do this either in a separate writing or in a written rental agreement or lease. You may not evict for nonpayment of any rent that came due during any period you were not in compliance with this requirement. If you have not done so, provide the tenant the required information. You then will have to wait until the next month's rent comes due, and give the tenant a three-day notice demanding rent—but only after you've complied. This law, designed to protect a tenant when a new owner takes over the property, can be abused by a tenant

who's paid the same landlord rent for months or even years, then stopped paying. If this is your situation, you could perhaps go ahead with a three-day notice and thereafter an unlawful detainer action based on rent that accrued before you started to comply with this requirement, but if the tenant contests the lawsuit, you could lose the case. (See Chapter 8 on contested cases, under the discussion of the tenants' affirmative defenses.)

Checklist for Uncontested Three-Day Notice Eviction (Nonpayment of Rent)

The checklist just above lists the steps involved in evicting on the grounds covered in this chapter, when the tenant defaults (doesn't contest the eviction). We cover some of the subjects (for example, filing a complaint and default judgments) in later chapters. As you work your way through the book you might want to return to this chart to see where you are in the process.

Preparing the Three-Day Notice to Pay Rent or Quit

Pay very close attention to the formalities of preparing and giving the notice. Any mistake in the notice, however slight, will give your tenants (or their attorney) grounds to contest the eviction lawsuit. At worst, a mistake in the three-day notice may render your unlawful detainer lawsuit "fatally defective"—which means you not only lose, but very likely will have to pay the tenant's court costs and attorneys' fees if the tenant is represented by a lawyer, and will have to start all over again with a correct three-day notice.

Requirements of a Three-Day Notice

The requirements for preparing a three-day notice differ according to when the unpaid rent was due. Here are the details.

Rent Due October 1, 2021 and Later

In addition to stating the correct amount of past-due rent and the dates for which it is due (see the next section), your three-day notice must contain all of the following:

- your tenant(s)'s name(s)
- a description of the property: street address and apartment or unit number, city, county, and state
- a demand that the tenant(s) pay the stated amount of rent due within three days or move. If you just demand the rent and do not set out the alternative of leaving, your notice is fatally defective.
- a statement that you will pursue legal action (and declare the lease/rental agreement "forfeited") if the tenant does not pay the entire rent due or move
- information on to whom, where, and how the rent is to be paid. This information must include either (1) for personal delivery of the rent, an address and the hours for delivery where the tenant can pay the rent in person, or (2) if the rent cannot be delivered in person, a mailing address with a statement that the date of payment will be the date of mailing as evidenced by a postmarked United States Postal Service proof of mailing to the listed name and address, or (3) the notice may specify the name, address, and account number for a financial institution within five miles of the apartment or rental property where the tenant can pay the rent by direct deposit.

- an indication—such as a signature by you, your manager, or other person you authorize to sign three-day notices—that the notice is from you. You don't need to date the notice, but it doesn't hurt. And,
- any language or attachment required by a local rent control or another ordinance.

 RENT CONTROL
Some rent control ordinances require Three-Day Notices to Pay Rent or Quit to contain special warnings. Check your ordinance if your property is subject to rent control. In most cases, you can edit the forms in our book for extra information to comply with your rent control ordinance requirement, but if you have any questions, consult with an attorney experienced in rent control in your community.

COVID-19 Rental Debt and Transition Period Rents

If any of the unpaid rent was for rental periods between July 1, 2021 and September 30, 2021, special rules attach to the notice. (For COVID recovery period rents from October 1, 2021, through June 30, 2022, see "Forms for COVID-19 Unpaid Rent" on page 31.) In addition to the information described above, C.C.P. § 1179.03 added all of the following:

- The notice is now a *fifteen (15) day notice*, not a three day notice.
- You must itemize the rent due by stating each month or rental period separately.
- The notice must inform tenants that they will not be evicted if, prior to the expiration of the notice, the tenant delivers a declaration of COVID-19-related financial distress.
- You must include the following language in your notice.

NOTICE FROM THE STATE OF CALIFORNIA: YOU MUST TAKE ACTION TO AVOID EVICTION.

If you are unable to pay the amount demanded in this notice because of the COVID-19 pandemic, you should take action right away.

IMMEDIATELY: Sign and return the declaration form included with your notice to your landlord within 15 days, excluding Saturdays, Sundays, and other judicial holidays. Sign and return the declaration even if you have done this before. You should keep a copy or a picture of the signed form for your records.

BEFORE SEPTEMBER 30, 2021: Pay your landlord at least 25 percent of any rent you missed between September 1, 2020, and September 30, 2021. If you need help paying that amount, apply for rental assistance. You will still owe the rest of the rent to your landlord, but as long as you pay 25 percent by September 30, 2021, your landlord will not be able to evict you for failing to pay the rest of the rent. You should keep careful track of what you have paid and any amount you still owe to protect your rights and avoid future disputes.

AS SOON AS POSSIBLE: Apply for rental assistance! As part of California's COVID-19 relief plan, money has been set aside to help renters who have fallen behind on rent or utility payments. If you are behind on rent or utility payments, YOU SHOULD COMPLETE A RENTAL ASSISTANCE APPLICATION IMMEDIATELY! It is free and simple to apply. Citizenship or immigration status does not matter. You can find out how to start your application by calling 1-833-430-2122 or visiting http://housingiskey.com right away.

When You Have Recently Acquired the Property

When you acquire property—whether by purchase at a foreclosure sale, ordinary purchase, or inheritance—you must notify tenants that you are the new owner. You're required to give them:

- your name, street address, and telephone number
- the name, street address, and telephone number of any manager or other person authorized to accept rent, and
- whether rent is to be paid personally (and if so, the usual days and hours that someone will be present to accept rent), by mail, or by deposit in a financial institution (with the details pertaining to forms and methods of payment). (Civil Code § 1962.)

If your tenants are being evicted for nonpayment, you cannot include, in your three-day notice, any rent that was due before you obtained title, unless you have complied with the requirements of Section 1962.

> **EXAMPLE:** Ted Tenant rents a house that his former landlord, Lottie, sold to Bob Buyer in June. Only in mid-August did Bob notify Ted in writing that Ted was to pay the rent to him and only then did he give Ted the other required information. Though Ted hasn't paid rent for several months, Bob can't use a three-day notice to ask for the rent that accrued on the first day of each of the months of June, July, or August. In September, Bob should prepare the three-day notice to demand September's rent only.

How to Determine the Amount of Rent Due

It's essential that you ask for the correct amount of rent in your three-day notice. That may seem easy, but a demand for an improper amount is the most common defect in a three-day notice. If, at trial, the court finds that the rent due at the time the three-day notice was served was less than the amount demanded in the notice (in other words, the notice overstated the rent), you will lose the lawsuit. (See *Ernst Enterprises, Inc. v. Sun Valley Gasoline, Inc.* (1983) 139 Cal. App. 3d 355 and *Nouratchan v. Miner* (1985) 169 Cal. App. 3d 746.)

To calculate the correct amount, follow these rules.

Rule 1: Never demand anything in a Three-Day Notice to Pay Rent or Quit other than the amount of the past due rent. Do not include late charges, bounced check or other fees of any kind, interest, utility charges, or anything else, even if a written lease or rental agreement says you're entitled to them. (Don't trust a sneaky late rent clause that describes late fees as "additional rent." That trick won't work in California.)

Does this mean that you cannot legally collect these charges? No. It simply means you can't legally include them in the Three-Day Notice to Pay Rent or Quit or recover them in an unlawful detainer lawsuit. You can deduct these amounts from the security deposit or sue for them later in small claims court. You can evict a tenant for failure to pay legitimate utility or other nonrent charges, even though you can't recover or ask for those charges in an unlawful detainer lawsuit. (See "Using the Three-Day Notice to Perform Covenant or Quit" in Chapter 4.)

When Your Tenant Is More Than 12 Months Late

In the unlikely event that your tenant is more than 12 months in arrears, you won't be able to demand back rent in excess of 12 months in your three-day notice. (C.C.P. § 1161(2).) You'll have to treat unpaid rent in excess of 12 months like late charges, in that you can offset it against the deposit when the tenant leaves, or you can sue for it later in small claims court (you'll have to file before the expiration of the statute of limitations (two or four years from the date it was due)). The most you can ask for in an unlawful detainer lawsuit is 12 months' rent.

Rule 2: Assuming the rent is due once a month and the tenant simply does not pay the rent for the month, you are entitled to ask for the full month's rent in your notice. The amount of rent due is not based on the date the three-day notice is served, but on the whole rental period. Thus, if rent is due in advance the first of every month, and you serve a three-day notice on the 5th, you should ask for the whole month's rent—that's what's overdue.

Rule 3: If the tenancy is already scheduled to terminate because you have given a 30-day, 60-day, or other notice to that effect, you must prorate the rent due. For example, if the tenant's $900 monthly rent is due June 1, but you gave her a 30-day notice about three weeks earlier, on May 10, the tenancy is terminated effective June 10. Your three-day notice served after June 1 should demand only $300, the rent for June 1 through 10. Because this can get tricky, we don't recommend terminating a tenancy in the middle of the month or another rental period. If you serve a three-day notice after having served a 30-day or 60-day notice, you risk confusing the tenant and losing an unlawful detainer action. (See Chapter 3.)

Rule 4: To arrive at a daily rental amount, always divide the monthly rent by 30. (Do this even in 28-, 29-, or 31-day months.)

Rule 5: If the tenant has paid part of the rent due, your demand for rent must reflect the partial payment. For example, if the monthly rent is $1,800 and your tenant has paid $800 of that amount, your three-day notice must demand no more than the $1,000 balance owed.

Resist any temptation to prorate the rental period in the notice (by asking for rent for the second half of the month when the tenant has paid half). Even though the tenant owes only a partial payment, the payment is for the entire month (or other rental period), not a portion of the period.

Rule 6: You do not have to credit any part of a security deposit (even if you called it last month's rent) toward the amount of rent you ask for in the three-day notice. In other words, you have a right to wait until the tenant has moved, to see if you should apply the deposit to cover any necessary damage repair or cleaning. Even if you called the money "last month's rent," the tenant is entitled to have this credited—before termination of the tenancy—only if and when the tenant has properly terminated the tenancy with a 30-day or 60-day notice, or has actually moved out.

Here are a few examples of how rent should be calculated for purposes of a three-day notice.

EXAMPLE 1: Tom has been paying $1,000 rent to Loretta on the first of each month, as provided by a written rental agreement. On October 6, Tom still hasn't paid his rent, and Loretta serves him with a three-day notice to pay the $1,000 or leave. (Loretta has, in effect, given Tom a five-day grace period; she could have given him the notice on October 2.) Even though the rental agreement provides for a $10 late charge after the second day, Loretta should not list that amount in the three-day notice.

EXAMPLE 2: Teresa's rent of $900 is due the 15th of each month for the period of the 15th through the 14th of the next month. Teresa's check for the period from October 15 through November 14 bounced, but Linda, her landlord, doesn't discover this until a month later, on November 15. Now Teresa not only refuses to make good on the check, but also refuses to pay the rent due for November 15 through December 14. It's now November 20. Teresa owes Linda $1,800 for the two-month period of October 15–December 14, and that's what the notice should demand. Linda should not add check-bouncing charges or late fees to the amount. And even though Teresa promises to leave "in a few days," rent for the entire period of October 15 through December 14 is already past due, and Linda has the right to demand it.

EXAMPLE 3: Terri and her landlord, Leo, agree in writing that Terri will move out on July 20. Terri's $900 rent is due the first of each month, in advance for the entire month. Terri will only owe rent for the first 20 days of July, due on the first day of that month. If Terri doesn't pay up on July 1, the three-day notice Leo should serve her shortly thereafter should demand this 20 days' rent, or 1/30 of the monthly rent ($900 ÷ 30 = $30 per day) for each of the 20 days, a total of $600.

EXAMPLE 4: Tony pays $950 rent on the first of each month under a one-year lease that expires July 31. On June 30, he confirms to his landlord, Lana, that he'll be leaving at the end of July, and he asks her to consider his $1,000 security deposit as the last month's rent for July. Lana should not formally agree to use the security deposit for the rent, because legally the deposit is not "rent" under California Civil Code § 1950.5. However, because a landlord may deduct from the security for a default in the payment of rent, as a practical matter, the unpaid rent will come from the deposit—but Lana should wait until after Tony moves out. Before Tony moves, he is entitled to an initial inspection of the condition of the apartment and a list of repairs necessary to avoid having his deposit charged for repair or other items. At that time, Lana can list the unpaid rent as a "charge" item if Tony does not pay the rent.

RESOURCE
*The California Landlord's Law Book:
Rights & Responsibilities*, **by Nils Rosenquest and Janet Portman (Nolo),** provides detailed information on how to deduct amounts, such as late fees or the cost of repairing damage, from the security deposit, and other issues relevant to preparing a three-day notice for nonpayment of rent. *Rights & Responsibilities* also covers rent control issues not covered in this book, such as rent formulas, rent calculations under state law rent control, and rent control board hearings.

Special Rules for Rent Control (State and Local)

You can't evict a tenant for refusal to pay a rent increase that was illegal under rent control (either too much or too soon), even if the tenant also refuses to pay the part of the rent that is legal under the law. That basic rule is the same under state rent control (the TPA) or local rent control ordinances.

EXAMPLE 1: Owsley rents out his Santa Monica studio for a reasonable $950 per month. After a year of renting to Tina on a month-to-month basis, Owsley gave Tina a notice raising the rent to $1,150. When Tina refused to pay the increase, Owsley served her with a three-day notice demanding that she pay the additional $200 or move. Unfortunately for Owsley, Santa Monica's rent control board allowed only a 7% increase that year, so that the most Owsley can legally charge is $1,016.50. Because the three-day notice demanded more rent than was legally due (under the rent control ordinance), the tenant, Tina, will win any lawsuit based on the three-day notice.

EXAMPLE 2: Suppose Tina refused to pay any rent at all, in protest of the increase. Tina does owe Owsley the old and legal rent of $950. But because Owsley's three-day notice demanded $1,150, more rent than was legally

due, the notice is defective. Owsley will lose any eviction lawsuit based on this defective notice, even if Tina refuses to pay even the legal portion of the rent, because the three-day notice must precisely demand the correct rent. Notice that Owsley could have given a three-day notice for the old, legal rent, without the increase. Such a notice might, however, constitute a waiver of the increase, requiring Owsley to give a new notice of increase to Tina. (Time- and face- saving tip: Any time the notice is illegal, whether it demands too much money or lacks a necessary disclosure, you should withdraw it quickly and either reissue it if it can be fixed or retract it in writing and collect the old, legal amount. It rarely pays to push a bad notice any more than it pays to push a bad hand at cards.)

A three-day notice is also defective under a rent control law (state or local) if the landlord at any time collected rents in excess of those allowed and failed to credit the tenant with the overcharges, even though the landlord now charges the correct rent and seeks to evict based only on nonpayment of the legal rent. Because the previously collected excess rents must be credited against unpaid legal rent, any three-day notice that doesn't give the tenant credit for previous overcharges is legally ineffective because it demands too much rent.

EXAMPLE: Lois rented the apartments in her Los Angeles building for $1,000 a month. In April, she served her tenant Taylor with a notice increasing the rent to $1,150, effective May 1. Taylor paid the increase (without complaint) in May and June. In July, when Taylor was unable to pay any rent at all, Lois learned, after checking with the Rent Adjustment Commission, that the maximum legal rent was $1,021. She therefore served Taylor with a three-day notice demanding this amount as the rent for July.

After filing an unlawful detainer complaint based on the nonpayment of this amount, Lois lost the case and had to pay Taylor's court costs and attorneys' fees. Why? First, since her rent increase notice had demanded an illegally high rent, it was void. The legal rent therefore was still $1,000. Second, in May and June, Lois collected a total of $258 more than that legal rent, which had to be credited against the $1000 Taylor did owe. Taylor therefore owed only $742. Since Lois's three-day notice demanded more than this, it was ineffective.

Some rent control ordinances impose special requirements on rent increase notices. Under state law for month-to-month tenancies, all that's required is a written notice of 30 days (60 days for a rent increase of 10% or more over 12 months) that clearly states the address of the property and the new rent (see Chapter 14 of *The California Landlord's Law Book: Rights & Responsibilities*). Quite a few rent-controlled cities require rent increase notices to list a justification or itemization of rent increases and other information. A rent increase notice that fails to comply with all requirements imposed by both state and local law has no effect. Therefore, any later Three-Day Notice to Pay Rent or Quit based on the tenant's failure to pay the increased amount is void because the rent increase notice was defective. In short, a landlord will lose any eviction lawsuit based on this sort of defective notice.

EXAMPLE: When Opal raised the rent on her Beverly Hills apartment unit from $1,900 to $1,975, an increase allowed under that city's rent control ordinance, she thought everything was okay. When she prepared her 30-day rent increase notice, however, she forgot about the part of the ordinance requiring a landlord to justify and itemize the rent increase and state in the notice that her records were open to inspection by the tenant. Opal collected the $1,975 rent for three months. The next month, when her tenant Renee failed to pay rent, Opal served her with a three-day notice demanding $1,975. When the case got to court, the judge told Opal her rent increase notice hadn't complied with city requirements and was ineffective, leaving the legal rent at $1,900. Since Renee had paid the extra $75 for three months, she was entitled to a $225 credit against this amount, so that she owed $1,675. Since Opal's three-day notice demanded $1,975, it, too, was ineffective, and Renee won the eviction lawsuit.

These problems occur most often in cities with "moderate" to "strict" rent control enforcement ordinances, which set fixed rents that a landlord cannot legally exceed without board permission.

These problems are less likely to occur in cities with "mild" rent control enforcement, including San Jose, Hayward, and Los Gatos, where if the tenant fails to contest a rent increase, the increase is usually considered legally valid. Even if the tenant does contest the increase in these "mild" enforcement cities, the proper legal rent will be quickly decided by a hearing officer, making it less likely the landlord will be caught by surprise later if the landlord has to evict for nonpayment of rent.

The moral of all this: Pay close attention to any rent control ordinance in the city in which your property is located. Ask yourself the following questions:

- Have you owned the premises at all times when the tenant was living there?
- If not, did the previous owner fully comply with your rent control law?

- Have you fully complied with notice requirements concerning any rent control program? Have you advised tenants of their rights, registered or verified the registration of the affected units (if required), and paid any administrative rent program fees?
- If so, have you fully complied with the notice requirements for rent increases and charged the correct rent?

If your answer is "no" to any of the four questions, your tenant might be due a refund before you can evict for nonpayment of rent.

If your answer to these questions is "yes," have you fully complied with all other provisions of the rent control ordinance? If so, you are probably in a position to legally evict the tenant for nonpayment of rent.

RENT CONTROL

Some rent control ordinances require landlords to give tenants printed forms that inform tenants of their rights when landlords terminate or otherwise change tenancy terms. These cities include Berkeley, Los Angeles, Palo Alto, and San Francisco, and we expect other cities to join the list. Be sure to check your rent control website for any similar requirements. State law does not require special language in the notice of rent increase, but it does require certain disclosures in the lease, especially with respect to exemptions, in order for the exemption to apply.

Good-Faith Mistakes

Cities that require registration of rents must limit the sanctions against landlords who make good-faith mistakes in the calculation of rents. (Civ. Code § 1947.7.)

How to Fill Out a Three-Day Notice

A sample Three-Day Notice to Pay Rent or Quit, and instructions for filling it out appear below.

Forms for Covid-19 Unpaid Rent

We strongly recommend you do not attempt an eviction based on **COVID transition period rent** or **COVID recovery period rent**, because the additional allegations and steps required make it nearly impossible to successfully prosecute an eviction to judgment. Collection proceedings or receipt of state rental assistance will be easier and more productive. Even as we go to press, the Legislature extended the recovery period to June 30, 2022, to facilitate landlords and tenants in rental assistance processing. However, if you wish to give a COVID debt period three day notice, you must use special forms when you demand rent that was due during the **COVID transition period** (September 1, 2020 through September 30, 2021) and the **COVID recovery period** (October 1, 2021 through June 30, 2022). You'll find these forms on this book's companion page. Fortunately, they are reasonably self-explanatory.

Transition period rent. If the tenant did not pay rent during the transition period and also after the transition period ended (September 30, 2021), you'll need to use two notices, not one.

Recovery period rent. When rent was unpaid during this time frame, use the standard three-day notice, but modify it as follows:

- Itemize the amount of rent demanded and the date each amount came due.
- Attach a Rental Assistance Program Notice to the Three-Day Notice to Pay Rent or Quit. The Assistance Notice must include the telephone number and Internet website address of the pertinent government rental assistance program.

(Refer to C.C.P. §1179.10 for details on recovery period notices.)

Three-Day Notice to Pay Rent or Quit

To: __Tyrone Tenant__
(name)

Tenant(s) in possession of the premises at __123 Market Street, Apartment 4__
(street address)

City of __San Diego__, County of __San Diego__, California.

Please take notice that the rent on these premises occupied by you, in the amount of $ __1,500__, for the period from __June 1, 20xx__ to __June 30, 20xx__, is now due and payable.

YOU ARE HEREBY REQUIRED to pay this amount within THREE (3) days from the date of service on you of this notice or to vacate and surrender possession of the premises. In the event you fail to do so, legal proceedings will be instituted against you to recover possession of the premises, declare the forfeiture of the rental agreement or lease under which you occupy the premises, and recover rents, damages, and costs of suit.

RENT IS TO BE PAID TO:

[X] the undersigned, or

[ ] the following person: ____

AT THE FOLLOWING ADDRESS: __123 Maple Street, La Mesa__

____, California, phone: (__619__) __555-4567__ ;

IN THE FOLLOWING MANNER:

[X] In person. Usual days and hours for rent collection are: __3 p.m. to 8 p.m. Monday through Saturday__

[ ] by mail to the person and address indicated above

[ ] by deposit to account ____ at ____, a financial institution located within 5 miles of your rental at, ____ California

[ ] by electronic funds transfer procedure previously established.

Date: __June 5, 20xx__   *Lou Landlord*

Owner/Manager

- -

Proof of Service

I, the undersigned, being at least 18 years of age, served this notice, of which this is a true copy, on ____, one of the occupants listed above as follows:

[ ] On ____, ____, I delivered the notice to the occupant personally.

[ ] On ____, ____, I delivered the notice to a person of suitable age and discretion at the occupant's residence/business after having attempted personal service at the occupant's residence, and business, if known. On ____, ____, I mailed a second copy to the occupant at his or her residence.

[ ] On ____, ____, I posted the notice in a conspicuous place on the property, after having attempted personal service at the occupant's residence, and business, if known, and after having been unable to find there a person of suitable age and discretion. On ____, ____, I mailed a second copy to the occupant at the property.

I declare under penalty of perjury under the laws of the State of California that the foregoing is true and correct.

Date: ____   ____
Signature

Sign Pay or Quit Notices Yourself

A pay or quit notice signed or even just prepared by your lawyer may trigger the Fair Debt Collection Practices Act. This act (15 U.S.C. §§ 1692 and following) governs debt collectors and requires, among other things, that debtors be given 30 days in which to respond to a demand for payment. A federal appellate court in New York has ruled that an attorney who signs a pay or quit notice is acting as a debt collector. Consequently, the tenant must have 30 days to pay or quit, regardless of the state's three-day provision. (*Romea v. Heiberger*, 163 F.3d 111 (2d Cir. 1998).)

Although this ruling applies only to Connecticut, New York, and Vermont landlords, legal scholars in California believe that the Ninth Circuit Court of Appeals (which hears California cases) would hold similarly. To easily protect yourself (or avoid the dubious honor of being the test case), if you use a lawyer, tell your lawyer that you want to sign pay or quit notices yourself, whether they are based on rent nonpayment or any other failure to honor monetary obligations under the lease.

Step 1: Fill In the Tenant's Name

The first blank is for the name(s) of the tenant(s) to whom the three-day notice is addressed. This normally should include the tenant(s) whose name(s) is (are) listed on a written lease or rental agreement, or with whom you orally entered into a rental agreement, plus the names, if known, of any other adult occupants or subtenants of the property. (C.C.P. § 1161(2).)

When you want to evict an adult who claims to be a tenant (or subtenant) but is not named on the lease or rental agreement, you must provide the person with notice of the unlawful detainer action and an opportunity to be heard. This usually means naming the person as a defendant in the complaint. For example, if a married couple occupies an apartment but only the husband signed the lease, the landlord must still name both the husband and wife as defendants.

Although this rule technically applies only to the unlawful detainer complaint (see Chapter 6), not necessarily to the three-day notice, you should nevertheless name all adult occupants in the notice. It's a good practice and will avoid omission of the subtenants who must be named in the notice. (C.C.P. § 1174.25; *Arrieta v. Mahon* (1982) 31 Cal. 3d 381, 182 Cal. Rptr. 770.)

Step 2: Fill In the Address

The next spaces are for the address of the premises. Include the street address, city and county, and apartment number if your tenant lives in an apartment or condominium unit.

In the unlikely event the unit has no street address, use the legal description of the premises from your deed to the property, along with an ordinary understandable description of where the place is located (for example, "the small log cabin behind the first gas station going north on River Road from Pokeyville"). You can retype the notice to make room for the legal description or staple a separate property description as an attachment to the notice and type "the property described in the attachment to this notice" in place of the address.

Step 3: Fill In the Rent Due

The next space is for the amount of rent due and the dates for which it is due. You must state this figure accurately. (See "How to Determine the Amount of Rent Due," above.)

Step 4. Fill In Payment Information

The next spaces tell the tenant to whom, where, and how to pay the rent, as follows.

Under "RENT IS TO BE PAID TO," check the box next to "the undersigned" if the person who signs the notice (such as the manager or owner) will receive the rent. If someone else will receive the rent, check the box next to "the following person" and list the name of that person.

Under "AT THE FOLLOWING ADDRESS," give the address where the rent should be paid (do not list a post office box unless you want the rent to be mailed to one). Give the telephone number of the person who will accept the rent.

Under "IN THE FOLLOWING MANNER," check one or more boxes indicating how the rent will be accepted. If you check "In person," list the days and hours when someone will be present to accept the rent. For example, the office hours for a resident manager might be "Monday through Friday, 9:00 AM through 5:00 PM." If you check "by mail …," rent is legally paid when mailed, regardless of when you receive it.

Do not check the "by deposit to account …" box, indicating the tenant must deposit the sum in your bank account, nor the "by electronic funds transfer procedure previously established," unless you have accepted rent one or both of these ways in the past. If you use the deposit to account option, make sure the bank branch address is correct and within five miles of the property, and that you list the correct account number.

 CAUTION

Do not omit any information on your three-day notice. Failure to include all of the information called for on the form may make the notice legally ineffective. If your tenant refuses to move and you attempt to evict on the basis of a legally defective three-day notice, you'll be tossed out of court and will have to begin all over, with a new three-day notice.

Step 5: Sign and Date the Notice and Make Copies

The "ultimatum" language—that the tenant either pay the rent within three days or move out, or you'll bring legal action—and the "forfeiture" language are already included in our printed form. (See the "YOU ARE HEREBY REQUIRED" paragraph.) All you need to add are your signature to the form and the date you signed it. The date is not legally required, but it helps to clarify when the

rent was demanded. This date must not be the same day the rent was due, but at least one day later.

Be sure to make several photocopies for your records; the original goes to the tenant. If you serve a notice on more than one tenant (see "Who Should Receive the Notice" in the next section), you can give the others copies.

Step 6: Complete the Proof of Service Box on Your Copy

At the bottom of the Three-Day Notice to Pay Rent or Quit is a "Proof of Service," which indicates the name of the person served, the manner of service, and the date(s) of service. You or whoever served the notice on the tenant should fill out the Proof of Service on your copy of the three-day notice and sign it. **You do not fill out the Proof of Service on the original notice that is given to the tenant.** If more than one person is served with the notice, there should be a separate Proof of Service (on a copy of the notice) for each person served. Save the filled-out Proof(s) of Service—you'll need this information when you fill out the complaint and other eviction forms discussed in Chapter 6.

Serving the Three-Day Notice on the Tenant

The law is very strict about when and how the Three-Day Notice to Pay Rent or Quit must be given to ("served on") your tenant(s). Even a slight departure from the rules may cause the loss of your unlawful detainer lawsuit if it is contested. As ever, if your property is covered by a local rent control ordinance, check for any special requirements, such as mandatory language to be included in the notice, before using the forms in this book. In most cases, you can edit the forms in our book to comply with your rent control ordinance requirement for extra information, but if you have any questions, consult with an attorney experienced in rent control in your community.

When to Serve the Notice

The three-day notice can be given to your tenant any day after the rent is due, but not on the day it's due. For example, if the rent is due on the first day of each month, a notice given to the tenant on that day has no legal effect. If the due date falls on a Saturday, Sunday, or holiday, rent is still due on that day, unless your lease or rental agreement specifies that it will be due on the next business day. The three-day notice cannot be given until the day after that.

EXAMPLE: Tyson pays monthly rent, due in advance on the first of each month. Tyson's lease states that rent is due on the next business day when the date falls on a Saturday, Sunday, or holiday. If the first falls on a Monday holiday, Tyson's rent is not legally due until Tuesday. This means the three-day notice cannot be served until Wednesday.

This is one of the many technicalities of eviction law that can haunt an unlawful detainer action from the very beginning. Bizarre as it sounds, if you give the notice only a day prematurely, and the tenant still doesn't pay the rent during the two to three weeks he or she contests the lawsuit, you will still lose the case if the tenant spots your mistake.

EXAMPLE: When Tiffany didn't pay her $1,000 rent to Leslie on Friday, January 1, Leslie prepared a Three-Day Notice to Pay Rent or Quit, giving it to Tiffany the next day. Unfortunately for Leslie, she forgot that her lease included a clause that specified that when the rent due date falls on a Saturday, Sunday, or holiday, the rent would be due on the next business day. Therefore, the rent wasn't actually due until January 4, even though Tiffany's lease said it was due on the first, because January 1, New Year's Day, was a legal holiday; January 2 was a Saturday; and January 3 was a Sunday. Oblivious to all this, Leslie waited the three days, and, as Tiffany still hadn't paid the rent, Leslie filed her unlawful detainer

suit on January 6. Tiffany contested it, and the case finally went to court on February 5. Even though Tiffany clearly owed Leslie the rent for January and February, Leslie lost the lawsuit because she gave Tiffany the three-day notice before the rent was legally past due, the judge ruled for Tiffany. Now Leslie will have to pay Tiffany's court costs as well as her own. Assuming Tiffany still has not paid the rent, Leslie can, of course, serve a new three-day notice and begin the eviction procedure again, poorer but wiser.

In *LaManna v. Vognar* ((1993) 4 Cal. App. 4th Supp. 4, 22 Cal. Rptr. 2d 501), a landlord lost a case for the same reason illustrated in the example above. The three-day notice was served on a Wednesday. The third day after that was a Saturday. The tenant had until the end of the following Tuesday to pay the rent because Saturday and Sunday were not business days and Monday was a legal holiday, Memorial Day. The landlord could not legally file the eviction lawsuit until Wednesday. Unfortunately, he filed one day early, on Tuesday, and lost the case as a result.

If You Routinely Accept Late Rent

No law gives tenants a five-day or any other grace period when it comes to paying the rent. If, however, you regularly allow your tenant to pay rent several days or even weeks late, you might have problems evicting the tenant. If your three-day notice demands the rent sooner than the tenant is accustomed to paying it, the tenant might be able to successfully defend an eviction based on that three-day notice.

EXAMPLE: You routinely allowed the tenant to pay by the fifth of the month, even though the rental agreement states that the rent is due on the first. If you now serve a notice on the second or third day of the month, the tenant may be able to convince a judge that you served the notice too early.

This is called an "estoppel defense" or "waiver" in legalese. This means that one person (you) who consistently fails to insist on strict compliance with the terms of an agreement (in this case, prepayment of rent on time) may be prevented or stopped ("estopped") from insisting on strict compliance at a later time.

To avoid problems, wait until after any traditional grace period (that is, one that you've given regularly in the past) has expired before serving the three-day notice. Or, if the tenancy is one from month to month, and the rental agreement requires that rent be paid on the first of the month, you can reinstate the original payment terms with a 30-day written notice. Doing so allows you to insist that rent be paid on the first of the month, regardless of past custom. (See *The California Landlord's Law Book: Rights & Responsibilities*, Chapter 3, for more information on and Sample Notice of Reinstatement of Terms of Tenancy.)

Grace periods. Rent is due on a certain day under many rental agreements (usually on the first of the month), but leases or rental agreements don't usually impose late charges until several days later. Even so, the rent is still "due" on the date the rental agreement or lease says it's due, and the Three-Day Notice to Pay Rent or Quit can be served the day after that (taking into account extension of the due date by Saturdays, Sundays, and holidays). Any so-called grace period, after which late charges kick in, has no effect on when the three-day notice can be served.

> **EXAMPLE:** Under the lease between Titus Tenant and Lisa Landlady, Titus's $900 rent is due on the first day of each month, with a $25 late charge if paid after the 5th. Despite this so-called five-day grace period, the three-day notice can be served on the day after the first of the month, assuming the first doesn't fall on a Saturday, Sunday, or holiday.

TIP

Generally, you should not serve a three-day notice before any late charge comes due. First, if the rental agreement or lease provides for a grace period and you never made a habit of insisting on the rent before the late charge came due, tenants might be able to successfully defend against the three-day notice if they were allowed to pay late with no consequences. (See "If You Routinely Accept Late Rent," above.)

Second, it isn't a good business practice to serve a three-day notice right away. It breeds unnecessary tenant resentment and, in effect, gives the tenant a three-day grace period anyway.

Who Should Serve the Three-Day Notice

Anyone at least 18 years old (including you) can legally give the three-day notice to the tenant. It's often best to have it served by someone else. That way, if the tenant refuses to pay the rent and contests the resulting eviction suit by falsely claiming he or she didn't receive the notice (this is rare), at trial, you can present the testimony of someone not a party to the lawsuit who is more likely to be believed by a judge. Of course, you must weigh this advantage against any time, trouble, or expense it takes to get someone else to accomplish the service and, if necessary, appear in court.

Who Should Receive the Notice

Ideally, each person named on the three-day notice should be personally handed a copy of it. This isn't always possible, though, and under certain circumstances it isn't necessary. If you rented your property to just one tenant, whose name alone appears on any written rental agreement or lease, serve that person with the three-day notice. (However, as discussed in the next section, you can sometimes actually give the notice to a co-occupant of the property who isn't listed on the lease if you can't locate the tenant who is listed on the lease.)

If you rented to two or more tenants whose names are all on the lease or rental agreement, it is legally sufficient to serve just one. (*University of Southern California v. Weiss* (1962) 208 Cal. App. 2d 759, 769.) If your agreement is with only one tenant and that tenant has a roommate who is not on the agreement, the notice must be served on both. (See *Briggs v. Electronic Memories & Magnetics Corp.* (1975) 53 Cal. App. 3d 900.) Doing so minimizes the possibility that a nonserved tenant will try to defend against any subsequent eviction lawsuit on the ground that he or she didn't receive the notice.

Under C.C.P. § 1162(2), notice of a curable breach, like nonpayment of rent, does not bind a subtenant unless the notice names the subtenant and the landlord serves the subtenant separately from the tenant. So, to avoid problems in the unlawful detainer action, you must name and serve any roommates or known adult occupants not named in the lease.

You normally have no obligation to serve the three-day notice on unknown occupants who are not named in the written rental agreement or lease and with whom you've had no dealings in renting the property. (See *Chinese Hospital Foundation Fund v. Patterson* (1969) 1 Cal. App. 3d 627, 632, and *Four Seas Investment Corp. v. International Hotel Tenants Ass'n* (1978) 81 Cal. App. 3d 604.) However, as discussed above (Step 1, under "How to Fill Out a Three-Day Notice"), it's best to serve all adult occupants of the premises.

How to Serve the Three-Day Notice on the Tenant

The law is very strict on how the three-day notice must be served on the tenant. It is not enough that you mail the notice or simply post it on the door. There are three legal methods of service for a three-day notice.

Personal Service

The best method of service of a three-day notice is to simply have someone over 18 hand your tenant the notice, ideally at the tenant's home. If the tenant to whom you're attempting to give the three-day notice never seems to be home, and you know where he or she is employed, you should try to personally serve him or her there.

If the tenant refuses to accept the notice, it is sufficient to drop or lay it at his or her feet. It is unnecessary and possibly illegal to force the notice on the tenant's person. If the tenant slams the door in your face before you can leave it at his or her feet, or talks to you through the door while refusing to open it, it's okay to slide the notice under the door or shout, "I'm leaving a notice on your doormat" while doing so.

Handing the notice to any other person, such as someone who lives with your tenant but is not listed as a cotenant on the written rental agreement, is not sufficient except as described just below under "Substituted Service on Another Person."

Substituted Service on Another Person

If you are unable to locate the tenant at either their home or place of employment, the law allows you to use "substituted service" in lieu of personally giving the notice to the tenant. In order to serve the notice this way, you must do all of the following:

1. Make at least one unsuccessful attempt to personally serve the tenant at home.
2. Make one unsuccessful attempt to serve the notice at work.
3. Leave the notice, preferably with an adult, at the tenant's home or workplace. (Although one California court ruled that a 16-year-old boy (but not a younger child) could be served a three-day notice on behalf of the tenant, the ruling is not binding on all California courts (*Lehr v. Crosby* (1981) 123 Cal. App. 3d Supp. 7).)

4. Mail a copy of the notice to the tenant at home by ordinary first-class mail. (C.C.P. § 1162(a)(2).)

Ask for the name of the person with whom you leave the notice; you'll need to include it in the complaint you'll file to begin your lawsuit (Chapter 6). If you can't get a name, you can just put a description of the person.

> ! **CAUTION**
> **Accomplishing substituted service.** Substituted service of the notice is not completed, and the three-day period specified in the notice does not start running, until you have left the copy with the "substitute" person and mailed the second copy to the tenant at home. The first day of the notice's three-day period is the day after both these steps are accomplished.

EXAMPLE: Tad should have paid you his rent on the first of the month. By the 5th, you're ready to serve him with a Three-Day Notice to Pay Rent or Quit. When you try to personally serve it on him at home, a somewhat hostile buddy of Tad's answers the door, saying he's not home. Your next step is to try Tad's workplace—the one listed on the rental application he filled out when he moved in. You go there only to find that Tad called in sick that day. You can give the notice to one of Tad's coworkers or to his friend at home, with instructions to give it to Tad when they see him. After that, you must mail another copy of the notice to Tad at home by ordinary first-class mail. Substituted service is complete only after both steps have been accomplished.

"Posting-and-Mailing" Service

If you can't find the tenant or anyone else at home or work (or if you don't know where the tenant is employed), you may serve the three-day notice through a procedure known as "posting and mailing" (often referred to as "nail-and-mail"). To serve the notice this way, you must do the following, in the order indicated:

1. Make at least one unsuccessful attempt to personally serve the tenant at home.
2. If you know where the tenant works, try unsuccessfully to serve him or her at work.
3. Post a copy of the notice on the tenant's front door.
4. Mail another copy to the tenant at home by first-class mail. (C.C.P. § 1162(a)(3) and *Hozz v. Lewis* (1989) 215 Cal. App. 3d 314.) The notice period does not begin to run until after mailing the notice, and you must post the notice before mailing it. Mailing the notice first does not satisfy the procedure and will not count as a valid nail-and-mail serve.

You might be tempted to send the letter by certified mail and save the mailing receipt the postal service gives you. *Do not do this.* The statute specifically requires service by first-class mail, and the courts require strict compliance with the statute. In some cases where the landlord sent the notice by certified mail and the tenant signed a receipt, the court accepted actual receipt of the notice in lieu of the nail-and-mail procedure. However, if the tenant never accepted the mailing, no actual receipt occurred and the landlord never completed service of the notice required by the statute.

EXAMPLE: Tyler's rent is due on the 15th of each month, but he still hasn't paid Lyle, his landlord, by the 20th. Lyle can seldom find Tyler (or anyone else) at home, and doesn't know where (or if) Tyler works. Because that leaves no one to personally or substitute serve with the three-day notice, Lyle has only the posting-and-mailing alternative. Lyle can tape one copy to the door of the property and mail a second copy to Tyler at that address by first-class mail. Lyle should begin counting the three days the day after both of these tasks are accomplished. The three-day period after which Lyle can bring an unlawful detainer lawsuit is counted the same way as if the notice were served personally.

Proof of Service. Be sure the person who serves the three-day notice completes the Proof of Service at the bottom on an extra copy of the notice (not the original notice that is given to the tenant— see Step 6, above).

After the Three-Day Notice Is Served

Your course of action after serving the three-day notice depends on whether the tenant pays the rent in full and stays or leaves.

The Tenant Stays

If the tenant offers the rent in full any time before the end of the three-day period, you must accept it if it's offered in cash, certified check, or money order. If you've routinely accepted rent payments by personal check, you must accept a personal check in response to a three-day notice unless you notified the tenant otherwise in the notice itself. You can insist, in the notice, on a cash payment only if both the following are true:

- The tenant has bounced a check to you within the previous three months.
- You've given the tenant a separate written notice (to which a copy of the bounced check must be attached) to pay cash only for as long as three months after the check bounced.

Such a notice can be given with the three-day notice, or earlier. (See Civil Code § 1947.3.)

If you refuse to accept the rent (or if you insist on more money than demanded in the three-day notice, such as late charges) and file your lawsuit anyway, your tenant will be able to contest it and win. (The only way to evict a month-to-month tenant who never pays until threatened with a three-day notice is to terminate the tenancy with a 30-day or 60-day notice—see Chapter 3.)

If a properly notified tenant doesn't pay before the notice period passes, the tenancy terminates.

You then have a legal right to the property, which you can enforce by bringing an unlawful detainer action. (See below and Chapter 6.)

 CAUTION
You do not have to accept rent after the end of the notice period. In fact, if you do accept rent (even partial payment), you reinstate the tenancy and waive your right to evict based on the three-day notice. For example, if on the third day after service of a three-day notice demanding $800 rent you accept $600, along with a promise to pay the remaining $200 "in a few days," you will have to start over again with a three-day notice demanding only the balance of $200, and base your lawsuit on that. If you proceed with the lawsuit based on the three-day notice demanding all the rent, the tenant might be able to successfully defend the lawsuit on the ground that you waived the three-day notice by accepting part of the rent. Of course, you might want the partial payment badly enough to be willing to serve a new notice. In that case, accept it with one hand and serve a three-day notice for the remaining unpaid amount with the other.

The Tenant Moves Out

Once in a great while, a tenant will respond to a Three-Day Notice to Pay Rent or Quit by actually moving out within the three days. When tenants don't pay the rent but simply move after receiving the three-day notice, they still owe you a full month's rent because rent is due in advance. The tenant's security deposit might cover all or most of the rent owed. If not, you might decide to sue the tenant in small claims court for the balance.

 RESOURCE
Nolo's book *Everybody's Guide to Small Claims Court in California*, by Cara O'Neill, shows how to sue in small claims court. (See the "Small Claims Court & Lawsuits" section of www.nolo.com for general information.)

> ### Holidays
>
> Many of the rules for counting calendar days direct you to omit Saturdays, Sundays, and holidays. In this context, a holiday is a day that the courts are closed, as declared by the California courts. The list is not the same as the list of federal holidays (the federal list is shorter). California court holidays (also referred to in our book as legal holidays, state holidays, and judicial holidays) are:
>
> | | |
> |---|---|
> | New Year's Day | Independence Day |
> | Dr. Martin Luther King, Jr. Day | Labor Day |
> | | Columbus Day |
> | Lincoln's Birthday | Veteran's Day |
> | President's Day | Thanksgiving |
> | Cesar Chavez Day | Day After Thanksgiving |
> | Memorial Day | Christmas Day |
>
> Be sure to check the calendar. As you know, some of these holidays come every year on the same date (New Year's, for example), while others change yearly (like Thanksgiving).

What if the tenant simply sneaks out within the three-day period, but doesn't give you the keys or otherwise make it clear he or she is turning over possession of the property to you? In that case, you can't legally enter and take possession unless you either use a procedure called "abandonment" or file an eviction suit anyway. If you file suit, you must serve the summons and complaint by posting and mailing, as described in "Serving the Papers on the Defendant(s): Service of Process" in Chapter 6, and obtain a judgment. (For more information on the abandonment alternative, and to decide whether it may be suitable under your circumstances, see *The California Landlord's Law Book: Rights & Responsibilities*, Chapter 19.)

When to File Your Lawsuit

As we have stressed, you cannot begin your unlawful detainer lawsuit until the three-day notice period expires. The rules for counting the days are as follows:

- Service is complete when you personally serve the three-day notice or, if you serve the notice by substituted service or posting-and-mailing service, three business days after you have both (1) mailed the notice and (2) either given it to another adult or posted it (as described above). Note: Saturday is not considered a business day for this purpose.
- If you serve more than one tenant with notices, but not all on the same day, start counting only after the last tenant is served.
- Do not count the day of service as the first day. The first day to count is the day after service of the notice was completed.
- Do not file your lawsuit on the third business day after service is complete. The tenant must have three full days after service to pay the rent or leave before you file suit.
- If the third day is a business day, you may file your lawsuit on the next business day after that.

To illustrate how the business day rule works, during a nonholiday week, if you serve a notice on Thursday, the first day will be Friday, the second day will be Monday (excluding Saturday and Sunday), and the third day will be Tuesday. (See C.C.P. §1161(2).)

In the distant past, some judges (particularly some in Los Angeles County) ruled that if you served your three-day notice by posting-and-mailing or by substituted service on another person—both of which involve mailing a second copy to the tenant—you had to wait an extra five days for the tenant to pay or move, before filing suit. A court decision settled that issue several years ago, and you do not have to wait an extra five days before filing your complaint. (*Losornio v. Motta* (1998) 67 Cal. App. 4th 110, 115.)

You should be prepared to bring this to the attention of the judge during any default hearing or trial if the judge or tenant raises the issue. (See "Taking a Default Judgment" in Chapter 7 and "Contested Cases" in Chapter 8.) You can file the unlawful detainer complaint the first business day after the notice expires.

Eviction by 30-Day or 60-Day Notice

FORMS IN THIS CHAPTER

Chapter 3 includes instructions for and a sample of the 30-Day Notice of Termination of Tenancy, the 60-Day Notice of Termination of Tenancy, and the 90-Day Notice of Termination of Tenancy. The Nolo website includes downloadable copies of all three forms. (See the appendix for the link to the forms in this book, and other information on using the forms.)

This chapter also includes a Checklist for 30- or 60-Day Notice Eviction that outlines the steps involved in evicting a tenant with a 30- or 60-day notice and the earliest times you can do each step.

The second most common basis for unlawful detainer lawsuits (after failure to pay rent) is the tenant's failure to move after receiving a 30-day notice terminating the tenant's month-to-month tenancy.

Overview of the Process

Before you can file an unlawful detainer lawsuit against a tenant, you must legally terminate the tenancy. If the tenant has a month-to-month tenancy, you can use a 30-day notice to terminate the tenancy if the tenant has occupied the rental for less than a year. In most cases, you must give a tenant 60 days' notice if he or she has lived in the property a year or more. (See "30-Day, 60-Day, and 90-Day Notices," below.) Also, a 90-day notice is required to terminate certain government-subsidized tenancies.

In most circumstances involving occupancies of less than one year, you don't have to state a reason for terminating the tenancy. This general rule, however, has some very important exceptions, particularly where just cause requirements come into play. These are discussed below.

If the tenant doesn't leave by the end of the 30- (or 60-) day notice period, you can file your lawsuit to evict the tenant.

Checklist for 30- or 60-Day Notice Eviction

Below is an overview of steps for evicting on the grounds covered in this chapter, assuming that the tenant defaults (doesn't contest the eviction). We cover some subjects, such as filing a complaint and default judgment, in later chapters. As you go through the book, you may want to return to this chart to see where you are in the process.

When a Tenancy Can Be Terminated With a 30-Day or 60-Day Notice

There are basically two types of residential tenancies. The first is a "fixed-term" tenancy, where the property is rented to the tenant for a fixed period of time, usually a year or more, and is formalized with a written lease or rental agreement. During this period, the landlord may not raise the rent and may not terminate the tenancy except for cause, such as the tenant's failure to pay the rent or violation of other lease terms.

This type of tenancy may not be terminated by a 30- or 60-day notice before the end of the fixed term.

Negotiating With Tenants

If a lease is in effect and for some important reason, such as your need to sell or demolish the building, you want the tenants out, you might try to negotiate with them. For example, offer them a month or two of free or reduced rent if they'll move out before their lease expires. Of course, any agreement you reach should be put in writing.

Exercise caution where rent control applies. San Francisco, for example, requires landlords to give tenants a buy-out disclosure notice concerning their rights, and to separately file a buy-out form with the rent board. (For further information and to access the notification form, Pre-Buyout Negotiations Disclosure Form Required by Ordinance Section 37.9E, type its exact name in your browser.)

Checklist for 30- or 60-Day Notice Eviction	
Step	**Earliest Time to Do It**
☐ 1. Prepare and serve the 30- or 60-day notice on the tenant.	Any time. Immediately after receipt of rent is best.
☐ 2. Prepare the summons (or summonses, if there is more than one tenant) and complaint and make copies. (Chapter 6)	The 30th or 60th day after service of the 30-day or 60-day notice is complete.
☐ 3. File the complaint at the courthouse and have the summons(es) issued. (Chapter 6)	The first business day after the notice period expires.
☐ 4. Have the sheriff, the marshal, a registered process server, or a friend serve the summons and complaint. (Chapter 6)	As soon as possible after filing the complaint and having the summons(es) issued.
☐ 5. Prepare Request for Entry of Default, Judgment, Declaration, and Writ of Possession. (Chapter 7)	While you're waiting for five-day (or 15-day, if complaint not personally served) response time to pass.
☐ 6. Call the court to find out whether or not tenant(s) have filed written response.	Just before closing on the fifth court day after service of summons, or early on the sixth day. (Do not count holidays that fall on weekdays, however. Also, if fifth day after service falls on weekend or holiday, count the first business day after that as the fifth day.)
☐ 7. Mail copy of Request for Entry of Default to tenant(s), file original at courthouse. Also file Declaration and Proof of Service, and have clerk issue Judgment and Writ for Possession for the property. (Chapter 7)	Sixth court day after service of summons and complaint. (Again, count first business day after fifth day that falls on weekend or holiday.)
☐ 8. Prepare letter of instruction for, and give writ and copies to, sheriff or marshal. (Chapter 7)	As soon as possible after above step. Sheriff or marshal won't evict for at least five days after posting notice.
☐ 9. Change locks after tenant vacates.	As soon as possible.
For Money Judgment	
☐ 10. Prepare Request for Entry of Default, Judgment, and, if allowed by local rule, declaration in lieu of testimony. (Chapter 7)	As soon as possible after property is vacant.
☐ 11. Mail Request for Entry of Default copy to tenant, file request at courthouse. If a declaration in lieu of testimony is allowed, file that too, and give clerk judgment and writ forms for money part of judgment. If testimony required, ask clerk for default hearing. (Chapter 7)	As soon as possible after above.
☐ 12. If testimony required, attend default hearing before judge, testify, and turn in your judgment form for entry of money judgment. (Chapter 7)	When scheduled by court clerk.
☐ 13. Apply security deposit to cleaning and repair of property, and to any rent not accounted for in judgment, then apply balance to judgment amount. Notify tenant in writing of deductions, keeping a copy. Refund any balance remaining. If deposit does not cover entire judgment, collect balance of judgment. (Chapter 9)	As soon as possible after default hearing. Deposit must be accounted for within three weeks of when the tenants vacate.

The second type of tenancy is a "periodic tenancy," a tenancy for an unspecified time in which the rent is paid every "period"—month, week, every other week, and so on. A periodic tenancy that goes from month to month may be terminated with a 30-day notice (subject to the two restrictions mentioned above).

Because the overwhelming majority of residential tenancies are periodic month-to-month tenancies, we assume 30 or 60 days is the correct notice using the procedures in this chapter.

How do you tell if your tenancy is month-to-month? If you have been accepting monthly rent from your tenant without a written agreement or if you have a written rental agreement that either is noncommittal about a fixed term or specifically provides for 30 days' notice to terminate the tenancy, the tenancy is from month to month. It is also a month-to-month tenancy if you (or the owner from whom you purchased the property) continued to accept rent on a monthly basis from a tenant whose lease had expired.

Impermissible Reasons to Evict With a 30- or 60-Day Notice

Except for tenancies subject to local or statewide just cause eviction laws (discussed below), a landlord can evict a tenant without a reason, but not for the wrong reason. This means you can't evict a tenant:

- because of race, immigration status, citizenship status, marital status, religion, sex, sexual preference, having children, national origin, age, or disability (see Gov't Code §§ 12955 and following (Fair Employment and Housing Act); C.C. §§ 51-53 (Unruh Civil Rights Act); 42 U.S.C. § 3604 (Federal Fair Housing Act))
- if the tenant exercised the "repair-and-deduct" remedy (by deducting the cost of habitability-related repairs from the rent) within the past

six months, unless the notice states a valid reason for terminating the tenancy, or
- because the tenant complained about the premises to local authorities, exercised rights given to tenants by law, or engaged in behavior protected by the First Amendment —for example, by organizing other tenants.

If you evict for an illegal reason, or if it looks like you are trying to, your tenant can defend the unlawful detainer lawsuit and sue you later for damages. Generally, if any of the elements listed below are present, you should think twice about evicting with a 30-day or 60-day notice that doesn't state a valid reason. Even though you state a valid reason, tenants can still sue if they believe the eviction was illegally motivated. Conversely, even if you state no reason, your eviction will be upheld if you prevail over the tenant's defense. The main purpose to stating a valid reason in a "retaliation presumed" termination notice (except in rent control areas where the reason must be stated) is to declare your legitimate reason for termination, which you can prove if the tenant raises a retaliation defense.

Think twice about evicting with such a notice, especially without a valid business reason, when any of the following are present:

- The tenant is a member of a racial, ethnic, or religious minority group.
- The tenant is gay or transgender.
- The tenant has children and your other tenants don't.
- The tenant has recently (say within six months) complained to the authorities about the premises.
- The tenant has recently (within six months) lawfully withheld rent.
- The tenant has organized a tenants' union.
- The tenant is disabled.
- The tenant is elderly.
- The tenant receives public assistance.

If none of these factors is present (and the premises are not covered by a rent control law or rented under a government-subsidized program), you will probably have no problem using a 30-day or 60-day notice, without specifying a reason, to terminate a tenancy.

RESOURCE

The California Landlord's Law Book: Rights & Responsibilities, **by Nils Rosenquest and Janet Portman (Nolo),** provides detailed information on antidiscrimination and illegal retaliation rules and other violations of tenant rights (such as reasonable notice of entry to make repairs) to help you avoid getting into trouble when evicting a tenant with a 30- or 60-day notice. *Rights & Responsibilities* also covers some rent control issues not covered completely in this book, such as rent control board hearings and the statewide rent control law.

Federal Housing Programs

"Section 8" refers to Section 8 of the United States Housing Act of 1937 (42 U.S.C. § 1437f), and "Section 236" refers to Section 236 of the National Housing Act of 1949 (12 U.S.C. § 1517z-1). Both are federal laws providing government housing assistance to low-income families. Terminating any Section 8 tenancy requires "cause" as defined under the lease, the Housing Assistance Payments contract, or applicable federal regulations. "Cause" under Section 8 leases differs from the typical "just cause" requirements imposed in rent control and eviction control statutes (described below in this chapter). (For additional information about the more stringent requirements for eviction from government-subsidized rentals, see Civ. Code § 1954.535 and the following cases: *Appel v. Beyer* (1974) 39 Cal. App. 3d Supp. 7; *Gallman v. Pierce* (1986, N.D. Cal.) 639 F. Supp. 472; *Mitchell v. Poole* (1988) 203 Cal. App. 3d Supp. 1; *Gersten Companies v. Deloney* (1989) 212 Cal. App. 3d 1119; and 24 C.F.R. §§ 450 and following, §§ 982 and following.)

30-Day, 60-Day, and 90-Day Notices

To terminate a month-to-month tenancy, you must give written notice to the tenant. Here's how much notice you need to give:

- 30 days' notice if your tenant has occupied the property for less than a year
- 60 days' notice if the tenant has been in the property a year or more, or
- 90 days' notice for certain government-subsidized tenancies.

Regardless of which notice is required, you must comply with just cause eviction provisions of any applicable rent control ordinances—which usually include listing the reason for the termination of tenancy.

30-Day Notice for Tenancies of Less Than a Year

If your tenant has occupied your property for less than a year, you must give 30 days' notice to terminate a residential month-to-month tenancy. (Civ. Code § 1946.1(c).) This is true even for tenancies of shorter periodic length, such as tenancies from week to week. (However, the *tenant* need give only a week's notice to terminate a week-to-week tenancy, and so forth.) Of course, you can give the tenant *more* than 30 days' notice if you want to. The requirement is that you give at least 30 days' written notice.

CAUTION

Landlords cannot reduce their notice period to less than 30 days. Although agreements reducing the landlord's notice period to as few as seven days were previously legal under Civ. Code § 1946, termination of residential tenancies, as opposed to commercial ones, is now governed by the newer Section 1946.1, which does not refer to the possibility of such a reduced notice period. We believe Civ. Code § 1946, with its language allowing the parties to agree in writing to a shorter notice period, no longer applies to residential tenancies.

One final word of caution: The "less than a year" requirement refers to how long the tenant has actually lived in the property, not the length of the most recent lease term. For example, if your tenant has lived in your rental house for the past year and a half, but signed a new six-month lease eight months ago (so that the lease expired and the tenancy is now month to month), you must give 60 days' notice. (See just below.) In other words, you start counting as of the date the tenant started living in the unit, not when you both signed the most recent lease or rental agreement.

60-Day Notices for Tenancies of a Year or More

If your tenant has occupied the premises for a year or more, you must deliver a 60-day notice to terminate a month-to-month tenancy. (Civ. Code § 1946.1.) Again, this is true even for periodic tenancies of shorter duration, such as week to week, and regardless of any provision in your rental agreement that specifies a shorter notice period.

This 60-day notice requirement does not work both ways. A month-to-month residential tenant who has occupied your property for a year or more does not have to give you 60 days' notice. The tenant need give you only 30 days' notice to terminate the tenancy.

If you give your tenant a 60-day notice, the tenant has the right to give *you* a written 30-day (or more) notice, which (as long as it's less than your 60-day notice) will terminate the tenancy sooner than the expiration of the 60-day notice that you delivered.

> EXAMPLE: Lois Landlord has rented to Terri Tenant for over a year. On March 1, Lois serves Terri with a 60-day notice, terminating her tenancy effective April 29. Terri, however, quickly finds a new place and now wants to leave sooner than that. So, on March 10, she gives Lois a written 30-day notice, which terminates her tenancy on April 9. Assuming she vacates on or before that date, Terri won't be responsible for any rent past April 9.

There is one extremely narrow exception to the rule that a landlord must give a tenant 60 days' notice of termination of a month-to-month tenancy, where the tenant has lived in the property a year or more. This is where the landlord is in the process of selling the property to an individual who is going to live in it. Even if the tenant has occupied the property for a year or more, the landlord can terminate the tenant's month-to-month tenancy with a 30-day notice if all the following are true:

- The property is a single-family home or condominium unit (as opposed to an apartment unit).
- You are selling the property to an actual ("bona fide") purchaser (as opposed to transferring it to a relative for less than fair market price, for example).
- The buyer is an individual (not a corporation, a partnership, or an LLC) who intends to occupy the property for a year.
- You and the buyer have opened an escrow account to hold money that will be transferred during the sale.
- You give the 30-day notice within 120 days of opening the escrow.
- You have never previously invoked this exception, with respect to this property.

Unless all the above things are true, you must give the tenant at least 60 days' written notice to terminate a month-to-month or other periodic tenancy, if the tenant has occupied the property for a year or more.

90-Day Notices to Terminate Government-Subsidized Tenancies

If you receive rent or other subsidies from federal, state, or local governments, you may evict only for certain reasons. Acceptable reasons for termination are usually listed in the form lease drafted by the agency or in the agency's regulations. If your tenants receive assistance from a local housing authority under Section 8 or another similar program of a federal, state, or local agency, you must very specifically state the reasons for termination in the 90-day notice, *not* a 30-day or 60-day notice, saying what acts the tenant did, and when, that violated the lease or otherwise constitute good cause for eviction. (Civ. Code § 1953.545; *Wasatch Property Management v. Del Grate*, (2005) 35 Cal. 4th 1111.) Allowable reasons for eviction are contained in the standard form leases the housing authority requires the landlord to use.

Keep in mind, however, that you cannot terminate for this reason until that tenant's initial rental term has elapsed. In addition, during the 90-day period prior to termination, you cannot increase the rent or otherwise require any subsidized tenants to pay more than they paid under the subsidy.

In some rent control cities, rent limits and eviction controls for unsubsidized housing also apply to Section 8 tenancies. The just causes to terminate in the HUD model lease do not take precedence over the rent ordinance when the local ordinance provides greater protection to the tenant. For example, if the rent ordinance imposes more just cause restrictions than the HUD model lease, that ordinance controls, and the tenant gets the benefit of the extra protections. Similarly, if a local ordinance is more expansive when defining who can qualify for an owner move-in than the definition provided by HUD, the local definition would apply.

Rent Control and Just Cause Eviction Ordinances

Just cause requirements for evictions, whether state or local, severely limit the reasons for which landlords can evict tenants. Landlords are authorized to terminate a month-to-month tenancy only for the reasons specifically listed in the particular law. Most just cause provisions also require that the reason be clearly stated on the notice (see below), as well as in a subsequent unlawful detainer complaint.

If your property is under state rent and eviction control, or in a city that requires just cause (see "Rent Regulation in California," in the Companion preface for a quick list), the usual rules for 30- or 60-day notice evictions simply do not apply. Even when an eviction is authorized under state law, a stricter local rent control ordinance or state just cause requirement may forbid it. For example, San Francisco's rent control ordinance, which does not permit eviction of a tenant solely on the basis of a change in ownership, was held to prevail over state law, which allows eviction for this reason if the tenancy is month to month. (*Gross v. Superior Court* (1985) 171 Cal. App. 3d 265.)

> **EXAMPLE:** You wish to terminate the month-to-month tenancy of a tenant who won't let you in the premises to make repairs, even though you have given reasonable notice (all ordinances consider this a just cause for eviction). You must give the tenant a 30-day (or 60-day) notice that complies with state law and that also states in detail the reason for the termination, listing specifics, such as dates the tenant refused to allow you in on reasonable notice. If the tenant refuses to leave and you bring an unlawful detainer suit, the complaint must also state the reason for eviction (this is usually done by referring to an attached copy of the 30-day or 60-day notice). If the tenant contests the lawsuit, you must prove at trial that the tenant repeatedly refused you access, as stated in the notice.

Statewide Just Cause Requirements

Civil Code § 1946.2 created a just cause requirement to terminate a lease on all covered units, but only after the tenant has lived in the unit for twelve months or more. The listed just causes fall into two categories—at fault and no fault.

The "at-fault" reasons are:

- failure to pay rent
- breach of a material term of the lease, provided that where the breach of the lease is curable, the tenant has been given an opportunity to cure the condition, but has failed to do so (see Chapter 4 concerning curable breaches)
- maintaining or committing a nuisance
- waste (causing serious damage to the property)
- refusal to sign a renewal lease or extension with similar terms
- criminal activity on the property or threats against the owner or agent
- assigning or subletting in violation of the lease
- denial of access to make repairs
- using the property for an illegal purpose
- failure of an employee, agent, or licensee to vacate after termination; and
- failure to vacate after giving notice of intent to terminate.

The "no fault" reasons are:

- Intent of owner or listed relative to occupy the unit
- withdrawal of the unit from the rental market
- compliance with government or court order that requires vacating the unit; and
- intent to demolish or substantially remodel the unit.

Where the termination is for a no-fault just cause, you must also pay the tenant relocation assistance of one month's rent. Payment can be made directly or by forgiving the last month's rent prior to the termination date.

As with local rent control ordinance requirements, the just cause must be stated in the notice. It's a good idea to include in the notice any facts supporting the at-fault cause.

Local Just Cause Requirements

Before you start an eviction by giving a 30-day or 60-day notice, you should check for any just cause requirements for your property in a current copy of your ordinance. Do this carefully. If you are confused, talk to your local landlords' association or an attorney in your area who regularly practices in this field.

Although cities' ordinances differ in detail, the basic reasons that constitute just cause are pretty much the same in all of them. Most rent control ordinances allow the following justifications for terminating a month-to-month tenancy with a 30-day or 60-day notice. These are similar to the statewide just cause requirements (we know this because the Legislature admitted to copying from a bunch of local ordinances!).

Nonpayment of Rent

Theoretically, you can use a 30-day or 60-day notice to evict a tenant who doesn't pay the rent, but it is a bad idea. You cannot get any money for the unpaid rent and must wait much longer to file an unlawful detainer. In addition, if you use a longer notice based on nonpayment of rent, you deprive tenants of their rights to a conditional notice that gives them the chance to stay if they pay the rent. Although the long notice gives more time, it's unconditional, unlike a three-day notice to pay rent or quit, which allows tenants to stay if they pay rent by the end of the notice period. In fact, C.C.P. § 1161(2)—which describes giving tenants a three-day notice and a chance to save their tenancy—may very well prohibit use of a 30-/60- day notice for unpaid rent, which lacks this saving option. So, you should almost always use a three-day notice instead (see Chapter 2). (*Saberi v. Bakhtiari* (1985) 169 Cal. App. 3d 509.)

Don't Get Tripped Up by Rent Control Violations

Any violation of a rent control ordinance by you can be used by a tenant to avoid eviction—even if the part of the ordinance you violated has nothing to do with the basis for eviction. For example, in many "strict" rent control cities, as well as in Los Angeles, where ordinances require landlords to register their properties with rent boards, a landlord who fails to register all the properties in a particular building cannot evict any tenant in any of the units for any reason—even if that particular unit is registered. In these cities, a tenant could be months behind in the rent and destroying the apartment, but the landlord would be legally unable to evict because the owner hadn't registered some other apartment in the same building with the rent board.

Similarly, a landlord's minor violation, such as failing to keep a tenant's security deposit in a separate account (if required), can be used by a tenant to defend an eviction based on the tenant's repeated loud parties. Problems of this sort can be avoided if you comply with every aspect of your city's ordinance.

Refusal to Allow Access

If, following receipt of a written warning from you, the tenant continues to refuse you or your agent access to the property (assuming you give the tenant proper notice of your need to enter), to show it to prospective buyers or to repair or maintain it, you may evict the tenant. (See *The California Landlord's Law Book: Rights & Responsibilities*, Chapter 13, for more on notice requirements.)

Most ordinances require that tenants be given a written warning before their tenancy is terminated by notice. Thus, if the tenant refuses you entry, you should serve a written demand that the tenant grant access followed by (or sometimes accompanied with) a three-day notice to cure or quit that demands access on a stated date and time at least three business days after service of the notice.

Check your ordinance to make sure you comply with its requirements for such a notice. Before you begin an eviction on this ground, you should be able to answer "yes" to all the following questions:

- Was your request to enter based on one of the reasons allowed by statute, such as to make repairs or show the property?
- Did you give your tenant adequate time to comply with the notice?
- Did you send a final notice setting out the tenant's failure to allow access and clearly stating your intent to evict if access was not granted?

You should use a curable three-day notice to evict on this ground. If the tenant doesn't comply, you can file the UD directly.

Landlord or Relative Move-In

A landlord who wants the premises to live in (or for a spouse, parent, or child) may use a 30-day or 60-day notice to ask the existing tenants to leave, provided the tenancy is month to month.

Some ordinances also allow landlords to evict tenants so that other relatives of the landlord (such as stepchildren, grandchildren, grandparents, or siblings) may move in. Because some landlords have abused this reason for eviction—for example, by falsely claiming that a relative is moving in—most cities strictly limit this option by requiring the termination notice to include detailed information, such as the name, current address, and phone number of the relative who will be moving in.

In addition, severe rent control cities forbid the use of this ground if the building has comparable vacant units into which the landlord or relative could move. Some cities allow only one unit per building to be occupied this way, and most cities do not allow nonindividual landlords (corporations or partnerships), or persons with less than a 50% interest in the building, to use this reason. Several cities go so far as to require landlords evicting for this reason to compensate the tenant who must move out.

Finally, rent control ordinances and state laws provide for heavy penalties against landlords who use a phony-relative ploy. State law requires that in rent control cities that mandate registration, landlords who evict tenants on the basis of wanting to move a relative (or the landlord) into the property must have their relative actually live there for six continuous months. (Civ. Code § 1947.10.) Individual cities may require a longer stay (San Francisco specifies 36 months). If the newcomer occupies the unit for less time than required, the tenant can sue the landlord in court for actual and punitive damages caused by the eviction.

Owners pay heavy penalties for intentional or even negligent violations of the occupancy rules. If a court determines that the landlord or relative never intended to stay in the unit, the tenant can move back in. The court can also award the tenant three times the increase in rent the tenant paid while living somewhere else, and three times the cost of moving back in. If the tenant decides not to move back into the old unit, the court can award three times the amount of one month's rent of the old unit and three times the costs incurred moving out of it. The tenant can also recover attorneys' fees and costs. (Civ. Code § 1947.10.)

Local ordinances provide much stiffer penalties. In the 90s, violations were priced in the low six figures. A court awarded one San Francisco tenant $200,000 for a wrongful eviction based on a phony-relative move-in. (*Beeman v. Burling* (1990) 216 Cal. App. 3d 1586, 265 Cal. Rptr. 719.) The price of such ploys has increased dramatically.

Now, verdicts and settlements in wrongful eviction suits have exceeded $2.4 *million*, with one couple receiving $3.5 million at trial. These verdicts are not covered by most insurance policies.

If you are planning to evict on the ground of renting the premises to a family member, you should be able to answer "yes" to all the following questions:

- Are you an "owner" as that term is described in your ordinance for the purpose of defining who has the right to possession?
- If a relative is moving in, does the relative qualify under the ordinance?
- Will the person remain on the premises long enough to preclude a later action against you by the tenant?
- Does your notice provide the information required by the ordinance?
- Are you prepared to pay the tenant compensation, if required by your local ordinance?

Remodeling

A landlord who wants possession of the property to conduct remodeling or extensive repairs can use a 30-day or 60-day notice to evict tenants in some circumstances if the tenancy is month to month. Because of the ease with which this ground for eviction can be abused, most cities severely limit its use. For instance, the Los Angeles ordinance requires that at least $10,000 or more per unit (depending on the size of the property) be spent on the repairs or remodeling before eviction on this ground is allowed, and some ordinances (for example, those in Berkeley and Santa Monica) allow this ground only where the repairs are designed to correct local health or building code violations. In some cities, once the repairs are made, the landlord must give the evicted tenant the right of "first refusal" to rerent the property.

All cities with just cause eviction provisions require that the landlord obtain all necessary building and other permits before eviction. Finally, most cities allow the tenant to sue the landlord for wrongful eviction if the work isn't accomplished within a reasonable time (usually six months) after the tenant leaves.

If you plan to evict using this ground, you should be able to answer "yes" to all the following questions:

- Is the remodeling really so extensive that it requires the tenant to vacate the property?
- Have you obtained all necessary permits from the city?
- Are you prepared to pay the tenant compensation if required by ordinance?
- Have you made all necessary arrangements with financing institutions, contractors, and so on, in order to make sure the work will be finished within the period required by the ordinance?
- Have you met all other requirements of your local ordinance, such as giving proper notice to the tenant, offering the tenant the right to relocate into any vacant comparable unit, or giving the tenant the opportunity to move back in once the remodeling work is finished?

Condominium Conversion and Demolition

A landlord may evict to permanently remove the property from the rental market by means of condominium conversion or "good-faith" demolition (not motivated by the existence of the rent control ordinance). But the notice of termination (which must specify the reason) is only the last step in a very complicated process for conversion or demolition.

A state statute, the Ellis Act, allows permanent removal as a ground for eviction, but cities can (and do) restrict application of the law, including requiring notice periods of more than 30 or even 60 days—in some cases, as much as 120 days or even a year. All cities allow these grounds to be used only after the landlord has obtained all the necessary permits and approvals. Most cities have very stringent condominium conversion or antidemolition ordinances that require all sorts of preliminary notices to tenants. Some limit the landlord's right to demolish residential rental property occupied by low-income or disabled tenants; others limit the ability of individual cities to impose restrictions on condominium conversions. Be sure to check for new legislation, on the state and local levels, if your eviction is a first step toward hoped-for condominium conversion. Hiring a lawyer to help you through the permit process is almost always a good idea.

Violation of Rental Agreement

If the tenant violates a significant provision of the rental agreement, you can use a 30-day or 60-day notice to initiate an eviction if the tenancy is month to month. This ground also justifies evicting with a three-day notice, but if you use this option, the tenant must, in some cases, be given the opportunity to correct the violation. (See Chapter 4.) As a general rule, however, you may use a 30-day or 60-day notice if the tenancy is month to month (for reasons discussed below), and the tenant cannot cure the violation.

 RENT CONTROL
Violation of new rental agreement terms. Some cities prohibit eviction for violation of a rental agreement provision that was added to the original rental agreement, either by means of a notice of change in terms of tenancy or by virtue of a new rental agreement signed after the original one expired.

Even in places without rent control, judges are reluctant to evict based on breaches other than nonpayment of rent. First, the breach must be considered "substantial"—that is, very serious. Second, you should be able to prove the violation with convincing testimony from a fairly impartial person, such as a tenant in the same building who is willing to testify in court. If you're unable to produce any witnesses who saw (or heard) the violation, or who heard the tenant admit to it, forget it.

Before you begin an eviction on this ground, you should be able to answer "yes" to the following questions:

- Was the violated provision part of the original rental agreement?
- If the provision was added later, does your ordinance allow eviction on this ground?
- Can you definitely prove the violation?
- Was the violated provision legal under state law and the ordinance?
- Have you given the tenant a previous warning letter as required by the lease, or the rent control ordinance or just cause for eviction ordinance?

Unauthorized Subletting and Assignment

In written rental agreements that restrict the tenant's right to sublet or assign, or that limit the number of occupants in the apartment, a tenant who subleases, assigns, or adds a new occupant without the landlord's approval violates the agreement. Outside of certain rent control jurisdictions, the breach may be curable or not curable, depending upon your specific lease.

As we explain in Chapter 18 of *The California Landlord's Law Book: Rights and Responsibilities*, if your lease defines unapproved subletting or assignment as a "material, noncurable" breach, the unapproved act justifies termination with a three-day notice to quit under C.C.P. §1161(3). But if the lease prohibits unauthorized subletting or assigning *but does not specifically include a provision defining the breach as a material, noncurable breach*, then the breach can be cured. In that event, you'll need to use a different notice, a three-day notice to cure or quit under C.C.P. §1161(2). Chapter 4 discusses these two types of notice.

Subleases and Assignments

A *sublease* involves leasing the premises to a subtenant for a period of time, such as during the tenant's absence while on vacation, after which the tenant returns and the subtenant leaves. Or, the tenant subleases part of the rental while still living there. An *assignment* involves turning the entire lease over to a new tenant (the "assignee"), when the original tenant has no plans to return. In each situation, the original tenant remains liable to the landlord for the entire rent, unless the landlord has explicitly relieved the tenant of that obligation. Assignments are better handled by terminating the original lease and entering into a new one with the proposed new occupant.

For example, ordinances often allow tenants to add a family member to the rental as long as the family member meets certain basic requirements. Family members include spouses, domestic partners, children, grandchildren, siblings, and grandparents. Similarly, a tenant can replace an outgoing approved occupant with a new occupant approved by the landlord. Many ordinances limit the landlord's right to disapprove proposed occupants or additions.

If a landlord reasonably refused to approve a proposed occupant (on the grounds of poor references, for instance), continued occupancy by the rejected occupant would give the landlord cause to terminate the lease. However, a landlord's unreasonable refusal to approve will furnish a defense to an eviction (an unreasonable refusal might include a personal dislike, without a valid business reason). Savvy tenants who propose adding a new occupant will document any approvals or, more importantly, disapprovals, by writing to the landlord summarizing the landlord's response. If the landlord fails to write back, disputing the tenant's account, that can be brought to the attention of a judge if the parties end up in court, arguing over whose version was agreed to.

(Failure to dispute the tenant's account is refutable evidence that the landlord agreed with it.) The lesson here is to never let the tenant have the last word unless you agree with it.

If your tenant has proposed a sublet or assignment, think twice before rejecting the applicant based on the applicant's credit score. As noted in "Subleases and Assignments," above, the original tenants remain responsible for the rent unless you explicitly relieve them of that duty. The subtenant's or assignee's ability to pay the original tenant is their business and technically not your concern; you simply have no financial stake in that relationship. However, if you will accept rent payments directly from the subtenant or assignee; or if the sublessee's or assignee's rent payments represent a large part of the total rent due, you arguably do have a financial stake in the sublease or assignment and can legitimately insist on a creditworthy subtenant or assignee.

Damage to the Premises

If the tenant is disturbing other tenants or seriously damaging the property, you can use a 30-day or 60-day notice to initiate an eviction procedure. Under state law, a three-day notice to quit that doesn't give the tenant the option of correcting the problem may also be used. Some rent control cities require that a landlord give the tenant a chance to correct the violation. (See Chapter 4.)

Illegal Activity on the Premises

If the tenant has committed (or, in some cities, been convicted of) serious illegal activity on the premises, a landlord may initiate an eviction by using a 30-day or 60-day notice when the tenancy is month to month. This ground also justifies using a three-day notice (discussed in Chapter 4), but you should use the longer one if possible (in most places, using the longer notice relieves you of the need to prove the activity). You should document

the illegal activity thoroughly (see Chapter 4), keeping a record of your complaints to police and the names of the persons with whom you spoke. And although not required by ordinance, it's often a good idea to first give the tenant written notice to cease the illegal activity. If the tenant fails to do so, the fact that you gave notice should help establish that there's a serious and continuing problem.

> **CAUTION**
> **Drug-dealing tenants.** As stated earlier, it is essential to do everything you can to evict any tenant who you strongly suspect is dealing illegal drugs on the property. A landlord who ignores this sort of problem can face severe liability.

Should You Use a Three-Day, 30-Day, or 60-Day Notice?

As we have pointed out, some reasons for eviction under a 30-day or 60-day notice, such as making too much noise or damaging the property, also justify evicting with a three-day notice, as described in Chapter 4.

When to Use a 30- or 60-Day Notice

If you can evict a tenant by using a three-day notice, why give the tenant a break by using a 30-day or 60-day notice? Simply because tenants are more likely to contest an eviction lawsuit that accuses them of misconduct and gives them a lot less time to look for another place to live. In places where you don't have to show just cause to give a 30-day or 60-day notice, you also avoid having to prove your reason for evicting (unless you must overcome a tenant's defense based on your supposed retaliation or discrimination).

Finally, if you base the three-day notice on trivial violations, such as a tenant's having a goldfish or parakeet contrary to a no-pets clause in the rental agreement, but you really want the tenant out because the two of you can't get along,

30-Day Notice of Termination of Tenancy

(Tenancy Less Than One Year)

To: _____ **Fill in tenant's name(s).** _____ ,

(name)

Tenant(s) in possession of the premises at _____ **List street address, including apartment number.** _____ ,

(street address)

City of _____ , County of _____ , California.

YOU ARE HEREBY NOTIFIED that effective THIRTY (30) DAYS from the date of service on you of this notice, the periodic tenancy by which you hold possession of the premises is terminated, at which time you are required to vacate and surrender possession of the premises. If you fail to do so, legal proceedings will be instituted against you to recover possession of the premises, damages, and costs of suit.

If you are in a rent control city or are otherwise required by law to state a reason for terminating a tenancy, insert it here. Be specific. You must also include any required disclosure statements under the law, such as an "advice regarding this notice" clause, together with any required attachments, such as an informational statement concerning assistance from the local rent board or agency.

NOTICE: State law permits former tenants to reclaim abandoned personal property left at the former address of the tenant, subject to certain conditions. You may or may not be able to reclaim property without incurring additional costs, depending on the cost of storing the property and the length of time before it is reclaimed. In general, these costs will be lower the sooner you contact your former landlord after being notified that property belonging to you was left behind after you moved out.

Date: _____ **date of notice** _____   _____ **owner's or manager's signature** _____

Owner/Manager

The instructions for completing the Proof of Service are the same as those described under the Three-Day Notice to Pay Rent or Quit (Chapter 2) with one exception— service by certified mail may be used.

Proof of Service

I, the undersigned, being at least 18 years of age, served this notice, of which this is a true copy, on _____ , _____ , one of the occupants listed above as follows:

☐ On _____ , _____ , I delivered the notice to the occupant personally.

☐ On _____ , _____ , I delivered the notice to a person of suitable age and discretion at the occupant's residence/business after having attempted personal service at the occupant's residence, and business, if known. On _____ , _____ , I mailed a second copy to the occupant at his or her residence.

☐ On _____ , _____ , I posted the notice in a conspicuous place on the property, after having attempted personal service at the occupant's residence, and business, if known, and after having been unable to find there a person of suitable age and discretion. On _____ , _____ , I mailed a second copy to the occupant at the property.

I declare under penalty of perjury under the laws of the State of California that the foregoing is true and correct.

Date: _____   _____

Signature

30-Day Notice of Termination of Tenancy
(Tenancy Less Than One Year)

To: _____Rhoda D. Renter_____,
                              (name)

Tenant(s) in possession of the premises at _____950 Parker Street_____,
                                                                          (street address)

City of _____Palo Alto_____, County of _____Santa Clara_____, California.

YOU ARE HEREBY NOTIFIED that effective THIRTY (30) DAYS from the date of service on you of this notice, the periodic tenancy by which you hold possession of the premises is terminated, at which time you are required to vacate and surrender possession of the premises. If you fail to do so, legal proceedings will be instituted against you to recover possession of the premises, damages, and costs of suit.

_____

_____

_____

_____

_____

_____

_____

_____

_____

NOTICE: State law permits former tenants to reclaim abandoned personal property left at the former address of the tenant, subject to certain conditions. You may or may not be able to reclaim property without incurring additional costs, depending on the cost of storing the property and the length of time before it is reclaimed. In general, these costs will be lower the sooner you contact your former landlord after being notified that property belonging to you was left behind after you moved out.

Date: _____August 3, 20xx_____   _____Lani Landlord_____
                                                                      Owner/Manager

- -

Proof of Service

I, the undersigned, being at least 18 years of age, served this notice, of which this is a true copy, on _____
_____, one of the occupants listed above as follows:

☐ On _____, _____, I delivered the notice to the occupant personally.

☐ On _____, _____, I delivered the notice to a person of suitable age and discretion at the occupant's residence/business after having attempted personal service at the occupant's residence, and business, if known. On _____, _____, I mailed a second copy to the occupant at his or her residence.

☐ On _____, _____, I posted the notice in a conspicuous place on the property, after having attempted personal service at the occupant's residence, and business, if known, and after having been unable to find there a person of suitable age and discretion. On _____, _____, I mailed a second copy to the occupant at the property.

I declare under penalty of perjury under the laws of the State of California that the foregoing is true and correct.

Date: _____   _____
                                                                                      Signature

you are likely to lose your unlawful detainer suit. Judges are not eager to let a tenant be evicted, with only three days' notice, for a minor breach of the rental agreement or causing an insignificant nuisance or damage. If, on the other hand, you use a 30-day or 60-day notice and rent in an area that does not require just cause to evict, you don't have to state a reason. In other words, by following this approach, you have one less significant problem to deal with.

When to Use a Three-Day Notice

If your tenant has an unexpired fixed-term lease, you cannot use an unconditional 30-day or 60-day notice to evict. You can evict only if the tenant violates the lease; in that case, the three-day notice must usually give the tenant the option of correcting the violation and staying in the premises.

Finally, you should use a three-day notice if your reason for evicting a month-to-month tenant is nonpayment of rent (and you want the rent). That's because you won't be able to sue for back rent in an unlawful detainer lawsuit based on a 30-day or 60-day notice (you'll have to bring a separate, small claims court suit to get the rent). Unless you are prepared to go to two courts (or want to forgo the back rent in favor of not having to prove a reason for the termination), you'll need to use a three-day notice. (*Saberi v. Bakhtiari*, (1985) 169 Cal. App. 3d 509.)

Preparing the 30-Day or 60-Day Notice

A sample 30-Day Notice of Termination of Tenancy, with instructions, appears above. The sample shown here is for a 30-day notice, but the 60-day notice is identical, except for the amount of the notice.

 FORM

Blank copies of the 30-, 60-, and 90-day notices can be downloaded from the Nolo website. (See the appendix for the link to the forms in this book, and other information on using the forms.)

As you can see, filling in the notice requires little more than setting out the name of the tenant, the address of the property, the date, and your signature.

List the names of all adult occupants of the premises, even if their names aren't on the rental agreement.

RENT CONTROL

Comply with rent control and other local ordinances that require just cause for eviction, and provide any additional information your ordinance requires on your 30- or 60-day notice. For example, San Francisco's ordinance requires that every notice on which an eviction lawsuit is based tell tenants that they may obtain assistance from that city's rent control board. San Francisco's Rent Board regulations require that the 30-day notice quote the section that authorizes evictions for the particular reason listed. San Francisco also requires attaching a form that advises the tenant that information can be obtained from the San Francisco Rent Board ("Notice to Tenant Required by Rent Ordinance § 37.9(c)," known as the "1007 form"). Failure to attach the advice form nullifies the validity of your termination notice. You'll find a blank copy of this form online by going to the "Forms Center" menu at the San Francisco Rent Board website (www.sfrb.org) and scrolling down to Form Number 1007).

In addition, many rent control ordinances require that the reason for eviction be stated in the notice. For example, under most just cause provisions, a notice based on the tenant's repeated refusal to allow the landlord access to the property on reasonable notice must state at least the dates and times of the refusals. And for terminations based on wanting to move in a relative or remodel the property, extra notice requirements are specified in detail in the ordinance or in regulations adopted by the rent control board.

Also, if your tenant has made a complaint to you or a local government agency, withheld rent because of a claimed defect in the property, or participated in tenant-organizing activity, be extra sure that your notice states legitimate, nonretaliatory reasons for terminating the tenancy. (Civ. Code § 1942.5(c); *Western Land Office, Inc. v. Cervantes* (1985) 174 Cal. App. 3d 724.)

Absent a just cause requirement, you should not list the reason for the termination unless you are in a high-risk situation as described in "Impermissible Reasons to Evict With a 30- or 60-Day Notice," above, or the rent control law or government regulation (for subsidized housing) requires it. If you do have to include the reason, you may wish to check with an attorney or other knowledgeable person in your area to make sure you state it properly and with specificity; doing so will help ensure that your tenant cannot complain that the notice is too vague or void under local law. Tenants and courts scrutinize the notice for defects and poor or defective wording will result in your losing the case.

Serving the Notice

The law sets out detailed requirements for serving a 30-day or 60-day notice on a tenant. If you don't comply with them, you could lose your unlawful detainer lawsuit.

When the Notice Should Be Served

A 30-day or 60-day notice can be served on the tenant on any day of the month. For example, a 60-day notice served on March 17 terminates the tenancy 60 days later, on May 16. The notice expires in 30 or 60 *calendar* days, not business days. (Remember to count 60 days, regardless of whether any intervening month has 28, 29, or 31 days.) This is true even if rent is paid for the period from the first to the last day of each month.

There's one exception: If your lease or rental agreement requires the landlord's termination notice to be served on a certain day, such as the first of the month, you must wait for that date before serving your notice (eliminate this provision in future leases). Be advised that attempting to limit the tenant to serving notice on the first, or any specified date, would not be upheld in court.

The best time to serve the notice is shortly after you receive and cash a rent check. Assuming the tenant paid on time, this means you'll give the notice toward the beginning of the month or rental period, so that the last day of the tenancy will fall only one or two days into the next month. The advantage is that you will already have the rent for almost all of the time the tenant can (legally) remain on the premises. If the tenant refuses to pay any more rent (for the day or two in the next month), you can just deduct it from the security deposit. (See Chapter 9.)

> EXAMPLE: Tess has been habitually late with the rent for the last five months of her seven-month occupancy, usually paying on the third day after receiving your three-day notice. On October 2, you knock on Tess's door and ask for the rent. If you luck out and get her to pay this time, cash the check and then serve Tess with a 30-day notice. The last day of the tenancy will be November 1, and she'll owe you only one day's rent. You can deduct this amount from the deposit before you return it, assuming you give the tenant proper written notice of what you are doing.
>
> Of course, if Tess doesn't pay her rent on the 2nd, you can resort to the usual three-day notice. If she still doesn't pay within three days, you can sue for nonpayment of rent as described in Chapter 2.

If you've already collected "last month's rent," you can serve the 30-day notice (assuming the tenancy has lasted less than a year) on the first day of the last month without worrying about collecting rent first. Do not, however, serve it so that the tenancy ends before the end of the period (the last month) for which you have collected rent. Accepting rent for a period beyond the date you set in the 30-day notice for termination of the tenancy is inconsistent with the notice and means you have effectively cancelled it. (See *Highland Plastics, Inc. v. Enders* (1980) 109 Cal. App. 3d Supp.1.)

If you serve the 30-day or 60-day notice in the middle of the month, your tenant may not be eager, when the next month comes around, to pay rent for the part of a subsequent month before the tenancy ends. If this happens and you can't settle the issue by talking to your tenant, you can take the prorated rent for the last portion of a month out of the security deposit. (See Chapter 9.) You could also serve the tenant with a Three-Day Notice to Pay Rent or Quit for the prorated rent due. We recommend against this, unless you've given a 60-day notice and the tenant refuses to pay the rent for the following full month. Using two notices increases the chances that you will make a procedural mistake. It complicates the eviction, increases hostility, and probably won't get the tenant out any faster.

Who Should Serve the Notice

The 30-day notice may be served by any person over age 18. (See Chapter 2.) Although you can legally serve the notice yourself, it's often better to have someone else serve it. That way, if tenants refuse to pay the rent and contest the eviction lawsuit by claiming they didn't receive the notice, you can present the testimony of someone not a party to the lawsuit who is more likely than you to be believed by a judge. Of course, you must weigh this advantage against any time, trouble, or expense it takes to get someone else to accomplish the service and, if necessary, appear in court.

Whom to Serve

As with three-day notices, you should try to serve a copy of the 30-day or 60-day notice on each tenant to whom you originally rented the property. (For advice, see "Who Should Receive the Notice" in Chapter 2.)

How to Serve the Notice on the Tenant

The notice may be served in any of the ways three-day notices can be served (see Chapter 2):
- by personal delivery to the tenant
- by substituted service on another person, plus mailing, or
- by posting and mailing.

In addition, the notice can be served by certified mail. The statute does not require that it be sent return receipt requested. The return receipt gives you proof that the tenant received the notice, but it also entails a risk, because a tenant can refuse the letter by refusing to sign the receipt. In any case, the post office gives you a receipt when you send anything by certified mail.

If you serve the notice by certified mail, we suggest that you give the tenant an extra five days (in addition to the 30 or 60 days) before filing suit. You may be wondering why, since you do *not* need to add the extra five days if you serve a three-day or other notice by substituted service plus mailing or by posting and mailing. (In Chapter 2, see "When to File Your Lawsuit" and its explanation of the *Losornio* case that established this rule.) The answer is that, in both a substituted service plus mailing situation and a posting plus mailing situation, there is a chance that the tenant will, in fact, get the benefit of the full period (the person you've served may give the tenant the notice, or the tenant may pick up the posted notice, within the three or 30 or 60 days). When you serve using certified mail only, however, there is no way that the tenant can get the benefit of the full 30 or 60 days, because the notice will necessarily sit in the post office and the mailbag for a day or two at least, and there is no alternative way to receive the notice. For this reason, we think that you should add the five days to service accomplished via certified mail only, although plausible arguments can be made to the contrary. It's best to take the time to serve the 30-day notice personally.

 TIP
Remember:

- Do not accept any rent whatsoever for any period beyond the day your tenant should be out of the premises under your notice.
- Accept only rent that you've prorated by the day up until the last day of tenancy, or you'll void your notice and have to start all over again with a new one.
- If you've given a 30-day notice, don't accept any rent at all if you collected "last month's rent" from the tenant, because that's what you apply to the tenant's last month or part of a month.
- Be sure the person serving the notice completes a Proof of Service at the bottom of an extra copy of the notice, indicating when and how the notice was served. (See "Preparing the Three-Day Notice to Pay Rent or Quit" in Chapter 2.)

When to File Your Lawsuit

Once your 30-day or 60-day notice is properly served, you must wait 30 or 35 (or 60 or 65) days before taking any further action. If you file an unlawful detainer complaint prematurely, you will lose the lawsuit and have to start all over again. Here's how to figure out how long you have to wait:

- Service is complete when you personally serve the notice, or after you have mailed it following substituted service or posting. If you serve it by certified mail, though, you should wait an extra five days before filing suit.

- If you serve more than one tenant with notices, but not all on the same day, start counting only after the last tenant is served.
- Do not count the day of service as the first day. The first day to count is the day after service of the notice was completed.
- The tenant gets 30 or 60 full days after service. Do not file your lawsuit until at least the 31st day (plus any five-day extension on account of serving by certified mail) after service is complete.
- If the 30th or 60th day is a business day, you may file your lawsuit on the next business day after that.
- If the 30th or 60th day falls on a Saturday, Sunday, or legal holiday, the tenant can stay until the end of the next business day. You cannot file your suit on that business day, but must wait until the day after that.

EXAMPLE: You personally served Tanya with her 30-day notice on June 3 (the day after she paid you the rent). June 4 is the first day after service, and July 3 is the 30th day. But July 3 is a Sunday, and July 4 is a holiday. This means Tanya has until the end of the next business day, July 5, to vacate. The first day you can file your suit is July 6.

If you had served Tanya on June 3 using any other method of service, she would have an additional five days to leave, and you could file suit on July 11 (or later if July 10 were a Saturday, Sunday, or holiday).

Once you have waited the requisite period, and the tenant has failed to leave, you can proceed to the next phase, which is filing an eviction complaint. We tell you how to do this in Chapter 6.

Eviction for Lease Violations, Property Damage, or Nuisance

FORMS IN THIS CHAPTER

Chapter 4 includes instructions for and samples of the Three-Day Notice to Perform Covenant or Quit and the Three-Day Notice to Quit, and the Nolo website includes downloadable copies of them. (See the appendix for the link to the forms in this book, and other information on using the forms.)

This chapter also includes a Checklist for Uncontested Nonrent Three-Day Notice Eviction, which outlines the steps involved in evicting a tenant with a three-day notice and the earliest times you can do each step.

This chapter is about using a three-day notice to evict tenants who:

- engage in highly disruptive activity (for example, making unreasonable noise, creating a nuisance, threatening neighbors)
- destroy part or all of the premises
- violate the lease or rental agreement on a substantial issue (for example, keeping a pet or subleasing without permission)
- make illegal use of the premises (for example, selling or even possessing illegal drugs or firearms), or
- fail to make a payment (other than rent) that is required under the lease or rental agreement (for example, late fee, security deposit upgrade, or utility surcharge). (If you want to evict the tenant for nonpayment of rent, use Chapter 2.)

When to Use a Three-Day Notice Eviction

For reasons covered in Chapter 3, in some situations you might prefer to use a 30-day or 60-day notice to terminate a month-to-month tenancy instead of the three-day notice. A three-day notice is allowed or required under circumstances such as a tenant's making unreasonable noise or violating the lease by keeping a pet. Typically, and we discuss this further below, you have to use a three-day notice if the problem can be cured or a law requires its use.

Why would you want to take the slower route with a 30-/60-day notice where you have a choice? Here's why:

- First, if you use a three-day notice, you will have to prove to the court your reason for eviction (the tenant's misconduct), whereas with a 30-day or 60-day notice, you don't have to (unless state or local law requires just cause).

Can You Evict Tenants Who Host Guests via Airbnb?

Airbnb and other online businesses are clearinghouses for short-stay (less than 30-day) vacation rentals. Especially in vacation destination cities, tenants have taken advantage of these services, essentially subletting their rentals and pocketing the money (at the same time, increasing wear and tear on the premises). This is a legal practice in most cities whose laws often, however, limit the number of short-stay days and require registration. Landlords universally dislike the practice, and many hope to prevent it with no-sublet clauses. However, the law is unclear whether standard no-sublet clauses can effectively forbid the practice of hosting guests via Airbnb and similar services.

For this reason, unless you have an absolutely airtight lease clause specifically prohibiting such rentals (the clause in the Nolo lease mentions Airbnb and similar services), you should seek the advice of an experienced attorney before evicting on this basis. Be sure your attorney is current on local rules, because these are changing rapidly. For example, San Francisco, which had long prohibited short-term residential rentals (less than 30 days), changed its rules to legalize and regulate short-term stays.

- Second, tenants who receive a three-day notice for misconduct are a lot more likely to defend the suit. They might want to vindicate their reputations, or get back at you, or simply want some additional time to move. By contrast, if you terminate a month-to-month tenancy with a 30-day or 60-day notice, the tenant has time both to move and to cool off emotionally, and might exit quietly without finding it necessary to shoot a hole in your water heater (or worse).

Checklist for Uncontested Nonrent Three-Day Notice Eviction	
Step	**Earliest Time to Do It**
☐ 1. Prepare and serve the three-day notice on the tenant. If covered by just cause, the notice may be an alternative ("cure or quit") notice.	Any day the tenant is in violation of the lease, has damaged the property, or has created a nuisance.
1(a). If the tenancy is subject to statewide just cause termination restrictions, prepare a noncurable three-day notice to quit. (C.C. § 1946.2(c)	After the curable notice has expired.
☐ 2. Prepare the summons (or summonses, if there is more than one tenant) and complaint and make copies. (Chapter 6)	When it's apparent the tenant(s) won't leave on time; don't sign and date it until the day indicated below in Step 3.
☐ 3. File the complaint at the courthouse and have the summons(es) issued. (Chapter 6)	The first business day after the lease term or tenant's notice period expires.
☐ 4. Have the sheriff, the marshal, a registered process server, or a friend serve the summons and complaint. (Chapter 6)	As soon as possible after filing the complaint and having the summons(es) issued.
☐ 5. Prepare Request for Entry of Default, Judgment, Declaration, and Writ of Possession. (Chapter 7)	While you're waiting for five-day (or 15-day, if complaint not personally served) response time to pass.
☐ 6. Call the court to find out whether or not tenant(s) has filed written response.	Just before closing on the fifth business day after service of summons, or early on the sixth day. (Do not count holidays that fall on weekdays, however. Also, if fifth day after service falls on weekend or holiday, count the first business day after that as the fifth day.)
☐ 7. Mail copy of Request for Entry of Default to tenant(s), file original at courthouse. Also file summons and declaration and have clerk issue judgment and writ for possession of the property. (Chapter 7)	Sixth business day after service of summons and complaint. (Again, count first business day after fifth day that falls on weekend or holiday.)
☐ 8. Prepare letter of instruction for, and give writ and copies to, sheriff or marshal. (Chapter 7)	As soon as possible after above step. Sheriff or marshal won't evict for at least five days after posting notice.
☐ 9. Change locks after tenant vacates.	As soon as possible.
For Money Judgment	
☐ 10. Prepare Request for Entry of Default, Judgment, and, if allowed by local rule, declaration in lieu of testimony. (Chapter 7)	As soon as possible after property is vacant.
☐ 11. Mail Request for Entry of Default copy to tenant, file request at courthouse. If declaration in lieu of testimony is allowed, file that, too, and give clerk judgment and writ forms for money part of judgment. If testimony required, ask clerk for default hearing. (Chapter 7)	As soon as possible after above.

Checklist for Uncontested Nonrent Three-Day Notice Eviction (continued)	
For Money Judgment (continued)	
☐ 12. If testimony required, attend default hearing before judge, testify, and turn in your judgment form for entry of money judgment. (Chapter 7)	When scheduled by court clerk.
☐ 13. Apply security deposit to cleaning and repair of property, and to any rent not accounted for in judgment, then apply balance to judgment amount. Notify tenant in writing of deductions, keeping a copy. Refund any balance remaining. If deposit does not cover entire judgment, collect balance of judgment. (Chapter 9)	As soon as possible after default hearing. Deposit must be accounted for within three weeks of when the tenants vacate.

- Third, to use a three-day notice successfully, the problem you're complaining about must be truly serious. A judge will not order an eviction based on a three-day notice for minor rental agreement violations or property damage. For example, if you base a three-day notice eviction on the fact that your tenant's parakeet constitutes a serious violation of the no-pets clause in the lease; or that one or two noisy parties or the tenant's loud stereo is a sufficient nuisance to justify immediate eviction, you may well lose. The point is simple: Any time you use a three-day notice for reasons short of a serious situation, your eviction attempt becomes dependent on the judge's (or a jury's) predilections on what is a serious problem and therefore more uncertain.

For these reasons, you should resort to three-day notice evictions based on something other than nonpayment of rent only when the problem is serious and time is very important.

Checklist for Uncontested Nonrent Three-Day Notice Eviction

Above is an overview of the steps involved in evicting on the grounds covered in this chapter when the tenant defaults (doesn't contest the eviction). We

cover some of the subjects (for example, filing a complaint and default judgments) in later chapters. As you work your way through the book, you may want to return to this chart to see where you are in the process.

Evicting a Tenant Who Is Dealing Drugs

If the tenant is dealing illegal drugs on the property, the problem is serious. A landlord who hesitates to evict a drug-dealing tenant (1) faces lawsuits from other tenants, neighbors, and local authorities; (2) may wind up liable for tens of thousands of dollars in damages; and (3) could even lose the property.

Fortunately, you won't be in the ridiculous position of having to argue about the seriousness of drug dealing. California law identifies such activity—or even mere possession of drugs like cocaine, heroin, and methamphetamine; or possession of illegal firearms on the premises—as an illegal nuisance. (C.C.P. § 1161(4), H&S § 115 71.1 (c), C.C. § 3485.)

It's easier to evict drug-dealing tenants with a 30-day or 60-day notice, where no just cause requirements apply. However, if the tenant has a fixed-term lease (which can't be terminated with a 30-day or 60-day notice), or if you have a just cause requirement to terminate, you will have no choice but to follow the procedures set forth in this chapter, by using a three-day notice to quit. (See "Using the Unconditional Three-Day Notice to Quit," below.) You should start by getting other tenants, and neighbors if possible, to document heavy traffic in and out of the tenant's home at odd hours.

In a contested case, proving drug dealing without assistance from law enforcement requires considerable evidence and can be difficult to document. Neighbors and tenants often do not want to testify in court. Experienced attorneys build cases with video and photographic evidence, and frequently hire private investigators to conduct investigations and even place the tenant under surveillance. Preparing a case like this is expensive, time-consuming, and generally beyond the ken of even the most energetic self-helper.

Fortunately, there's a simpler way to get rid of your drug-dealing resident. Instead of trying to make a case for drug dealing, consider a case based upon breach of the rental agreement (violation of the lease's use clause, which limits use to residential activities only; or the nuisance clause, which prohibits activity that substantially interferes with the comfort or safety of other residents). Proving a breach of the lease or other nuisance requires less evidence than you'd need to prove drug dealing directly, but successfully obtaining a judgment usually depends on the testimony (and not just letters) from other residents or neighbors. The bottom line is that if you're dealing with a drug-dealing situation, you'd be wise to hire an attorney.

The Two Types of Three-Day Notices

Two kinds of three-day notices are covered here. The first is called a Notice to Perform Covenant or Quit and is like the three-day notice used for nonpayment of rent (see Chapter 2) in that it gives tenants the option of staying if they correct their behavior within the three-day period. If they don't, then the tenancy is considered terminated. Most three-day notices fit into this category.

The other type of three-day notice simply tells the tenant to move out in three days. There is no option to correct the behavior. This kind of unconditional notice is allowed only in certain circumstances, described below.

We strongly recommend that you use the conditional notice if any guesswork is involved. The consequences of using the unconditional notice can be drastic if the judge later disagrees with you and thinks that the situation called for a conditional notice. In that event, the judge will rule that your unconditional three-day notice was void; you will lose the lawsuit, be liable for the tenant's court costs and attorneys' fees, and have to start all over again with a new notice.

Type of Notice Used in Rent Control (Just Cause) Situations

The type of notice you must deliver (and the number of notices you must give!) depends on whether the property is covered by rent control (statewide or a local rent ordinance). Here are the rules:

- If no law (the TPA or a local ordinance) requires just cause to terminate, you can give a "standard" three-day notice to cure or quit, like the sample form below.
- If the property is covered by statewide just cause limitations under Civ. Code § 1942.6, you should first serve a notice to cure or quit, listing the cause and the breach; then, if the tenant neither cures nor quits, serve a noncurable three-day notice on the same ground. Both are discussed below.
- If you are covered by a local rent control ordinance (or if both the TPA and a local ordinance apply, but the local one has more requirements), things get complicated.

The TPA appears to require two three-day notices, delivered one after the other—a curable notice and a noncurable notice. Prepare them like this:

- First, prepare and serve the warning, or "cease and desist" notice, required by the local ordinance.
- Then depending on the situation and facts underlying the tenant's breach, prepare and serve a conditional *or* unconditional three-day notice to quit. This final step (conditional or unconditional) requires a judgment call on whether the violation qualifies as deserving of a chance to be stopped, thus saving the tenancy. If the problem can be fixed by a relatively simple act, such as making a payment or getting rid of a pet, use the conditional notice. If you're unsure about applicable eviction regulations or have any doubt about the validity of your grounds for eviction, consulting with a landlord-tenant specialist will be well worth the price.

If you attempt to evict a tenant in violation of a city's ordinance, you could be facing more than an unsuccessful eviction. Depending on the circumstances and the city, tenants may come back at you with a suit of their own, alleging any number of personal injuries—even if the tenant defaults or loses in the underlying eviction action.

Some rent control cities preclude eviction for violations of a lease provision if the provision was added unilaterally to the original agreement, either by means of a notice of change of terms in tenancy or by virtue of a new lease signed by the tenant after the previous one expired. In such cities, a landlord who, for example, rented to a tenant with a pet couldn't later change the terms of the rental agreement with a 30-day notice saying no pets are allowed, then evict for violation of that term after it goes into effect. (Los Angeles's ordinance specifically forbids just this sort of eviction.) Eviction on the basis of violating a unilateral lease change could allow a landlord who does not have grounds for eviction to evade the just cause requirement. By changing the lease terms and hoping the tenant will violate the new clause, the landlord will have ensured the tenant's breach.

Even in cities that do permit eviction based on after-added clauses, the clauses still must be legal and reasonable. Also, every city's ordinance makes it illegal for a landlord to attempt to evade its provisions. An unreasonable change in the rental agreement that ensures a tenant's breach will most likely be considered an attempt to circumvent any just cause requirement and a court will not enforce it.

The state just cause statute does not speak directly to this issue. An inference exists that you cannot enforce a unilateral change in terms of the tenancy, because the law only enforces the tenant's refusal to sign a substantially similar lease or extension. However, it is difficult to rely on an inference and no published cases have discussed unilateral changes to leases under the state just cause requirement. From a policy perspective, the tenant has a better defense to unilateral enforcement than a landlord has the right to terminate, especially if a court or jury thinks the landlord's change was unreasonable or unfair.

If your property is located in a rent control city that provides for just cause eviction (see Chapter 3), be sure to check a current copy of your ordinance for additional eviction and notice requirements that might apply.

Using the Three-Day Notice to Perform Covenant or Quit

In most situations, you'll use a conditional three-day notice, giving the tenant the option of correcting the violation or moving out.

When to Use a Conditional Three-Day Notice

If tenants who have violated a provision of the lease or rental agreement can correct their behavior, your three-day notice must give them that option. As mentioned, most lease violations are correctable. For instance:

- The tenant who violates a "no-pets" clause can get rid of the pet.
- The tenant who has failed to pay separate charges for utilities, legitimate late charges, or an installment toward an agreed-on security deposit can make the payment.
- Tenants who violate a lease clause requiring them to allow you reasonable access to the property can let you in (on proper notice— see *The California Landlord's Law Book: Rights & Responsibilities*, Chapter 13).

The list of potentially correctable lease violations is endless. As a general rule, if the violation isn't of the type listed below in "When to Use an Unconditional Three-Day Notice," it's probably correctable, and you should use a three-day notice giving the tenant the option of correcting the violation.

Before using the violation-of-lease ground to evict a tenant, ask yourself the following questions:

- Was the violated provision part of the original lease or rental agreement?
- If the provision was added later, does a rent control ordinance in your city preclude eviction on this ground?
- If the violation is correctable (most are), does your three-day notice give the tenant an option to cure the defect?
- Does your city's rent control ordinance impose special requirements on the notice, such as a requirement that it state the violation very specifically, be preceded by a "cease-and-desist" notice, or include a notation that assistance is available from the rent board?

- Did you give the required prior warning notice?

Preparing a Conditional Three-Day Notice

If you opt for the conditional notice, your three-day notice to perform the lease provision (often termed a covenant or promise) or quit should contain all of the following:

- the tenant's name. List the names of all adult occupants of the premises, even if they did not sign the original rental agreement or lease. (See Chapter 2 for advice.)
- the property's address, including apartment number if applicable
- a very specific statement as to which lease or rental agreement provision has been violated, and how

    EXAMPLE: "You have violated the Rules and Regulations incorporated by Paragraph 21 of the lease, prohibiting work on motor vehicles in the parking stalls, in the following manner: by keeping a partially dismantled motor vehicle in your parking stall."

- a demand that within three days the tenant either comply with the lease or rental agreement provision or leave the premises, including the particular action that must be taken to cure the breach

    EXAMPLE: "You must either (a) restore the vehicle to working and drivable condition and refrain from further repairs in your parking stall or the parking area, or (b) remove the vehicle entirely from your parking stall and the parking area; or if you do not cure said breach as indicated, vacate and deliver possession of the premises to the undersigned, (etc.)."

Three-Day Notice to Perform Covenant or Quit

To: _____ Tammy Tenant _____ ,
(name)

Tenant(s) in possession of the premises at ____ 1234 4th Street _____ ,
(street address)

City of ____ Monterey _____ , County of ____ Monterey _____ , California.

YOU ARE HEREBY NOTIFIED that you are in violation of the lease or rental agreement under which you occupy these premises because you have violated the covenant to:

pay agreed installments of the security deposit in the amount of $50 per month on the first day of each month

(in addition to the rent) until paid _____

_____

in the following manner:

failing to pay the $50 on the first day of the month of September 20xx* _____

_____

YOU ARE HEREBY REQUIRED within THREE (3) DAYS from the date of service on you of this notice to remedy the violation and perform the covenant or to vacate and surrender possession of the premises.

If you fail to do so, legal proceedings will be instituted against you to recover possession of the premises, declare the forfeiture of the rental agreement or lease under which you occupy the premises, and recover damages and court costs.

Date: ____ Sept. 25, 20xx _____   ____ Leo Landlord _____
                                              Owner/Manager

- -

Proof of Service

I, the undersigned, being at least 18 years of age, served this notice, of which this is a true copy, on _____ , one of the occupants listed above as follows:

☐ On _____ , _____ , I delivered the notice to the occupant personally.

☐ On _____ , _____ , I delivered the notice to a person of suitable age and discretion at the occupant's residence/business after having attempted personal service at the occupant's residence, and business, if known. On _____ , _____ , I mailed a second copy to the occupant at his or her residence.

☐ On _____ , _____ , I posted the notice in a conspicuous place on the property, after having attempted personal service at the occupant's residence, and business, if known, and after having been unable to find there a person of suitable age and discretion. On _____ , _____ , I mailed a second copy to the occupant at the property.

I declare under penalty of perjury under the laws of the State of California that the foregoing is true and correct.

Date: _____   _____
                                  Signature

* Where statewide just cause applies, add the following language as a new paragraph: "The just cause for termination of your tenancy is that, pursuant to Civ. Code § 1946.2(b)(1)(B), you have breached a material term of the lease, as described in Paragraph (3) of Section 1161 of the Code of Civil Procedure, including, but not limited to, violation of a provision of the lease after being issued a written notice to correct the violation." If you issue a second notice for incurable breach, use the same language for the just cause.

Three-Day Notice to Perform Covenant or Quit

To: __Lester Lessee_____ ,
        (name)

Tenant(s) in possession of the premises at ____123 Main Street, Apartment 4_____ ,
                                                    (street address)

City of _____San Jose_____ , County of ____Santa Clara_____ , California.

YOU ARE HEREBY NOTIFIED that you are in violation of the lease or rental agreement under which you occupy these premises because you have violated the covenant to:

____refrain from keeping a pet on the premises_____

_____

_____

in the following manner:
____by having a dog and two cats on premises*_____

_____

YOU ARE HEREBY REQUIRED within THREE (3) DAYS from the date of service on you of this notice to remedy the violation and perform the covenant or to vacate and surrender possession of the premises.

If you fail to do so, legal proceedings will be instituted against you to recover possession of the premises, declare the forfeiture of the rental agreement or lease under which you occupy the premises, and recover damages and court costs.

Date: __*November 6, 20xx*_____   __*Linda Landlord*_____
                                                    Owner/Manager

- -

Proof of Service

I, the undersigned, being at least 18 years of age, served this notice, of which this is a true copy, on _____ , one of the occupants listed above as follows:

☐ On _____ , _____ , I delivered the notice to the occupant personally.

☐ On _____ , _____ , I delivered the notice to a person of suitable age and discretion at the occupant's residence/business after having attempted personal service at the occupant's residence, and business, if known. On _____ , _____ , I mailed a second copy to the occupant at his or her residence.

☐ On _____ , _____ , I posted the notice in a conspicuous place on the property, after having attempted personal service at the occupant's residence, and business, if known, and after having been unable to find there a person of suitable age and discretion. On _____ , _____ , I mailed a second copy to the occupant at the property.

I declare under penalty of perjury under the laws of the State of California that the foregoing is true and correct.

Date: _____   _____
                                                    Signature

* Where statewide just cause applies, add the following language as a new paragraph: "The just cause for termination of your tenancy is that, pursuant to Civ. Code § 1946.2(b)(1)(B), you have breached a material term of the lease, as described in Paragraph (3) of Section 1161 of the Code of Civil Procedure, including, but not limited to, violation of a provision of the lease after being issued a written notice to correct the violation." If you issue a second notice for incurable breach, use the same language for the just cause.

- a statement that you will pursue legal action or declare the lease or rental agreement "forfeited" if the tenant does not cure the violation or move within three days, and
- the date and your (or your manager's) signature.

Two sample Three-Day Notices to Perform Covenant or Quit appear above, and instructions follow. To complete the Proof of Service on this form follow the instructions described under the Three-Day Notice to Pay Rent or Quit. (See Chapter 2.)

FORM

A blank copy of the Three-Day Notice to Perform Covenant or Quit is available for downloading from the Nolo website. (See the appendix for the link to the forms in this book, and other information on using the forms.)

Using the Unconditional Three-Day Notice to Quit

Under certain circumstances, the three-day notice need not offer the option of correcting the violation or leaving.

When to Use an Unconditional Three-Day Notice

There are four situations when you need not give the tenant the option of correcting the problem:

- **Improper subletting.** The tenant has sublet all or part of the premises to someone else, contrary to an express provision in the rental agreement or lease. (However, in rent control cities, additional provisions or regulations may prohibit unconditional termination. See the discussion in Chapter 3.)
- **Nuisance.** The tenant is causing a legal nuisance on the premises. This means seriously interfering with neighbors' ability to live normally in their homes, for example, by repeatedly playing excessively loud music

late at night, by conducting dogfights or cockfights on the premises (C.C.P. § 1161(4), Civ. Code § 3482.8), or by selling illegal drugs on the premises.
- If you are tempted to use this ground, be sure that you can prove the problems with convincing testimony from a fairly impartial person, such as a tenant in the same building who is willing to testify in court. If you're unable to produce any witnesses, or can't produce independent objective evidence (such as definitive video) forget it.
- **Damage or waste.** The tenant is causing a great deal of property damage ("waste," in legalese). Forget about evicting on this ground for damage caused by carelessness. It works only in extreme cases, such as where a tenant shatters numerous windows, punches large holes in walls, or the like. Again, you must be able to prove the damage convincingly.

RENT CONTROL

Some rent control cities require that you give tenants a written notice directing them to stop damaging the property and pay the estimated cost of repairs before you can evict using this ground. You can satisfy this requirement by either a Three-Day Notice to Perform Covenant or Quit, or a cease and desist notice, followed by a Three-Day Notice to Quit.

- **Drugs or illegal use.** The tenant is using the property for an illegal purpose (running a house of prostitution, dealing illegal hard drugs or making illegal firearms or ammunition, like ghost guns, or possibly operating a legitimate business in violation of local zoning laws). It is unclear just how serious the illegal activity must be to justify eviction, because are very few court decisions have dealt with this question, but use of the property should be integral to the criminal violation and the violation needs to be serious.

Three-Day Notice to Quit

(Improper Subletting, Nuisance, Waste, or Illegal Use)

To: __Ronald Rockland_____ ,
(name)

Tenant(s) in possession of the premises at __1234 Diego Street, Apartment 5_____ ,
(street address)

City of __San Diego_____ , County of __San Diego_____ , California.

YOU ARE HEREBY NOTIFIED that you are required within THREE (3) DAYS from the date of service on you of this notice to vacate and surrender possession of the premises because you have committed the following nuisance, waste, unlawful use, or unlawful subletting:

__You committed a nuisance on the premises by holding several loud boisterous parties at which music was played__

__at an extremely loud volume, and at which intoxicated guests milled about outside the front door to the premises__

__and shouted obscenities at passersby every night from February 26th through 28th, 20xx, resulting in multiple__

__police calls and substantially interfering with the comfort and quiet enjoyment of other residents and tenants.__

__[If you are subject to statewide rent control, add the following: The just cause for termination of your tenancy__

__is that, pursuant to Civ. Code § 1946.2(b)(1)(D), you are maintaining, committing, or permitting the maintenance of__

__commission of a nuisance as described in paragraph (4) of Section 1161 of the Code of Civil Procedure."]__

As a result of your having committed the foregoing act(s), the lease or rental agreement under which you occupy these premises is terminated. If you fail to vacate and surrender possession of the premises within three days, legal proceedings will be instituted against you to recover possession of the premises, damages, and court costs.

Date: __March 1, 20xx_____   __Laura Landlord_____
                                                Owner/Manager

- -

Proof of Service

I, the undersigned, being at least 18 years of age, served this notice, of which this is a true copy, on _____
_____ , one of the occupants listed above as follows:

☐ On _____ , _____ , I delivered the notice to the occupant personally.

☐ On _____ , _____ , I delivered the notice to a person of suitable age and discretion at the occupant's residence/business after having attempted personal service at the occupant's residence, and business, if known. On _____ , _____ , I mailed a second copy to the occupant at his or her residence.

☐ On _____ , _____ , I posted the notice in a conspicuous place on the property, after having attempted personal service at the occupant's residence, and business, if known, and after having been unable to find there a person of suitable age and discretion. On _____ , _____ , I mailed a second copy to the occupant at the property.

I declare under penalty of perjury under the laws of the State of California that the foregoing is true and correct.

Date: _____   _____
                                       Signature

Infractions, like traffic tickets or even using the barbeque on "spare the air days" do not qualify for an illegal purpose eviction. You just can't use an "illegal purpose" reason to evict for minor transgressions. However, use or possession (or worse) of hard drugs or illegal firearms or ammunition (or both) on the premises, on even a single occasion, can be a basis for eviction on this ground where the violation is serious.

You should keep in mind two major qualifications concerning illegal purpose. First, the criminal activity must be on the property or involve the property. Criminal activity outside of the property does not form a basis for eviction. Even if your tenants steal cars for a living (and deliver them to a chop shop), as long as they don't bring their work home, you can't evict for it.

Second, possession offenses must involve illegal substances or items. Possession of a firearm or ammunition in itself is legal. Using the firearm might present a different story. Because most "illegal purpose" evictions usually fall somewhere in between, if the tenancy is month to month, avoid using a three-day notice to evict on this ground. Instead, use a 30-day or 60-day notice, which doesn't require you to state a reason for the eviction.

> **CAUTION**
>
> **Use the exact language from the Civil Code.** The various just causes are separate subsections in Civ. Code § 1946.2. Where the form asks you to recite the just cause for termination of the tenancy, you should quote the exact wording of the cause subsection. The above example pertains to nuisance. So, if the termination is based on waste, illegal subletting, or criminal activity, you must refer to and quote the corresponding subsection in your notice.

Because you might have to prove the illegal activity in court, make sure to make appropriate complaints to the relevant authorities before filing for eviction. Keep a record of the dates and times of your complaints, and the name(s) of the person(s) with whom you spoke. You will also have to document the tenant's transgressions, so a log of illegal actions, including dates and times, as well as supporting evidence (like security video) may be crucial. You should also file police reports where warranted, such as where thefts have occurred on the property, but you should identify your tenant only where you have eyewitnesses or direct evidence of the tenant's wrongdoing. And, although not required by ordinance, your record of having given the tenant written notice to cease the illegal activity should also help establish that there's a problem.

- **State just cause uncorrected notices.** Under the statewide just cause eviction controls, if the tenant fails to cure the breach within the three-day cure period, you can (and should) serve a noncurable three-day notice under C.C.P. §1161(4). Civil Code § 1942.6 states that the landlord "may" serve a noncurable notice if the tenant doesn't fix the problem. It is not clear whether "may" means "must," but experienced landlord attorneys consider this second notice to be the safest route to follow.

You also need to maintain copies of any warning letters required under the local rent control ordinance, and should have a written record of any complaints from neighbors and tenants, plus copies of any police reports related to the tenant. Be sure to preserve any video or photographic evidence.

Evictions based on intensive proof of facts create the trickiest trial problems for landlords in contested matters. Rules of evidence prevent you from just "telling your story," and technical requirements, such as the hearsay rule, could block admission of letters from other residents or neighbors. Trial judges hold individuals to the same rules and standards that attorneys must follow, and judges cannot assist self-represented parties (people who do not have attorneys) at trial. Consequently, any landlord attempting a tenant fault-based eviction (such as breach of the lease, nuisance, or illegal use or activity) should have the evidence ready even before giving the notice to quit. If in doubt, seek the assistance of an experienced attorney, if only to help you prepare the case.

RENT CONTROL

No rent control ordinance requires the tenant be given a chance to correct illegal use of property. Some cities, however, allow eviction on this ground only if the tenant is convicted of illegal activity.

Preparing an Unconditional Three-Day Notice

If you opt for the unconditional three-day notice, it must contain the following:

- the tenant's name. List the names of all adult occupants of the premises, even if they didn't sign the original lease or rental agreement. (See Chapter 2 for advice.)
- the property's address
- a specific statement as to how and approximately when the tenant violated the rental agreement or lease in a way that can't be corrected—for example, if the tenant sublet (in violation of a lease clause that specifies that so doing is grounds for termination and eviction), created a nuisance, damaged the premises, or illegally used the premises. This is the most important part of the notice, and must be drafted very carefully to clearly tell tenants what they are doing wrong. Failure

to be very specific regarding dates, times, and conduct could render the notice void—another reason why a 30-day or 60-day eviction or, at least, a conditional three-day notice is usually preferable.

RENT CONTROL

Again, many rent control ordinances that provide for just cause for eviction require that the reason to use an unconditional three-day notice be stated even more specifically than is required under state law. Check your ordinance.

- a demand that the tenant leave the premises within three days
- an unequivocal statement that the lease is forfeited and that you will take legal action to remove the tenant if he or she fails to vacate within three days, and
- the date and your (or your manager's) signature.

A sample unconditional Three-Day Notice to Quit appears above, and instructions follow. To complete the Proof of Service on this form, follow the instructions described under the Three-Day Notice to Pay Rent or Quit. (See Chapter 2.)

FORM

A blank copy of the Three-Day Notice to Quit is available for downloading from the Nolo website. (See the appendix for the link to the forms in this book, and other information on using the forms.)

Serving the Three-Day Notice (Either Type)

You can serve a three-day notice telling a tenant to either comply with a lease provision or vacate any day the tenant is in violation of the lease, but not before. For example, if your tenants inform you of their intent to move in a pet Doberman in violation of the "no pets" clause in the lease, you can serve them with a conditional three-day notice only as soon as they get the dog. You can't get the jump on them by anticipating the violation. The same is true of an unconditional Three-Day Notice to Quit. You can serve the notice any time after the tenant has illegally sublet, caused a nuisance, severely damaged the property, or used the property for an illegal purpose.

When to Serve Notice

What happens if you've accepted rent for a whole month and then want to give your tenant a three-day notice? Should you wait awhile? Here are some general rules about when to serve your tenants with three-day notices:

- **Serve a conditional notice right after you learn of the breach** *and* **gather the facts, not after you accept rent.** To enforce a lease (which includes your right to terminate it for specified misbehavior), the law requires you to act quickly once you know of the breach. It is tempting to first accept rent to minimize your costs, but you cannot take rent while the breach is happening (and you know about it) if you want to enforce the lease (that is, terminate). Otherwise, by accepting next month's rent, the court will view you as having waived, or forgiven, the breach.

- **Serve an** *unconditional* **notice as close as possible to the end of a rental period.** If you serve the notice right after you've collected the rent in advance for a whole month, the tenants may claim that by accepting the rent (assuming you knew about the problem) you gave up your right to complain. However, if you can prove that you became aware of a noncorrectable violation only a few days after having accepted rent, don't worry. If

you get the tenants out within the month for which the tenants had already paid rent, the tenants do not get a refund for the days they paid for but didn't get to enjoy. By breaching the lease or rental agreement, the tenants forfeited their right to occupy the premises, even though they'd already paid the rent.

- **Never give a tenant an unconditional Three-Day Notice to Quit concurrently with a Three-Day Notice to Pay Rent or Quit.** The two are contradictory, one telling the tenant he or she can stay if the rent is paid, the other telling the tenant to move no matter what. Also, do not give the tenant an unconditional Three-Day Notice to Quit along with a 30-day or 60-day Notice of Termination of Tenancy. These two are contradictory as well, giving two different time periods within which the tenant must leave unconditionally.

Who Should Serve the Three-Day Notice

As with a Three-Day Notice to Pay Rent or Quit, anyone over 18 can serve the notice, including you. (See Chapter 2.)

Whom to Serve

As with other three-day notices, you should try to serve a copy of the notice on each tenant to whom you originally rented the property, plus any other adult living there. (See Chapter 2.)

How to Serve the Notice

The three-day notice must be served in one of three ways:
- personal service on the tenant(s)
- substituted service and mailing, or
- posting and mailing.

You may not serve the notice by certified mail, which may be used only for 30-day or 60-day notices terminating month-to-month tenancies. Chapter 2 explains how to accomplish service.

Accepting Rent After the Notice Is Served

With *conditional* three-day notices, don't accept any rent unless the tenant has cured the violation within three days—in which case you can't evict, and the tenant can stay. If the tenant doesn't correct the violation within three days, don't accept any rent unless you want to forget about evicting for the reason stated in the notice.

Don't accept rent after you've served an *unconditional* three-day notice unless you want to give up on the eviction. Acceptance of the rent will be considered a legal admission that you decided to forgive the violation and go on collecting rent rather than complain about the problem.

> **EXAMPLE:** You collected a month's rent from Peter on March 1. On March 15, Peter threw an extremely boisterous and loud party that lasted until 3 a.m. Despite your warnings the next day, he threw an identical one that night. He did the same on the weekend of March 22–23. You served him an unconditional Three-Day Notice to Quit on the 25th of the month, but he didn't leave and you therefore have to bring suit. The rent for March is already paid, but you can't accept rent for April or you'll give up your legal right to evict on the basis of the March parties. However, you can get a court judgment for the equivalent of this rent in the form of "damages" equal to one day's rent for each day from April 1 until Peter leaves or you get a judgment.

When to File Your Lawsuit

Once you have properly served the notice, you will need to wait for the appropriate number of days to pass before you take the next step, filing your lawsuit. Here is how to compute this period:

- If you serve more than one tenant with notices, but not all on the same day, start counting only after the last tenant is served.
- Do not count the day of service as the first day. The first day to count is the day after service of the notice was completed.
- Do not file your lawsuit on the third business day after service is complete. The tenant must have three full business days after service before you file suit.
- If the third day is a business day, you may file your lawsuit on the next business day after that.
- If the third day falls on a Saturday, Sunday, or legal holiday, the tenant has until the end of the next business day to correct the violation (if the notice was conditional) or move. You cannot file your suit on that business day, but must wait until the day after that.

> **EXAMPLE:** On November 11, Manuel personally served Maria with a conditional three-day notice at home. The first day after service is Friday the 12th, the second day is Saturday the 13th, and the third day is Sunday the 14th. Because the second day falls on a Saturday, the count is suspended until Monday, which becomes the second day, and the third day falls on Tuesday. The notice will therefore expire at the end of Tuesday the 16th. Only on Wednesday the 17th can Manuel file suit.

Once you have waited the requisite period, and the tenant has failed to leave (or correct the violation if your notice was conditional), you can proceed to the next phase, which is filing an eviction complaint. We tell you how to do this in Chapter 6.

Eviction Without a Three-Day or Other Termination Notice

There are just two situations in which you may file an eviction lawsuit against a tenant without first giving a written three-day, 30-day, or 60-day notice. As long as the property is not subject to just cause eviction controls, those situations are:

- when the tenant refuses to leave after a fixed-term lease expires, and you haven't renewed it or converted it into a month-to-month tenancy by accepting rent after expiration of the lease term, and
- when your month-to-month tenant terminates the tenancy by giving you a 30-day notice, but then refuses to move out as promised.

RENT CONTROL

Rent control laws requiring just cause for eviction, under both statewide law (the TPA) and in many cities, limit evictions or add requirements for eviction. In rent- and eviction- controlled tenancies, you cannot terminate (let alone evict) without notice and a recognized cause. The mere expiration of the lease term is not sufficient cause to justify terminating the tenancy. So, what happens when the lease expires? The tenant stays in place.

Unless the tenant voluntarily leaves, the lease automatically converts to a month-to-month rental agreement, which is effectively the same as an open-ended lease. The landlord cannot enforce the end of the term by evicting the tenant, but you can enforce the extension of the term with a new (nearly identical) agreement. Check the rent control chart, whose link is on this book's companion page and a copy of your city's rent control ordinance if your property is subject to rent control.

Lease Expiration

Unlike a month-to-month tenancy, a fixed-term tenancy ends on the date stated in the lease. No further notice is strictly necessary. However, unless you are careful you could find yourself inadvertently renewing the lease or converting it into a month-to-month tenancy. Here are the basic rules:

- If you simply continue to accept monthly rent after the termination date, the fixed-term tenancy is automatically converted to a month-to-month tenancy. (Civ. Code § 1945.) It must be terminated with a 30-day or 60-day notice. (See Chapter 3.)
- If the lease has a renewal or holdover provision, your acceptance of rent may automatically operate to renew the lease for another full term, or as a month-to-month tenancy, depending on the wording of the lease.

EXAMPLE: Masao rented his house to Yuko under a six-month lease for January 1 through June 30. Although Masao assumed Yuko would leave on June 30, Yuko remained there the next day. When she offered Masao the rent on July 1, Masao accepted it, believing this was preferable to filing an eviction lawsuit, but he told Yuko she could stay only one month more. At the end of July, however, Yuko's lawyer told Masao that Yuko was entitled to stay under her now month-to-month tenancy until and unless Masao terminates it with a proper 30-day notice. Masao gave Yuko a written 30-day notice on July 31, which meant Yuko didn't have to move until August 30.

In this example, Masao could have given Yuko a one-month extension without turning the tenancy into one from month to month if he had given her a notice extending the term of the lease for one month, with a fixed expiration date of July 31. Alternatively, he could have presented Yuko with an amendment to the lease, extending the term for one month, and requiring that Yuko sign the amendment staying the extra month.

Notice to Tenant That Lease Will Not Be Renewed

November 3, 20xx
950 Parker Street
Berkeley, CA 94710

Leo D. Leaseholder
123 Main Street, Apt. #4
Santa Rosa, CA 95403

Dear Mr. Leaseholder:

As you know, the lease you and I entered into on January 1 of this year for the rental of the premises at 123 Main Street, Apartment 4, Santa Rosa, is due to expire on December 31, slightly less than two months from now.

I have decided not to extend the lease for any period of time, even on a month-to-month basis. Accordingly, I will expect you and your family to vacate the premises on or before December 31. You have the right to request an initial move-out inspection, and to be present at that inspection, provided you request it no more than two weeks prior to your move-out date. I will return your security deposit to you in the manner prescribed by Section 1950.5 of the California Civil Code, within three weeks after you move out. If I make any deductions from your deposit, you also have the right to receive copies of invoices or receipts for work needed to remedy damage beyond normal wear and tear or to perform necessary cleaning.

Sincerely,

Lenny D. Landlord

Lenny D. Landlord

Reminding the Tenant Before the Lease Expires

To avoid an inadvertent extension of the lease or its conversion into a month-to-month tenancy, it is always a good idea to inform a fixed-term tenant in writing and well in advance, that you don't intend to renew the lease. While not required, such a notice will prevent a tenant from claiming that you granted a verbal extension. It will also prevent any holdover provision in the lease (increasing rent when tenants don't leave as scheduled) from taking effect. Fixed-term tenants who know a month or two in advance that you want them out at the end of a lease term are obviously in a good position to leave on time. Tenants who realize that the lease is up only when you refuse their rent and demand that they leave immediately are not. Your letter might look something like the one shown above.

The letter isn't a legally required notice but is sent to show your intent to assert your right to possession of the property at the expiration of the lease and covers one legally required base in the process. (The part of the letter telling the tenant of the right to an initial move-out inspection and to be present *is* legally required, as is the part concerning the tenant's right to invoices and receipts. See *The California Landlord's Law Book: Rights & Responsibilities*, Chapters 5 and 18.)

The letter doesn't have to be served in any particular way and can be mailed first class. However, if you're afraid the tenants will claim they never received the letter, you may want to send it certified mail, return receipt requested.

Make Sure the Tenancy *Is* for a Fixed Term

If you want to evict a tenant who stays after the lease expires, you should make sure that the tenant had a lease for a fixed-term tenancy. Because the titles of standard rental forms try to make one size fit all, the title may be "rental agreement" or "lease" and sometimes none of the above. You need to look at the substantive provisions of the document if you are in doubt. (We discuss this in detail in *The California Landlord's Law Book: Rights & Responsibilities*, Chapter 2.)

If the agreement lists a specific expiration date with the total amount of rent to be collected over the term, chances are it's a lease. In other circumstances, the lease will contain checkboxes—one for the ending date and a second to be "month to month." If the fixed date is checked but not the month to month, you can assume it is a fixed-term type of lease agreement.

In other cases, a clearly written lease might use this language:

> The term of this rental shall begin on _____ , 20___ , and shall continue for a period of _____ months, expiring on _____ , 20___ .

As discussed above, the big exception to the rule that no notice is required to end a fixed-term tenancy is when you have, by word or action, allowed the lease to be renewed, either for another full term (if there's a clause to that effect in the lease) or as a month-to-month tenancy (if you have a month-to-month holdover provision or continued to accept monthly rent after the end of the term).

Must You Have a Reason for Not Renewing a Lease?

A landlord's reason for refusing to renew a lease is treated the same way as is a landlord's reason for terminating a month-to-month tenancy with a 30-day or 60-day notice when just cause does not apply. (See Chapter 3.) In general, as long as there's no just cause eviction control, you don't have to give a reason for refusing to renew the lease. (For just cause eviction control, see Chapter 3.) But, as with your initial rental decision, you cannot base your refusal on retaliatory or discriminatory motives. Laws against illegal discrimination apply to nonrenewal of fixed-term tenancies to the same extent that they apply to termination of month-to-month tenancies.

RENT CONTROL

In rent control cities with just cause ordinances, or under the TPA statewide rent control, expiration of a fixed-term lease will not be one of the just causes for termination unless the tenant refuses to sign a new agreement on nearly identical terms and conditions. Most ordinances don't require you to give the tenant any specific renewal notice for a month-to-month renewal term, although a few require that the tenant be requested in writing to sign the new lease. If you want to renew for an additional fixed term, such as one year, you should give notice of that renewal. Otherwise, the tenant will expect the term to revert to a month-to-month tenancy under the Civil Code.

The best practice is to personally hand tenants a letter, at least 30 days before the lease expires, requesting that they sign the new lease (attached to the letter) and return it to you before the current one expires. Be sure to keep a copy of the letter and proposed new lease for your own records. Even if all this isn't required by your city, it will make for convincing documentation if the tenant refuses to sign and you choose to evict for this reason.

The tenant's refusal to sign a new lease does not revoke the old lease. It *does* furnish just cause to terminate under the TPA and many local rent control ordinances. If the tenant refuses to sign a new written lease, the old written lease remains in effect. The landlord can terminate by using a "cure or quit" notice of termination, giving the tenant one more chance to sign. A refusal to sign at that point gives you just cause to evict.

How to Proceed

You may begin an unlawful detainer suit immediately if all of the following are true:

- You conclude that your tenant's fixed-term tenancy has expired.
- You have not accepted rent for any period beyond the expiration date.
- The tenant refuses to move.

Instructions on how to begin the suit are set out in Chapter 6.

Checklist for Uncontested "No-Notice" Eviction

Step	Earliest Time to Do It
☐ 1. Prepare the summons(es) and complaint and make copies. (Chapter 6)	When it's apparent the tenant(s) won't leave on time; don't sign and date it until the day indicated below in Step 3.
☐ 2. File the complaint at the courthouse and have the summons(es) issued. (Chapter 6)	The first court day after the lease term or tenant's notice period expires.
☐ 3. Have the sheriff, the marshal, a registered process server, or a friend serve the summons and complaint. (Chapter 6)	As soon as possible after filing the complaint and having the summons(es) issued.
☐ 4. Prepare Request for Entry of Default, Judgment, Declaration, and Writ of Possession. (Chapter 7)	While you're waiting for five-day (or 15-day, if complaint not personally served) response time to pass.
☐ 5. Call the court to find out whether or not tenant(s) filed a written response.	Just before closing on the fifth court day after service of summons, or early on the sixth day. (Do not count holidays that fall on weekdays, however. Also, if fifth court day after service falls on weekend or holiday, count the first business day after that as the fifth day.)
☐ 6. Mail copy of Request for Entry of Default to tenant(s), file original at courthouse. Also file declaration and have clerk issue judgment and writ for possession of the property. (Chapter 7)	Sixth court day after service of summons and complaint. (Again, count first business day after fifth day that falls on weekend or holiday.)
☐ 7. Prepare letter of instruction for, and give writ and copies to, sheriff or marshal. (Chapter 7)	Sixth day after service of summons and complaint. (Again, count first business day after fifth day that falls on weekend or holiday.)
☐ 8. Change locks.	As soon as tenant vacates or sheriff carries out the writ of possession by removing the tenant.

For Money Judgment

Step	Earliest Time to Do It
☐ 9. Prepare Request for Entry of Default, Judgment, and, if allowed by local rule, declaration in lieu of testimony. (Chapter 7)	As soon as possible after property is vacant.
☐ 10. Mail Request for Entry of Default copy to tenant, file request at courthouse. If a declaration in lieu of testimony is allowed, file that, too, and give clerk judgment and writ forms for money part of judgment. If testimony required, ask clerk for default hearing. (Chapter 7)	As soon as possible after above.
☐ 11. If testimony required, attend default hearing before judge, testify, and turn in your judgment form for entry of money judgment. (Chapter 7)	When scheduled by court clerk.
☐ 12. Apply security deposit to cleaning and repair of property, and to any rent not accounted for in judgment, then apply balance to judgment amount. Notify tenant in writing of deductions, keeping a copy. Refund any balance remaining. If deposit does not cover entire judgment, collect balance of judgment. (Chapter 9)	As soon as possible after default hearing. Deposit must be accounted for within three weeks of when the tenants vacate.

Termination by the Tenant

Except in rent control cities (but not in TPA properties, as explained below), you can also evict a tenant without written notice when the tenant terminates a month-to-month tenancy by serving you with a legally valid 30-day notice but refuses to leave after the 30 days. (As we saw in Chapter 3, although you must give 60 days' notice of termination of tenancy to tenants who have lived in the premises a year or more, they need only give you 30 days' notice.)

Your ability to file for eviction without first terminating in this situation does not apply if the property is subject to statewide eviction control. Under statewide eviction control, the tenant's

---

What To Do When Tenants Change Their Minds and Don't Move Out

Now and then, month-to-month tenants who have given notice change their minds and decide to stay in their rental. Or, tenants whose leases are up fail to move out, contrary to the termination date in their lease. Often, the landlord has already advertised and rerented the unit. What are your options if this happens to you? It depends on whether your rental is subject to local rent control and/or eviction control laws.

Non-rent-control rentals. Your month-to-month tenant's decision to terminate the rental became effective when it was delivered to you. Similarly, your lease-holding tenant lost the right to occupy as of the termination date. If the tenant fails to move out as specified in the notice or in the lease, the tenant becomes a hold-over. As long as you do not accept rent (or do anything else that indicates that you've accepted this tenant's continued residence), you may proceed with an eviction, as described in this book.

Rent-controlled tenancies. The answer is quite different here. Eviction controls prevent a landlord from evicting when tenants change their minds and do not move out at the end of the thirty-day notice. Put another way, voluntary termination by the tenant is not a "just cause" for eviction under local rent control laws. Local rent control ordinances do not permit you to enforce

a tenant's notice to vacate when the tenant chooses not to honor it. But it is one of the at-fault just causes to terminate under the statewide eviction control law and can be enforced by you.

For these reasons, it's risky to sign a new rental agreement with new tenants promising delivery of the premises before the current tenant has actually moved out. Your rental agreement with the new tenants probably includes a clause limiting your damages in case you cannot deliver the premises as promised (limiting them to sums previously paid, such as the deposit and advance rent), but that's not the end of the matter. More than one unhappy canceled tenant has posted negative comments about landlords on rental websites, which are increasingly relied upon by prospective tenants.

Practical reasons also support waiting to show a rental and sign up new tenants until after the coast is clear. Because you'll often need to clean, repaint, or refresh a unit at turnover time, it will look better after that process than it will when the current tenant's belongings are still there, usually in the cluttered state of being packed up. A clean, empty unit will be more attractive and easier to rent.

In the long run, you'll be better off with a small vacancy during the marketing period than dealing with an unhappy, canceled tenant.

failure to move after giving notice forms one of the at-fault just causes permitting termination and eviction. In other words, you'll need to terminate with an at-fault cure or quit notice, giving the tenant one last chance to move out.

Again, if you accept rent for a period after the time the tenant is supposed to leave, you've reinstated the tenancy on a month-to-month basis and cannot evict without notice.

If only one of several cotenants who signed the rental agreement terminates the tenancy, the others may stay unless the tenant who signed the notice was acting on their behalf as well.

Because the tenant's notice may be unclear in this respect or may be invalid for other reasons (such as failure to give a full 30 days' notice), some landlords follow a tenant's questionable termination notice with a definite 30-day notice of their own. This avoids the problem of relying on a tenant's notice, rerenting the property and then not being able to deliver the apartment to the new tenant. However, this technique is not possible if the tenant has stayed a year or more, in which case a 60-day notice is required, or if eviction control applies.

If you choose not to serve your own 30-day or 60-day notice and instead want to evict on the basis that the tenant has not vacated in accordance with the tenant's own 30-day notice, proceed to Chapter 6 for how to file an unlawful detainer complaint. If you do decide to serve a 30-day or 60-day notice of your own, turn to Chapter 3.

Checklist for Uncontested "No-Notice" Eviction

Above is a checklist listing the steps required in this type of eviction, assuming the tenant does not answer your unlawful detainer complaint (that is, the tenant defaults). At this point, much of the outline may not make sense to you, as you have not yet read the chapters on filing the unlawful detainer complaint, taking a default judgment, or enforcing the judgment. As you proceed through those chapters (or Chapter 8, if the tenant contests your action), you may want to return to this chapter to keep in touch as to where you are in the process.

Filing and Serving Your Unlawful Detainer Complaint

FORMS IN THIS CHAPTER

Chapter 6 includes instructions for and samples of the following forms:

- Summons—Unlawful Detainer—Eviction
- Complaint—Unlawful Detainer
- Civil Case Cover Sheet
- Plaintiff's Mandatory Cover Sheet and Supplemental Allegations – Unlawful Detainer
- Proof of Service of Summons, and
- Application and Order to Serve Summons by Posting for Unlawful Detainer.

The Nolo website includes downloadable copies of these forms, as well as the Civil Case Cover Sheet Addendum, Statement of Location, and statewide Prejudgment Claim of Right to Possession that are discussed in this chapter, but for which sample forms are not shown.

You can also download fillable Judicial Council forms from the California Courts website: www.courts.ca.gov/forms.htm

Always check for the most recent date on any Judicial Council form. Due to the passage of COVID-related legislation, the forms have changed frequently since 2020. Never use an out-of-date form, because the courts will not accept them.

After you have legally terminated your tenant's tenancy by properly serving the appropriate termination notice (or the tenancy has ended because a lease expired or the tenants terminated it themselves), you can begin an unlawful detainer lawsuit to evict the tenant. Chapters 2 through 5 provide the necessary forms and procedures to terminate a tenancy. The checklists included at the start of Chapters 2 through 5 are useful in understanding where you are in the process.

This chapter tells you how to prepare and file a complaint, supplementary allegations, the summons, and the collateral documents that initiate your lawsuit.

How to Use This Chapter

The COVID pandemic caused a number of changes in unlawful detainer pleading and court rules, making the complaint and supplemental allegations more complicated, and delaying when you can file for nonpayment of rent. All of this means you will need to proceed carefully as you draft the papers, because there are many more parts to be completed.

The reason you're evicting (nonpayment of rent, for example) and the kind of notice you use to terminate the tenancy (Three-Day Notice to Pay Rent or Quit, for example) determine the actual wording of your unlawful detainer complaint and supplemental allegations. To keep you from getting confused, we label the parts of our discussion that apply to each type of eviction.

As you go through the instructions on how to fill out the complaint, simply look for the number of your "home" chapter (the one you used to prepare the termination notice) and start reading. You needn't pay attention to the material following the other symbols.

Key to Symbols in This Chapter

 Evictions based on nonpayment of rent—Three-Day Notice to Pay Rent or Quit (Chapter 2)

Evictions based on a 30-day or 60-day notice (Chapter 3)

Evictions based on lease violations, damage, or nuisance—Three-Day Notice to Quit or Three-Day Notice to Perform Covenant or Quit (Chapter 4)

Evictions based on termination of tenancy without notice (Chapter 5)

If a paragraph is relevant only to certain types of evictions, only the appropriate symbols will appear. In addition, we occasionally refer you to the chapter you started with (for example, Chapter 2 for evictions based on nonpayment of rent). We also alert you to the special requirements of rent control ordinances.

Okay, let's start.

When to File Your Unlawful Detainer Complaint

   If you terminated the tenancy with a three-day, 30-day, or 60-day notice, you can file your unlawful detainer complaint the day after the notice period expires. (See "Preparing the Complaint," below, for details on doing this.) You must be careful not to file your complaint prematurely. If you file before the notice period is over, there is no basis for the suit because the tenancy never properly terminated. If the tenant files a written response to your lawsuit, you will lose.

It is therefore very important to correctly calculate the length of the notice period. We explained how to do this in the chapter you started out in (for example, Chapter 2 for evictions based on nonpayment of rent, Chapter 3 for evictions based on a 30-day notice). If necessary, go back to the chapter covering your type of eviction and review how to determine when the notice period ends.

Then return here for instructions on how to fill in and file your unlawful detainer complaint.

If, as discussed in Chapter 5, the tenancy has already ended without a three-, 30-, or 60-day notice—that is, if a lease has expired or the tenant terminated the tenancy with a proper notice to you—you may file your complaint at any time after the end of the term.

Where to File Suit

California's Superior Courts hear all evictions. Most large counties divide their Superior Courts into "divisions" or "branches." (A notable exception is San Francisco, whose Superior Court has no civil divisions or branches.)

All California courts have websites. You can reach them by going to a central website: www.courts.ca.gov/find-my-court.htm Once you get to this main website, you'll see links to the Superior Courts.

File your lawsuit in the division or district where the property is located. You can find nearly all the information concerning where to file, plus local court procedures, on the various courts' websites.

Check the court's website for information on where to file. In our form example in this chapter (below), the property is in Hollywood and filed in downtown Los Angeles in the Stanley Mosk Courthouse. If the property were in North Hollywood, the case would be filed in the Burbank courthouse.

We made the example a little complicated to illustrate some of the additional parts that must be included in a complaint in a rent control situation. Your filing will be less complicated in San Mateo County, for example, where all filings are centrally located, or if there are no rent or eviction controls affecting your property.

Look through the website carefully. Busy courts no longer respond to telephone calls seeking general information, and many clerks' offices have reduced hours to the public. COVID has caused many changes in rules and procedures (we will introduce you to remote conferencing in later chapters). Courts rely upon their websites to provide information to the public. Attempting to obtain information over the telephone can be difficult if not impossible.

Even for lawyers, correctly following court procedures is challenging. Court procedures are decidedly not "user friendly." Even lawyers frequently have to correct papers before filing, and courts make no official distinction between attorneys and people who represent themselves (described as "self-represented litigants"). However, because so many people act without an attorney, many courts maintain an online self-help center for people who represent themselves. The court will provide that information on its website.

Finally, resign yourself to the distinct possibility that you might have to go to the courthouse more than once before the clerk will accept your papers for filing. Clerks cannot give legal advice, but they might offer assistance concerning local procedures and point you towards local rules and assist you in how to fill out forms. Your chances for help will increase if you are polite and patient. Although court clerks exist to serve the courts, not the public, most clerks will go out of their way to help people if they can.

Preparing the Summons

The first legal form that you'll need to start your lawsuit is the summons. The summons is a message from the court to each defendant (person being sued). It states that you have filed a complaint against the defendant, and that if the defendant doesn't file a written response to the complaint within five days, the court may grant you judgment for eviction and money damages.

FORM

Blank copies of the Summons—Unlawful Detainer—Eviction (Judicial Council form SUM-130) and Proof of Service of Summons (Judicial Council form POS-010) are available for download from the Nolo website. (See the appendix for the link to the forms in this book, and other information on using the forms.)

The form is filled out in the same way no matter what the ground for the eviction you are using.

Fill out the summons as follows.

Step 1: "NOTICE TO DEFENDANT:"

You should name as defendants the following individuals:

- All adults who live in the property, whether or not you made any agreement with them; and
- Any tenants who entered into the original rental agreement and have since sublet the property. (Such tenants are still legally in possession of the property through their subtenants.) If none of the original tenants are verifiably there, however, the current tenants are probably "assignees," not subtenants, and you shouldn't name the original tenants as defendants. (See *The California Landlord's Law Book: Rights & Responsibilities*, Chapter 10, for more discussion of the subtenant/assignee distinction.)

It is not enough to name the person you think of as the "main" tenant. For example, if a husband and wife reside on the property and are listed as tenants in your lease, and the wife's brother also lives there, you must list all three as defendants. The sheriff or marshal will not evict any occupant not named as defendant who claims to have moved in before you filed suit. You may then have to go back to court to evict the person you forgot to sue. (Meanwhile, this person will be free to invite the evicted tenants back as "guests.")

Also, below the defendants' names, type "DOES 1 to 10." This phrase indicates that you are also naming unknown defendants in your lawsuit, just in case you later find out that there are unauthorized occupants living on the premises in addition to the known tenants. You can list a number greater or less than 10, but 10 fits the great majority of situations. If you are concerned that your tenant has been running a guesthouse or even a "hacker hotel," you may wish to increase the number of potential unknown occupants.

Finally, the names and "Does" must exactly match the defendants' line on the complaint. For example, if you name "Joe Tenant, Tina Tenant; Does 1 to 10" in the complaint, you must type it exactly the same way on the summons. We discuss this in more detail in "Preparing the Complaint," Item 5.

Step 2: "YOU ARE BEING SUED BY PLAINTIFF:"

Type in the name of the plaintiff, who is the person suing. Here are the rules to figure out who this should be:

- The plaintiff must be an owner. If you are the sole owner of the property, you must be listed as plaintiff (but see fourth rule below).

  If you hired a management company to negotiate and sign the lease, you as the owner must still be the plaintiff. The property management firm or agent cannot be a plaintiff. (See C.C.P. § 367.) Some property managers and management companies have successfully brought unlawful detainer actions in their own behalf, without being called on it by a judge. Still, a competent tenant's attorney will raise this issue and win, perhaps even getting a judgment against the manager or management company for court costs and attorneys' fees.

- If there are several owners, they don't all have to be named as plaintiffs—the co-owner who rented to the tenant, or who primarily deals with the tenant, should be named. Or, name the co-owner who regularly deals with the manager, if there is one. One very important exception concerns evictions in rent-controlled properties for an owner or relative move-in ("OMI"): If you are alleging an OMI as your just cause, you need to include every owner of the property as a named plaintiff.

- As noted, the plaintiff must be an owner of the property (such as you or your spouse). An "owner" can also have some ownership interest, such as when the unit is owned by tenants in common (either one can be named as a plaintiff).

- If the lease or rental agreement lists a fictitious business name (for example, "Pine Street Apartments") as the landlord, you cannot sue (either under that name or under your own name) unless the business name is registered with the county. (See Bus. & Prof. Code §§ 17918 and following.) If the name is registered, list it as the plaintiff if the property is owned by a partnership. If you own the property alone but use the business name, put your name followed by "dba Pine Street Apartments." (The dba means "doing business as.") If the name isn't registered, go down to the county clerk's office and get the process started. This involves filling

out a form, paying a fee, and arranging to have the name published. (More extensive information on how to handle fictitious business names can be found online. Simply search for "fictitious business name [your county]," and most of the necessary information should come up.)

EXAMPLE 1: Jack Johnson and Jill Smith, a partnership named "Jack & Jill Partnership," own a five-unit apartment building they call "Whispering Elms." Their rental agreements list Whispering Elms as the landlord, and the name is properly registered with the county as a fictitious business name. They should enter "Jack Johnson and Jill Smith, a partnership, dba Whispering Elms" as the plaintiff.

EXAMPLE 2: Jill Smith owns the building herself, but her rental agreements list Whispering Elms as the landlord, and the name is on file with the county. The plaintiff in her eviction suit should be "Jill Smith, dba Whispering Elms."

- If a corporation is the owner of the property, the corporation itself must be named as plaintiff and represented by an attorney. Even if you're president and sole shareholder of a corporation that owns the property, unless you're a lawyer you cannot represent the corporation in court. (*Merco Construction Engineers, Inc. v. Municipal Court* (1978) 21 Cal. 3d 724, 147 Cal. Rptr. 631.)

Step 3: (Item 1 on the form)
"The name and address of the court is:"

Put the name and street address of the court, "Superior Court of California," the county, and the division or branch in which your rental property is located, if applicable. (See "Where to File Suit," above.)

SUMMONS
(CITACIÓN JUDICIAL)
UNLAWFUL DETAINER—EVICTION
(RETENCIÓN ILÍCITA DE UN INMUEBLE—DESALOJO)

SUM-130

<table>
<tr><td>FOR COURT USE ONLY
(SOLO PARA USO DE LA CORTE)</td></tr>
</table>

NOTICE TO DEFENDANT:
(AVISO AL DEMANDADO):
TERRENCE D. TENANT;TILLIE D. TENANT; DOES 1 to 10

(Step 1)

YOU ARE BEING SUED BY PLAINTIFF:
(LO ESTÁ DEMANDANDO EL DEMANDANTE):
LENNY D. LANDLORD

(Step 2)

NOTICE! You have been sued. The court may decide against you without your being heard unless you respond within 5 days. You have 5 DAYS, not counting Saturdays and Sundays and other judicial holidays, after this summons and legal papers are served on you to file a written response at this court and have a copy served on the plaintiff.

A letter or phone call will not protect you. Your written response must be in proper legal form if you want the court to hear your case. There may be a court form that you can use for your response. You can find these court forms and more information at the California Courts Online Self-Help Center (*www.courts.ca.gov/selfhelp*), your county law library, or the courthouse nearest you. If you do not file your response on time, you may lose the case by default, and your wages, money, and property may be taken without further warning from the court.

There are other legal requirements. You may want to call an attorney right away. If you do not know an attorney, you may want to call an attorney referral service. If you cannot afford an attorney, you may be eligible for free legal services from a nonprofit legal services program. You can locate these nonprofit groups at the California Legal Services website (*www.lawhelpca.org*), the California Courts Online Self-Help Center (*www.courts.ca.gov/selfhelp*), or by contacting your local court or county bar association.

¡AVISO! Usted ha sido demandado. Si no responde dentro de 5 días, el tribunal puede emitir un fallo en su contra sin una audiencia. Una vez que le entreguen esta citación y papeles legales, solo tiene 5 DÍAS, sin contar sábado y domingo y otros días feriados del tribunal, para presentar una respuesta por escrito en este tribunal y hacer que se entregue una copia al demandante.

Una carta o una llamada telefónica no lo protege. Su respuesta por escrito tiene que estar en formato legal correcto si desea que procesen su caso en la corte. Es posible que haya un formulario que usted pueda usar para su respuesta. Puede encontrar estos formularios de la corte y más información en el Centro de Ayuda de las Cortes de California (www.sucorte.ca.gov), en la biblioteca de leyes de su condado o en la corte que le quede más cerca. Si no presenta su respuesta a tiempo, puede perder el caso por falta de comparecencia y se le podrá quitar su sueldo, dinero y bienes sin más advertencia.

Hay otros requisitos legales. Es recomendable que llame a un abogado inmediatamente. Si no conoce a un abogado, puede llamar a un servicio de remisión a abogados. Si no puede pagar a un abogado, es posible que cumpla con los requisitos para obtener servicios legales gratuitos de un programa de servicios legales sin fines de lucro. Puede encontrar estos grupos sin fines de lucro en el sitio web de California Legal Services, (www.lawhelpcalifornia.org), en el Centro de Ayuda de las Cortes de California, (www.sucorte.ca.gov) o poniéndose en contacto con la corte o el colegio de abogados local.

FEE WAIVER: If you cannot pay the filing fee, ask the clerk for a fee waiver form. **NOTE**: The court has a statutory lien for waived fees and costs on any settlement or arbitration award of $10,000 or more in a civil case. The court's lien must be paid before the court will dismiss the case.

EXENCIÓN DE CUOTAS: Si no puede pagar la cuota de presentación, pida al secretario de la corte que le dé un formulario de exención de pago de cuotas. AVISO: Por ley, la corte tiene derecho a reclamar las cuotas y los costos exentos con un gravamen sobre cualquier cantidad de $10,000 ó más recibida mediante un acuerdo o una concesión de arbitraje en un caso de derecho civil. Tiene que pagar el gravamen de la corte antes de que la corte pueda desestimar el caso.

(Step 3)

1. The name and address of the court is:
   (El nombre y dirección de la corte es):
   Superior Court, County of Los Angeles, 111 North Hill Street, Los Angeles, CA 90012

CASE NUMBER *(número del caso):*
(Leave blank - Court will assign)

(Step 4)

(Step 5)

2. The name, address, and telephone number of plaintiff's attorney, or plaintiff without an attorney, is: *(El nombre, la dirección y el número de teléfono del abogado del demandante, o del demandante que no tiene abogado, es):*
   Lenny D. Landlord, 12345 Angeleno St., Los Angeles, CA 90028; Tel -213-555-6789

Form Adopted for Mandatory Use
Judicial Council of California
SUM-130 [Rev. January 1, 2022]

SUMMONS—UNLAWFUL DETAINER—EVICTION

Page 1 of 2

Code of Civil Procedure, §§ 412.20, 415.45, 1167
www.courts.ca.gov

SUM-130

PLAINTIFF *(Name):* LENNY D. LANDLORD	CASE NUMBER:
DEFENDANT *(Name):* TERRENCE D. TENANT;TILLIE D. TENANT; DOES 1 to 10	(Leave blank - Court will assign)

Step 8

Step 6

3. *(Must be answered in all cases)* An **unlawful detainer assistant (Bus. & Prof. Code, §§ 6400–6415)** [✗] did **not** [ ] did for compensation give advice or assistance with this form. *(If plaintiff has received **any** help or advice for pay from an unlawful detainer assistant, complete item 4 below.)*

4. **Unlawful detainer assistant** *(complete if plaintiff has received any help or advice for pay from an unlawful detainer assistant):*

Step 9

  a. Assistant's name:

  b. Telephone no.:

  c. Street address, city, and zip:

  d. County of registration:

  e. Registration no.:

  f. Registration expires on *(date)* :

Date: *(Fecha)*   Clerk, by *(Secretario)*   , Deputy *(Adjunto)*

(For proof of service of this summons, use Proof of Service of Summons (form POS-010).)
(Para prueba de entrega de esta citatión use el formulario Proof of Service of Summons (form POS-010).)

[SEAL]

Step 7

5. **NOTICE TO THE PERSON SERVED:** You are served

  a. [X] as an individual defendant.

  b. [ ] as the person sued under the fictitious name of *(specify):*

  c. [ ] as an occupant.

  d. [ ] on behalf of *(specify):*

  under: [ ] CCP 416.10 (corporation). [ ] CCP 416.60 (minor).

     [ ] CCP 416.20 (defunct corporation). [ ] CCP 416.70 (conservatee).

     [ ] CCP 416.40 (association or partnership). [ ] CCP 416.90 (authorized person).

     [ ] CCP 415.46 (occupant). [ ] other *(specify):*

  e. [X] by personal delivery on *(date):*

SUM-130 [Rev. January 1, 2022]   **SUMMONS—UNLAWFUL DETAINER—EVICTION**   Page 2 of 2

Step 4: "CASE NUMBER:"

Leave this space blank. The court clerk will fill in the case number when you file your papers.

Step 5: (Item 2)
"The name, address, and telephone number of plaintiff's attorney, or plaintiff without an attorney, is:"

Place your name and mailing address along with a telephone number at which you can be reached. Because your tenant will receive a copy of the summons, he or she will see this address (to which the tenant must mail a copy of any written response) and telephone number. To place some distance between you and the tenant, list a business address or post office box and a business telephone number.

Step 6: (Item 3)
"An unlawful detainer assistant (B&P §§ 6400-6415) ☐ did not ☐ did for compensation give advice or assistance with this form."

A nonattorney who is paid to fill out unlawful detainer paperwork must be registered and bonded. This law does not apply, however, to property owners or to managers who prepare such forms for their employers in the ordinary course of their duties (neither does it apply to attorneys). If you are such a property manager or owner, put an X next to the words "did not."

If you are paying a paralegal or another person to fill out or otherwise process your papers (other than just having a process server serve them), or to advise you on filling out the forms, he or she must be registered with the county and bonded, and the "did" box must be checked. That person's name, address, phone number, and registration information must be listed on this page of the summons form.

Step 7: (Item 5)
"NOTICE TO THE PERSON SERVED: You are served ..."

This part of the summons is for the process server to complete. The server needs to identify the defendant as an individual or as someone who represents a business entity. In residential eviction proceedings, the defendant will always be an individual, so you should put an X in Box 5a. The process server will complete the rest of the form when he or she completes the service. (See below for more information on serving the summons and completing this part of the form.)

Step 8: Complete the Caption on Page Two.

Enter the names of the plaintiff(s) and defendant(s), just as you did when filling out the top of the form on Page 1. Do so even if you won't be filling out Item 4 on this page (see instructions for Step 9).

Step 9: (Item 4)
If you used an unlawful detainer assistant, supply the information called for.

If you checked the box "did not" because you did not use an unlawful detainer assistant skip this step. If you received any advice or help for pay from an assistant and checked the box "did," provide the necessary information.

Preparing the Complaint

In the unlawful detainer complaint, you allege why the tenant should be evicted. The complaint also formally requests a judgment for possession of the premises and any sums that you may be owed as back rent (in nonpayment of rent evictions), damages, court costs, and attorneys' fees. The original of your unlawful detainer complaint is filed with the court. A copy is given to (served on) each defendant along with a copy of the summons. (See "Serving the Papers on the Defendant(s): Service of Process," below.) Together, filing and serving the complaint and summons initiate the lawsuit.

To fill out the complaint correctly, you need to know whether your property is located in an area covered by rent control—either statewide or local. To find this out, consult the list of rent control cities in the Rent Control Chart on Nolo.com (see this book's companion page for the link). Many rent control ordinances that require just cause for eviction require that the complaint (as well as the three-, or 30-, or 60-day notice) include a specific statement of reasons for the eviction. This requirement is satisfied by attaching a copy of the notice to the complaint and by making an allegation (that is, checking a box; see Item 6c, below) in the complaint that all statements in the notice are true. Some ordinances also require complaints to allege compliance with the rent control ordinance. And, even if the ordinance does not require it, the Judicial Council Form has a box for it. If you don't comply with these requirements, the tenant can defend the unlawful detainer suit on that basis.

Although many of these specific rent control requirements are listed in our online rent control chart, we can't detail all the rent control ordinance subtleties, and we can't guarantee that your ordinance hasn't been changed since this book was printed. Therefore, it is absolutely essential that you have a current copy of your ordinance and rent board regulations at the ready when you're planning an eviction in a rent control city.

Completing the complaint is going to be complicated due to COVID-related allegations and forms. As with the summons, the unlawful detainer complaint is completed by filling in a standard form. But don't let this lull you into a false sense of security. If you make even a seemingly minor mistake, such as forgetting to check a box, checking one you shouldn't, or filling in wrong or contradictory information, it will increase the chances that your tenant can and will successfully contest the action, costing you time and money.

Pay very close attention to the following instructions. This chapter includes directions on filling in each item of the complaint plus a completed sample form.

COVID-19 Rent Debt

New rules of pleading change the allegations and procedures required to evict for nonpayment of COVID-19 rental debt. If you want to evict for COVID **transition rents** (C.C.P. §1179.03 (9/1/20-9/30/21)) or **recovery period** rent (C.C.P. §1179.10 (10/1/21-3/31/22)), you cannot obtain a summons for the unlawful detainer until after you have sought rental assistance from the state or local programs. (C.C.P. §1179.11.) Also, **transition period** rents require a special 15-day notice, while **recovery period** rents require a modified three-day notice with a Rental Assistance Program advisory. Finally, default and trial judgments are suspended pending the rental assistance application process.

We have not included instructions and forms for evictions based on COVID **transition** or **recovery period** rent, because the process is so complicated you will need the assistance of an attorney to proceed successfully to the end (with the term "successfully" being relative).

In fact, in view of the availability of statewide rental assistance and the ongoing reluctance of many courts to evict for nonpayment of COVID period rents, we do not recommend even making an attempt to evict based upon nonpayment of **protected period**, **transition period**, or even **recovery period** rents. The time and cost to pursue an eviction for COVID rental debt will exceed what you could expect to collect long before you reach the end of the process.

You can try to collect any COVID-19 rental debt not covered by state rental assistance by filing a lawsuit in small claims court. The Legislature has suspended the cap ($10,000) on small claims actions when an owner is suing for COVID rent. (C.C.P. § 116.223.)

FORM

A blank copy of the Complaint—Unlawful Detainer (Judicial Council form UD-100) is available for downloading from the Nolo website. (See the appendix for the link to the forms, and other information on using them.)

Make single-sided copies of all pleadings. At one time, court forms were prepared as double-sided documents, but with greater use of electronic filing and scanning, double-sided copying might present difficulties. Using single-sided copies, although it consumes more paper, is a safer practice.

    At the top of the form, type your name, address, and telephone number in the first box that says "Attorney or Party Without Attorney." Your email address is optional, and we recommend that you fill it in. After the words "Attorney For," just put the words "Plaintiff in Pro Per," to indicate that you're representing yourself. In the second box, you will need to fill in the county, division, and court address, as you did on the front of the summons. In the third box, fill in the plaintiff's (your) and defendants' names in capital letters. As with the summons, leave blank the box in the upper right corner of the form which is for court use only. Also, leave blank the box labeled "CASE NUMBER."

Put an X in the box next to the space labeled "DOES 1 to _____ ," and put "10" in the space after that. This allows you to name five more defendants later, if, for example, you find out the names of unauthorized occupants of the premises.

If you want to name more defendants later, you can amend (change) your complaint and add the names of the new defendants in exchange for each of your fictional "Doe" defendants. However, you can only do this one time without the court's permission, and it is beyond the scope of this book to explain how to do so.

Put an X in the two boxes next to the words "ACTION IS A LIMITED CIVIL CASE" and the words "does not exceed $10,000" (assuming the rent due is less than $10,000). Do not check any other boxes in this area. This tells the clerk to charge you the lower filing fee (around $240) for a case involving a relatively small amount of money. (If you don't check these boxes, or check the wrong ones, you could be charged $385 to $435.)

Item 1: PLAINTIFF and DEFENDANT Names

    Type your name after the words "PLAIN-TIFF (name each)" and type the defendants' names after the words "DEFENDANT (name each)" using upper case for the caption and title sections, and mixed case for the names after that (for example, SMITH in the caption, but Joe Smith for the remainder of the complaint).

Item 2: Plaintiff Type

  Item 2a: State whether the plaintiff is an individual, a public agency, a partnership, or a corporation. If, as in most cases, the plaintiff is an adult individual—you—who is an owner of the property, type an X in Box (1) next to the words "an individual over the age of 18 years."

Do not check the box next to the words "a partnership" unless you listed the partnership as the plaintiff on the summons. (See Step 2 in "Preparing the Summons," above.) If you are a partnership, you will need to complete and attach the Partnership Verification form. More on this later in the chapter.

If you are a corporation, you cannot do this yourself. Corporate landlords must be represented by an attorney—in which case you should not be doing the eviction lawsuit on your own.

UD-100

ATTORNEY OR PARTY WITHOUT ATTORNEY	STATE BAR NUMBER:	FOR COURT USE ONLY

NAME: Lenny D. Landlord

FIRM NAME:

STREET ADDRESS: 12345 Angeleno Street

CITY: Los Angeles   STATE: CA   ZIP CODE: 90028

TELEPHONE NO.: 213-555-6789   FAX NO.:

EMAIL ADDRESS: LDLXX321@ispofchoice.com

ATTORNEY FOR (name): Plaintiff in Pro Per

SUPERIOR COURT OF CALIFORNIA, COUNTY OF LOS ANGELES

STREET ADDRESS: 111 North Hill Street

MAILING ADDRESS:

CITY AND ZIP CODE: Los Angeles, California 90012

BRANCH NAME:

PLAINTIFF: LENNY D. LANDLORD

DEFENDANT: TERRENCE D. TENANT; TILLIE D. TENANT

[x] DOES 1 TO 10

COMPLAINT—UNLAWFUL DETAINER*	CASE NUMBER:
[x] COMPLAINT [ ] AMENDED COMPLAINT (Amendment Number):	Leave blank - court will fill in

Jurisdiction *(check all that apply):*

[x] **ACTION IS A LIMITED CIVIL CASE**

Amount demanded [x] **does not exceed $10,000.**

[ ] **exceeds $10,000 but does not exceed $25,000.**

[ ] **ACTION IS AN UNLIMITED CIVIL CASE** (amount demanded exceeds $25,000)

[ ] **ACTION IS RECLASSIFIED** by this amended complaint or cross-complaint *(check all that apply):*

    [ ] **from unlawful detainer to general unlimited civil** (possession not in issue). [ ] **from limited to unlimited.**

    [ ] **from unlawful detainer to general limited civil** (possession not in issue). [ ] **from unlimited to limited.**

1. *PLAINTIFF (name each):*
    Lenny D. Landlord

    alleges causes of action against DEFENDANT (name each):
    Terrence D. Tenant, Tillie D. Tenant

2. a. Plaintiff is (1) [x] an individual over the age of 18 years. (4) [ ] a partnership.
                (2) [ ] a public agency. (5) [ ] a corporation.
                (3) [ ] other *(specify):*

    b. [ ] Plaintiff has complied with the fictitious business name laws and is doing business under the fictitious name of *(specify):*

3. a. *The venue is the court named above because defendant named above is in possession of the premises located at (street address, apt. no., city, zip code, and county):*
    3815 Gower Canyon Avenue, Apt. 3, Los Angeles, California 90028 (Los Angeles County)

    b. The premises in 3a are *(check one)*

        (1) [x] within the city limits of *(name of city):* Los Angeles

        (2) [ ] within the unincorporated area of *(name of county):*

    c. The premises in 3a were constructed in *(approximate year):* 1929

4. Plaintiff's interest in the premises is [x] as owner [ ] other *(specify):*

5. The true names and capacities of defendants sued as Does are unknown to plaintiff.

***NOTE:** Do not use this form for evictions after sale (Code Civ. Proc., § 1161a).*

Page 1 of 4

Form Approved for Optional Use		
Judicial Council of California	**COMPLAINT—UNLAWFUL DETAINER**	Civil Code, § 1940 et seq.;
UD–100 [Rev. September 1, 2020]		Code of Civil Procedure, §§ 425.12, 1166
		www.courts.ca.gov

Item 2b: Type an X in the box if you included a fictitious business name when you identified the plaintiff in the summons (see Step 2 in "Preparing the Summons," above). Type the fictitious business name in the space provided.

Item 3: Address of Rental Property and Venue

    List the street address of the rental property, including apartment number if applicable, the city and county in which it is located, and the zip code. You will also need to include the city limits allegation (Subparagraph (b)) and the approximate construction date (Subparagraph (c)).

> EXAMPLE:
> a. 123 Main Street, Apartment 4, San Jose 95123 County of Santa Clara.
> b. (1) [X] "San Jose, California"
> c. 1957

Item 4: Plaintiff's Interest

    If you are an owner of the property, type an X in the box next to the words "as owner."

Item 5: Unknown Defendants

    You don't need to do anything here. This allegation applies only if there are unauthorized subtenants or long-term "guests" in the property, but you don't know their names. If you later learn the real name of a "John Doe," this allegation makes it easier for you to file an "amended" complaint, giving the correct name(s). Filing an amended complaint gets a bit tricky. If you need help, contact a lawyer to help you.

    PLAINTIFF and DEFENDANT.

At the top of the second page of the complaint is a large box labeled "PLAINTIFF (Name)" and "DEFENDANT (Name)." Here, type in capital letters the names of the first-listed plaintiff and defendant the same way their names are listed on the front caption under "PLAINTIFF" and "DEFENDANT." Where there are multiple plaintiffs or defendants, you list only the first one here, followed by "et al."

Item 6: Landlord and Tenant's Agreement

    Item 6a: This item calls for basic information about the terms of the tenancy.

On the first line (beginning with "On or about"), fill in the date on which you agreed to rent the property to your tenant. This is the date the agreement was made, not the date the tenant moved in. If a written lease or rental agreement is involved, the date should be somewhere on it. If it's an oral agreement and you can't remember the exact date, don't worry. The approximate date is okay.

It's very common for tenants with leases to stay beyond the lease expiration date, with the full knowledge and blessing of the landlord. When the landlord continues to accept rent, these tenants become month-to-month tenants, subject to the same terms and conditions of the original lease. If the tenant you're evicting stayed on in this way, use the date that the original lease was signed. If you asked this tenant to sign a new lease when the old one expired (this is the better practice), use the date that the latest lease was signed, and refer to this lease for all other information that's called for in the complaint.

Then, as defendant, fill in the names of the persons with whom you made the oral agreement or who signed a written agreement or lease. In the case of an oral agreement, list the name(s) of the person(s) with whom you or a manager or another agent originally dealt in renting the property. Don't worry if the list of people with whom the oral or written agreement was made does not include all the current adult occupants. Occupants who didn't make the original agreement are subtenants or assignees (see *The California Landlord's Law Book: Rights & Responsibilities*, Chapter 10) and are accounted for in Item 6c (below).

If some of the original tenants have moved out, they should not be listed in Item 6a, since you are not permitted to name them as defendants. You list here only those person(s) who entered into the rental agreement *and* still live in the property.

The boxes after Line (1) of Item 6a (beginning with the words "agreed to rent the premises as a") indicate the type of tenancy you and your tenant(s) originally entered into:

- If the tenancy was from month to month (see Chapter 3), check that box.
- If the tenancy was not originally month to month, type an X in the "other tenancy" box.
  - For a fixed-term tenancy, type "fixed-term tenancy for _____ months," indicating the number of months the lease was to last.
  - The "other tenancy" box can also be used to indicate periodic tenancies other than from month to month, such as week-to-week tenancies.
  - If the tenancy began for a fixed period (one year is common), but the term has expired and the tenancy is now month to month, indicate it as it originally was (fixed term). You can note in Item 6d (see below) that the tenancy subsequently changed to month to month.

The boxes after Line (2) in Item 6a (beginning with the words "agreed to pay rent of") has a space for you to fill in the amount of the rent when the tenant originally rented the premises. If the rent has increased since then, say so in Item 6d (see below). Next indicate how often the rent was payable (again, when the tenancy began; changes since then should be indicated in Item 6d). In the rare cases where the rent was not payable monthly, put an X in the "other" box and type in the appropriate period (for example, weekly or bimonthly).

At Line (3) of Item 6a, check "first of the month" if the rent was payable then. If it was payable on any other day (for example, on the 15th of each month, or every Monday), instead check the box next to "other day (*specify*):" and type in when the rent did come due.

    Item 6b: This item tells whether the rental agreement or lease was oral or written and whether you, an agent, or a previous owner entered into it with the tenant. Check either the "written" box or the "oral" box on the first line. If there was a written agreement with the first tenants, but only an oral agreement with subsequent occupants, the latter are most likely subtenants under the written agreement. So you need only check the "written" box.

Also put an X in one of the four boxes below it. Check the box labeled "plaintiff" if you—the plaintiff—signed the written rental agreement or lease or made the oral agreement with the tenant. If a manager, an agent, or another person did this, check the box labeled "plaintiff's agent" instead. If the tenant was renting the property before you owned it, and you didn't have a new rental agreement or lease signed, the tenant is there because of some sort of agreement with the previous owner—in legalese, your "predecessor in interest"—and you should check that box.

    Item 6c: If the occupants you're trying to evict are all named in Item 6a (because you entered into a written or oral rental agreement or lease with them), leave Box c blank and go on to Item 6d. If you're not sure whether the tenants are properly named in 6a, or should instead be listed in 6c, do what many attorneys do, as a catch-all: In 6c, check Boxes (1) and (2) (subtenants and assignees), plus (3) ("Other"—write in "co-occupants whose status is unknown"). Don't remove their names from 6a. Listing the occupants in both places classifies all the unknown occupants in one category or another.

UD-100

PLAINTIFF: LENNY D. LANDLORD DEFENDANT: TERRENCE D. TENANT; TILLIE D. TENANT	CASE NUMBER: Leave blank - court will fill in

6. a. On or about *(date):* Jan. 2, 20xx

        defendant (name each):
        Terrence D. Tenant, Tillie D. Tenant

        (1) agreed to rent the premises as a [**✗**] month-to-month tenancy [ ] other tenancy *(specify):*
        (2) agreed to pay rent of $ 1,650   payable [**✗**] monthly [ ] other *(specify frequency):*
        (3) agreed to pay rent on the [**✗**] first of the month [ ] other day *(specify):*

    b. This [**✗**] written [ ] oral agreement was made with
        (1) [**✗**] plaintiff.   (3) [ ] plaintiff's predecessor in interest.
        (2) [ ] plaintiff's agent. (4) [ ] Other *(specify):*

    c. [**✗**] The defendants not named in item 6a are
        (1) [**✗**] subtenants.
        (2) [**✗**] assignees.
        (3) [**✗**] Other *(specify):* co-occupants whose status is unknown

    d. [**✗**] The agreement was later changed as follows *(specify):*
    Rent lawfully increased 3% to $1,699.50 on January 2, 20xx+1

    e. [**✗**] A copy of the written agreement, including any addenda or attachments that form the basis of this complaint, is attached and labeled Exhibit 1. *(Required for residential property, unless item 6f is checked. See Code Civ. Proc., § 1166.)*

    f. [ ] *(For residential property)* A copy of the written agreement is **not** attached because *(specify reason):*
        (1) [ ] *the written agreement is not in the possession of the landlord or the landlord's employees or agents.*
        (2) [ ] *this action is solely for nonpayment of rent (Code Civ. Proc., § 1161(2)).*

7. The tenancy described in 6 *(complete (a) or (b))*

    a. [**✗**] is **not** subject to the Tenant Protection Act of 2019 (Civil Code, § 1946.2). The specific subpart supporting why tenancy is exempt is *(specify):* Civil Code §1946.2(g)(1)(A)

    b. [ ] is subject to the Tenant Protection Act of 2019.

8. *(Complete only if item 7b is checked. Check all applicable boxes.)*

    a. [ ] The tenancy was terminated for at-fault just cause (Civil Code, § 1946.2(b)(1)).

    b. [ ] The tenancy was terminated for no-fault just cause (Civil Code, § 1946.2(b)(2)) and the plaintiff *(check one)*

        (1) [ ] waived the payment of rent for the final month of the tenancy, before the rent came due, under section 1946.2(d)(2), in the amount of $

        (2) [ ] provided a direct payment of one month's rent under section 1946.2(d)(3), equaling $ to *(name each defendant and amount given to each):*

    c. [ ] Because defendant failed to vacate, plaintiff is seeking to recover the total amount in 8b as damages in this action.

9. a. [**✗**] Defendant *(name each):* Terrence D. Tenant, Tillie D. Tenant

    was served the following notice on the same date and in the same manner:

        (1) [ ] 3-day notice to pay rent or quit   (5) [ ] 3-day notice to perform covenants or quit
        (2) [**✗**] 30-day notice to quit   *(not applicable if item 7b checked)*
        (3) [ ] 60-day notice to quit   (6) [ ] 3-day notice to quit under Civil Code, § 1946.2(c)
        (4) [ ] 3-day notice to quit   Prior required notice to perform covenants served *(date):*
                                             (7) [ ] Other *(specify):*

COMPLAINT—UNLAWFUL DETAINER

If, however, some of the persons you named as defendants were not named in Item 6a (for example, adults who later moved in without your permission), check Box c and one of the three boxes below it to indicate whether these defendants are "subtenants" (usually) or "assignees" (rarely).

Here's a brief explanation.

Subtenants. If any of the original tenants listed in Item 6a still live in the premises with these defendants, check the "subtenants" box, because these people are essentially renting from the original tenants, not from you.

> **EXAMPLE:** Larry rented to Tim and Twyla ten years ago. Tim and Twyla signed a month-to-month rental agreement that is still in effect (though Larry has increased the rent since then). Last year, Twyla moved out and Twinka moved in with Tim. Larry never had Twinka sign a new rental agreement.
>
> What is the current status of Tim and Twinka? Tim is still renting from Larry under the old rental agreement, but Twinka is actually renting from Tim—even if she pays the rent to Larry herself. Twinka is a subtenant and should be listed under Item 6c. Tim and Twyla, the original tenants, are listed in Item 6a.

Assignees. On the other hand, if none of the original tenants lives on the premises and you don't expect any of them to return, chances are that the current occupants are "assignees"—unless you had them sign or enter into a new rental agreement. An assignee is someone to whom the former tenants have, in effect, turned over all of their legal rights under the lease.

> **EXAMPLE:** Lana rented one of her apartments to Toby and Toni five years ago. Three years ago, Toby and Toni left and, without telling Lana, had Toby's cousin Todd move in. Although Lana could have objected under the rental agreement clause prohibiting subletting and

assignment, she didn't. She accepted rent from Todd, but never had Todd sign a new rental agreement, so he's an "assignee" of Toby's and Toni's. In this situation, Lana would name only Todd as defendant, but list Toby and Toni as the persons in Item 6a to whom she originally rented. (This is true even though Item 6a asks you to list "defendants." Toby and Toni aren't actually defendants, because they no longer live there; the form isn't perfectly designed for every situation.) In Item 6c, you should check the "assignees" box to indicate that Todd, not named in 6a, is an assignee of the persons who are named.

Sometimes you'll have trouble determining the definitive status of other occupants. Are they subtenants, assignees, co-tenants, or subsequent occupants under a rent control ordinance? Unfortunately, the official fillable form permits you to electronically mark only one of the three boxes. If necessary, you can check Box (3)—"other"—and state, "co-occupants whose status is unknown."

 Item 6d: Box d should be checked if there was a change in any of the information provided in Item 6a since the original tenancy began. For instance, if the rent is higher now than it was at first, this is the place for you to say so, especially if your eviction is for nonpayment of rent and you are seeking unpaid rent. If there have been several rent increases, list them all, in chronological order.

> **EXAMPLE 1:** Leon rented his property on a month-to-month basis to Teresa on January 1, 20xx, for $1,100 per month. (This date and former rent amount should be listed in Item 6a.) On July 1, 20xx, Leon gave Teresa a 60-day notice (required for rent increases of more than 10%), that her rent would be increased from $1,100 per month to $1,200, effective

September 1, 20xx. Leon should check Box d under Item 6 and after the words "The agreement was later changed as follows (specify):" type the following:

> "On July 1, 20xx, Plaintiff notified defendant in writing that effective September 1, 20xx, the rent would be increased to $1,200 each month."

EXAMPLE 2: Teresa's neighbor, Juan, moved into one of Leon's apartments on January 1, 20xx. On December 1, Leon told Juan his rent would go from $1,100 to $1,200, effective January 1,"On July 1, 20xx, Plaintiff notified defendant in writing that effective September 1, 20xx, the rent would be increased to $900 each month."20xx. However, Leon forgot to give Juan the required written 30-day notice to increase the rent. Still, Juan paid the increased rent for several months, beginning in January. Even though Leon should have raised the rent with a written notice, Juan effectively "waived" or gave up his right to a written notice by paying the increase anyway. (Note: This may not be true in a rent control city, especially if the increased rent exceeds the legal rent for the property.) Now, in June 20xx, Juan won't pay the rent (or move) and Leon has to sue him. Check Box d under Item 6 and type in the following:

> "On December 1, 20xx, plaintiff notified defendant that effective January 1, 20xx, the rent due would be increased to $1,200 each month, and defendant agreed to and did pay the increased rent on its effective date."

Another common event that should be recorded in Item 6d is any change in the type of tenancy (for example, from a fixed-term lease to a month-to-month tenancy).

> "On July 1, 20xx, Plaintiff notified defendant in writing that effective September 1, 20xx, the rent would be increased to $1,200 each month."

EXAMPLE: On June 1, you rented your property to Leroy for one year under a written lease. Leroy didn't leave on June 1 of the following year and paid you the usual rent of $900, which you accepted. Although the original tenancy was one for a fixed term, as should be indicated in Item 6a, it is now month to month. (See Chapter 5.) Check Box d in Item 6 and type the following:

> "On June 1, 20xx, after expiration of the lease term, defendant remained in possession and paid $900 rent, which plaintiff accepted, so as to continue the tenancy on a month-to-month basis."

Item 6d should also be filled out for changes in the rental period (for example, from bimonthly to monthly) and changes in the date when the rent was due (for example, from the 15th of the month to the first). Simply put, Item 6d is your chance to bring the court up to date as to your current arrangements with your tenants.

You may find that there isn't enough space on the complaint form to type in all the required information for this item. If you can't fit it in with three typewritten lines that go right up against each margin, type the words "see Attachment 6d" and add all the necessary information on a sheet of white typing paper labeled "Attachment 6d." This attachment is stapled to the complaint, along with the "Exhibit" copies of the lease/rental agreement and three-day, 30-day, or 60-day notice discussed below. (Be sure to add one more page to the number of pages listed in Item 1 if you do this.)

Item 6e: If the rental agreement is oral, skip this box and Item 6f, and go on to Item 7. If the rental agreement or lease is in writing, put an X in this box if you have the original or a copy of it. Attach a photocopy (not a signed duplicate) of the lease or rental agreement to the complaint (unless you can't find an original or copy). Write "EXHIBIT 1" on the bottom of the copy. (If you and the tenants signed a new lease or rental agreement after having signed an older version, you need only attach a copy of the most recent lease or rental agreement.) You must include copies of any written amendments or addenda. Finally, keep track of the correct number of pages attached to the complaint, which you'll need to list in Item 20 (count two printed sides of one page as two pages).

> **TIP**
>
> **If you're seeking to evict because of nonpayment of rent, you aren't legally required to attach a copy of the rental agreement, but we think it's a good practice.** Doing so might defeat a tenant's objection to the complaint for failure to include a contract. This argument would give the tenant a way to delay the proceeding. In addition, if the tenant defaults, you will have to furnish the lease. Similarly, if the tenant contests the lawsuit, the judge who hears the case will have to look at the lease, and if you've taken the extra step now to attach all relevant documents, the court might be favorably impressed with the way you put your case together.

   Item 6f: This question asks you to explain why, if there is a written rental agreement or lease, you have not attached a copy of it to the complaint. (You're not required to do so in rent nonpayment cases even if you have a copy, though we suggest that you do if you have one and leave this box unchecked.) If your rental agreement is oral, skip this item and go to Item 7. Also skip it if you are attaching a copy of the rental agreement or lease.

If you haven't attached a copy of a lease or rental agreement, put an X in the box next to Item 6f. Also put an X either in Box (1) if you simply don't have an original or copy of the lease or rental agreement, or in Box (2) if your lawsuit is based on nonpayment of rent, and (against our advice) you decide not to attach a copy.

Item 7: Statewide Rent Control

This is the section where you indicate whether you are subject to the Tenant Protection Act (TPA) just cause provisions. It is a matter of checking one of the two boxes—yes or no. If the answer is "no," you will have to cite the statutory exemption section, which in nearly all cases will be found in Civ. Code § 1946.2(g). If you are in a rent control city, the subsection will be either Subsection (g)(1A) or (B).

8. Statewide Just Cause

Complete this section if the TPA applies to your unit, as you indicated in Section 7. If it does, check the applicable box for the just cause under the notice to terminate. You should know the just cause from the notice you issued earlier, but you can find the list in Civ. Code § 1946.2 as well.

Box (a) refers to at-fault terminations (breach of the lease, nonpayment of rent, nuisance, waste, and so on). Box (b) refers to no-fault causes for which relocation expenses must be paid directly or by waiver of the last month's rent (owner or relative moving in, demolition, removal from rental housing, and so on). Check Box (c) if you paid relocation fees but the tenant didn't move out.

> **EXAMPLE:** George Tenant, the defendant, occupies the premises that are covered by the TPA. The landlord, Fred, served a three-day notice to cure or quit, followed by a three-day notice to quit, because George kept smoking in the common areas in violation of the lease and refused to cease after receiving a warning. Fred filled out Paragraphs 7 and 8 by checking Box 7(b) and Box 8(a).

9: Notice

   Check the box immediately following the number 9 to indicate that a notice to quit was served on at least one of the tenants, and fill in the name of the defendant to whom the notice was given. If you served more than one defendant, list all of their names. You will also list the other names and method of service in Items 9f and Attachment 10c, below.

 Leave Items 9 and 9a through 9f blank if your eviction is being brought under Chapter 5 of this book (that is, if no notice was given the tenant).

 Item 9a: Check Box (1), labeled "3-day notice to pay rent or quit." Also check Box (7) and enter the title of any additional documents required by the local rent control ordinance.

 Item 9a: Check Box (2) labeled "30-day notice to quit" if that is what you used because the tenancy was for less than a year. (See Chapter 3.) If you had to give a 60-day notice because your tenant occupied the premises for a year or more, check Box (3) next to the words "60-day notice to quit." Also check Box (7) and enter the title of any additional documents required by the local rent control ordinance.

If you used a 90-day notice of termination of tenancy because the tenancy was government subsidized, check Box (7) next to the words "Other (*specify*):" and type the words "90-day notice to quit."

 Item 9a: Check either Box (5) labeled "3-day notice to perform covenants or quit" (the conditional notice), or Box (6) "3-day notice to quit" (the unconditional notice), depending on which type of notice you served. Also check box (7) and enter the title of any

additional documents required by the local rent control ordinance.

    PLAINTIFF and DEFENDANT. At the top of the second page of the complaint is a large box labeled "PLAINTIFF (Name)" and "DEFENDANT (Name)." Here, type in capital letters the names of the first-listed plaintiff and defendant the same way their names are listed on the front caption under "PLAINTIFF" and "DEFENDANT." Where there are multiple plaintiffs or defendants, you list only the first one here, followed by "ET AL."

  Item 9b: List the date the period provided in your three-day notice expired. This is the third business day, not counting the day the notice was served or intervening weekends and holidays after the three-day notice was personally served. (See Chapters 2 and 4 for several detailed examples.) If you used substituted service for your notice or are unsure of your notice's expiration date, return to your "home" chapter (Chapter 2 or 4) and compute the correct expiration date in accordance with our instructions.

 Item 9c: List the date the period provided in your 30-day or 60-day notice expired. This is the 30th day (or the 60th day) after the notice was personally served (don't count the day the notice was served), except that when the 30th or 60th day falls on a weekend or legal holiday, the last day is the next business day. (See the detailed examples in Chapter 3 to get a better handle on this.) If you used substituted service or are unsure of the proper expiration date, return to Chapter 3 and compute the proper expiration date in accordance with our instructions.

 CAUTION
Don't file until the three, 30, or 60 days have expired.

Be sure you do not file your papers with the court (see below) until after the date you indicate in Item 9b. Otherwise, the complaint will be premature, and you may lose the case and have to pay the tenant's court costs.

   Item 9c: You don't need to fill in a box or add information on this one, which just says that everything in the notice you served (a copy of which you will attach to the complaint) is true.

  Item 9d: Put an X in this box. This indicates that your three-day notice contained an "election of forfeiture"—legalese for a statement in the notice that the tenancy is ended if the notice is not obeyed. The form notices in this book include a forfeiture statement.

 Item 9d: Leave this item blank, since 30-day and 60-day notices do not require a notice of forfeiture.

   Item 9e: Check this box. Label the bottom of your copy of the three- or 30-day notice "EXHIBIT 2" (even if you don't have an Exhibit 1), and remember to staple it to your complaint. Including a copy of your termination notice is essential. We strongly recommend attaching a copy of the 3 day to pay or quit notice as well, along with the any collateral documents required by the local rent control ordinance, even though they might not be strictly required by the Judicial Council form.

   Item 9f: Put an X in Box 9f only if (1) there are two or more defendants, *and* (2) you served *two* or more of them with the notice on a different date or in a different manner. (Although the form contemplates checking this box also if two or more defendants were served with different notices, we do not recommend such a procedure.) For example, if Tillie Tenant and Sam Subtenant were each served with a three-day notice on a different

day, or if one was served personally and the other served by substituted service and mailing (see Chapter 2), then Lenny Landlord would check this box. However, do not check the box if the two or more defendants are all cotenants on a written lease or rental agreement and you served just one of them on behalf of all tenants.

If you check Item 9f, you should also put an X in Item 10c of the complaint form. At this point, the information in Item 10a on content and service of the notice will apply only to the person(s) whose name(s) is listed in Item 9a. You will have to state on a separate page labeled "Attachment 10c," how any other persons were served in a different manner or on a different date. Before doing that, however, you complete Items 10a and 10b of the complaint form.

 Item 9f: Leave Item 9f blank if your eviction is being brought under Chapter 5 of this book—that is, if no notice was served on any tenant.

Item 10: Service of Notice

   This part of the eviction form asks for the details on how you performed service of process. You have a choice: You can complete Item 10a or you can demonstrate your service compliance by checking Item 10d and supplying as Exhibit 3 a written, signed proof of service indicating when and how the notice was served. Which method is preferable? We suggest doing both—completing Item 10(a) as to the first defendant and attaching proofs of service for everyone under 10(d). The form no longer permits you to enter the information for all defendants in 10. So you will have to enter the information for the first defendant on the form and then all other defendants in Attachment 10(c). The attachment should label the first proof of service, described in 9a as "Exhibit 3" and the second and succeeding proofs of service, described in 10(c), as "Exhibit 3a," "Exhibit 3b," and so on.

Labeling the exhibits involves no more than writing, on the bottom of the page of the exhibit in uppercase letters "EXHIBIT" followed by the number. Because so many pleadings are scanned or filed electronically, for ease of reading we recommend taking the extra step to separate each exhibit with a slip sheet (or blank piece of paper) that has the word "Exhibit" and the number for the following exhibit.

Slip sheets are not strictly required but make it easier for the court to find your papers and exhibits. If the day comes that you are required to submit all your papers electronically, as many attorneys must now do, slip sheets also make bookmarking the electronic version much simpler.

Remember, if you have multiple defendants served different ways, you'll need to add separate attachment pages for each.

 Leave Items 10a and 10b and 10c blank, because no notice was served on your tenant.

  Item 10a: If the defendant listed in Item 9a was personally served with the notice, check Box (1) (next to the words "by personally handing a copy to defendant on (*date*)") and type the date the tenant was handed the notice.

Box (2) in Item 10a, next to "by leaving a copy with ...," should be checked instead only if you used "substituted service," that is, you gave the notice to someone at the tenant's home or workplace and mailed a second copy. On the same line, list the name (or physical description if name is unknown) of the person to whom the notice was given. On the next two lines, fill in the date you delivered the notice, check a box to indicate whether the notice was served at the residence or business address, and list the date the second copy was mailed to the residence address. Then go on to Item 8b.

If you had to resort to "posting and mailing" service because you couldn't find anyone at the defendant's home or place of employment, check Box (3) next to the words "by posting a copy on the premises on (*date*)" and insert the date the notice was

posted. Ignore the box by the words "AND giving a copy to a person found residing at the premises." Below that, list the date the copy of the notice was mailed to the residence address. Next, check one of the two boxes (in front of phrases beginning with "because") to indicate why you used posting-and-mailing service. In almost all residential cases you should check the second box, next to the phrase "because no person of suitable age or discretion can be found there." Leave blank the box next to the phrase "because defendant's residence and usual place of business cannot be ascertained"—after all, you always know the defendant's residence address in a residential eviction.

 The fourth box in Item 10a, followed by the words *"Not for 3-day notice"* in parentheses, obviously should be used only if your eviction was preceded by a 30-day or 60-day notice (see Chapter 3) which you served by certified or registered mail.

   Item 10a: The last (fifth) box in Item 10a should not be checked. It applies only to some commercial tenancies—a subject beyond the scope of this book.

  Item 10b: Put an X in this box and again list the name(s) of any defendant you served with a termination notice (as you did in Item 7a), only if all of the following are true: (1) There are two or more defendants, (2) two or more of the defendants both signed the written lease or rental agreement, and (3) you did not serve all of the signers of the lease or rental agreement with a notice. You should only use this box if you served a 30-/60- day notice, not a three-day notice. (See *Four Seas Investment Corp. v. International Hotel Tenants' Assn* (1978) 81 Cal. App.3d 604, 611-12.) In that case, Item 10a should list "Terrence Tenant" as the one served with a notice, Item 9f should not be checked and Item 10b should be checked. At Item 10b, "Terrence Tenant" should again be listed as the person who was served on behalf of the other tenant(s) on the lease or rental agreement.

UD-100

PLAINTIFF: LENNY D. LANDLORD DEFENDANT: TERRENCE D. TENANT; TILLIE D. TENANT	CASE NUMBER: Leave blank - court will fill in

9. b. (1) On *(date):* April 9, 20xx   the period stated in the notice checked in 9a expired at the end of the day.

        (2) Defendants failed to comply with the requirements of the notice by that date.

  c. All facts stated in the notice are true.

  d. [✗] The notice included an election of forfeiture.

  e. [✗] A copy of the notice is attached and labeled Exhibit 2. *(Required for residential property. See Code Civ. Proc., § 1166. When Civil Code, § 1946.2(c), applies and two notices are required, provide copies of both.)*

  f. [✗] One or more defendants were served (1) with the prior required notice under Civil Code, § 1946.2(c), (2) with a different notice, (3) on a different date, or (4) in a different manner, as stated in Attachment 10c. *(Check item 10c and attach a statement providing the information required by items 9a–e and 10 for each defendant and notice.)*

10. a. [✗] The notice in item 9a was served on the defendant named in item 9a as follows:

        (1) [✗] By personally handing a copy to defendant on *(date):* April 4, 20xx

        (2) [ ] By leaving a copy with *(name or description):*

        a person of suitable age and discretion, on *(date):*   at defendant's

        [ ] residence   [ ] business   AND mailing a copy to defendant at defendant's place of residence

        on *(date):*   because defendant cannot be found at defendant's residence or usual place of business.

        (3) [ ] By posting a copy on the premises on *(date):*

        [ ] AND giving a copy to a person found residing at the premises AND mailing a copy to defendant at the premises

        on *(date):*

          (a) [ ] because defendant's residence and usual place of business cannot be ascertained OR

          (b) [ ] because no person of suitable age or discretion can be found there.

        (4) [ ] *(Not for 3-day notice; see Civil Code, § 1946, before using)* By sending a copy by certified or registered mail addressed to defendant on *(date):*

        (5) [ ] *(Not for residential tenancies; see Civil Code, § 1953, before using)* In the manner specified in a written commercial lease between the parties

  b. [ ] *(Name):*

    was served on behalf of all defendants who signed a joint written rental agreement.

  c. [✗] *Information about service of notice on the defendants alleged in item 9f is stated in Attachment 10c.*

  d. [✗] *Proof of service of the notice in item 9a is attached and labeled Exhibit 3.*

11. [ ] *Plaintiff demands possession from each defendant because of expiration of a fixed-term lease.*

12. [✗] *At the time the 3-day notice to pay rent or quit was served, the amount of **rent due** was* $1,699.50

13. [✗] *The fair rental value of the premises is* $56.65   per day.

14. [ ] *Defendant's continued possession is malicious, and plaintiff is entitled to statutory damages under Code of Civil Procedure section 1174(b). (State specific facts supporting a claim up to $600 in Attachment 14.)*

15. [ ] *A written agreement between the parties provides for attorney fees.*

16. [✗] *Defendant's tenancy is subject to the local rent control or eviction control ordinance of (city or county, title of ordinance, and date of passage):*
Rent Stabilization Ordinance of the City of Los Angeles, LA Municipal Code, Chapter XV, City of Los Angeles, enacted 1979, as amended.

Plaintiff has met all applicable requirements of the ordinances.

17. [ ] *Other allegations are stated in Attachment 17.*

18. Plaintiff accepts the jurisdictional limit, if any, of the court.

COMPLAINT—UNLAWFUL DETAINER

Item 10c: If you put an X in Box 9f, you did so because (1) there are two or more defendants, *and* (2) you served two or more defendants with the same notice on a different date or in a different manner. (You generally will not check Box 9f or 10c if you checked Box 10b to indicate you served one cotenant, but not other written-lease cotenants.) If you did put an X in Box 9f, do so in Box 10c also. You will then also need to add an extra piece of typing paper titled "Attachment 10c to Complaint—Unlawful Detainer." On that attachment, you need to explain how the defendant(s) other than the one whose name is mentioned in Item 9a was served in a different manner or on a different date. Use the format of the wording in Item 10a(1), (2), (3), (4), or (5) (certified mail service of 30-day or 60-day notice only).

TIP
You can use Judicial Council form MC-025 (Attachment to Judicial Council Form) instead of blank paper to write the 10c attachment (or any other attachment). The MC-025 form comes preformatted and looks more professional to the judge reading your complaint. The sample Form 10c attachment allegation in this chapter uses MC-025 as its base.

For example, where Items 9 and 10 show you served Tillie D. Tenant personally with a three-day notice to pay rent or quit on April 4, and you served Sam Subtenant on April 6 by substituted service, Boxes 9f and 10c should be checked, and Attachment 10c would state, "Defendant Sam Subtenant was served the three- day notice to pay rent or quit, alleged in Item 8, by leaving a copy with Terrence D. Tenant, a person of suitable age and discretion, on April 6, 20xx, at his residence, and by mailing a copy to him on April 7, 20xx, because he could not be found at his residence or place of business."

  Item 10d: If you wish, you may check this box to indicate that instead of using Items 9a through 9c above to describe how the notice was served, you're attaching as Exhibit 3 a written, signed proof of service indicating when and how the notice was served. See the discussion at the beginning of Item 10 for the pros and cons of using Item 10d.

Item 11: Expiration of Lease

   Do not use this box. It does not apply in evictions based on three-day, 30-day, or 60-day notices.

Check this box if you are proceeding under Chapter 5 on the grounds that your fixed-term lease expired. Do not check it if the reason for the eviction is that the tenant failed to vacate on time after serving you with a 30-day notice.

Item 12: Rent Due

 Put an X in Box 12. At the end of the sentence following the box, put the amount of rent you demanded in the three-day notice.

Your complaint will be susceptible to a delaying motion if it ambiguously states that the rent due was something other than that stated on the attached three-day notice, so do not under any circumstances list a different amount.

   Leave this box blank. It is solely for evictions based on a Three-Day Notice to Pay Rent or Quit. (See Chapter 2).

Item 13: Daily Rental Value

   Check Box 13 and list the daily prorated rent. This is the monthly rent divided by 30 or, if the rent is paid weekly, the weekly rent divided by seven. For example, if the rent is $450 per month, the daily rental value is $450 ÷ 30, or $15. Round the answer off to the nearest penny if it doesn't come out even. This figure is the measure of the "damages" you suffer each day the tenant stays after the end of the rental period.

Item 14: Landlord's Right to Statutory Damages

    Statutory damages are damages that the landlord can recover if the judge finds that the tenant acted particularly badly (the code uses the word "malicious"). Judges rarely, if ever, give statutory damages, and for this reason, we recommend that you not check this box. If you were to check it, you'd be claiming that the tenant is being "malicious" in staying when he or she should leave, and you are asking for up to $600 in punitive damages in addition to the rent. (The law does not allow you to ask for more. Before 1994, a landlord could recover "treble damages," or three times the rent the tenant owed, but now you can recover only $600 if you can convince a judge the tenant acted maliciously.) If you do check this box, you must then add an Attachment 14 in which you state— in very specific detail—the acts of the tenant that you think show a malicious intent. Because only $600 of a probably uncollectible judgment is at stake, because the requirements for alleging and proving malicious intent are very technical, and because judges seldom award these types of extra damages, we do not recommend seeking this sum. Also, demanding extra money based on the tenant's maliciousness may provoke a delaying response on the part of the tenant. You're almost always better off leaving Item 14 blank.

Rent vs. Damages

It's important to understand the legal difference between "rent" and "damages," because you'll need to list them appropriately on your complaint:

- Rent is money that the tenant owes you, a debt that arose before the three-day notice for the use of the premises expired. It includes unpaid rent up to that date, but nothing else.
- Damages arise during the period when the tenant deprives the landlord from taking back the property, after the termination notice expires and before the landlord gets a judgment from the court. For example, suppose that after you file the unlawful detainer action, the tenant remains in the apartment, up until the date of judgment. Your damages are the equivalent of the daily rent (called the daily rental value) from the date the notice expired through the date of judgment.

The difference between "rent" and "damages" is illustrated as follows: On February 1, Tim doesn't pay his landlord Lenny the monthly $900 rent. On February 6, Lenny serves Tim a three-day notice. After the three days have elapsed, and Tim still hasn't paid the rent, the tenancy is terminated. Lenny brings an unlawful detainer action to enforce that termination, and gets a judgment against Tim on March 10. Lenny is still entitled to the $900 rent for February, since it was all due as rent before the tenancy was terminated.

Because the termination of the tenancy was effective in February, Tim owes no "rent" as such for his stay during March. What Tim does owe Lenny for those ten days is money to compensate Lenny for being unable to rerent the property during that time. Assuming that Lenny could have gotten the same rent from a new tenant, namely $900 per month or $30 per day, the "damages" for those ten days would be $300 in addition to the $900 rent, for total rent and damages of $1,200.

Item 15: Attorneys' Fees

   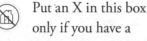 Put an X in this box only if you have a written rental agreement or lease (a copy of which should be attached to the complaint—see Item 6e) —and it has a clause specifically providing that you (or the prevailing party in a lawsuit) are entitled to attorneys' fees. A clause referring only to "costs" or "court costs" isn't enough.

To be entitled to a court judgment for attorneys' fees, you must also be represented by an attorney. Since you're representing yourself, you won't be entitled to attorneys' fees even if you win. Still, you should fill in this part just in case your tenant contests the lawsuit and you later hire a lawyer.

Item 16: Rent/Eviction Control Ordinance

   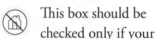 This box should be checked only if your property is subject to a local rent control law or just cause eviction ordinance. (See "Rent Control and Just Cause Eviction Ordinances" in Chapter 3 for a list.) When you put an X in this box, you declare under penalty of perjury that you have complied with all rent ceiling, registration, and other applicable requirements under the ordinance. Be sure you have. If you haven't, or if you're not sure, do some research. (Check your latest rent control ordinance.)

Once you're sure you are in compliance, type in the name of the city or county, the title of the ordinance, a citation to where it can be found in the municipal laws, and the date it went into effect. Much of this information is listed in the California Rent Control Chart, online on Nolo.com, but because rent control ordinances are constantly changing, you should also call the local rent control board for the latest information (and check the website).

Item 17: Other Allegations

   This box does not have to be checked in cases based on standard three-day, 30-day, or 60-day notices.

Special situations may require additional allegations, as when terminating a Section 8 tenancy, terminating a resident manager, satisfying extra local rent control requirements, or you seek to evict based on nonpayment of COVID-19 rental debt. If you face such a situation, you are best advised to consult an attorney or experienced paralegal.

 Check this box if you're suing a tenant who won't leave after having terminated a month-to-month tenancy by giving you at least 30 days' written notice. You'll have to add an extra paper titled "Attachment 17" to the complaint. Using a blank sheet of typing paper or Judicial Council form MC-025, and type a statement based on this model:

Attachment 17

On ____(date)__ , 20__ , defendants served plaintiff a written notice terminating their month-to-month tenancy no sooner than 30 days from the date of service of the notice, for the termination to be effective on ____(date)__ , 20__ . That period has elapsed, and defendants have failed and refused to vacate the premises.

RENT CONTROL

Extra required allegations. Some rent control cities require landlords to make additional allegations. For example, Berkeley requires landlords to allege that they are in compliance with the "implied warranty of habitability." Attachment 17 can also be used for this sort of required allegation. The landlord might allege, for example, "Plaintiff is in full compliance with the implied warranty to provide habitable premises with respect to the subject property." Or, that "Plaintiff seeks possession in good faith and without ulterior motive and that the ground listed in the notice is the dominant motive under which possession is sought." Carefully consult the requirements of your local rent control ordinance.

Item 18: Jurisdictional Limit of the Court

    This statement just means you are not asking for more money than the court has the power to give.

Item 19: Plaintiff Requests

 Here you list what you want the court to grant. Because you want "possession of the premises" and court costs such as court filing fees, in any unlawful detainer action, there is no box to check for "a" or "b." Put Xs in Boxes c, e, and g. Also, put an X in Box d if your lease or rental agreement has an attorneys' fees clause. (See Item 5.)

Fill in the amount of past-due rent in the space provided following Box c, again making sure this is the same amount stated in Item 12 and in the three-day notice. In the space after the word "(date)" to the lower right of Box g, list the date for the next day following the rental period for which the rent is due.

> **EXAMPLE 1:** Larry Landlord served Tanya Tenant with a three-day notice, demanding $900 rent for the month of September, or September 1 through 30. The first day after that rental period is October 1, 20xx. Larry should put that date after "(date)" in Box g, to ask the court to award him 1/30th of the monthly rent ($30) for each day after October 1 that Tanya stays.

> **EXAMPLE 2:** Louise Landowner served Tom Tenant with a three-day notice, demanding $1,000 monthly rent that was due on July 15. Since this rent is due in advance, it covers July 15 through August 14. Louise should put the next day after that, August 15, 20xx, after "(date)" in Box g.

 Put Xs in Boxes e and f for evictions based on both conditional three-day notices to perform covenant or quit and unconditional three-day notices. In the space after the word "(date)" below Box g, list the *day after* the three-day notice expiration date you listed in Item 9b(1). Don't check Box c, since you can only collect back rent in evictions for nonpayment of rent. You may, however, put an X in Box d if your lease or rental agreement has an attorneys' fees clause. (See Item 15.)

  Put an X in Box g only. In the space after the word "(date)" below Box f, list the *day after* the 30-day notice expiration date, or the *day after* the fixed-term lease expired. For example, if you or the tenant gave a 30-day notice on July 1, the last day the tenant could legally stay was July 31, and you list August 1, 20xx, here. Or, if the tenant's lease expired on December 31, 20xx (and you didn't accept rent after that), list the next day, January 1, 20xx.

Don't check Box c, because it only applies in evictions for nonpayment of rent. Don't check Box e, which only applies in evictions based on three-day notices to quit. (See Chapters 2 and 4.) You may, however, put an X in Box d if your lease or rental agreement has an attorneys' fees clause (see Item 15.) and Box f if you have credited relocation expenses in the notice.

    Do not check Box h unless you insist on asking for extra "statutory damages" of up to $600 on account of the tenant's malicious conduct, in which case you will have also checked Item 14. (Once again, we do not recommend doing this.)

  Box i is a hangover category of relief— traditionally, as a catchall, complaints requested, "Such other and further relief as the court deems just and proper." You can insert this if you are feeling very "old school" or leave the box blank.

Item 20: Number of Pages Attached

    List the number of pages to be attached to the complaint, counting each page of every copy of a rental agreement or lease (Exhibit 1) and three-day, 30-day, or 60-day notice (Exhibit 2), as well as any attachments. (Count each printed side of a piece of paper as a page.) Do not count the pages of the complaint. Thus, for a complaint that attached a one-page lease and a one-page three-day, 30-day, or 60-day notice, the number of added pages should be "2."

Item 21: Unlawful Detainer Assistant

    The law requires that a nonattorney who is paid to fill out unlawful detainer paperwork must be registered and bonded. This law does not apply, however, to property owners or to managers who prepare such forms for their employers in the ordinary course of their duties (neither does it apply to attorneys). If you are such a property manager or owner, put an X next to the words "did not" in Item 21, and leave the rest of the item blank. If you are paying a paralegal or another person to fill out or otherwise process your papers (other than just having a process server serve them), or to advise you on filling out the forms, he or she must be registered with the county and bonded, and the "did" box must be checked on Item 21. (In that case, the assistant should be filling out the forms, saving you for other things.) That person's name, address, phone number, and registration information must then be listed on Item 21 of the complaint form. (If you let an unregistered person prepare your forms for a fee and he or she filled out the "did not"

box, remember, *you're* the one declaring, under penalty of perjury, to the truth of the form when you sign it!)

Verification and Plaintiffs' Names, Dates, and Signatures

Type your name in the spaces indicated below Item 21 and, under the heading "VERIFICATION," type in the date and sign the complaint in both places.

    The two lines side by side above the word "Verification" are the first of two places to sign and type the name(s) of the plaintiff(s). The name of each person who is listed on the complaint (and summons) as a plaintiff should be typed in the space to the left. Their signatures go on the space to the right. For more than one plaintiff, it's okay to either separate the names and signatures by commas, with all names on one line, or to list one above the other.

Under the Verification heading, you state under penalty of perjury that all the allegations in the complaint are true. A name and signature—but only of one plaintiff even if there are several—is required here, too. The plaintiff with the most knowledge about the matter should type his or her name and the date in the space to the left and sign in the space at the right.

   Be sure the date you sign is at least one day after the date in Item 9b of the complaint—the date the notice period legally expired.

If a partnership is named as plaintiff, the verification printed on the form does not apply. Attach instead a form for the verification of a partnership. (See the form, "Verification of Partnership by Plaintiff," listed in the appendix.)

PLAINTIFF: LENNY D. LANDLORD	CASE NUMBER:
DEFENDANT: TERRENCE D. TENANT; TILLIE D. TENANT	Leave blank - court will fill in

19. **PLAINTIFF REQUESTS**

a. possession of the premises.

b. costs incurred in this proceeding:

c. [**✗**] past-due rent of $ 1,699.50

d. [ ] reasonable attorney fees.

e. [**✗**] forfeiture of the agreement.

f. [ ] damages in the amount of waived rent or relocation assistance as stated in item 8: $

g. [**✗**] damages at the rate stated in item 13 from

date: May 1, 20xx

for each day that defendants remain in possession through entry of judgment.

h. [ ] statutory damages up to $600 for the conduct alleged in item 14.

i. [**✗**] other *(specify):*
Such other and further relief as the Court deems just and proper.

20. [**✗**] Number of pages attached *(specify):*   1

UNLAWFUL DETAINER ASSISTANT (Bus. & Prof. Code, §§ 6400–6415)

21. [ ] *(Complete in all cases.)* An unlawful detainer assistant [**✗**] did **not** [ ] did for compensation give advice or assistance with this form. (*If declarant has received **any** help or advice for pay from an unlawful detainer assistant, complete a–f.*)

a. Assistant's name:

b. Street address, city, and zip code:

c. Telephone no.:

d. County of registration:

e. Registration no.:

f. Expires on *(date):*

Date: April 10, 20xx

Lenny D. Landlord
_____
(TYPE OR PRINT NAME)

▶ _____
(SIGNATURE OF PLAINTIFF OR ATTORNEY)

VERIFICATION

(Use a different verification form if the verification is by an attorney or for a corporation or partnership.)

I am the plaintiff in this proceeding and have read this complaint. I declare under penalty of perjury under the laws of the State of California that the foregoing is true and correct.

Date: April 10, 20xx

Lenny D. Landlord
_____
(TYPE OR PRINT NAME)

▶ _____
(SIGNATURE OF PLAINTIFF)

Preparing the Civil Case Cover Sheet

This form must be filed with the court at the same time as your complaint. Its purpose is to tell the court what kind of a civil case you're filing, and it's used when filing any type of civil case. (The second page is full of information and instructions that are either irrelevant to your case or unnecessary in light of the information you're getting from this book.) We've preprinted this form with all the information needed to tell the court clerk you're filing an unlawful detainer action to evict the tenant from a residence (as opposed to a commercial building). You need only do the following:

- Type your name, address, and telephone number in the box at the left top of the page, and the court's name, including division, and address in the box below that.
- In the third box near the top of the page, entitled "CASE NAME," type in capital letters the last name of the first plaintiff (you) before the "vs." and the last name of the first defendant after the "vs." For example, if Leslie Smith and Laura Smith-Jones are suing Don Brown and Debra Miller, the case name is "SMITH vs. BROWN."
- Leave the CASE NUMBER box blank. As for Items 1 through 4 on this form, put Xs as indicated on the sample Civil Case Cover Sheet form. (These are always the same in residential unlawful detainer actions.)
- In Item 5, check "is not" (your eviction case won't be a class action lawsuit). Ignore Item 6 (it's highly unlikely that you'll have another, related case ongoing when you file your eviction lawsuit).
- Put the date and type your name in capital letters, in the spaces provided (labeled "Date" and "(TYPE OR PRINT NAME)"). Then sign the form at the lower right in the space provided.
- You will need to make only one copy for your records, which the court clerk will date-stamp and return to you. You do not need to serve any copies on the tenant(s) along with copies of the summons and complaint.

 FORM
A blank copy of the Civil Case Cover Sheet (Judicial Council form CM-010) can be downloaded from the Nolo website. (See the appendix for the link to the forms, and other information on using them .)

In Los Angeles County, you'll also need to complete the Civil Case Cover Sheet Addendum and Statement of Location, which you'll file with your regular cover sheet. This form tells the court what kind of unlawful detainer action you're commencing (if the eviction is based on the tenant's drug use or sales, your case will proceed quickly), and why you've chosen this courthouse location. Complete the "Short Title" information at the top of each page by listing your name and the last name of the first defendant (for example, Landlord vs. Tenant). On the second page near the bottom of Column Two, check Box A6020 (Unlawful Detainer—Residential) or A6022 (Unlawful Detainer—Drugs). In Column Three, circle Reason 6 (the rental property should be within the area served by the courthouse you've chosen). On Page 4, under Item III, check Box 6 and include the rental property's address.

 FORM
A blank copy of the Los Angeles form Civil Case Cover Sheet Addendum and Statement of Location can be downloaded from the Nolo website. (See the Appendix for the link to the forms, and other information on using them.) This form can also be filled out online at www.lasuperiorcourt.org/forms/pdf/LACIV109.pdf and printed.

 TIP
Use the Internet to identify the correct court branch in Los Angeles. Go to the L.A. County Superior Court website (www.lasuperiorcourt.org) and choose "Locations" under "About The Court." Then select the "Filing Court Locator." After entering the zip code of the rental property, you'll learn the proper courthouse for your case.

ATTORNEY OR PARTY WITHOUT ATTORNEY *(Name, State Bar number, and address):*
Lenny D. Landlord
12345 Angeleno Street, Los Angeles, California 90028

TELEPHONE NO.: 213-555-6789   FAX NO. *(Optional):*
E-MAIL ADDRESS: LDLXX321@ispofchoice.com
ATTORNEY FOR *(Name):* in Pro Per

FOR COURT USE ONLY

SUPERIOR COURT OF CALIFORNIA, COUNTY OF LOS ANGELES
STREET ADDRESS: 111 North Hill Street
MAILING ADDRESS:
CITY AND ZIP CODE: Los Angeles, California 90012
BRANCH NAME:

CASE NAME:
LANDLORD V. TENANT, ET AL.

CIVIL CASE COVER SHEET	**Complex Case Designation**	CASE NUMBER: Leave blank - court will fill in
[ ] Unlimited [x] Limited (Amount demanded exceeds $25,000) (Amount demanded is $25,000 or less)	[ ] Counter [ ] Joinder Filed with first appearance by defendant (Cal. Rules of Court, rule 3.402)	JUDGE: DEPT.:

Items 1–6 below must be completed (see instructions on page 2).

1. Check **one** box below for the case type that best describes this case:

Auto Tort
[ ] Auto (22)
[ ] Uninsured motorist (46)
Other PI/PD/WD (Personal Injury/Property Damage/Wrongful Death) Tort
[ ] Asbestos (04)
[ ] Product liability (24)
[ ] Medical malpractice (45)
[ ] Other PI/PD/WD (23)
Non-PI/PD/WD (Other) Tort
[ ] Business tort/unfair business practice (07)
[ ] Civil rights (08)
[ ] Defamation (13)
[ ] Fraud (16)
[ ] Intellectual property (19)
[ ] Professional negligence (25)
[ ] Other non-PI/PD/WD tort (35)
Employment
[ ] Wrongful termination (36)
[ ] Other employment (15)

Contract
[ ] Breach of contract/warranty (06)
[ ] Rule 3.740 collections (09)
[ ] Other collections (09)
[ ] Insurance coverage (18)
[ ] Other contract (37)
Real Property
[ ] Eminent domain/Inverse condemnation (14)
[ ] Wrongful eviction (33)
[ ] Other real property (26)
Unlawful Detainer
[ ] Commercial (31)
[x] Residential (32)
[ ] Drugs (38)
Judicial Review
[ ] Asset forfeiture (05)
[ ] Petition re: arbitration award (11)
[ ] Writ of mandate (02)
[ ] Other judicial review (39)

Provisionally Complex Civil Litigation (Cal. Rules of Court, rules 3.400–3.403)
[ ] Antitrust/Trade regulation (03)
[ ] Construction defect (10)
[ ] Mass tort (40)
[ ] Securities litigation (28)
[ ] Environmental/Toxic tort (30)
[ ] Insurance coverage claims arising from the above listed provisionally complex case types (41)
Enforcement of Judgment
[ ] Enforcement of judgment (20)
Miscellaneous Civil Complaint
[ ] RICO (27)
[ ] Other complaint *(not specified above)* (42)
Miscellaneous Civil Petition
[ ] Partnership and corporate governance (21)
[ ] Other petition *(not specified above)* (43)

2. This case [ ] is [x] is not complex under rule 3.400 of the California Rules of Court. If the case is complex, mark the factors requiring exceptional judicial management:
a. [ ] Large number of separately represented parties
b. [ ] Extensive motion practice raising difficult or novel issues that will be time-consuming to resolve
c. [ ] Substantial amount of documentary evidence
d. [ ] Large number of witnesses
e. [ ] Coordination with related actions pending in one or more courts in other counties, states, or countries, or in a federal court
f. [ ] Substantial postjudgment judicial supervision

3. Remedies sought *(check all that apply):* a. [x] monetary b. [x] nonmonetary; declaratory or injunctive relief c. [ ] punitive
4. Number of causes of action *(specify):* One
5. This case [ ] is [x] is not a class action suit.
6. If there are any known related cases, file and serve a notice of related case. *(You may use form CM-015.)*
Date: April 10, 20xx
LENNY D. LANDLORD
(TYPE OR PRINT NAME)   *Lenny D. Landlord*
                                         (SIGNATURE OF PARTY OR ATTORNEY FOR PARTY)

NOTICE
• Plaintiff must file this cover sheet with the first paper filed in the action or proceeding (except small claims cases or cases filed under the Probate Code, Family Code, or Welfare and Institutions Code). (Cal. Rules of Court, rule 3.220.) Failure to file may result in sanctions.
• File this cover sheet in addition to any cover sheet required by local court rule.
• If this case is complex under rule 3.400 et seq. of the California Rules of Court, you must serve a copy of this cover sheet on all other parties to the action or proceeding.
• Unless this is a collections case under rule 3.740 or a complex case, this cover sheet will be used for statistical purposes only.

Page 1 of 2

Form Adopted for Mandatory Use
Judicial Council of California   **CIVIL CASE COVER SHEET**   Cal. Rules of Court, rules 2.30, 3.220, 3.400–3.403, 3.740; Cal. Standards of Judicial Administration. std. 3.10

Plaintiff's Mandatory Supplemental Allegations— Unlawful Detainer

> **FORM**
>
> **A blank copy of the form, Plaintiff's Mandatory Supplemental Allegations—Unlawful Detainer (UD-101) can be downloaded from the Nolo website. (See the appendix for the link to the forms, and other information on using them.)**

This is a new form required by the COVID-19 Tenant Relief Act. We strongly recommend avoiding any eviction based on COVID transition or recovery period rents, making the form (and your life in court) much simpler. This form may be required until June 30, 2022 if the State extends the COVID recovery period after March 31, 2022. Check the Judicial Council website for the most recent form.

This is how you fill out the new form:
1. Fill in the court, caption, and parties just as you have on the complaint.
2. Check the various boxes with the requested information. Item 1 requests the party information and Item 2 basic background pertaining to COVID relief eligibility. Box 2a will be "residential" and 2b depends on the cause for the notice. Only if you want to evict for nonpayment of rent should you check "yes" on 2b.
3. Item 3 checks eligibility for COVID relief, which applies only to tenancies with rent due between March 1, 2020, and March 31, 2022. If the cause for eviction does not involve rent between those two periods, check "no" and skip to the end of the form.

If you check yes on Box 3a, proceed to Box 3b. Again, if you check "no", you can skip to end of the form. If you check "yes", you will have to complete all the following provisions concerning your COVID compliance.

Compliance depends upon each individual case and the circumstances. We cannot give specific instructions pertaining to COVID relief compliance, because the answers depend upon each landlord's actions.

The succeeding boxes and questions are largely self-explanatory. The only trick question is Item 4(b), referring to Civil Code Section 1940(b). That box should be "no" because Section 1940(b) refers to temporary lodging in hotels.

After you reach the end of the form, you must sign and verify the form just as you do on the complaint. That means that if the plaintiff is a partnership, you will have to use the Partnership Verification form listed in the Appendix.

Getting the Complaint and Summons Ready to File

Now that you have filled out the complaint, go through the instructions again and double-check each step, using the sample complaint form set out on the preceding few pages as a guide.

Finally, place the pages of the complaint in the following order:
1. Unlawful detainer complaint (front facing you, on top)
2. Attachments, in numerical order if there are more than one
3. Exhibit 1 (copy of written rental agreement) if applicable (see Item 6e, above)
4. Exhibit 2 (copy of three-day, 30-day, or 60-day notice) if notice was served (see Item 7, above), and
5. Exhibit 3 (copy of proof of service of the notice).

Fasten them with a paper clip for now.

UD-101

ATTORNEY OR PARTY WITHOUT ATTORNEY	STATE BAR NUMBER:	FOR COURT USE ONLY

NAME: Lenny D. Landlord

FIRM NAME:

STREET ADDRESS: 12345 Angeleno Street

CITY: Los Angeles   STATE: CA   ZIP CODE: 90028

TELEPHONE NO.: 213-555-6789   FAX NO.:

EMAIL ADDRESS: LDLXX321@ispofchoice.com

ATTORNEY FOR (name): Plaintiff in Pro Per

SUPERIOR COURT OF CALIFORNIA, COUNTY OF LOS ANGELES

STREET ADDRESS: 111 North Hill Street

MAILING ADDRESS:

CITY AND ZIP CODE: Los Angeles, California 90012

BRANCH NAME:

PLAINTIFF: LENNY D. LANDLORD

DEFENDANT: TERRENCE D. TENANT; TILLIE D. TENANT, et al.

PLAINTIFF'S MANDATORY COVER SHEET AND SUPPLEMENTAL ALLEGATIONS—UNLAWFUL DETAINER	CASE NUMBER: [Leave blank]

All plaintiffs in unlawful detainer proceedings must file and serve this form. Filing this form complies with the requirement in Code of Civil Procedure section 1179.01.5(c).

- *Serve this form and any attachments to it with the summons.*
- *If a summons has already been served without this form, then serve it by mail or any other means of service authorized by law.*
- *If defendant has answered prior to service of this form, there is no requirement for defendant to respond to the supplemental allegations before trial.*

To obtain a summons in an unlawful detainer action for nonpayment of rent on a residential property filed before March 31, 2022, a plaintiff must verify that they applied for governmental rental assistance that was not granted, or that the tenancy began after September 30, 2021. (See item 3.)

To obtain a judgment in an unlawful detainer action for nonpayment of rent on a residential property, a plaintiff must verify that no rental assistance or other financial compensation has been received for the amount demanded in the notice or accruing afterward, and that no application is pending for such assistance. To obtain a default judgment, plaintiff must use Verification by Landlord Regarding Rental Assistance—Unlawful Detainer (form UD-120) to make this verification and provide other information required by statute.

1. PLAINTIFF *(name each):*
   Lenny D. Landlord

   alleges causes of action in the complaint filed in this action against DEFENDANT *(name each):*
   Terrence D. Tenant, Tillie D. Tenant, Does 1 to 10

2. **Statutory cover sheet allegations** (Code Civ. Proc., § 1179.01.5(c))

   a. This action seeks possession of real property that is *(check all that apply):*   [x] Residential   [ ] Commercial
   (If "residential" is checked, complete items 3 and 4 and all remaining items that apply to this action. If only "commercial" is checked, no further items need to be completed except the signature and verification on page 5; a summons may be issued.)

   b. This action is based, in whole or in part, on an alleged default in payment of rent or other charges. [x] Yes   [ ] No

3. **Verifications required for issuance of summons—residential** (Code Civ. Proc., § 1179.11(a))

   a. Is this action based, in whole or in part, on a defendant's nonpayment of rent or other financial obligation during the period between March 1, 2020, and March 31, 2022? [ ] Yes   [x] No
   (If no is checked, no further items need to be completed except the signature and verification on page 5, and item 12 if the action is based in whole or in part on nonpayment of rent during some other time frame; a summons may be issued.)

   b. Is this action on a tenancy that was initially established before October 1, 2021?   [ ] Yes   [ ] No
   (If no is checked, the further items that need to be completed are the signature and verification on page 5, and items 10 or 11, and 12 if the action is based in whole or in part on nonpayment of rent; a summons may be issued. (See Code Civ. Proc., § 1179.09(h) to learn more about what "initially established" means.)

Form Adopted for Mandatory Use
Judicial Council of California
UD-101 [Rev. October 1, 2021]

**PLAINTIFF'S MANDATORY COVER SHEET AND
SUPPLEMENTAL ALLEGATIONS—UNLAWFUL DETAINER**

Code of Civil Procedure, § 1179.01 et seq.
www.courts.ca.gov

UD-101

PLAINTIFF: LENNY D. LANDLORD DEFENDANT: TERRENCE D. TENANT; TILLIE D. TENANT, et al.	CASE NUMBER: [Leave blank]

3. c. *If you answered yes to questions 3a and 3b above, you must check either (1) or (2) below, or a summons may not be issued.*

    (1) ☐ Before filing the complaint in this action, plaintiff applied for governmental rental assistance to cover the rent or other financial obligations demanded in this action, but the application was denied **and** a copy of a final decision denying the assistance is attached.

        Note that a "final decision" does not include rejection based on plaintiff not completing the application or doing so correctly, notification that the application is pending further action, or notification that plaintiff or defendants applied to the wrong government agency. (Code Civ. Proc., § 1179.09(d).)

    or

    (2) ☐ Before filing the complaint in this action, plaintiff completed an application for governmental rental assistance to cover the rent or other financial obligations demanded in this action, including all the required contact information and documentation, **and all** of the following are true:

        (a) At least 20 days have passed since the **later** of either (*check one*):

            ☐ The date the plaintiff submitted the completed application, or
            ☒ The date the plaintiff served the three-day notice underlying the complaint.

        and

        (b) Plaintiff has not received any notice from the governmental agency to which defendant has applied for governmental rental assistance to cover the rent or other financial obligations demanded from the defendant in this action.

        and

        (c) Plaintiff has not received a communication from the defendant that defendant has applied for governmental rental assistance to cover the rent or other financial obligations demanded from the defendant in this action.

4. **Tenants subject to COVID-19 Tenant Relief Act** (Code Civ. Proc., § 1179.02(h))

    a. (1) One or more defendants in this action is a natural person: ☐ Yes   ☐ No
       (2) Identify any defendant not a natural person:

       (If no is checked, then no further items need to be completed except the signature and verification, and item 12 if the action is based on nonpayment of rent.)

    b. (1) All defendants named in this action maintain occupancy as described in Civil Code section 1940(b). ☐ Yes   ☐ No
       (2) Identify any defendant who does not:

       (If yes is checked, then no further items need to be completed except the signature and verification, and item 12 if the action is based on nonpayment of rent.)

5. ☐ **Unlawful detainer notice expired before March 1, 2020**
    The unlawful detainer complaint in this action is based solely on a notice to quit, to pay or quit, or to perform covenants or quit, in which the time period specified in the notice expired before March 1, 2020. *(If this is the only basis for the action, no further items need to be completed except the signature and verification on page 5. (Code Civ. Proc., § 1179.03.5(a)(1).))*

6. ☐ **Rent or other financial obligations due between March 1, 2020, and August 31, 2020 (protected time period)**
    The unlawful detainer complaint in this action is based, at least in part, on a demand for payment of rent or other financial obligations due in the protected time period. *(Check all that apply.)*

    a. ☐ Defendant *(name each):*

    was provided all the required versions of the "Notice from the State of California" required by Code of Civil Procedure section 1179.04. *(Provide information regarding service of the notice or notices in item 8 below.)*

    b. ☐ Defendant *(name each):*

    was served with at least 15 days' notice to pay rent or other financial obligations, quit, or deliver a declaration, and an unsigned declaration of COVID-19–related financial distress, in the form and with the content required in Code of Civil Procedure section 1179.03(b) and (d).

        *(If the notice identified defendant as a **high-income tenant** and requested submission of documentation supporting any declaration the defendant submits, complete item 9 below. (Code Civ. Proc., § 1179.02.5(c).))*

        (If filing form UD-100 with this form and item 6b is checked, specify this 15-day notice in item 9a(7) on form UD-100, attach a copy of the notice to that complaint form, and provide all requested information about service on that form.)

**PLAINTIFF'S MANDATORY COVER SHEET AND
SUPPLEMENTAL ALLEGATIONS—UNLAWFUL DETAINER**

UD-101

PLAINTIFF: LENNY D. LANDLORD DEFENDANT: TERRENCE D. TENANT; TILLIE D. TENANT, et al.	CASE NUMBER: [Leave blank]

6. c. Response to notice *(check all that apply):*

    (1) ☐ Defendant *(name each):*

        delivered a declaration of COVID-19–related financial distress on landlord in the time required. (Code Civ. Proc., § 1179.03(f).)

    (2) ☐ Defendant *(name each):*

        did *not* deliver a declaration of COVID-19–related financial distress on landlord in the time required. (Code Civ. Proc., § 1179.03(f).)

7. ☐ **Rent or other financial obligations due between September 1, 2020, and September 30, 2021 (the transition time period)** The unlawful detainer complaint in this action is based, at least in part, on a demand for payment of rent or other financial obligations due during the transition time period.

    a. ☐ Defendant *(name each):*

        was provided all the required versions of the "Notice from the State of California" as required by Code of Civil Procedure section 1179.04. *(Provide information regarding service of the notice or notices in item 8 below.)*

    b. ☐ Defendant *(name each):*

        was served with at least 15 days' notice to pay rent or other financial obligations, quit, or deliver a declaration, and an unsigned declaration of COVID-19–related financial distress, in the form and with the content required in Code of Civil Procedure section 1179.03(c) and (d).

        *(If the notice identified defendant as a **high-income tenant** and requested submission of documentation supporting any declaration the defendant submits, complete item 9 below. (Code Civ. Proc., § 1179.02.5(c).))*

        (If filing form UD-100 with this form and item 7b is checked, specify this 15-day notice in item 9a(7) on form UD-100, attach a copy of the notice to that complaint form, and provide all requested information about service on that form.)

    c. Response to notice *(check all that apply):*

        (1) ☐ Defendant *(name each):*

            delivered a declaration of COVID-19–related financial distress on the landlord in the time required. (Code Civ. Proc., § 1179.03(f).)

        (2) ☐ Defendant *(name each):*

            did *not* deliver a declaration of COVID-19–related financial distress on the landlord in the time required. (Code Civ. Proc., § 1179.03(f).))

    d. ☐ Rent or other financial obligations due:

        (1) Rent or other financial obligations in the amount of $_____ was due between September 1, 2020, and September 30, 2021.

        (2) Payment of $_____ for that period was received by September 30, 2021.

8. **Service of Code of Civil Procedure Section 1179.04 Notice from the State of California** *(You must complete this item if you checked item 6 or 7 above. Section 1179.04 provides three separate versions of a "Notice from the State of California" that the landlord was to provide to tenants at different times during the pandemic (the notices referenced in item 6a and 7a above). This item addresses when and how those notices were provided.)*

    a. **September 2020 Notice.** Plaintiff provided the required notice for tenants who, as of September 1, 2020, had any unpaid rent or other financial obligations due any time between March 1, 2020, and August 31, 2020 (Code Civ. Proc., § 1179.04(a)), to defendants identified in 6a or as follows:

        (1) ☐ By sending a copy by mail addressed to each named defendant on *(date):*

        (2) ☐ By personally handing a copy to each named defendant on *(date):*

**PLAINTIFF'S MANDATORY COVER SHEET AND
SUPPLEMENTAL ALLEGATIONS—UNLAWFUL DETAINER**

<table>
<tr><td>PLAINTIFF: LENNY D. LANDLORD
DEFENDANT: TERRENCE D. TENANT; TILLIE D. TENANT, et al.</td><td>CASE NUMBER:
[Leave blank]</td></tr>
</table>

UD-101

8. a. (3) ☐ By some other method of service described in Code of Civil Procedure section 1162. (*If this box is checked, describe the method and date of service on an attached page (you can use form MC-025) and title it Attachment 8a.*)

   (4) ☐ In different ways for different defendants. (*If this box is checked, describe the method and date of service for each defendant on an attached page (you can use form MC-025) and title it Attachment 8a.*)

   (5) ☐ Plaintiff was not required to serve the September 2020 notice on the named defendants.

b. **February 2021 Notice.** Plaintiff provided the required notice for tenants who as of February 1, 2021, had unpaid rent or other financial obligations due any time after March 1, 2020, (Code Civ. Proc., § 1179.04(b)) to defendants identified in 6a and 7a as follows:

   (1) ☐ By sending a copy by mail addressed to each named defendant on *(date):*

   (2) ☐ By personally handing a copy to each named defendant on *(date):*

   (3) ☐ By some other method of service described in Code of Civil Procedure section 1162. (*If this box is checked, describe the method and date of service on an attached page (you can use form MC-025) and title it Attachment 8b.*)

   (4) ☐ In different ways for different defendants. (*If this box is checked, describe the method and date of service for each defendant on an attached page (you can use form MC-025) and title it Attachment 8b.*)

   (5) ☐ Plaintiff was not required to serve the February 2021 notice on the named defendants.

c. **July 2021 Notice.** Plaintiff provided the required notice for tenants who as of July 1, 2021, had unpaid rent or other financial obligations due any time after March 1, 2020, (Code Civ. Proc., § 1179.04(c)) to defendants identified in 6a and 7a as follows:

   (1) ☐ By sending a copy by mail addressed to each named defendant on *(date):*

   (2) ☐ By personally handing a copy to each named defendant on *(date):*

   (3) ☐ By some other method of service described in Code of Civil Procedure section 1162. (*If this box is checked, describe the method and date of service on an attached page (you can use form MC-025) and title it Attachment 8c.*)

   (4) ☐ In different ways for different defendants. (*If this box is checked, describe the method and date of service for each defendant on an attached page (you can use form MC-025) and title it Attachment 8c.*)

   (5) ☐ Plaintiff was not required to serve the July 2021 notice on the named defendants.

9. ☐ **High-income tenant.** The 15-day notice in item 6b or 7b above identified defendant as a high-income tenant and requested submission of documentation supporting the tenant's claim that tenant had suffered COVID-19–related financial distress. Plaintiff had proof before serving that notice that the tenant has an annual income that is at least 130 percent of the median income for the county the rental property is located in and not less than $100,000. (Code Civ. Proc., § 1179.02.5.)

  a. ☐ The tenant did not deliver a declaration of COVID-19–related financial distress within the required time. (Code Civ. Proc., § 1179.03(f).)

  b. ☐ The tenant did not deliver documentation within the required time supporting that the tenant had suffered COVID-19–related financial distress as asserted in the declaration. (Code Civ. Proc., § 1179.02.5(c).)

10. ☐ **Rent or other financial obligations due between October 1, 2021, and March 31, 2022 (recovery period rental debt).** The unlawful detainer complaint in this action is based, at least in part, on a demand for payment of rent or other financial obligations due during the recovery period. *(Check a or b.)*

  a. ☐ Defendant *(name each):* Terrence D. Tenant, Tilly D. Tenant

was served with at least 3 days' notice to pay rent or other financial obligations or quit, in a notice that included the name, website address, and phone number of the governmental rental assistance program for the locality in which the property at issue is located, as well as all other content required by Code of Civil Procedure section 1179.10.

(If filing form UD-100 with this form and this item is checked, specify this notice in item 9a(7) on form UD-100, attach a copy of the notice to that complaint form, and provide all requested information about service on that form.)

  b. ☐ Plaintiff has checked no in item 3b and the special notice to quit required by Code of Civil Procedure section 1179.10 does not apply in this action.

**PLAINTIFF'S MANDATORY COVER SHEET AND
SUPPLEMENTAL ALLEGATIONS—UNLAWFUL DETAINER**

PLAINTIFF: LENNY D. LANDLORD DEFENDANT: TERRENCE D. TENANT; TILLIE D. TENANT, et al.	CASE NUMBER: [Leave blank]

UD-101

11. ☐ **Rent or other financial obligations due after March 31, 2022.** (*Only applicable if action is filed on or after April 1, 2022.*) The only demand for rent or other financial obligations on which the unlawful detainer complaint in this action is based is a demand for payment of rent due after March 31, 2022.

12. ☐ **Statements regarding rental assistance** (*Required in all actions based on nonpayment of rent or any other financial obligation. Plaintiff must answer all the questions in this item and, if later seeking a default judgment, will also need to file Verification Regarding Rental Assistance—Unlawful Detainer (form UD-120).*)

   a. Has plaintiff received rental assistance or other financial compensation from any other source corresponding to the amount demanded in the notice underlying the complaint? ☐ Yes ☐ No

   b. Has plaintiff received rental assistance or other financial compensation from any other source for rent accruing *after* the date of the notice underlying the complaint? ☐ Yes ☐ No

   c. Does plaintiff have any pending application for rental assistance or other financial compensation from any other source corresponding to the amount demanded in the notice underlying the complaint? ☐ Yes ☐ No

   d. Does plaintiff have any pending application for rental assistance or other financial compensation from any other source for rent accruing *after* the date on the notice underlying the complaint? ☐ Yes ☐ No

13. ☐ **Other allegations** Plaintiff makes the following additional allegations: (*State any additional allegations below, with each allegation lettered in order, starting with (a), (b), (c) etc. If there is not enough space below, check the box below and use form MC-025, title it Attachment 13, and letter each allegation in order.*) ☐ Other allegations are on form MC-025.

14. ☐ Number of pages attached *(specify):*

Date: April 10, 20xx _____

Lenny D. Landlord _____   ▶ _____
       (TYPE OR PRINT NAME)   (SIGNATURE OF PLAINTIFF OR ATTORNEY)

VERIFICATION

(*Use a different verification form if the verification is by an attorney or for a corporation or partnership.*)

I am the plaintiff in this proceeding and have read this complaint. I declare under penalty of perjury under the laws of the State of California that the foregoing is true and correct.

Date: April 10, 20xx _____

Lenny D. Landlord _____   ▶ _____
       (TYPE OR PRINT NAME)   (SIGNATURE)

UD-101 [Rev. October 1, 2021]   **PLAINTIFF'S MANDATORY COVER SHEET AND**   Page 5 of 5
              SUPPLEMENTAL ALLEGATIONS—UNLAWFUL DETAINER

MC-025

SHORT TITLE:	CASE NUMBER:
Landlord v. Tenant	

ATTACHMENT *(Number):* 10c

(This Attachment may be used with any Judicial Council form.)

1. The notice attached as Exhibit 2 and referenced in Paragraph 9a was served on defendant, Tillie D. Tenant as follows:

(a) By leaving a copy with Terrence D. Tenant, a person of suitable age and discretion on April 4, 20xx, and by mailing a copy to defendant's residence on April 4, 20xx because defendant cannot be found at defendant's residence or usual place of business.

(b) Proof of service of the notice has been attached and labeled as Exhibit 3a.

(If the item that this Attachment concerns is made under penalty of perjury, all statements in this Attachment are made under penalty of perjury.)

Page ___1___ of ___1___

(Add pages as required)

Form Approved for Optional Use
Judicial Council of California
MC-025 [Rev. July 1, 2009]

ATTACHMENT
to Judicial Council Form

www.courtinfo.ca.gov

Before you take the summons, Civil Case Cover Sheet, Plaintiff's Mandatory Cover Sheet and Supplemental Allegations, and complaint to court for filing and stamping, you need to:

- Make one copy of the complaint and the mandatory cover sheet/supplemental allegations (together with attachments and exhibits) for your records, plus one copy to be served on each defendant (make extra copies if you think you might need to serve some occupants). You'll file the original with the court. Make sure to copy all the pages of the complaint, using a one-sided copying process if possible.
- Make two copies of the summons for each defendant (and any occupants you think you might need to serve), and one for your records. For example, if you named three defendants in your complaint, make seven copies of the summons.
- Make one copy of the Civil Case Cover Sheet (or the Civil Case Cover Sheet Addendum and Statement of Location if your property is in Los Angeles County) for your records. Because this form is not served on the defendant, you don't need to make any more.

Filing Your Complaint and Getting Summonses Issued

To file your unlawful detainer complaint, follow these steps (see the sidebar below for an alternative, however):

Step 1: Take the originals and all the copies of your papers to the court's "civil" filing window at the courthouse and tell the clerk you want to file an unlawful detainer action.

Step 2: Give the clerk the original Civil Case Cover Sheet, complaint, and mandatory cover sheet/supplemental allegations to be filed with the court. Ask the clerk to file-stamp each of your copies and give them back to you. The clerk will rubber-stamp each of the copies with the date, the word "FILED," and insert a case number.

Step 3: Give the clerk one copy of the summons per defendant and ask the clerk to "issue" a summons for each. The clerk will stamp the court seal on each of these summonses and fill in the date of issuance; these are now original summonses, and the clerk will give them back to you or give you copies instead.

Some courts no longer issue the original summons, but retain it and file it automatically. In that case, you serve a copy of the summons and file a proof of service using the Judicial Council Proof of Service of Summons, Form POS-010. In addition, the court may issue only one original summons for all defendants. The issuance of one original does not pose a problem, because each defendant receives only a copy of the summons, never the original.

Hire the Process Server to Do Most of the Work

For the sake of convenience and efficiency, most attorneys do not file their own papers in court. Instead, they use a service. Most registered process servers and legal service providers include court filing among their available services. These businesses know the courts and local filing procedures, and process servers will often bundle the initial complaint filing with service of the papers for an additional fee.

Servers or agencies can file the complaint, get the summons issued, and prepare the papers for service. They will often take care of minor form mistakes on the spot, eliminating repeated court trips. Of course, they also serve the papers and prepare the necessary proof of service and due diligence statement. Many services will also prepare the papers necessary to obtain a post-and-mail order if the tenant has been avoiding or "ducking" service.

Step 4: Give the clerk the other copies of the summons (remember, you will have two copies for each defendant), telling the clerk they are copies to be "conformed." The clerk will stamp them with the date, but not the court seal. Staple one of these summons copies to the front of each complaint copy. Both should be served on the defendants at the same time. (The original summonses are returned to the clerk after the copies are served—see below.)

Step 5: Pay the court filing fee of around $240, though the exact amount varies, depending on the county.

Serving the Papers on the Defendant(s): Service of Process

After you've filed your unlawful detainer complaint and had the summonses issued, a copy of the summons, the complaint, and the mandatory cover sheet/supplemental allegations must be served on each person you're suing. This is called "service of process," and it's an essential part of your lawsuit.

The summons tells defendants that they must file a written response to the allegations in your complaint within five days of the date of service or lose by "default." Unlike service of notices to quit, where service on one tenant is often considered service on others, each person sued must be separately served with copies of the summons and complaint.

If you don't follow service rules to the letter, you lose. For example, a "shortcut" service of summons and complaint, where the papers are given to the first person who answers the door at the property, instead of being properly handed to the defendant, is not valid. This is true even if the papers nevertheless are eventually given to the right person. (If the defendant cannot be found, the strict requirements of "substituted service"—discussed in "Substituted Service on Another Person," below—must be followed. These requirements include repeated attempts to personally serve, followed by mailing a second copy.)

Who Must Be Served

Each defendant listed in the summons and complaint must be served. *You must serve every adult*, even when the defendants live under the same roof or are married. For instance, if you don't serve a particular defendant, it's just as if you never sued her in the first place; the court can't enter a judgment against her, and she cannot be evicted when the sheriff or marshal comes later on. She not only will be allowed to stay, but may even be free to invite the evicted codefendants back in as "guests." (Minor children are evicted along with their parents, without the necessity of naming them as defendants and serving them with complaints.)

Service on Unknown Occupants (Optional)

If you don't serve copies of the summons and complaint on everyone residing in the property as of the date you filed the complaint, the eviction may be delayed even after you've gotten a judgment and arranged for the sheriff or marshal to evict. That's because occupants who weren't served with the summons and complaint were never really sued in the first place. After you get a court order for possession and the sheriff posts the property with a notice advising the occupants they have five days to move or be bodily evicted, the unserved occupants can file a Claim of Right to Possession with the sheriff and stop the eviction until you redo your lawsuit to get a judgment against them. (C.C.P. § 1174.3.) Coping with this problem is difficult, time-consuming, beyond the scope of this book, and a lawyer is almost a necessity.

How can you avoid this? State law gives you an option: A sheriff, marshal, or registered process server, when serving the summons and complaint on the named defendants, can ask whether there are any other occupants of the property that haven't been named. If there are occupants who aren't named, the sheriff, marshal, or registered process server can then serve each of them, too, with a blank Prejudgment Claim of Right to Possession form and an extra copy of the summons and complaint, and indicate this on the proof of service. In most situations, the unnamed occupants have ten days from the date of service to file any Claim of Right to Possession; they can't file it later when the sheriff is about to evict. If anyone does file a claim, he or she is automatically added as a defendant. (The court clerk is supposed to do that and notify you of such by mail.) The person filing a claim then has five days to respond to the summons and complaint. If they don't, you can obtain a default judgment for possession (see Chapter 7) that includes the new claimant as well as the other named defendants.

> **CAUTION**
>
> **Consult with counsel if your eviction involves a foreclosed property.** The Prejudgment Claim form asks you to indicate whether these unnamed occupants are residing in a foreclosed property. Foreclosure evictions, either by you or one begun by a previous owner from whom you've bought the property, involve additional tenant rights and complications, including extended notice periods. This area of the law is changing, and new procedures might affect your termination rights. You would be well advised to work with an experienced attorney in these situations. (See Chapter 11 of this book for further information.)

Even when a valid pretrial claim does not exist, the mere filing of a claim by any person will delay the eviction at least several days, if not one or two weeks. For this reason, most attorneys automatically instruct the registered server to carry out the Prejudgment Claim of Right to Possession procedure. When this procedure is carried out, an unknown occupant will be less likely to file such a claim, since the threat of eviction is not as immediate as when the sheriff offers this opportunity only days before the actual eviction. (C.C.P. §§ 415.46, 1174.25.) This optional procedure may not be necessary if you have no reason to believe there are occupants of the property whose names you don't know and have no concern about a delay. Because only a sheriff, marshal, or private process server can serve the papers when you follow this procedure, the eviction may be more costly or proceed more slowly. Also, if you use this option, you will have to wait ten days from service, rather than the usual five, to obtain a judgment that would include unnamed occupants.

> **FORM**
>
> **A blank copy of the Prejudgment Claim to Right of Possession can be downloaded from the Nolo website.** (See the appendix for the link to the forms in this book, and other information on using the forms.)

If you want to have any unknown occupants served, you will need to make as many extra copies of the summons and complaint and claim form as you anticipate need to be served on unknown occupants. Fill out the caption boxes at the top of the Prejudgment Claim of Right to Possession form as you have on your other court forms, and leave the rest of it blank. Your instructions to the process server, sheriff, or marshal should include a statement something like this: "Enclosed are two additional sets of copies of the summons and complaint, together with a blank Prejudgment Claim of Right to Possession form; please serve the same on any unnamed occupants of the premises pursuant to C.C.P. § 415.46. Please indicate this type of service on your Proof of Service."

Who May Serve the Papers: Process Servers

The law forbids you (the plaintiff) from serving a summons and complaint yourself, but any other person 18 or older and not named as a plaintiff or defendant in the lawsuit can do it. You can have a marshal or sheriff's deputy, a professional process server, or just an acquaintance or employee serve the papers. (If you have a friend or employee serve the papers, have that person read the part of this chapter on how to serve the papers and fill out the "Proof of Service" on the original summons.) However, if you use the optional procedure shown in the section above for serving a Claim of Right to Possession on any unnamed occupants, you must use a marshal or sheriff's deputy or registered process server. An ordinary individual cannot serve the Claim of Right to Possession.

What about having your spouse serve the papers? Although no statute or case law specifically disallows spouses not named in the complaint from serving papers for the named spouse, this isn't a good idea. Because spouses almost always share an ownership interest in real estate (even when the property is in only one spouse's name), a judge could rule, if the tenant contests service, that the unnamed spouse is a "party" because he or she partly owns the property.

Some landlords prefer to have a marshal or deputy sheriff serve the papers to intimidate the tenant and give the impression, however false, that the forces of the law favor the eviction. Not all counties provide this service, however, and in those that do, sheriff's deputies and marshals are occasionally slow and sometimes don't try very hard to serve a person who is avoiding service by hiding or saying she is someone other than the defendant. To have a marshal or deputy serve the summons and complaint, go to the marshal's office or the civil division of the county sheriff's office, pay the $40 fee for each defendant to be served, and fill out a form, which asks for information on the best hours to find the defendant at home or work, general physical descriptions, and so on.

Professional process-serving firms are commonly faster and are often a lot more resourceful at serving evasive persons. They are also a little more expensive, but the money you'll save in having the papers served faster (and therefore in being able to evict sooner) might justify the extra expense. If you have an attorney, ask your lawyer to recommend a good process-serving firm, or check the Web or yellow pages for process servers in the area where the tenant lives or works.

Take care to serve the tenant well within 60 days of the filing of your complaint. By state law, the court has the power to dismiss your eviction lawsuit if the proof of service of the summons has not been filed with the court within 60 days of the filing of the complaint. The dismissal, if it happens, will be "without prejudice," which means that you can start over with a new lawsuit—but you will have lost time and money in the meantime. (Code of Civil Procedure § 1167.1.)

Marshals and Sheriffs

Marshals are the enforcement officers for the courts. They serve court papers, enforce civil court judgments, and physically evict tenants who refuse to leave the property following a judgment of eviction. Los Angeles County and some others have marshal's offices separate from sheriff's offices, but in many other counties—especially in Northern California—the sheriff is designated as the marshal.

How the Summons and Complaint Copies Are Served

SKIP AHEAD
If you use a sheriff, marshal, or professional process server, you can skip this section.

There are only three ways to serve a defendant legally. Again, pay close attention to the rules for the method you use.

Remember that only copies of the summons, not the originals with the court seals, should be served on the defendant. If you mistakenly serve the original, you'll have to prepare a Declaration of Lost Summons After Service, Judicial Council Form SUM-300.

Personal Service

For personal service, the copy of the Summons and of the Complaint must be handed to the defendant by the server. The person serving the papers can't simply leave them at the defendant's workplace or in the mailbox. If the defendant refuses to take the paper, acts hostile, or attempts to run away, the process server should simply put the papers on the ground as close as possible to the defendant's feet and leave. The person serving the papers should never try to force a defendant to take them—it's unnecessary and may subject the process server (or even you) to a lawsuit for battery.

Personal service of the papers is best; if you have to resort to either of the other two methods, the law allows the defendant an extra ten days (15 days instead of five) to file a written response to the complaint. It is therefore worthwhile to make several attempts at personal service at the defendant's home or workplace.

Before personally serving the papers, the process server must check Boxes 4a and 5 on the bottom of the first page of the summons copies to be served and fill in the date of service in the space following Box 4. (See the sample summons in "Preparing the Summons," above.) It's better for the process server to fill the information in on the summons copy in pencil before service—so it can be changed later if service isn't effected that way or on that date. This is also less awkward than doing it right there just as you've located the angry defendant.

Some individuals have developed avoidance of the process server into a high (but silly) art. It is permissible, and may be necessary, for the person serving the papers to use trickery to get the defendant to open the door or come out of an office and identify him- or herself. One method that works well is for the process server to carry a wrapped (but empty) package and a clipboard, saying he or she has a "delivery" for the defendant and requires the defendant's signature on a receipt. The delivery, of course, is of the summons and complaint. If all else fails, your process server might have to resort to a "stakeout" and wait for the defendant to appear. It's obviously not necessary to serve the defendant inside his or her home or workplace. The parking lot is just as good.

(Nearly) All Is Fair in Love and Service of Process

Process servers frequently resort to legal subterfuge to get someone to open the door. We know of one former process server who got very creative.

He purchased a FedEx shirt and brown shorts at a Goodwill store, and showed up at the door of a witness who had been craftily avoiding service. Having waited for the target's birthday, in his "uniform" he carried a brown box labeled "FPD Flowers." After he knocked on the door and recognized the target, he asked, "Are you the birthday boy?"

And when he got a delighted, "Yes!" he handed the witness the flowers—along with a subpoena.

When serving more than one defendant, it's sometimes difficult to serve the remaining defendant after having served one. For example, if one adult in the family customarily answers the door and is served the papers, it's unlikely that she will cooperate by calling the other defendant to the door so that your process server can serve that person too. So, when one person answers the door, the process server should ask whether the other person is at home. Usually the defendant who answers the door will stay there until the other person comes to the door—at which time your process server can serve them both by handing the papers to each individual or laying them at their feet.

Substituted Service on Another Person

If your process server makes three unsuccessful attempts to serve a defendant at home and/or work, at times you would reasonably expect the defendant to be there, the server can give the papers to another person at the defendant's home, workplace, or usual mailing address (other than a U.S. Postal Service mailbox) with instructions to that person to give papers to the defendant.

If the papers are left at the defendant's home, they must be given to "a competent member of the household" who is at least 18 years old. In addition, the server must mail a second copy of the summons and complaint to the defendant at the place where the summons was left. (C.C.P. § 415.20(b).) This is called "substituted service."

Before the law permits substituted service, you (or your server) must establish "due diligence," meaning they have made at least three attempts on three different days during three different work shifts. Once the service is complete, the law allows the defendant ten extra days (for a total of about 15 days) to respond to the summons and complaint.

So using this method instead of personal service means that the eviction will be delayed ten days, but over the time that it takes to process most cases through the court system, the ten days rarely matter. In most instances, it's better to get a professional process server to make a substituted service than try to stake out the tenants to get everyone personally. After all, if the tenants are going to make the serve easy, you would have been able to serve them personally on the first or second attempt.

If you send a relative or friend to try to serve a tenant at work, you could regret it, as service at work is likely to create a lot of hostility. It might even prompt the tenant to go out and get a lawyer, when he or she otherwise might have simply moved out.

Post Office Boxes

A tenant who is never home to be served (and no one ever answers the door at the tenant's home) *cannot* be served at a "usual mailing address" if that address happens to be a post office box at a U.S. Postal Service public post office. However, a tenant who rents a box at a *private* post office (such as the UPS Store) and regularly uses that address and box may be served there by substituted service on the person in charge of the mail drop, followed by mailing a second copy of the summons and complaint (from a real U.S. Postal Service mailbox). This method should never be your first attempt at service, however, because it will qualify at best as a substituted service.

EXAMPLE: You name Daily and Baily as defendants. When your process server goes to serve the papers, only Daily is home. He serves Daily personally. Baily, however, has to be served before you can get a judgment against him. Two more attempts to serve Baily fail, when Daily answers the door and refuses to say where Baily is. The process server uses the substituted service technique and gives Daily another set of papers—for Baily—and mails still another set addressed to Baily. Service is not legally effective until the tenth day after giving the papers to Daily and mailing a second copy of the papers to Baily. This means that you'll have to wait these ten days, plus the five court day "response time," (see "What Next?" below) for a total of 15 plus days, before you can take a default judgment against Baily.

Before serving the papers by substituted service, the process server should check Box 3 on the bottom front of the summons copy and also check the box next to "CCP 416.90 (individual)" and should write in the name of the defendant served this way (not the person to whom the papers are given) after the words "On behalf of." Of the boxes below Box 3 and indented, check the box labeled "other" and add "C.C.P. § 415.20" after it to indicate that substituted service was used.

Although the three unsuccessful attempts necessary to use substituted service can be made at the tenant's home, work, or both, it's best to try the tenant's home only. Serving someone at their place of employment can create unnecessary hostility, and should be used as a last resort.

A sample Declaration re Reasonable Diligence for Substituted Service of Summons on Individual form is shown below.

If the process server plans to serve a Prejudgment Claim to Right of Possession (see "Service on Unknown Occupants (Optional)," above), the server should check Box c next to the words, "as an occupant," and also Box d, next to "CCP 415.46 (occupant)."

The process server must fill out the Proof of Service of Summons and sign and date a declaration detailing his or her attempts to locate the defendant for personal service. This declaration is attached to the original summons. A sample is shown below.

"Posting-and-Mailing" Service

Not infrequently, a process server cannot serve a defendant personally or by substituted service. For example, if your tenant lives alone and is deliberately avoiding service, and you don't know where he works (he's no longer at the job listed several months ago on his application), the law

provides that your process server can post copies of the summons and complaint on his front door and mail a second set of copies—after obtaining a court order.

As with substituted service, this posting-and-mailing method, often referenced as "nail and mail" also gives the defendant an extra ten days to file a response with the court, and so ten more days (total of 15 days) must go by before you can get a default judgment.

Judges closely scrutinize posting and mailing applications for errors, so we strongly recommend that you let a process server or a lawyer handle it. There are many ways to make a mistake, and, if you do, your whole lawsuit will be delayed.

Before you can use posting and mailing, you must get written permission from a judge. Your process server must show that he or she has made at least three, and preferably four, unsuccessful attempts to serve the papers at different and reasonable times, covering all possible work shifts on different days. Too many attempts at the wrong times do not work—another good reason to let someone experienced handle it. A sample form for Los Angeles (Application and Order to Serve Summons by Posting for Unlawful Detainer) to obtain court permission to "nail and mail" the summons is shown below. Keep in mind, though, that this sample should be adapted to your own situation.

 FORM
A blank copy of the Los Angeles form Application and Order to Serve Summons by Posting for Unlawful Detainer can be downloaded from the Nolo website. (See the appendix for the link to the forms in this book, and other information on using the forms.) Also, the Los Angeles County version of this form can be found at: www.lacourt.org/forms/all.

1
2
3
4
5
6
7
8
9
10
11
12
13
14
15
16
17
18
19
20
21
22
23
24
25
26
27
28

DECLARATION RE REASONABLE DILIGENCE FOR

SUBSTITUTED SERVICE OF SUMMONS ON INDIVIDUAL

I, SARAH SERVER, declare:

I am over the age of 18 years and not a party to this action.

On August 13, 20xx, I served the summons and complaint on defendant Terrence Tenant by leaving true copies thereof with Teresa Tenant at defendant's place of residence and mailing a second set of copies thereof addressed to defendant at his place of residence.

Prior to using substituted service to serve defendant Terrence Tenant, I attempted on the following occasions to personally serve him:

1. On August 10, 20xx, at 5:30 P.M., I knocked on the front door of defendant's residence. A woman who identified herself as Teresa Tenant answered the door. I asked her whether I could see either Terrence or Tillie Tenant and she replied, "They're not at home."

2. On August 12, 20xx, at 3:00 P.M., I went to defendant Terrence Tenant's place of employment, Bob's Burgers, 123 Main Street, Los Angeles, and was told that defendant Terrence Tenant had recently been fired.

3. On August 13, 20xx, at 7:00 A.M., I again went to defendant's home. Again, Teresa Tenant answered the door and said that Terrence Tenant was not home. I then gave her the papers for Terrence Tenant.

I declare under penalty of perjury under the laws of the State of California that the foregoing is true and correct.

Date: August 13, 20xx

Sarah Server
SARAH SERVER

Declaration re Reasonable Diligence for Substituted Service of Summons on Individual

NAME, ADDRESS, AND TELEPHONE NUMBER OF ATTORNEY OR PARTY WITHOUT ATTORNEY:	STATE BAR NUMBER	*Reserved for Clerk's File Stamp*
LENNY D. LANDLORD 12345 Angeleno Street Los Angeles, CA 90010 Tel: 213-555-6789 ATTORNEY FOR (Name): Plaintiff in Pro Per		

SUPERIOR COURT OF CALIFORNIA, COUNTY OF LOS ANGELES

COURTHOUSE ADDRESS:
110 N. Grand Avenue, Los Angeles, CA 90012

PLAINTIFF:
LENNY D. LANDLORD

DEFENDANT:
TERRENCE D. TENANT, TILLIE D. TENANT

APPLICATION AND ORDER TO SERVE SUMMONS BY POSTING FOR UNLAWFUL DETAINER	CASE NUMBER: A-123456-B

1. I am the ☒ plaintiff   ☐ plaintiff's attorney   ☐ other (specify):_____

2. I apply for an order pursuant to Code of Civil Procedure section 415.45 to permit service by posting of the summons and complaint on defendant(s). *Specify name(s):* _____
   _____ Terrence D. Tenant, Tillie D. Tenant _____
   _____
   _____
   _____

3. The complaint seeks possession of property location at: _6789 Angel St., Apt. 10, Los Angeles,_
   _Los Angeles County, California_____. The property is ☒ residential   ☐ commercial.

4. The notice to quit, or pay rent or quit, was served by: ☐ personal service   ☐ substituted service
   ☒ posting and mailing ☐ other *(specify):*_____

5. At least three attempts to serve in a manner specified in Code of Civil Procedure, Article 3, (other than posting or publication) are required. List attempts to serve, if made by declarant, or attach declaration(s) of process server(s) stating attempts to locate and serve the defendants. If service not made, please explain.

DATE	TIME	REASON SERVICE COULD NOT BE MADE/REMARKS
8/10/xx	5:30 p.m.	Minor daughter answered through door, refused to open and said her parents were not home.
8/12/xx	3:00 p.m.	Defendant not present at place of employment, manager said fired two weeks earlier.
8/13/xx	7:15 p.m.	No one answered the door, though lights on and both defendants' vehicles in driveway.

☒ Declaration(s) of process server stating attempts to locate and serve the defendant(s) is attached and incorporated into this application by reference

LACIV 107 (Rev. 01/07) LASC Approved 10-03	**APPLICATION AND ORDER TO SERVE SUMMONS BY POSTING FOR UNLAWFUL DETAINER**	Code Civ. Proc., § 415.45 Page 1 of 2

Short Title	Case Number
LANDLORD V. TENANT	A-123456-B

6. Service ☒ has ☐ has not been attempted during regular business hours at the place(s) of employment of the defendant(s). If not, state reason: ☐ the place(s) of employment of the defendant(s) is not known. ☒ Other *(specify)*: ___Service was attempted 8/12/xx at defendant's former place of employment, but process server was advised that defendant was fired two weeks before. Employment address of Tillie Tenant is unknown.___

7. Service ☒ has ☐ has not been attempted at the "residence" of the defendant(s). If not, state reasons: ☐ The place of residence of the defendant(s) is not known.
☐ Other *(specify)*: _____
_____
_____

8. Other: _____
_____
_____

9. Did the plaintiff pay for help from a registered unlawful detainer assistant (Bus. and Prof. Code, §§ 6400-5415) who helped prepare this form? ☐ Yes ☒ No If yes, complete the following information:
Name of Unlawful Detainer Assistant: _____; Telephone Number: (   )
_____ Address *(Mailing address, city and Zip code)*: _____
_____
Registration #: _____; County of Registration: _____.

I declare under penalty of perjury under the laws of the State of California, that the foregoing is true and correct.		
DATE	TYPE OF PRINT DECLARANT'S NAME	DECLARANT'S SIGNATURE
Aug. 13, 20xx	LENNY D. LANDLORD	*Lenny D. Landlord*

FINDINGS AND ORDER

THE COURT FINDS:
1. The defendant(s) named in the application cannot with reasonable diligence be served in any manner specified in Code of Civil Procedure, Article 3.
2. (a) A cause of action exists against the defendant(s) named in the application; **and/or** (b) defendant(s) named in the application has or claims an interest in real property in California that is subject to the jurisdiction of the court; **and/or** (c) the relief demanded in the complaint consists wholly or partially in excluding the defendant(s) from any interest in the property.

THE COURT ORDERS:
The defendant(s) named in the application may be served by posting a copy of the summons and complaint on the premises in a manner most likely to give actual notice to the defendant(s), and by immediately mailing, by certified mail, a copy of the summons and complaint to the defendant(s) at his/her last known address.

Dated: _____   _____   _____
                                        Judicial Officer   Div/Dept.

POS-010

ATTORNEY OR PARTY WITHOUT ATTORNEY *(Name, State Bar number, and address):* LENNY D. LANDLORD 12345 ANGELENO STREET LOS ANGELES, CA 90010 TELEPHONE NO.: 213-555-6789 FAX NO. *(Optional):* E–MAIL ADDRESS *(Optional):* ATTORNEY FOR *(Name):* Plaintiff in Pro Per	FOR COURT USE ONLY

SUPERIOR COURT OF CALIFORNIA, COUNTY OF LOS ANGELES
STREET ADDRESS: 110 North Hill Street
MAILING ADDRESS: Same
CITY AND ZIP CODE: Los Angeles, CA 90012
BRANCH NAME: CENTRAL DISTRICT/DOWNTOWN BRANCH

PLAINTIFF/PETITIONER: LENNY D. LANDLORD DEFENDANT/RESPONDENT: TERRENCE D. TENANT, TILLIE D. TENANT	CASE NUMBER:
PROOF OF SERVICE OF SUMMONS	Ref. No. or File No.:

(Separate proof of service is required for each party served.)

1. At the time of service I was at least 18 years of age and not a party to this action.

2. I served copies of:
   a. ☐ summons
   b. ☒ complaint
   c. ☐ Alternative Dispute Resolution (ADR) package
   d. ☐ Civil Case Cover Sheet *(served in complex cases only)*
   e. ☐ cross-complaint
   f. ☐ other *(specify documents):*

3. a. Party served *(specify name of party as shown on documents served):*

   TERRENCE D. TENANT

   b. ☐ Person (other than the party in item 3a) served on behalf of an entity or as an authorized agent (and not a person under item 5b on whom substituted service was made) *(specify name and relationship to the party named in item 3a):*

4. Address where the party was served: 3815 Gower Canyon Avenue, Apt. 3, Los Angeles, CA 90028

5. I served the party *(check proper box)*
   a. ☒ **by personal service.** I personally delivered the documents listed in item 2 to the party or person authorized to receive service of process for the party (1) on *(date):* April 12, 20xx (2) at *(time):* 6 PM
   b. ☐ **by substituted service.** On *(date):* at *(time):* I left the documents listed in item 2 with or in the presence of *(name and title or relationship to person indicated in item 3):*

      (1) ☐ **(business)** a person at least 18 years of age apparently in charge at the office or usual place of business of the person to be served. I informed him or her of the general nature of the papers.

      (2) ☐ **(home)** a competent member of the household (at least 18 years of age) at the dwelling house or usual place of abode of the party. I informed him or her of the general nature of the papers.

      (3) ☐ **(physical address unknown)** a person at least 18 years of age apparently in charge at the usual mailing address of the person to be served, other than a United States Postal Service post office box. I informed him or her of the general nature of the papers.

      (4) ☐ I thereafter mailed (by first-class, postage prepaid) copies of the documents to the person to be served at the place where the copies were left (Code Civ. Proc., § 415.20). I mailed the documents on *(date):* from *(city):* **or** ☐ a declaration of mailing is attached.

      (5) ☐ I attach a **declaration of diligence** stating actions taken first to attempt personal service.

Page 1 of 2

Form Adopted for Mandatory Use Judicial Council of California POS-010 [Rev. January 1, 2007]	**PROOF OF SERVICE OF SUMMONS**	Code of Civil Procedure, § 417.10

PLAINTIFF/PETITIONER: LENNY D. LANDLORD	CASE NUMBER:
DEFENDANT/RESPONDENT: TERRENCE D. TENANT	

5. c. ☐ **by mail and acknowledgment of receipt of service.** I mailed the documents listed in item 2 to the party, to the address shown in item 4, by first-class mail, postage prepaid,

    (1) on *(date):*   (2) from *(city):*

    (3) ☐ with two copies of the *Notice and Acknowledgment of Receipt* and a postage-paid return envelope addressed to me. *(Attach completed* Notice and Acknowledgement of Receipt.*)* (Code Civ. Proc., § 415.30.)

    (4) ☐ to an address outside California with return receipt requested. (Code Civ. Proc., § 415.40.)

  d. ☐ **by other means** *(specify means of service and authorizing code section):*

      ☐ Additional page describing service is attached.

6. The "Notice to the Person Served" (on the summons) was completed as follows:
  a. ☒ as an individual defendant.
  b. ☐ as the person sued under the fictitious name of *(specify):*
  c. ☐ as occupant.
  d. ☐ On behalf of *(specify):*
    under the following Code of Civil Procedure section:

☐ 416.10 (corporation)	☐ 415.95 (business organization, form unknown)
☐ 416.20 (defunct corporation)	☐ 416.60 (minor)
☐ 416.30 (joint stock company/association)	☐ 416.70 (ward or conservatee)
☐ 416.40 (association or partnership)	☐ 416.90 (authorized person)
☐ 416.50 (public entity)	☐ 415.46 (occupant)
	☐ other:

7. **Person who served papers**
  a. Name: Sam D. Server
  b. Address: 1000 A Street, Los Angeles, CA 90010
  c. Telephone number: 213-555-1234
  d. **The fee** for service was: $ 50.00
  e. I am:
    (1) ☒ not a registered California process server.
    (2) ☐ exempt from registration under Business and Professions Code section 22350(b).
    (3) ☐ a registered California process server:
      (i) ☐ owner ☐ employee ☐ independent contractor.
      (ii) Registration No.:
      (iii) County:

8. ☒ **I declare** under penalty of perjury under the laws of the State of California that the foregoing is true and correct.

    or

9. ☐ **I am a California sheriff or marshal and** I certify that the foregoing is true and correct.

Date: April 13, 20xx

Sam D. Server   ▶ *Sam D. Server*

_____   _____
(NAME OF PERSON WHO SERVED PAPERS/SHERIFF OR MARSHAL)   (SIGNATURE)

Filling Out the Proof of Service of Summons Form

Once the process server has served the copies of the summonses, the server must fill out a "Proof of Service of Summons" form and staple it to the original summons. (Remember, there is one original summons for each defendant.) If you use a sheriff, marshal, or registered process server, that person should do this for you. So, even where two or more defendants are served at the same time and place by the same process server, two separate Proofs of Service should be filled out. When this form is filled out and returned to the court clerk (see Chapter 7), it tells the clerk that the tenant received notice of the lawsuit, an essential element of your lawsuit. Here's how to complete the Proof of Service of Summons (a sample is shown below). The process server must fill out a Proof of Service of Summons for each defendant.

FORM

A blank copy of the Proof of Service of Summons (Judicial Council form POS-010) can be downloaded from the Nolo website. (See the appendix for the link to the forms in this book, and other information on using the forms.)

In the box at the top of the form, fill in the plaintiff's and defendant's names, and leave blank the box entitled "case number."

Item 2: Check the box next to "complaint." If a sheriff, marshal, or registered process server served a Prejudgment Claim of Right to Possession using the optional procedure discussed above, that person should also check the box next to "other (*specify documents*)" and add, "Prejudgment Claim of Right to Possession."

Item 3a: Type the name of the defendant for whom this summons was issued and on whom the copies were served.

Item 3b: Leave this box blank (it's for the unlikely event that your tenant has a designated agent who will accept service of process).

Item 4: Type the address where the defendant (or the person given the papers by substituted service) was served.

Item 5: If the defendant was personally served, check Box a and list the date and time of service on the same line in Subitems (1) and (2).

If the defendant was served by substituted service on another person, check Box b, list the date and time the papers were given to this other person, and type the name of that other person in the space just below the first two lines. If you don't know the name of that person, insert the word "co-occupant," "coworker," or whatever other word (such as "spouse of defendant") describes the relationship of the person to the defendant. Check the box in Subitem (1) or (2) to indicate whether the papers were left with this other person at the defendant's business or home. Then, indicate in Subitem (4) the date that additional copies of the summons and complaint were mailed to the defendant (at the home or business address where the papers were left), and the city (or nearest post office branch) from which the second set was mailed. Do not check Subitem (3), but do check Subitem (5). Be sure to attach the original Declaration re Reasonable Diligence for Substituted Service of Summons on Individual signed and dated by the process server, to the Proof of Service of Summons.

If you used service by posting and mailing, after getting permission from a judge, check Box d on the second page and after the words "by other means (specify means of service and authorizing code section)" enter the words "C.C.P. § 415.45 pursuant to Court's order, by posting copies of summons and complaint on front door to premises at [*list full street address*] on [*list date posted*], and mailing copies thereof on [*list date of mailing, or words* "same date" *if applicable*] by certified mail addressed to defendant at that address."

Item 6: The alphabetical boxes here (a through d) are the same as those on Item 4 on the front of the summons (however, Box d includes more options). If personal service was used, check Box a.

If substituted service was used, check Box d, and also the box next to "CCP 416.90 (authorized person)." Also type the name of the defendant served by substituted service (not the one to whom the papers were given) on Line c.

For posting-and-mailing service, check Box a.

Items 7–9, Date and Signature: In the spaces below Item 7, list the home or business address and telephone number of the process server. Next to "The fee for service," list the amount you paid, if applicable, to the person who served the summons. Under e, check Box 1 to indicate that this person is not a registered process server. (If you do use a registered process server, they will fill out the Proof of Service of Summons for you.) Do not check Box 2 unless the person who served the papers is an attorney or licensed private investigator, or an employee of either. Then, check Box 8 and have the person who served the papers date and sign the Proof of Service of Summons at the bottom. Do not check Box 9.

What Next?

Tenants have a choice after being properly served with your summons and complaint: They can do nothing and lose automatically (in legalese, default), or they can fight the suit. They must decide what to do within five days (15 days if they weren't personally served with the summons and complaint).

If the tenant doesn't file some kind of written response with the court within five days, you can get a default judgment by filing a few documents with the court. No court hearing is necessary. Chapter 7 tells you how to do this.

Taking a Default Judgment

 FORMS IN THIS CHAPTER

Chapter 7 includes instructions for and samples of the following forms:

- Request for Entry of Default
- Judgment—Unlawful Detainer
- Writ of Execution
- Declaration Regarding Daily Rental Value
- Declaration Regarding Lost Lease
- Application for Issuance of Writ of Execution, Possession or Sale
- Declaration in Support of Default Judgment for Rent, Damages, and Costs
- Declaration in Support of Default Judgment for Damages and Costs
- Request for Court Judgment, and
- Judgment—Unlawful Detainer By Court.

You can download these forms from the Nolo website, plus the Request for Dismissal and Judicial Council form Declaration for Default Judgment by Court, which are covered in this chapter, but for which a sample is not shown. (See the appendix for the link to the forms in this book, and other information on using the forms.)

If your tenant does not contest the unlawful detainer lawsuit by filing a written response to your complaint, you win the lawsuit almost automatically. The tenant has "defaulted," and you are entitled to obtain a "default judgment" from the court clerk for possession of the property. Most unlawful detainer actions are uncontested and wind up as defaults. By submitting more papers and, where required, appearing before a judge, you can also obtain a separate default judgment for some or all of the money the tenant owes you.

You can obtain a default judgment if all of the following requirements are satisfied:

- The tenancy was properly terminated (covered in Chapter 2, 3, 4, or 5 depending on the type of termination).
- The summons and complaint were properly served on all the tenants (covered in Chapter 6).
- At least five court days (Saturday, Sunday, and judicial holidays do not count) have elapsed from the date the tenant was personally served with the summons and complaint (15 days if you used substituted service or a court order).
- The tenants have not filed a written response to your complaint by the time you file your request for a default judgment.

This chapter tells you when and how you can obtain a default judgment. (Refer to the checklist in your "home" chapter for a step-by-step outline of the process.)

When Can You Take a Default?

The law gives a defendant who was personally served with the summons and complaint at least five court days to respond to your unlawful detainer complaint. You can't take a default judgment until this response period has passed. You will have to wait at least six court days before you can get a default judgment from the court clerk. This is because you don't count the day of service or court holidays, which include statewide legal holidays, or weekends.

A tenant who was served with the complaint and summons by substituted or posting-and-mailing service has an extra ten days to respond (by filing an answer or a motion to the substance of your complaint). Thus, you must count 10 days from the date of mailing *plus* 5 court days. The last day will always be a court day.

Because you don't want to give the tenant any more time to file a written response than you have to, you should be prepared to "take a default" against one or all of the defendants on the first day you can. If the defendant beats you to the courthouse and files an answer, you can't take a default.

How do you know whether the tenants have in fact defaulted (and are not contesting the eviction)? Although tenants are supposed to mail you a copy of any response filed, they might not do so or might wait until the last day to file and mail you a copy. To find out whether they have filed anything, call the court clerk on the first day after the response period has expired.

When you call to ask about any response, the clerk will first ask you for information about yourself. (Code of Civil Procedure Section 1161.2 restricts public access to unlawful detainer records.) You might have to give the clerk your name, affirm you are the plaintiff in pro per, the case number stamped on the summons and complaint, and the exact address of the apartment as written in the complaint. If you have provided all the required information, you can then ask if a response has been filed.

Most tenants don't file a written response. If no response has been filed, you can visit the courthouse when it opens that same day to obtain the default judgment. If, however, you find to your dismay that the tenant or his or her lawyer has filed a response to your lawsuit, it will probably take you a few more weeks to evict. (See Chapter 8 on contested eviction lawsuits.)

EXAMPLE 1: Your process server personally served Leon with the summons and complaint on Tuesday, August 2. You can take a default if Leon doesn't file a response within five court days, not counting the day of service. The first day after service is Wednesday, August 3. Because August 5 falls on a Friday, the count is suspended to Monday, August 8, when it resumes. Leon has until the end of Tuesday, August 9, to file his response and prevent a default. If he hasn't filed by the end of that business day, you can get a default judgment against him the next day, Wednesday, August 10.

EXAMPLE 2: Angela is a codefendant with Leon, but neither you nor your process server can locate her at home or work. She is served by substituted service on August 7, when the papers are given to Leon to give to her, and a second set of papers is mailed to her that same day. Service will be complete ten days after mailing, which means the count of the five days starts on August 17, assuming that the 17th is not a weekend or judicial holiday. You start counting five court days from the 17th, and that will be the last day to answer. If she doesn't file a response by the end of the business day, you can take a default against her on the next business day. (As a practical matter, you should probably wait until the 23rd to take Leon's default too, because you won't get Angela out or the property back any sooner by taking Leon's default first—and it's more paperwork.)

> **CAUTION**
>
> **Don't accept rent now.** Do not accept any rent from your tenant during (or even after) the waiting period (also called "response time"), unless you want to allow the tenant to stay. This is true whether you are evicting for nonpayment of rent, termination by 30-day or 60-day notice, breach of the lease, or any other reason. If you do accept rent, you will "waive," or give up, your right to sue, and the tenant can assert that as a defense in the answer. In rent nonpayment cases, if you care more about getting your rent than getting the tenant out, you should at least insist that the tenant pay all the rent plus the costs of your lawsuit, including any costs to serve papers. Don't be foolish enough to accept partial rent payment with a promise to pay more later. If you do, and it's not forthcoming, you will very likely have to start all over again with a new three-day notice and new lawsuit.
>
> There is one exception to this rule: when you are trying to collect or evict based on nonpayment of COVID-19 rental debt. Evicting for COVID-19 rental debt is so complicated, it is usually worth taking a part payment of at least one month's rent. However, before you take the money, you should try to negotiate for payment of court costs and an enforceable payment plan from the tenant as part of the acceptance.

The Two-Step Default Judgment Process

As part of evicting a tenant, normally you will obtain two separate default judgments:

- **Default Judgment for Possession of property.** It's fairly easy to get a Judgment for Possession of your property on the day after the tenant's response time passes by simply filing your default papers with the court clerk.

- **Default judgment for any money you are entitled to.** Getting a default judgment for back rent, damages, and court costs you requested in your complaint is more time-consuming; you have to either go before a judge or submit a declaration setting forth the facts of the case. (See "Getting a Money Judgment for Rent and Costs," below.) And because the judge can award you damages (prorated rent) covering only the period until the date of judgment, your money judgment won't include any days after you get the judgment and before the tenant is actually evicted.

(*Cavanaugh v. High* (1960) 182 Cal. App. 2d 714, 723.) For example, a judgment cannot say, "$10 per day until defendant is evicted." Prorated daily damages end on the day of the money judgment. The actual eviction won't occur for at least ten days after the possession default is entered unless, of course, the tenant leaves voluntarily before then.

For this reason, it's best to first get a clerk's default Judgment for Possession and then wait until the tenant leaves before you go back to court to get the money part of the judgment.

If you do get the money part of the judgment before the tenant is evicted, you are still entitled to the prorated rent for the time between money judgment and eviction. You can deduct this amount from any security deposit the tenant paid you. This isn't quite as good as waiting, because it means less of the security deposit will be available if the place is damaged or dirty. If you wait to enter the default as to rent until after the tenant leaves, you can get a judgment for the entire amount of rent due and still leave the deposit available to take care of cleaning and repairs.

Getting a Default Judgment for Possession

To obtain a default Judgment for Possession of the property, you must fill out and file at least five documents:

- a Request for Entry of Default
- a Request for Dismissal dismissing all the Doe defendants (not all courts require this step)
- a Clerk's Judgment for Possession (this is the Judgment—Unlawful Detainer form)
- a Writ of Possession for the property (this is the Writ of Execution form)
- a Declaration re: Daily Rental Value (or local court form equivalent), and
- a Declaration re: Lost Original (some courts require you to submit a copy of the rental agreement or lease.

Because you want to get your tenant out as fast as possible, you might as well prepare the default judgment forms during your five-day (or 15-day) wait. If the tenant files a response in the meantime, you won't be able to obtain a default judgment, and this work will be wasted. However, the time it takes to prepare these forms is not great. And because of the high percentage of cases that end in defaults, it's a worthwhile gamble.

If the tenant voluntarily moved out after being served with the summons and complaint, he or she still is required to answer the complaint within five days. Assuming the tenant does not, you should still go ahead and get a money judgment for any rent owed, by skipping to "Getting a Money Judgment for Rent and Costs," below.

Preparing Your Request for Entry of Default for Possession

Your request for the clerk to enter a default and a Judgment for Possession of the premises is made on a Judicial Council form called a Request for Entry of Default. In it, you list the names of the defendants against whom you're taking defaults and indicate that you want a "clerk's judgment" that says you are entitled to possession of the property.

If you're suing more than one occupant of the property, and they were all served with the summons and complaint on the same day, you can get a default judgment against them all on the same day, by filing one set of papers with all their names on each form.

On the other hand, if you're suing more than one person and they were served on different days (or by different methods), each will have a different date by which he or she must respond. Your best bet is to prepare one set of papers with all the defaulting defendants' names on them, wait until the response time has passed for all defendants, and take all the defaults simultaneously.

You can fill out a separate set of papers for each defendant and take each defendant's default as soon as the waiting period for each defendant has passed, but there's normally no reason to, unless the tenants with later response times have already moved out or there is something special about the tenants with earlier response times (for example, they have potential retaliation or discrimination claims) that makes it advisable to take their default as soon as possible and get them out of the case. More paperwork is involved, and a default judgment against one tenant won't usually help you get the property back any sooner—you still have the others to deal with.

 FORM

A blank copy of the Request for Entry of Default (Judicial Council form CIV-100) can be downloaded from the Nolo website. (See the appendix for the link to the forms and related information.)

On the front of the form, fill in the caption boxes (your name, address, phone, and the words "Plaintiff in Pro Per" after the words "Attorney For;" the name and address of the court; the name of the plaintiff and defendants; and the case number) just as they are filled out on the complaint. Put Xs in the boxes next to the words "ENTRY OF DEFAULT" and "CLERK'S JUDGMENT." Then fill in the following items.

Item 1a: Enter the date you filed the complaint. This should be stamped in the upper right corner of your file-stamped copy of the complaint.

Item 1b: Type your name, because you're the plaintiff who filed the complaint.

Item 1c: Put an X in the box and type in the names of all the defendants against whom you are having the defaults entered.

Item 1d: Leave this box blank.

Item 1e: Put an X in Box e. This tells the clerk to enter Judgment for Possession of the property. If you used the optional procedure in Chapter 6, "Service on Unknown Occupants," by which a sheriff, marshal, or registered process server served a Prejudgment Claim of Right to Possession on unnamed occupants, also check Box (1). Leave Boxes (2) and (3) blank.

Items 2a–2f: Because you're asking only for possession of the property at this point, don't fill in any dollar amounts. Just type "possession only" in the "Amount" and "Balance" columns of 2a (Demand of Complaint), and enter 0 on other lines.

Item 2g: Type the daily rental value, listed in Item 13 of the Complaint, in the space with the dollar sign in front of it. Then, enter the date you put in Box 19g of the Complaint.

EXAMPLE 1: May Li's $900 June rent was due on June 1. On June 7, you served her a Three-Day Notice to Pay Rent or Quit, which demanded the rent for the entire month. Monthly rent of $900 is equivalent to $30 per day. List this amount in Item 2g of the Request for Entry of Default form. Then, since the last day of the rental period for which you demanded the $900 rent was June 30, type in the next day, July 1. That is the date the prorated daily "damages" begin, at $30 per day, and it should be listed in Complaint Item 19g and Item 2g of the Request for Entry of Default form.

EXAMPLE 2: You terminated Mortimer's month-to-month tenancy by serving a 30-day notice on September 10. The 30th day after this is October 9. The day after that, October 10, is the day you are entitled to prorated daily rent. That date should be listed in Item 2g of the Request for Entry of Default form and in Complaint Item 19g. Since Mortimer's monthly rent was $1,750, the dollar figure is $1,750 ÷ 30, or $58.33 per day. That amount should be listed here (Item 2g) as well as in Complaint Item 13.

Item 3: Put an "X" in this box to indicate the case is an unlawful detainer proceeding.

Enter the date you'll be filing the default papers with the court and type in your name opposite the place for signature. Now turn to Page 2.

CIV-100

ATTORNEY OR PARTY WITHOUT ATTORNEY:	STATE BAR NO:	FOR COURT USE ONLY
NAME: Lenny D. Landlord		
FIRM NAME:		
STREET ADDRESS: 12345 Angeleno Street		
CITY: Los Angeles STATE: CA ZIP CODE: 90028		
TELEPHONE NO.: 231-555-6789 FAX NO.:		
E-MAIL ADDRESS: LDLXX321ispofchoice.com		
ATTORNEY FOR (name): Plaintiff in pro per		

SUPERIOR COURT OF CALIFORNIA, COUNTY OF LOS ANGELES
STREET ADDRESS: 111 North Hill Street
MAILING ADDRESS:
CITY AND ZIP CODE: Los Angeles, California 90012
BRANCH NAME:

Plaintiff/Petitioner: Lenny D. Landlord
Defendant/Respondent: Terence D. Tenant, et al.

REQUEST FOR [x] **Entry of Default** [x] **Clerk's Judgment**	CASE NUMBER:
(Application) [ ] **Court Judgment**	A-12345-B (as assigned by Court)

Not for use in actions under the Fair Debt Buying Practices Act (Civ. Code, § 1788.50 et seq.) *(see CIV-105)*

1. TO THE CLERK: On the complaint or cross-complaint filed
   a. on *(date):* April 11, 20XX
   b. by *(name):* Lenny D. Landlord
   c. [x] Enter default of defendant *(names):*
      Terence D. Tenant, Tillie D. Tenant

> Check this box if you served the Prejudgment Claim of Right to Possession with the Summons

   d. [ ] I request a court judgment under Code of Civil Procedure sections 585(b), 585(c), 989, etc., against defendant *(names):*

      (Testimony required. Apply to the clerk for a hearing date, unless the court will enter a judgment on an affidavit under Code Civ. Proc., § 585(d).)
   e. [x] Enter clerk's judgment
      (1) [x] for restitution of the premises only and issue a writ of execution on the judgment. Code of Civil Procedure section 1174(c) does not apply. (Code Civ. Proc., § 1169.)
          [x] Include in the judgment all tenants, subtenants, named claimants, and other occupants of the premises. The *Prejudgment Claim of Right to Possession* was served in compliance with Code of Civil Procedure section 415.46.
      (2) [ ] under Code of Civil Procedure section 585(a). *(Complete the declaration under Code Civ. Proc., § 585.5 on the reverse (item 5).)*
      (3) [ ] for default previously entered on *(date):*

2. **Judgment to be entered.**

	Amount	Credits acknowledged	Balance
a. Demand of complaint	$ Possession only	$	$ Possession only
b. Statement of damages*			
(1) Special	$ 0.00	$	$ 0.00
(2) General	$ 0.00	$	$ 0.00
c. Interest	$ 0.00	$	$ 0.00
d. Costs *(see reverse)*	$ 0.00	$	$ 0.00
e. Attorney fees	$ 0.00	$	$ 0.00
f. **TOTALS**	$ 0.00	$	$ 0.00

   g. **Daily damages** were demanded in complaint at the rate of: $ 56.65   per day beginning *(date):* May 1, 20xx
   (* Personal injury or wrongful death actions; Code Civ. Proc., § 425.11.)

3. [x] *(Check if filed in an unlawful detainer case.)* **Legal document assistant or unlawful detainer assistant** information is on the reverse *(complete item 4).*

Date: April 27, 20xx

Lenny D. Landlord
(TYPE OR PRINT NAME)

▶ *Lenny D. Landlord*
(SIGNATURE OF PLAINTIFF OR ATTORNEY FOR PLAINTIFF)

FOR COURT USE ONLY	(1) [ ] Default entered as requested on *(date):*
	(2) [ ] Default NOT entered as requested *(state reason):*

Clerk, by _____, Deputy   Page 1 of 2

Form Adopted for Mandatory Use
Judicial Council of California CIV-100
[Rev. January 1, 2020]

REQUEST FOR ENTRY OF DEFAULT
(Application to Enter Default)

Code of Civil Procedure, §§ 585–587, 1169
www.courts.ca.gov

CIV-100

Plaintiff/Petitioner: Lenny D. Landlord Defendant/Respondent: Terence D. Tenant, et al.	CASE NUMBER: A-12345-B (as assigned by Court)

4. **Legal document assistant or unlawful detainer assistant (Bus. & Prof. Code, § 6400 et seq.).** A legal document assistant or unlawful detainer assistant ☐ did ☒ did **not** or compensation give advice or assistance with this form. If declarant has received **any** help or advice for pay from a legal document assistant or unlawful detainer assistant, state:

    a. Assistant's name: c. Telephone no.:

    b. Street address, city, and zip code: d. County of registration:

                                                       e. Registration no.:

                                                       f. Expires on *(date):*

5. ☒ **Declaration under Code Civ. Proc., § 585.5** *(for entry of default under Code Civ. Proc., § 585(a)).* This action

    a. ☐ is ☒ is not   on a contract or installment sale for goods or services subject to Civ. Code, § 1801 et seq. (Unruh Act).

    b. ☐ is ☒ is not   on a conditional sales contract subject to Civ. Code, § 2981 et seq. (Rees-Levering Motor Vehicle Sales and Finance Act).

    c. ☐ is ☒ is not   on an obligation for goods, services, loans, or extensions of credit subject to Code Civ. Proc., § 395(b).

6. **Declaration of mailing (Code Civ. Proc., § 587).** A copy of this *Request for Entry of Default* was

    a. ☐ **not mailed** to the following defendants, whose addresses are unknown to plaintiff or plaintiff's attorney *(names):*

    b. ☒ **mailed** first-class, postage prepaid, in a sealed envelope addressed to each defendant's attorney of record or, if none, to each defendant's last known address as follows:

       (1) Mailed on *(date):* April 27, 20xx   (2) To *(specify names and addresses shown on the envelopes):* Terence D. Tenant, 3815 Gower Canyon Ave., Apt. 3, Los Angeles, CA 90028 (See attached for additional defendants)

I declare under penalty of perjury under the laws of the State of California that the foregoing items 4, 5, and 6 are true and correct.

Date: April 27, 20xx

Lenny D. Landlord	▶ *Lenny D. Landlord*
(TYPE OR PRINT NAME)	(SIGNATURE OF DECLARANT)

7. **Memorandum of costs** *(required if money judgment requested).* Costs and disbursements are as follows (Code Civ. Proc., § 1033.5):

    a. Clerk's filing fees .... $

    b. Process server's fees .... $

    c. Other *(specify):* $

    d. $

    e. **TOTAL** .... $

    f. ☐ Costs and disbursements are waived.

    g. I am the attorney, agent, or party who claims these costs. To the best of my knowledge and belief this memorandum of costs is correct and these costs were necessarily incurred in this case.

I declare under penalty of perjury under the laws of the State of California that the foregoing is true and correct.

Date:

(TYPE OR PRINT NAME)	▶ (SIGNATURE OF DECLARANT)

8. **Declaration of nonmilitary status** *(required for a judgment).* No defendant named in item 1c of the application is in the military service as that term is defined by either the Servicemembers Civil Relief Act, 50 U.S.C. App. § 3911(2), or California Military and Veterans Code sections 400 and 402(f).

I declare under penalty of perjury under the laws of the State of California that the foregoing is true and correct.

Date: April 27, 20xx

Lenny D. Landlord	▶ *Lenny D. Landlord*
(TYPE OR PRINT NAME)	(SIGNATURE OF DECLARANT)

CIV-100 [Rev. January 1, 2020]   **REQUEST FOR ENTRY OF DEFAULT**   Page 2 of 2
                                               (Application to Enter Default)

Caption: Type the names of the plaintiff and defendant, just as you did on the second page of the Proof of Service of Summons. (See "Filing Your Complaint and Getting Summonses Issued" in Chapter 6.)

Item 4: As we saw when preparing the complaint ("Preparing the Complaint," Item 19, in Chapter 6), you must indicate if an "unlawful detainer assistant" or a "legal document preparer" (a bonded paralegal) advised or assisted you. Assuming you are using this book on your own, put an "X" in the "did not" box. If you are paying a legal document or unlawful detainer assistant to help with the Request for Entry of Default, then you would put an "X" in the "did" box and fill in the remainder of Item 4 (for advice, see the instructions for Item 19 of the complaint). Otherwise, do not complete the rest of Item 4.

Item 5: Put an X next to Item 5 and check the boxes next to the words "is not" in Items a, b, and c. (This is a general-purpose form, and none of these items applies to unlawful detainer lawsuits. Even so, many clerks insist that these items be checked, and doing so is easier than arguing.)

Item 6: Check Box 6b. (You don't check Box 6a because obviously you know the tenant's most recent address—at your property.) Then, type the date you'll mail the defendants their copies, and their mailing address, under Headings (1) and (2). Below that, again type in the date you'll be filing the papers, and your name opposite the place for signature. Make sure that the mailing date is the same or before the date you sign the form.

If you cannot fit all the names and addresses in Box (b)(2), you will need to attach an extra page. If so, type "See attachment for additional defendants," then fill in Attachment 1 with the names and addresses. A sample of Attachment 1 is below.

 FORM

A blank copy of Attachment to the Request for Entry of Default (Judicial Council Form MC-025) can be downloaded from the Nolo Website. (See the appendix for the link to the forms in this book and other information on using the forms.)

Item 7: Leave this entire item blank. You'll list your court costs when you file for your money judgment after the tenant is evicted.

Item 8: If none of the defendants against whom you're taking a default judgment is on active duty in the U.S. Armed Forces (Army, Navy, Marines, Air Force, and Coast Guard), or is a member of the Public Health Service or National Oceanic and Atmospheric Administration, or is in the National Guard and called to active service for more than a month, check the box. Then, simply enter the date you'll file the papers and type your name opposite the place for you to sign.

SEE AN EXPERT

Special rules for the military. If a defendant, or spouse of a defendant, is on active duty in the military, that servicemember or spouse may obtain a 90-day stay on written request, and the court has discretion to grant additional stays. Such a servicemember is also entitled to set aside a default and/or default judgment within 60, and in some cases 90, days. Situations like this are fairly complicated and beyond the scope of this book. See an attorney if a person you're suing is in the military and refuses to leave after being served with the summons and complaint. (Servicemembers' Civil Relief Act 50 U.S.C. App. §§ 3931 and following.) Some landlords take the expedient shortcut of complaining to their military tenant's commanding officer about nonpayment of rent or other problems. This often works a lot faster than the legal process.

Make two copies of the completed (but unsigned) form. Don't sign the Request for Entry of Default until you have mailed a copy to the defendant. (See below.)

MC-025

SHORT TITLE:	CASE NUMBER:
Landlord v. Tenant	

ATTACHMENT *(Number):* _____

(This Attachment may be used with any Judicial Council form.)

6. Declaration of Mailing (C.C.P. §587) -- cont'd

A copy of this Request for Entry of Default was mailed first class, postage prepaid, in a sealed envelope address to each defendant's attorney of record or, if none, to each defendant's last known address, mailed on April 27, 20xx, addressed as follows:

Tillie D. Tenant
3815 Gower Canyon Ave., Apt. 3
Los Angeles, CA 90028

(If the item that this Attachment concerns is made under penalty of perjury, all statements in this Attachment are made under penalty of perjury.)

Page ___1___ of ___1___

(Add pages as required)

Form Approved for Optional Use

ATTACHMENT

www.courtinfo.ca.gov

Preparing the Request for Dismissal of the Doe Defendants

Many courts require you to dismiss the fictitious or Doe defendants before you can obtain a default. Follow these instructions to do so.

FORM

A blank copy of the Request for Dismissal (Judicial Council Form CIV-110) is available for downloading from the Nolo website. (See the appendix for the link to the forms in this book and other information on using the forms.)

To fill out the form, begin by supplying the information on the top left caption boxes just as you have done in other forms. Note that the form has separated the fields for the city, state, and zip code. Don't forget to put in the case number.

Box 1: Check the following: (a)(2) [Without prejudice], (b)(1) [Complaint], and (b)(6) [Other]. In the field that says "Other (*specify*)," type "Does 1–5 ONLY."

Box 2: Check "did not."

Date and Sign: After Box 2, enter the date and your name. Check the box "Party without Attorney." Check the box "Plaintiff/Petitioner" under your signature line. Then print and sign. Do not fill out anything else. The form is finished and must be submitted as part of the default package.

Preparing the Judgment Issued by the Clerk for Possession of the Premises

The judgment form provides the legal basis for issuance of a Writ of Possession, the document authorizing the sheriff or marshal to evict the tenant. You will present it to the clerk with the Request for Entry of Default.

FORM

A blank copy of the Judgment—Unlawful Detainer (Judicial Council form UD-110) can be downloaded from the Nolo website. (See the appendix for the link to the forms in this book, and other information.)

As with the summons, complaint, and Request for Entry of Judgment, there is a statewide form for a judgment in an unlawful detainer case. This Judgment—Unlawful Detainer form can be used in various situations. In the instructions below, we show you how to fill it out as a default judgment issued by the clerk, for possession of the property. (As we'll see below, this form is filled out in a different way to obtain a default judgment for monetary sums, after the tenant has vacated the property. This form can also be used in contested cases; see "Responding to the Answer" and "Preparing for Trial" in Chapter 8.)

This Judgment—Unlawful Detainer form is not difficult to fill out. Enter the names and addresses of the landlord and tenant, the court name and address, and the case number as you have done on previous forms. (There's also an optional line where you can enter your email address. We advise that you not do so. The court will not communicate with you via email, and because this document is a public record, anyone who looks at it will have your address. Also, you can omit your fax number.) In the box containing the words "JUDGMENT—UNLAWFUL DETAINER," put an X in the boxes next to the words "By Clerk," "By Default," and "Possession Only."

Item 1: Put an X in Item 1 next to the words "BY DEFAULT," and also in Box 1d next to the words "Clerk's Judgment."

UD-110

ATTORNEY OR PARTY WITHOUT ATTORNEY *(Name, state bar number, and address)*: **LENNY D. LANDLORD** 1234 Angeleno Street Los Angeles, CA 90010 TELEPHONE NO.: 213-555-6789 FAX NO. *(Optional)*: 213-555-5678 E-MAIL ADDRESS *(Optional)*: ATTORNEY FOR *(Name)*: Plaintiff in Pro Per	FOR COURT USE ONLY

SUPERIOR COURT OF CALIFORNIA, COUNTY OF LOS ANGELES
STREET ADDRESS: 111 North Hill Street
MAILING ADDRESS: Same
CITY AND ZIP CODE: Los Angeles, CA 90012
BRANCH NAME:

PLAINTIFF: LENNY D. LANDLORD

DEFENDANT: TERRENCE D. TENANT, TILLIE D. TENANT

JUDGMENT—UNLAWFUL DETAINER	CASE NUMBER:
[X] **By Clerk** [X] **By Default** [ ] **After Court Trial** [ ] **By Court** [X] **Possession Only** [ ] **Defendant Did Not** **Appear at Trial**	A-12345-B

JUDGMENT

1. [X] **BY DEFAULT**
   a. Defendant was properly served with a copy of the summons and complaint.
   b. Defendant failed to answer the complaint or appear and defend the action within the time allowed by law.
   c. Defendant's default was entered by the clerk upon plaintiff's application.
   d. [X] **Clerk's Judgment** (Code Civ. Proc., § 1169). For possession only of the premises described on page 2 (item 4).
   e. [ ] **Court Judgment** (Code Civ. Proc., § 585(b)). The court considered
      (1) [ ] plaintiff's testimony and other evidence.
      (2) [ ] plaintiff's or others' written declaration and evidence (Code Civ. Proc., § 585(d)).

2. [ ] **AFTER COURT TRIAL.** The jury was waived. The court considered the evidence.
   a. The case was tried on *(date and time)*:

      before *(name of judicial officer)*:

   b. Appearances by:
      [ ] Plaintiff *(name each)*:   [ ] Plaintiff's attorney *(name each)*:
                                                             (1)
                                                             (2)

      [ ] Continued on *Attachment* 2b (form MC-025).

      [ ] Defendant *(name each)*:   [ ] Defendant's attorney *(name each)*:
                                                             (1)
                                                             (2)

      [ ] Continued on *Attachment* 2b (form MC-025).

   c. [ ] Defendant did not appear at trial. Defendant was properly served with notice of trial.

   d. [ ] A statement of decision (Code Civ. Proc., § 632) [ ] was not [ ] was   requested.

Page 1 of 2

PLAINTIFF: LENNY LANDLORD	CASE NUMBER:
DEFENDANT: TERRENCE D. TENANT, ET AL.	A-12345-B

JUDGMENT IS ENTERED AS FOLLOWS BY: ☐ THE COURT ☒ THE CLERK

3. **Parties.** Judgment is

   a. ☒ for plaintiff *(name each):* Lenny Landlord

   and against defendant *(name each):* Terrence D. Tenant, Tillie D. Tenant

   ☐ Continued on *Attachment* 3a (form MC-025).

   b. ☐ for defendant *(name each):*

4. ☒ Plaintiff ☐ Defendant is entitled to possession of the premises located at *(street address, apartment, city, and county):*
   3815 Gower Canyon Ave, Apt. 3, Los Angeles, CA 90028 (Los Angeles County)

5. ☐ Judgment applies to all occupants of the premises including tenants, subtenants if any, and named claimants if any (Code Civ. Proc., §§ 715.010, 1169, and 1174.3).

   > check box 5 only if you had a Prejudgment Claim of Right of Possession served (see Chapter 6); otherwise, ignore it

6. **Amount and terms of judgment**

   a. ☐ Defendant named in item 3a above must pay plaintiff on the complaint:

(1) ☐	Past-due rent	$	
(2) ☐	Holdover damages	$	
(3) ☐	Attorney fees	$	
(4) ☐	Costs	$	
(5) ☐	Other *(specify):*	$	
(6)	**TOTAL JUDGMENT**	$	

   b. ☐ Plaintiff is to receive nothing from defendant named in item 3b.
   ☐ Defendant named in item 3b is to recover costs: $
   ☐ and attorney fees: $.

   c. ☐ The rental agreement is canceled. ☐ The lease is forfeited.

7. ☐ **Conditional judgment.** Plaintiff has breached the agreement to provide habitable premises to defendant as stated in *Judgment—Unlawful Detainer Attachment* (form UD–110S), which is attached.

8. ☐ **Other** *(specify):*

   ☐ Continued on *Attachment* 8 (form MC-025).

Date: _____ ☐ _____
                                             JUDICIAL OFFICER

Date: _____ ☐ Clerk, by _____ , Deputy

(SEAL)	**CLERK'S CERTIFICATE** *(Optional)*
	I certify that this is a true copy of the original judgment on file in the court.
	Date:
	Clerk, by _____ , Deputy

UD-110 [New January 1, 2003]   **JUDGMENT—UNLAWFUL DETAINER**   Page 2 of 2

Item 2: Leave this part blank and proceed to Page 2 of the form. At the top of Page 2, fill in the names, in capitals, of the plaintiff (you), the first-named defendant (followed by "ET AL." if there is more than one defendant), and the court case number. After the words "JUDGMENT IS ENTERED AS FOLLOWS BY:" put an X in the box following the words "THE CLERK."

Item 3: Put an X in Box 3a and type, in upper and lower case, the names of the plaintiff(s) and the names of all defendants against whom you're obtaining the clerk's default judgment for possession. Leave Box 3b blank.

Item 4: Put an X in the box next to the word "Plaintiff" (leave the box next to "Defendant" blank) and list the address of the property including street address, any apartment number, city, zip code, and county.

Item 5: If you used the optional procedure in Chapter 6 to have Prejudgment Claim of Right to Possession served on unnamed occupants by a sheriff, marshal, or registered process server, check this box. Otherwise, leave it blank.

Items 6–8: Leave all these boxes blank.

After you fill out the Judgment—Unlawful Detainer form, make one copy for your records and three for the court filing. You will file this with the court clerk as discussed below (see "Filing the Forms and Getting the Writ of Possession Issued").

Preparing the Writ of Possession

The next form you need is the Writ of Possession. (The name of the preprinted form you'll use is a Writ of Execution. It's a multipurpose one for use as a writ of "possession," ordering the sheriff or marshal to put you in possession of real property; or as a writ of "execution," which requests enforcement of a money judgment.) Like the summons, the Writ of Possession is "issued" by the court clerk, but you have to fill it out and give it to the clerk with the other default forms. (See below.) The clerk will issue the writ as soon as court files contain the Judgment for Possession. The original

and copies of the Writ of Possession are given to the sheriff or marshal, who then "executes" the judgment by evicting the tenants against whom you obtained the judgment. You will also need to prepare a Declaration Re: Daily Rental Value.

 FORM

A blank copy of the Writ of Execution for possession (Judicial Council form EJ-130) and an Application for Issuance of Writ of Execution and Declaration Re: Daily Rental Value can be downloaded from the Nolo website. (See the appendix for the link to the forms in this book, and other information on using the forms.)

On the Writ of Execution, the usual information goes in the big boxes at the top of the writ form—your name, address, phone number, the name and address of the court; the names of plaintiffs and defendants; and the case number. For the reasons previously explained, we suggest that you omit your email address, which is optional. Also put an X in the box next to the words "Original judgment Creditor" in the top large box and in the boxes next to the words "POSSESSION OF" and "Real Property" as shown. Also, check the box next to the words "Limited Civil Case." Fill out the rest of the writ according to these instructions.

Item 1: Type the name of the county in which the property is located. The sheriff or marshal of that county will perform the eviction.

Item 2: Nothing need be filled in here.

Item 3: Put an X in the box next to the words "original judgment creditor" and type your name and the names of any other plaintiffs. You are "judgment creditors" because you won the judgment.

Item 4: Type in the names of up to two defendants and list the residence address. If you got a judgment against more than two persons, check the box next to the words "additional judgment debtors on next page." List the other names and address in the space provided (Item 21) on Page 2 of the form.

EJ-130

ATTORNEY OR PARTY WITHOUT ATTORNEY: STATE BAR NO.:	FOR COURT USE ONLY
NAME: Lenny D. Landlord	
FIRM NAME:	
STREET ADDRESS: 12345 Angeleno Street	
CITY: Los Angeles STATE: CA ZIP CODE: 90028	
TELEPHONE NO.: 213-555-6789 FAX NO.:	
EMAIL ADDRESS: LDLXXX@ispofchoice.com	
ATTORNEY FOR (name): in pro per	
[ ] ATTORNEY FOR [x] ORIGINAL JUDGMENT CREDITOR [ ] ASSIGNEE OF RECORD	

SUPERIOR COURT OF CALIFORNIA, COUNTY OF LOS ANGELES
STREET ADDRESS: 111 N. Hill Street
MAILING ADDRESS:
CITY AND ZIP CODE: Los Angeles, CA 90012
BRANCH NAME:

PLAINTIFF/PETITIONER: Lenny D. Landlord	CASE NUMBER:
DEFENDANT/RESPONDENT: Terrence D. Tenant, et al.	A-12345-B

WRIT OF	[ ] EXECUTION (Money Judgment)		[x] Limited Civil Case (including Small Claims)
	[x] POSSESSION OF	[ ] Personal Property	[ ] Unlimited Civil Case (including Family and Probate)
	[ ] SALE	[x] Real Property	

1. **To the Sheriff or Marshal of the County of:** Los Angeles
   You are directed to enforce the judgment described below with daily interest and your costs as provided by law.
2. **To any registered process server:** You are authorized to serve this writ only in accordance with CCP 699.080 or CCP 715.040.
3. (Name): *Terrence D. Tenant and Tillie D. Tenant*
   is the [x] original judgment creditor [ ] assignee of record whose address is shown on this form above the court's name.

4. **Judgment debtor** (name, type of legal entity if not a natural person, and last known address):

   Terrance D. Tenant
   3815 Gower Canyon Ave., Apt. 3
   Los Angeles, CA 90028

   [ ] Additional judgment debtors on next page

5. **Judgment entered** on (date): 4/22/20xx
   (See type of judgment in item 22.)

6. [ ] Judgment renewed on (dates):

7. **Notice of sale** under this writ:
   a. [x] has not been requested.
   b. [ ] has been requested (see next page).
8. [ ] Joint debtor information on next page.

[SEAL]

9. [x] Writ of Possession/Writ of Sale information on next page.
10. [ ] This writ is issued on a sister-state judgment.
    —— For Items 11–17, see form MC-012 and form MC-013-INFO.
11. Total judgment (as entered or renewed) $ Possession only
12. Costs after judgment (CCP 685.090) $
13. Subtotal (add 11 and 12) $ _____ 0.00
14. Credits to principal (after credit to interest) $
15. Principal remaining due (subtract 14 from 13) $ _____ 0.00
16. Accrued interest remaining due per CCP 685.050(b) (not on GC 6103.5 fees) $
17. Fee for issuance of writ (per GC 70626(a)(I)) $
18. **Total amount due** (add 15, 16, and 17) $ _____ 0.00
19. **Levying officer:**
    a. Add daily interest from date of writ (at the legal rate on 15) (not on GC 6103.5 fees) . . . . $ 0.00
    b. Pay directly to court costs included in 11 and 17 (GC 6103.5, 68637; CCP 699.520(j)) . . . . $ 0.00
20. [ ] The amounts called for in items 11–19 are different for each debtor. These amounts are stated for each debtor on Attachment 20.

Date: _____   Clerk, by _____, Deputy

NOTICE TO PERSON SERVED: SEE PAGE 3 FOR IMPORTANT INFORMATION.

Page 1 of 3

Form Approved for Optional Use
Judicial Council of California
EJ-130 [Rev. September 1, 2020]

WRIT OF EXECUTION

Code of Civil Procedure, §§ 699.520, 712.010, 715.010
Government Code, § 6103.5
www.courts.ca.gov

EJ-130

Plaintiff/Petitioner: Lenny D. Landlord	CASE NUMBER:
Defendant/Respondent: Terrence D. Tenant, et al.	A-12345-B

21. [x] Additional judgment debtor(s) *(name, type of legal entity if not a natural person, and last known address):*

Tillie D. Tenant
3815 Gower Canyon Ave., Apt. 3
Los Angeles, CA 90028

22. The judgment is for *(check one):*

a. [ ] wages owed.
b. [ ] child support or spousal support.
c. [x] other.

23. [ ] Notice of sale has been requested by *(name and address):*

24. [ ] Joint debtor was declared bound by the judgment (CCP 989-994)

a. *on (date):*
b. name, type of legal entity if not a natural person, and last known address of joint debtor:

a. *on (date):*
b. name, type of legal entity if not a natural person, and last known address of joint debtor:

c. [ ] Additional costs against certain joint debtors are itemized: [ ] below [ ] on Attachment 24c.

25. [x] (Writ of Possession or Writ of Sale) **Judgment** was entered for the following:

a. [x] Possession of real property: The complaint was filed on *(date):* April 10, 20xx
   (Check (1) or (2). Check (3) if applicable. Complete (4) if (2) or (3) have been checked.)

   (1) [x] The *Prejudgment Claim of Right to Possession* was served in compliance with CCP 415.46. The judgment includes all tenants, subtenants, named claimants, and other occupants of the premises.

   (2) [ ] The *Prejudgment Claim of Right to Possession* was NOT served in compliance with CCP 415.46.

   (3) [ ] The unlawful detainer resulted from a foreclosure sale of a rental housing unit. (An occupant not named in the judgment may file a *Claim of Right to Possession* at any time up to and including the time the levying officer returns to effect eviction, regardless of whether a *Prejudgment Claim of Right to Possession* was served.) *(See CCP 415.46 and 1174.3(a)(2).)*

   (4) If the unlawful detainer resulted from a foreclosure (item 25a(3)), or if the *Prejudgment Claim of Right to Possession* was not served in compliance with CCP 415.46 (item 25a(2)), answer the following:

   (a) The daily rental value on the date the complaint was filed was $

   (b) The court will hear objections to enforcement of the judgment under CCP 1174.3 on the following dates *(specify):*

Item 25 continued on next page

EJ-130

Plaintiff/Petitioner: Lenny D. Landlord	CASE NUMBER:
Defendant/Respondent: Terrence D. Tenant, et al.	A-12345-B

25. b. ☐ Possession of personal property.

☐ If delivery cannot be had, then for the value *(itemize in 25e)* specified in the judgment or supplemental order.

c. ☐ Sale of personal property.

d. ☐ Sale of real property.

e. The property is described ☒ below ☐ on Attachment 25e.
3815 Gower Canyon Ave., Apt. 3, Los Angeles, CA 90028

NOTICE TO PERSON SERVED

WRIT OF EXECUTION OR SALE. Your rights and duties are indicated on the accompanying *Notice of Levy* (form EJ-150).

WRIT OF POSSESSION OF PERSONAL PROPERTY. If the levying officer is not able to take custody of the property, the levying officer will demand that you turn over the property. If custody is not obtained following demand, the judgment may be enforced as a money judgment for the value of the property specified in the judgment or in a supplemental order.

WRIT OF POSSESSION OF REAL PROPERTY. If the premises are not vacated within five days after the date of service on the occupant or, if service is by posting, within five days after service on you, the levying officer will remove the occupants from the real property and place the judgment creditor in possession of the property. Except for a mobile home, personal property remaining on the premises will be sold or otherwise disposed of in accordance with CCP 1174 unless you or the owner of the property pays the judgment creditor the reasonable cost of storage and takes possession of the personal property not later than 15 days after the time the judgment creditor takes possession of the premises.

EXCEPTION IF RENTAL HOUSING UNIT WAS FORECLOSED. If the residential property that you are renting was sold in a foreclosure, you have additional time before you must vacate the premises. If you have a lease for a fixed term, such as for a year, you may remain in the property until the term is up. If you have a periodic lease or tenancy, such as from month-to-month, you may remain in the property for 90 days after receiving a notice to quit. A blank form *Claim of Right to Possession and Notice of Hearing* (form CP10) accompanies this writ. You may claim your right to remain on the property by filling it out and giving it to the sheriff or levying officer.

EXCEPTION IF YOU WERE NOT SERVED WITH A FORM CALLED PREJUDGMENT CLAIM OF RIGHT TO POSSESSION. If you were not named in the judgment for possession and you occupied the premises on the date on which the unlawful detainer case was filed, you may object to the enforcement of the judgment against you. You must complete the form *Claim of Right to Possession and Notice of Hearing* (form CP10) and give it to the sheriff or levying officer. A blank form accompanies this writ. You have this right whether or not the property you are renting was sold in a foreclosure.

WRIT OF EXECUTION

If you have five or more judgment debtors, use the first box in Item 21 for the third debtor, then type the words, "See Attachment 21 for additional judgment debtors" in the second box in Item 21. To prepare your attachment, follow these steps:

1. Start with either the MC-025 Judicial Council Form or a piece of blank pleading paper, which is available for downloading on the Nolo website. You may also find blank pleading paper in your business software. If using the MC-025 form or on the blank pleading paper, put the short case name (such as, SMITH V. JONES) in capitals at the top left (SHORT TITLE) and the court case number at the top right.

2. After the word "Attachment" add the number 21.

3. Below that line, list the names and addresses (the premises address) for each occupant against whom you have a judgment.

Item 5: Fill in the date the judgment was entered by the court. If nothing goes wrong, this should be the date you take the papers down to the courthouse. However, it might be a different date, depending on the court's processing times.

Item 6: Leave this blank— nothing needs to be filled in here.

Item 7: Only Box a, next to the words "has not been requested," should be checked.

Item 8: Leave Box 8 blank—it does not apply here.

Item 9: Put an X in Box 9. On Page 2 of the form, at Item 25, check Boxes 25 and 25a and enter the date the complaint was filed. Then, if you used the optional procedure in Chapter 6 ("Service on Unknown Occupants"), by which a sheriff, marshal, or registered process server served a Prejudgment Claim of Right to Possession on unnamed occupants, put an X in Box (1). Otherwise, put an X in Box (2) and list the daily rental value of the property in Item 25a(4)(a)— the same as in Item 11 of the complaint. For

Item 25a(4)(b), call the court clerk for a future date (two to three weeks away), in case a person not named in the writ filed a postjudgment Claim of Right to Possession, and list that date in the space provided. Under e, list the complete street address, including apartment number if any, city, and county of the property.

Items 10–20: These items apply only when you get a money judgment, and should not be filled in on this writ, which reflects only a Judgment for Possession of the property. (Later, after you have a default hearing before a judge and get a money judgment, you will fill out another writ (of execution) and fill in Items 10–20—see "Getting a Money Judgment for Rent and Costs," below.) Instead, simply type the words "POSSESSION ONLY" next to Item 11. Type "0.00" (zeros) next to Items 18 and 19a. Put "0.00" in Item 19b because it always applies, even when collecting the money part of the judgment, which we discuss in Chapter 9.

You should make one copy of the Writ of Possession for your own records and three copies per defendant to give to the sheriff or marshal.

Preparing the Declaration Re: Daily Rental Value

In order to obtain a writ of possession, you have to provide a declaration under penalty of perjury concerning the daily rental value, the amount that you pleaded in the complaint. To fill out the declaration, use the Declaration (Judicial Council form MC-030). A sample declaration is below.

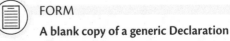

FORM

A blank copy of a generic Declaration (Judicial Council Form MC-030) can be downloaded from the Nolo website. (See the appendix for the link to the forms and other information on using them.)

MC-030

ATTORNEY OR PARTY WITHOUT ATTORNEY *(Name, State Bar number, and address):*

LENNY D. LANDLORD
1234 Angeleno Street
Los Angeles, CA 90010

TELEPHONE NO.: 213-555-6789   FAX NO. *(Optional):*
E-MAIL ADDRESS *(Optional):*
ATTORNEY FOR *(Name):* Lenny D. Landlord in pro per

FOR COURT USE ONLY

SUPERIOR COURT OF CALIFORNIA, COUNTY OF   LOS ANGELES
STREET ADDRESS: 111 North Hill Street
MAILING ADDRESS:
CITY AND ZIP CODE: Los Angeles, CA 90012
BRANCH NAME:

PLAINTIFF/PETITIONER: Lenny D. Landlord
DEFENDANT/RESPONDENT: Terence D. Tenant, et al

DECLARATION

CASE NUMBER:
A-12345-B

I, Lenny D. Landlord, declare that:

1. I am the owner of the premises involved in the above-entitled matter.

2. I hereby apply to this court for the issuance of a writ of execution for restitution of possession for the property described in Paragraph 24(a) on the Writ of Execution.

3. The daily rental value of the premises at the time of the filing of the Unlawful Detainer was $56.65 per day, which is the same amount stated in Paragraph 25(a) of the Writ of Execution.

4. This declaration has been executed at Los Angeles, California, on the date indicated below.

I declare under penalty of perjury under the laws of the State of California that the foregoing is true and correct.

Date: 2/22xx

Lenny D. Landlord
(TYPE OR PRINT NAME)

Lenny D. Landlord
(SIGNATURE OF DECLARANT)

☐ Attorney for [X] Plaintiff ☐ Petitioner ☐ Defendant
☐ Respondent ☐ Other *(Specify):*

MC-030

ATTORNEY OR PARTY WITHOUT ATTORNEY *(Name, State Bar number, and address):*	FOR COURT USE ONLY
LENNY D. LANDLORD 1234 Angeleno Street Los Angeles, CA 90010 TELEPHONE NO.: 213-555-6789 FAX NO. *(Optional):* E-MAIL ADDRESS *(Optional):* ATTORNEY FOR *(Name):* Lenny D. Landlord in Pro Per	

SUPERIOR COURT OF CALIFORNIA, COUNTY OF   LOS ANGELES
STREET ADDRESS: 111 North Hill Street
MAILING ADDRESS:
CITY AND ZIP CODE: Los Angeles, CA 90012
BRANCH NAME:

PLAINTIFF/PETITIONER: Lenny D. Landlord

DEFENDANT/RESPONDENT: Terence D. Tenant

DECLARATION	CASE NUMBER: A-12345-B

I, Lenny D. Landlord, declare:

1. I make this declaration of my own personal knowledge, and if called to testify, could testify competently thereto.

2. I am the plaintiff and custodian of records for the plaintiff and manage the premises that are the subject of this unlawful detainer action. Due and reasonable diligence has been made to locate the original lease; however, it cannot be located at this time. I request that this court accept the attached copy, which is a true and correct copy of the original lease.

3. This declaration is executed at Los Angeles, California as of the date indicated below.

I declare under penalty of perjury under the laws of the State of California that the foregoing is true and correct.

Date: 2/22xx

Lenny D. Landlord
_____
(TYPE OR PRINT NAME)

Lenny D. Landlord
_____
(SIGNATURE OF DECLARANT)

☐ Attorney for ☒ Plaintiff ☐ Petitioner ☐ Defendant
☐ Respondent ☐ Other *(Specify):*

DECLARATION

Follow these steps to complete your declaration.

Caption: Enter your name and address, telephone number, and your capacity ("Plaintiff in pro per") at the top of the form. Next, fill in the name and location of the court and the case number.

Body: In the body of the declaration, type the following, entering the correct daily rental value (it must be identical to the amount stated in the complaint), and the appropriate place of signing:

"I, [*owner's name*], declare that:

1. I am the owner of the premises involved in the above-entitled matter.

2. I hereby apply to this court for the issuance of a writ of execution for restitution of possession for the property described in Paragraph 24(a) on the Writ of Execution.

3. The daily rental value of the premises at the time of the filing of the Unlawful Detainer was $ [*daily rental value*] per day, which is the same amount stated in Paragraph 25(a) of the Writ of Execution.

4. This declaration has been executed at [*city or county name*], California, on the date indicated below."

Date and sign: Date and sign the declaration, and check the box as to your capacity (Plaintiff). You do not have to notarize this form.

Filing the Forms and Getting the Writ of Possession Issued

On the day after the response period ends, after you have made sure that the tenant did not file an answer (see the first section in this chapter), mail a copy of the Request for Entry of Default to the tenant(s) at the property's street address. Then sign your name on the three places on the original. (Technically, if you sign this form before you mail the copy to the tenant(s), you will be committing perjury, because in one of the places on the form you state under penalty of perjury that a copy was mailed—before you signed.)

Then take the following forms to the courthouse:

- the original summons for each defendant (if not previously filed), stapled to the Proof of Service of Summons completed and signed by the process server (see Chapter 6)

- the original plus at least two copies of the Request for Entry of Default

- the original plus three copies of the Judgment for Possession (this is the Judgment—Unlawful Detainer form)

- the original plus three copies per defendant of the Writ of Possession (this is the Writ of Execution form)

- the original or a copy of the rental agreement or lease. Not all courts require you to submit exhibits for a clerk's default, but some do. If you have any doubts, it's better to submit a complete package.

- a declaration re: lost original if you submit a copy of the lease (see the sample above). Again, not all courts require a declaration before they will accept a copy, but none prohibit it, either. At worst, the clerk will return the form when you try to file it, and

- a copy of the termination notices with signed proofs of service. While you should have attached the notices and proofs of service to the complaint, due to filing and scanning backlogs, the clerk may not have immediate access to the paper files or scanned documents in the current electronic file. Including these copies with the package makes it more convenient for the clerk—and that can only help your situation.

Give the court clerk the originals and copies of all the forms you've prepared. Tell the clerk that you're returning completed summonses in an unlawful detainer case and that you want him or her to:

- enter a default Judgment for Possession of the premises, and

- issue a Writ of Possession.

NAME, ADDRESS, AND TELEPHONE NUMBER OF ATTORNEY OR PARTY WITHOUT ATTORNEY	STATE BAR NUMBER	*Reserved for Clerk's File Stamp*
Lenny D. Landlord 12345 Angeleno Street Los Angeles, CA 90028 Tel: 213-555-6789		

ATTORNEY FOR (Name): in Pro Per

SUPERIOR COURT OF CALIFORNIA, COUNTY OF LOS ANGELES

COURTHOUSE ADDRESS:

111 North Hill Street, Los Angeles, CA 90012

PLAINTIFF:

Lenny D. Landlord

DEFENDANT:

Terence D. Tenant, Tillie D. Tenant

APPLICATION FOR ISSUANCE OF **WRIT OF EXECUTION, POSSESSION OR SALE**	CASE NUMBER: A-12345-B

I, Lenny D. Landlord _____ declare under penalty of perjury under the laws of the State of California:

1. I am the Plaintiff _____ in the above-entitled action.

2. The following ☑Judgment / ☐Order was made and entered on April 22, 20xx _____.
   ☐Judgment was renewed on _____.

3. Judgment/Order as entered/renewed provides as follows:

   Judgment Creditor: (name and address)

   Lenny D. Landlord
   1234 Angeleno St.
   Los Angeles, CA 90028

   Judgment Debtor: (name and address)

   Terence D. Tenant   Tillie D. Tenant
   3815 Gower Canyon Ave., Apt. 3   3815 Gower Canyon Ave., Apt. 3
   Los Angeles, CA 90028   Los Angeles, CA 90028

   Amount of Order and/or Description of Property:
   Possession only: residential rental property

4. ☑ (Unlawful Detainer Proceedings Only) The daily rental value of the property as of the date the complaint was filed is $ 56.65 _____.

5. ☑ This is an unlawful detainer judgment, and a Prejudgment Claim of Right to Possession was served on the occupant(s) pursuant to Code of Civil Procedure section 415.46. Pursuant to Code of Civil Procedure sections 715.010 and 1174.3, this writ applies to all tenants; subtenants, if any; named claimants, if any; and any other occupants of the premises.

6. ☐ This is a Family Law Judgment/Order entitled to priority under Code of Civil Procedure section 699.510.

7. This writ is to be issued to: ☑ Los Angeles County   ☐ Other (Specify):_____

Case Title:	Case Number:
Landlord v. Tenant	A-12345-B

INSTRUCTIONS

Fill in date below showing total of amount ordered (do not show separate amounts for principal, fees and pre-judgment costs and interest), amount actually paid, date paid and whether applied to order and/or to accrued interest if accrued interest is claimed, and balance due. Due date of costs of enforcement is the date they were added to the judgment pursuant to a cost bill after judgment, not date incurred.

Failure to claim interest shall be deemed a waiver thereof for the purpose of this writ only.

ON INSTALLMENT ORDERS: EACH PAYMENT ORDERED AND DUE DATE MUST BE STATED SEPARATELY.
PERSON TO WHOM AMOUNT IS ORDERED PAID MUST SIGN DECLARATION.

TOTAL ORDERED PAID		ACTUALLY PAID			BALANCE DUE	
DUE DATE	AMOUNT	DATE PAID	ON ORDER	ON ACCRUED INTEREST	ON ORDER	ON ACCRUED INTEREST
N/A		N/A			N/A	

There is actually remaining due on said order the sum of $_____ plus $_____ accrued costs plus
$_____ accrued interest plus $_____ interest per day accruing from date of this application to date of
writ, for which sum it is prayed that a writ of possession/sale/execution issue in favor of
Lenny D. Landlord
_____
(Judgment Creditor)

and against Terence D. Tenant, Tillie D. Tenant
_____
(Judgment Debtor)

to the County of Los Angeles
_____

I declare under penalty of perjury under the laws of the State of California that the foregoing is true and correct.

Executed on 4/22/20xx
_____

_____
(Signature)

**APPLICATION FOR ISSUANCE OF
WRIT OF EXECUTION, POSSESSION OR SALE**

Code Civ. Proc., § 712.010

The clerk will file the originals of the summonses, the Proofs of Service of the Summons, the Request for Entry of Default, and the Judgment, but will hand you back the original writ, stamped. The clerk should also file-stamp and hand back to you any copies you have offered for stamping. You will have to pay a $25 fee for issuance of the writ.

In Los Angeles and Orange Counties, you must fill out a special "local" form before the clerk will issue you a Writ of Possession. The local form substitutes for the Declaration Re: Daily Rental Value in this case.

The Los Angeles form is called an Application for Issuance of Writ of Execution, Possession or Sale, and is filled out as shown above.

 FORM

A blank copy of the Los Angeles writ form can be downloaded from the Nolo website. (See the appendix for the link to the forms in this book, and other information on using the forms.) This Los Angeles County form can also be downloaded at www.lacourt. org/forms/all.

In Los Angeles and other counties, clerks won't enter default judgments over the counter. Instead, you must either come back several days later for your default judgment and writ, or leave a self-addressed, stamped envelope with your papers and the $25 fee so the clerk can send it to you.

The Orange County form (Application for Writ of Possession—Unlawful Detainer, Number L-1051) is simple and needs no instructions from us. You can download the form from the Orange County website at www.occourts.org/formslocal/ l1051.pdf. Other counties may also require you to use their own, similar forms—be sure to call the clerk and check it out before heading to the courthouse.

Having the Marshal or Sheriff Evict

Once the court clerk issues the Writ of Possession and gives you the original (plus stamped copies), you are responsible for taking it to the sheriff or marshal, who will carry out the actual eviction. You can get the marshal's or sheriff's location from the court clerk, or search the sheriff's website.

Take the original of the Writ of Possession, plus three copies for each defendant you're having evicted, to the office of the marshal or civil division of the sheriff's office (whichever your county has). You will pay a $145 fee, which is recoverable from the tenant. You must also fill out a set of instructions telling the sheriff or marshal to evict the defendants. Usually the sheriff or marshal has a particular form of instructions, but you can prepare the instructions in the form of a signed letter. A sample letter is shown below.

Within a few days (or weeks, in large urban areas) a deputy sheriff or marshal will go to the property and serve the occupants (either personally or by posting and mailing) with a five-day eviction notice that says, in effect, "If you're not out in five days, a deputy will be back to throw you out." (Many sheriffs and marshals will specify the next business day if the fifth day falls on a weekend or holiday.) In most cases, tenants leave before the deadline. If the property is still occupied after five days, call the marshal's or sheriff's office to ask that the defendants be physically evicted. Many sheriff's or marshal's offices don't automatically go back to perform the eviction, so it's up to you to call them if they don't call you. (Ask about their practice when you deliver the writ of possession.)

You should meet the sheriff or marshal at the property at the eviction time. You should also schedule a locksmith to meet you at the premises at the same time. The marshal or sheriff will not break in if the tenant has changed the locks, and you will need a locksmith to make the entry. The locksmith should also change the locks after the tenant has been removed. If you think the ex-tenants will try to move back into the premises, you may wish to supervise, to make sure they really move their things out. If they try to stay there against your wishes or to reenter the premises, they are criminal trespassers, and you should call the police.

Sample Letter of Instructions for Sheriff or Marshal

August 18, 20xx
12345 Angeleno Street
Los Angeles, CA 90010

Los Angeles County Marshal
Civil Division
210 W. Temple
Los Angeles, CA 90012

Re: Landlord v. Tenant
    Los Angeles County Superior Court
    Los Angeles District, Case No. A-12345-B

Please serve the writ of execution for possession of the premises in the above-referenced action on Terrence D. Tenant and Tillie D. Tenant and place the plaintiff in possession of the premises at 3815 Gower Canyon Ave., Apt. 3, Los Angeles, California. You may call me at 213-555-6789 to schedule the final posting/eviction date.

Sincerely,
Lenny D. Landlord
Lenny D. Landlord

People the Sheriff or Marshal Will Not Remove

If you did not have the Prejudgment Claim of Right to Possession forms served (as discussed in Chapter 6), the sheriff or marshal will not physically remove a person who:

• was not named as a defendant in your suit, and

• has filed—before the final eviction date —a written claim that he or she was in possession of the premises when you filed your suit, or had a right to be in possession before you filed your suit.

For example, if you rented to a husband and wife, sued and served them both with summonses and complaint, and got judgments against them both, the sheriff or marshal will refuse to evict the wife's brother who files a claim stating that he moved in months ago at her invitation, even though the rental agreement had a provision prohibiting this. (The optional procedure in Chapter 6 is a sort of preventive step to make sure that such unknown occupants can't wait to do this until the sheriff comes, and must do it early in the proceeding.)

If an unknown occupant does file a claim with the sheriff or marshal before the final eviction date, the eviction will be delayed until a later hearing where the person must show why he or she should not be evicted, too. This involves procedures that are beyond the scope of this book. See an attorney if you encounter this problem.

What Happens to the Tenant's Belongings?

As for the tenant's belongings, the deputy who carries out the eviction will not allow the tenants to spend hours moving their belongings out, nor will their possessions be placed on the street. Rather, the tenant will be allowed to carry out one or perhaps a few armloads of possessions. The remainder will be locked in the unit. Of course, you should change the locks or the tenant may just go right back in. This does not mean you have a right to hold the tenant's possessions for ransom until the back rent is paid. Doing that is illegal and could subject you to a lawsuit. You have the right only to insist on "reasonable storage charges" equal to 1/30th of the monthly rent for each day, starting with the day the deputy sheriff or marshal performs the eviction, as a condition of releasing the property.

Don't be too insistent on this, though. You don't want to have to store a bunch of secondhand possessions on the property and be unable to rent the premises to a rent-paying tenant, nor do you particularly want to front moving and storage charges to have the belongings hauled off to a storage facility. (See *The California Landlord's Law Book: Rights & Responsibilities*, Chapter 21, for a detailed discussion of what you can legally do with a tenant's abandoned property.) Given this reality, it's amazing how many landlords and tenants who've been at each other's throats can suddenly be very reasonable and accommodating when it comes to arranging for the tenants to get their locked-up belongings back.

Getting a Money Judgment for Rent and Costs

Once the tenants have moved out of the premises, you should seek a judgment for the money they owe you. Although a court clerk can give you a Judgment for Possession of the Premises, a money judgment for the rent and court costs (including filing, process server, writ, and sheriff's fees) has to be approved by a judge, either on the basis of your written declaration or at a hearing. You must also prepare a Request for Entry of Default (the same form you used earlier, filled out differently) and a Judgment form.

Unlawful detainer money judgments against tenants are notoriously difficult to collect and the watchword for collection is "patience." (We discuss collection procedures, as well as the likelihood of success, in Chapter 9.) So why bother getting a judgment? First, you've done most of the work already, and there isn't much more involved. Second, the law gives you ten years to collect at 10% interest per year (and another ten years if you renew your judgment), and you might someday find the tenant with some money. Even if you do

not actively pursue collection, the judgment sits as a trap waiting for the right circumstances. And third, the judgment will show up on the tenant's credit report, which will motivate the tenant to pay it off.

Determining Rent, Damages, and Costs

The first step is figuring out how much money you're entitled to. You won't know for sure how much this is until the tenant leaves. Use the following guidelines and worksheets.

 Nonpayment of rent cases. You are entitled to:

- **Overdue rent.** This is the amount of rent you demanded in the three-day notice.

  EXAMPLE: You served your three-day notice on August 3 for $900 rent due on the 1st and covering August 1 to 31. You got a default Judgment for Possession on the 16th (such a fast result is rare), and your default hearing is scheduled for August 23. You are entitled to judgment for the entire $900 rent for August, even if the tenant leaves before the end of the month. Typically, the default hearing will occur after the end of the rental period.

Get What You're Due

Some judges believe that you're not entitled to the rent for the entire month if you get your judgment before the month is up. This is wrong; rent payable in advance accrues and is due in its entirety for the whole period, without proration on a daily basis. (See *Friedman v. Isenbruck* (1952) 111 Cal. App. 2d 326, 335, 224 P.2d 718; and *Rez v. Summers* (1917) 34 Cal. App. 527, 168 P. 156.)

- **Leases.** A tenant who was evicted while renting under a fixed-term lease is legally liable to you for the balance of the rent on the lease, less what you can get from a replacement tenant. (See *The California Landlord's Law Book: Rights & Responsibilities*, Chapter 2.) However, you have to bring a separate lawsuit to recover this amount. The judgment in an unlawful detainer is limited to the rent the tenant owed when served with a three-day notice, plus prorated daily rent up until the date of judgment.

- **Damages.** If, after you obtained a default Judgment for Possession, the tenant stayed past the end of the period for which rent was due, you are entitled to an additional award of "damages at the rate of reasonable rental value" for each day the tenant stayed beyond the initial rental period. You specified the reasonable daily rental value (1/30th of one month's rent) in Item 13 of the complaint.

  EXAMPLE: You were patient and didn't serve your three-day notice until the 17th of August. You got a default Judgment for Possession on September 6, and your tenant was evicted on September 21. You are entitled to a judgment for the $900 rent for August. In addition, you're entitled to prorated daily damages for each of the days in September the tenant stayed, at the rate of 1/30th of $900 or $30 for each, or $620. The total is $1,520.

- **Your court costs.** This does not include things like copy fees or postage, but does include fees you had to pay court clerks, the process server, and the sheriff or marshal.

You cannot get a judgment in this proceeding for the costs of repairing or cleaning the premises, but you can deduct them from the security deposit. If the deposit won't cover cleaning and repair costs, you'll have to go after the difference in a separate suit in small claims court, or superior court if the costs are high enough to justify it.

You do not need to credit the security deposit when you seek your money judgment. If there is anything left over after you pay for cleaning and repairs, the balance is credited against the judgment after you obtain it, not before. (For more information on how to itemize and return security deposits, see *The California Landlord's Law Book: Rights & Responsibilities*, Chapter 20.)

EXAMPLE: : Lola obtained a judgment for $1,680, including rent, prorated damages, and court costs. She holds her tenant's $800 security deposit. The cost of cleaning and repairing is $200, and Lola subtracts this from the deposit; the remaining $600 of the deposit is applied against the $1,680 judgment, so that the tenant owes Lola $1,080 on the judgment.

Worksheet #1

Calculating Amount of Judgment:
Eviction Based on Nonpayment of Rent

Overdue Rent:
(amount demanded in three-day notice) $ 900

Damages:
 15 days × $ 30 (daily rental value)   = $ 450

Court Costs:
$ 240   filing fee
$ 75   process server
$ 25   process server
$ 145   sheriff's or marshal's fee $ 485
                                    Total $ 1,835

 30-day or 60-day notice cases.
You are entitled to:
- Prorated daily "damages" at the daily rental value for each day the tenant stayed beyond the 30-day (or 60-day) notice period. You are not entitled to judgment for any rent or damages that accrued before the 30 days (or 60 days) passed. You can, however, deduct this amount from the security deposit; see Chapter 9. The daily rental value is listed in Item 13 of the complaint.

- Court costs, including your filing, service of process, writ, and sheriff's or marshal's fees.

EXAMPLE: You served Jackson, whose $1,400 rent is due on May 15, with a 60-day termination notice on April 1. This means he is required to leave on May 31. He pays the rent for the period of April 15 through May 14, but refuses to leave on the 31st and refuses to pay the $746.72 prorated rent, due on May 15, for the period of May 15 through 31 (1/30th of the $1,400 monthly rent, or $46.67 per day, for 16 days). On June 1, you sue on the 60-day notice, and finally get Jackson out on June 25. In this kind of unlawful detainer suit, you are entitled to judgment for prorated daily "damages" only for the period of June 1 (the day after he should have left under the 60-day notice) through June 25 (the day he left), for a total of $1,166.75 (25 x $46.67 per day), and your court costs.

To be paid for the earlier period of May 15 through May 31, you'll have to either sue him in small claims court (usually not worth the trouble) or deduct it from any security deposit he paid.

Lease violation cases.
You are entitled to:

- "damages," prorated at the rate of 1/30th the monthly rent (you listed this figure in Item 13 of the complaint) for each day beyond the expiration of the three-day notice period that the tenant stayed and for which you haven't already been paid in the form of rent, and
- court costs—filing, service, and writ fees.

The amount of your money judgment may be quite small, and you may get a judgment only for your court costs, particularly if you accepted the regular monthly rent in advance for the month during which you served the three-day notice.

EXAMPLE: Say you accepted the regular monthly rent of $1,000 from Ron when it was due the first of the month. Two weeks later, Ron begins having loud parties. You give Ron a written warning, but it continues. On the 16th, at the urging of all your other tenants who threaten to move, you give Ron an unconditional three-day notice to quit.

Ron doesn't move, and you file suit on the 20th and take a default Judgment for Possession on the 26th. The marshal posts a five-day eviction notice on the 28th, giving Ron until the 3rd of the next month before he gets the boot. Ron leaves on the 2nd, so you're out only two days' prorated rent or damages at the reasonable rental value of $33.33 per day (1/30th x $1,000 per month), for a grand total of $66.66 plus court costs.

If Ron had misbehaved earlier, and you had served the three-day notice only a few days after that, having collected rent on the first of the month, you might even have gotten Ron out before the end of the month. In that case, your judgment would have been for court costs only. Ron isn't entitled to a prorated refund for the last few days of the month for which he paid but didn't get to stay, since he "forfeited" his rights under the rental agreement or lease—including any right to stay for days prepaid.

No-notice cases.
You are entitled to:

- prorated daily "damages" at the daily rental value (you listed this figure in Item 13 of the complaint) for each day beyond the date of termination of tenancy (either the date the lease expired or the termination date of the 30-day notice the tenant gave you), and
- court costs, including filing, service, and writ fees.

EXAMPLE: Hilda sued Sally, whose six-month lease expired June 30. Even if Sally hadn't paid all the $1,800 rent for June, Hilda would be entitled only to prorated daily damages (rental value per day) of $60 ($1,800 divided by 30) per day for each day beyond June 30 that Sally stayed in possession of the premises. So, if Hilda got Sally out by July 25, Hilda would be entitled to damages of 25 x $60, or $1,500, plus costs.

Past due rent. You cannot seek past due rent unless the three-day notice was based on nonpayment of rent. So, if Sally hadn't paid all her rent when it was due in early June, Hilda should have used a three-day notice and the eviction procedure in Chapter 2.

Worksheet #2

Calculating Amount of Judgment:
Eviction Based on 30-Day or 60-Day Notice
Violation of Lease, or No Notice

Overdue Rent:

(past due rent—not demanded in notice) $ _____0_____

Damages:

__25__ days × $ __60__ (daily rental value) = $ __1,500__

Court Costs:

$ __240__ filing fee

$ __75__ process server

$ __25__ writ fee

$ __145__ sheriff's or marshal's fee $ __485__

Total $ __1,985__

Preparing the Request for Entry of Default (Money Judgment)

You must complete a second Request for Entry of Default form to get your money judgment. A sample is shown below.

Fill in the caption boxes the same way you did for the first Request for Entry of Default form. (See above.) This time, though, put an X only in the box next to the words "COURT JUDGMENT." Do not put an X in any other box, not even the "Entry of Default" box, since the defendant's default has already been entered. Then fill in the numbered items as follows.

Item 1a: Enter the date you filed the complaint and your name, just as you did in the first Request for Entry of Default.

Item 1b: Type your name.

Item 1c: Leave this box blank. The clerk already entered the defaults of the defendants when you filed your first Request for Entry of Default.

Item 1d: Put an X in this box. This asks the clerk to schedule a "default hearing" in front of a judge. (Some courts instead accept a written declaration that says what you'd say in front of the judge. See below.) Type the defendants' names.

Item 1e: Leave these boxes blank. This is only for a clerk's judgment, and the clerk can't enter a money judgment in an unlawful detainer case.

Items 2a-f: In the line entitled "a. Demand of complaint," list in the "Amount" column the total of rent demanded in the three-day notice and on Paragraph 19(c). You will add the daily rental damages in your declaration in support.

Don't list anything next to Lines b, b(1), or b(2) entitled "Statement of damages." This does not apply to unlawful detainer cases.

Next to "c. Interest" and "e. Attorney fees," enter "0.00." Next to "d. Costs," enter the total of the filing fee, the process server's fee for serving all the defendants, and other court costs tallied in Item 7. (See below.) Total these amounts at Item 2f. Under the "Credits Acknowledged" column, list all amounts and the total as "0.00," since the defendant has not paid you anything. Don't include the security deposit. Finally, under "Balance," list the same amounts as under the "Amount" column.

CIV-100

ATTORNEY OR PARTY WITHOUT ATTORNEY:	STATE BAR NO:	*FOR COURT USE ONLY*

NAME: Lenny D. Landlord
FIRM NAME:
STREET ADDRESS: 12345 Angeleno Street
CITY: Los Angeles   STATE: CA   ZIP CODE: 90028
TELEPHONE NO.: 231-555-6789   FAX NO.:
E-MAIL ADDRESS: LDLXX321ispofchoice.com
ATTORNEY FOR (name): Plaintiff in pro per

SUPERIOR COURT OF CALIFORNIA, COUNTY OF LOS ANGELES
STREET ADDRESS: 111 North Hill Street
MAILING ADDRESS:
CITY AND ZIP CODE: Los Angeles, California 90012
BRANCH NAME:

Plaintiff/Petitioner: Lenny D. Landlord
Defendant/Respondent: Terence D. Tenant, et al.

REQUEST FOR (Application)	☐ **Entry of Default** ☒ **Court Judgment**	☐ **Clerk's Judgment**	CASE NUMBER: A-12345-B (as assigned by Court)

Not for use in actions under the Fair Debt Buying Practices Act (Civ. Code, § 1788.50 et seq.) *(see CIV-105)*

1. TO THE CLERK: On the complaint or cross-complaint filed
   a. on *(date):* April 11, 20XX
   b. by *(name):* Lenny D. Landlord
   c. ☐ Enter default of defendant *(names):*

   d. ☒ I request a court judgment under Code of Civil Procedure sections 585(b), 585(c), 989, etc., against defendant *(names):*
   Terence D. Tenant, Tillie D. Tenant
   (Testimony required. Apply to the clerk for a hearing date, unless the court will enter a judgment on an affidavit under Code Civ. Proc., § 585(d).)
   e. ☐ Enter clerk's judgment
   (1) ☐ for restitution of the premises only and issue a writ of execution on the judgment. Code of Civil Procedure section 1174(c) does not apply. (Code Civ. Proc., § 1169.)
   ☐ Include in the judgment all tenants, subtenants, named claimants, and other occupants of the premises. The *Prejudgment Claim of Right to Possession* was served in compliance with Code of Civil Procedure section 415.46.
   (2) ☒ under Code of Civil Procedure section 585(a). *(Complete the declaration under Code Civ. Proc., § 585.5 on the reverse (item 5).)*
   (3) ☒ for default previously entered on *(date):* April 28, 20xx

2. **Judgment to be entered.**

	Amount	Credits acknowledged	Balance
a. Demand of complaint	$ 1699.50	$ 0.00	$ 1699.50
b. Statement of damages*			
(1) Special		$	
(2) General		$	
c. Interest	$ 0.00	$ 0.00	$ 0.00
d. Costs (see reverse)	$ 520.00	$ 0.00	$ 520.00
e. Attorney fees	$ 0.00	$ 0.00	$ 0.00
f. **TOTALS**	$ 2219.50	$ 0.00	$ 2219.50

   g. **Daily damages** were demanded in complaint at the rate of: $ 56.65   per day beginning *(date):* May 1, 20xx
   (* Personal injury or wrongful death actions; Code Civ. Proc., § 425.11.)

3. ☒ *(Check if filed in an unlawful detainer case.)* **Legal document assistant or unlawful detainer assistant** information is on the reverse *(complete item 4).*

Date: May 20, 20xx

Lenny D. Landlord
(TYPE OR PRINT NAME)

Lenny D. Landlord
(SIGNATURE OF PLAINTIFF OR ATTORNEY FOR PLAINTIFF)

FOR COURT USE ONLY	(1) ☐ Default entered as requested on *(date):* (2) ☐ Default NOT entered as requested *(state reason):*	

Clerk, by _____, Deputy   Page 1 of 2

Form Adopted for Mandatory Use
Judicial Council of California CIV-100
[Rev. January 1, 2020]

REQUEST FOR ENTRY OF DEFAULT
(Application to Enter Default)

Code of Civil Procedure, §§ 585–587, 1169
www.courts.ca.gov

CIV-100

Plaintiff/Petitioner: Lenny D. Landlord	CASE NUMBER:
Defendant/Respondent: Terence D. Tenant, et al.	A-12345-B (as assigned by Court)

4. **Legal document assistant or unlawful detainer assistant (Bus. & Prof. Code, § 6400 et seq.).** A legal document assistant or unlawful detainer assistant ☐ did ☒ did **not** or compensation give advice or assistance with this form. If declarant has received **any** help or advice for pay from a legal document assistant or unlawful detainer assistant, state:

  a. Assistant's name:

  b. Street address, city, and zip code:

  c. Telephone no.:

  d. County of registration:

  e. Registration no.:

  f. Expires on *(date):*

5. ☒ **Declaration under Code Civ. Proc., § 585.5** *(for entry of default under Code Civ. Proc., § 585(a)).* This action

  a. ☐ is ☒ is not on a contract or installment sale for goods or services subject to Civ. Code, § 1801 et seq. (Unruh Act).

  b. ☐ is ☒ is not on a conditional sales contract subject to Civ. Code, § 2981 et seq. (Rees-Levering Motor Vehicle Sales and Finance Act).

  c. ☐ is ☒ is not on an obligation for goods, services, loans, or extensions of credit subject to Code Civ. Proc., § 395(b).

6. **Declaration of mailing (Code Civ. Proc., § 587).** A copy of this *Request for Entry of Default* was

  a. ☐ **not mailed** to the following defendants, whose addresses are unknown to plaintiff or plaintiff's attorney *(names):*

  b. ☒ **mailed** first-class, postage prepaid, in a sealed envelope addressed to each defendant's attorney of record or, if none, to each defendant's last known address as follows:

    (1) Mailed on *(date):* May 20, 20xx

    (2) To *(specify names and addresses shown on the envelopes):* Terence D. Tenant, 3815 Gower Canyon Ave., Apt. 3, Los Angeles, CA 90028
    (See attached for additional defendants)

I declare under penalty of perjury under the laws of the State of California that the foregoing items 4, 5, and 6 are true and correct.

Date: May 20, 20xx

Lenny D. Landlord
(TYPE OR PRINT NAME)

▶ *Lenny D. Landlord*
(SIGNATURE OF DECLARANT)

7. **Memorandum of costs** *(required if money judgment requested).* Costs and disbursements are as follows (Code Civ. Proc., § 1033.5):

  a. Clerk's filing fees .... $ 250

  b. Process server's fees .... $ 100

  c. Other *(specify):* Writ $ 25

  d. Sheriff's eviction fee $ 145

  e. **TOTAL** .... $ 520

  f. ☐ Costs and disbursements are waived.

  g. I am the attorney, agent, or party who claims these costs. To the best of my knowledge and belief this memorandum of costs is correct and these costs were necessarily incurred in this case.

I declare under penalty of perjury under the laws of the State of California that the foregoing is true and correct.

Date: May 20, 20xx

Lenny D. Landlord
(TYPE OR PRINT NAME)

▶ *Lenny D. Landlord*
(SIGNATURE OF DECLARANT)

8. **Declaration of nonmilitary status** *(required for a judgment).* No defendant named in item 1c of the application is in the military service as that term is defined by either the Servicemembers Civil Relief Act, 50 U.S.C. App. § 3911(2), or California Military and Veterans Code sections 400 and 402(f).

I declare under penalty of perjury under the laws of the State of California that the foregoing is true and correct.

Date: May 20, 20xx

Lenny D. Landlord
(TYPE OR PRINT NAME)

▶ *Lenny D. Landlord*
(SIGNATURE OF DECLARANT)

CIV-100 [Rev. January 1, 2020]

REQUEST FOR ENTRY OF DEFAULT
(Application to Enter Default)

Page 2 of 2

Item 2g: List the same prorated daily rent amount and the same date from which you are asking for prorated daily damages that you did in the original Request for Entry of Default.

Item 3: Put an "X" in this box, to indicate the case is an unlawful detainer proceeding. Then, fill in the date you'll be filing the default papers with the court, type your name opposite the place for signature, and sign the form.

CAPTION, Second page: Type the names of the plaintiff and defendant, just as you did on the second page of the Proof of Service of Summons.

Items 4 and 5: Fill in these items exactly the same as you did in the original Request for Entry of Default.

Item 6: Fill in this item exactly as you did in the first Request for Entry of Default, checking Box b and entering the date of mailing of this second one to the defendant's address. (Even though the defendant has moved now, after eviction, that's still his address as last known to you, and your mail could be forwarded.) Mail copies to the tenants and put "ADDRESS CORRECTION AND FORWARDING REQUESTED" on the envelopes. This will help you locate them when you go to collect your money judgment. (See Chapter 9.)

Item 7: This is where you total your court costs. List the clerk's filing fee and your process server's fee in Items 7a and b. Charges for service of the notice do not qualify as "costs" and cannot be included in the amount. In Item 7c, "Other," type in "writ fee" and add the cost of the Writ of Possession. Below that, in Item d, add the sheriff's eviction fee. Total these items at Item 7e. This total should also be listed on Item 2d on the front. Date and sign where indicated.

Item 8: Date and sign the Declaration of Nonmilitary Status the same way you did on the original Request for Entry of Default.

Preparing a Declaration as to Rent, Damages, and Costs

Most courts allow you, and many require you, to prepare a written declaration under penalty of perjury in lieu of testifying before a judge at a default hearing. The judge simply reads the declaration's statements about rent, damages, and court costs, and awards you a judgment without a hearing. In the Central Division of Los Angeles County, you must use a declaration; default hearings are not held. If you want to get your money judgment this way rather than attending a default hearing, call the court and ask whether it accepts declarations in lieu of testimony in unlawful detainer default cases. If you'd rather testify in person, or if the court doesn't allow declarations, proceed to "Preparing the Proposed Judgment," below.

The Judicial Council offers a statewide form for this type of declaration—the Declaration for Default Judgment by Court (Judicial Council form UD-116). Technically, the form is optional, so you don't have to use it. However, all courts must accept it, and we prefer to use Judicial Council forms where available in the name of uniformity and predictability.

 RENT CONTROL
If your property is rent or eviction controlled, you may have to include additional statements in the declaration. These could include representing that you complied with the particular rent ordinance, reciting the just cause that underlies your eviction, and giving a statement of good faith and lack of ulterior motive.

Sample Declaration for Nonpayment of Rent—Page 1

1   Name: LENNY D. LANDLORD
    Address: 12345 ANGELENO STREET
2   LOS ANGELES, CA 90010
    Phone: 213-555-1234
3
    Plaintiff in Pro Per
4

5

6

7

8   SUPERIOR COURT OF CALIFORNIA, COUNTY OF _____ LOS ANGELES _____

9   _____ LOS ANGELES _____ DIVISION

10 LENNY D. LANDLORD _____   ) Case No. A-12345-B _____
                  Plaintiff,   )
11   ) DECLARATION IN SUPPORT OF DEFAULT
            v.   ) JUDGMENT FOR RENT, DAMAGES, AND COSTS
12   )
    TERRENCE D. TENANT, et al. _____)
13   Defendant(s).   )
) (C.C.P. SECS. 585(d), 1169)
14

15   I, the undersigned, declare:

16   1. I am the plaintiff in the above-entitled action and the owner of the premises at ____ 6789 Angel Street, ____

17 ____ Apartment 10 _____, City of

18 ____ Los Angeles _____, County of _____ Los Angeles _____, California.

19   2. On ____ August 1 _____, ____ 20xx ____, defendant(s) rented the premises from me

20 pursuant to a written/oral [cross out one] agreement under which the monthly rent was $ ____ 900.00 ____ payable in

21 advance on the ____ first _____ day of each month.

22   3. The terms of the tenancy [check one]:

23   ☒ were not changed; or

24   ☐ were changed, effective _____, _____, in that monthly rent was validly

25   and lawfully increased to $_____ by ☐ agreement of the parties and subsequent payment of

26   such rent; or

27   ☐ [month-to-month tenancy only] service on defendant(s) of a written notice of at least 30 days, setting forth the

28   increase in rent.

Sample Declaration for Nonpayment of Rent—Page 2

1   4. The reasonable rental value of the premises per day, that is, the current monthly rent divided by 30, is $ ___30.00___ .

2   5. Pursuant to the agreement, defendant(s) went into possession of the premises.

3   6. On ___August 3___ , ___20xx___ , defendant(s) were in default in the payment of rent in the amount

4   of $___900.00___ , and I caused defendant(s) to be served with a written notice demanding that defendant(s) pay that

5   amount or surrender possession of the premises within three days after service of the notice.

6   7. Defendant(s) failed to pay the rent or surrender possession of the premises within three days after service of the notice,

7   whereupon I commenced this action, complying with any local rent control or eviction protection ordinance applicable, and caused

8   Summons and Complaint to be served on each defendant. Defendant(s) have failed to answer or otherwise respond to the Complaint

9   within the time allowed by law.

10   8. Defendant(s) surrendered possession of the premises on ___September 7___ , ___20xx___ , after entry of

11   a clerk's Judgment for Possession and issuance of a Writ of Execution thereon.

12   9. The rent was due for the rental period of ___August 1___ , ___20xx___ , through

13   ___August 31___ , ___20xx___ . After this latter date, and until defendant(s) vacated the premises, I

14   sustained damages at the daily reasonable rental value of $___30.00___ , for total damages of $___210.00___ .

15   10. I have incurred filing, service, and writ fees in the total amount of $___465.00___ in this action.

16   11. If sworn as a witness, I could testify competently to the facts stated herein.

17   I declare under penalty of perjury under the laws of the State of California that the foregoing is true and correct.

18   Date: ___September 12___ , ___20xx___

19   *Lenny D. Landlord*
       Plaintiff in Pro Per

20

21

22

23

24

25

26

27

28

Sample Declaration for Violation of Lease—Page 1

1	Name: LORNA D. LANDLADY
	Address: 3865 Oak Street
2	Anaheim, CA 92801
	Phone: 818-555-1234
3	
	Plaintiff in Pro Per
4	

5

6

7

8   SUPERIOR COURT OF CALIFORNIA, COUNTY OF ORANGE

9   CENTRAL ORANGE COUNTY JUDICIAL DIVISION

10 LORNA D. LANDLADY   ) Case No. 5-0368
         Plaintiff,   )
11   ) DECLARATION IN SUPPORT OF DEFAULT
       v.   ) JUDGMENT FOR DAMAGES AND COSTS
12   )
    TERESA A. TENANT, et al.   )
13   Defendant(s).   ) (C.C.P. SECS. 585(d), 1169)
    _____)

14

15

16   I, the undersigned, declare:

17   1. I am the plaintiff in the above-entitled action and the owner of the premises at 15905 Lafayette Street,

18   Apartment 202, City of Anaheim, County of Orange, California.

19   2. On September 1, 20xx, defendant(s) rented the premises from me pursuant to a written one-year lease

20   under which the monthly rent was $900.00 payable in advance on the first day of each month. The terms of

21   the agreement have not been changed.

22   3. Pursuant to the agreement, defendants went into possession of the premises.

23   4. Defendants last paid rent on March 1, 20xx, for March.

24   5. On March 14, 20xx, Teresa began having loud parties that would begin around noon and last until

25   about 4 a.m. On the 14th, my other tenants began to complain and threaten to move. I went to the apartment

26   above, and the floor was vibrating from all the noise. I knocked at Teresa's door, but apparently no one could

27   hear the knocking, with the music as loud as it was. Finally, I just walked in, found Teresa, and asked her to

28

Declaration in Support of Default Judgment for Damages and Costs   Page 1 of 2

Sample Declaration for Violation of Lease—Page 2

1 turn down the music. She did, but she turned it back up when I left. The same thing happened the next two

2 days.

3   6. On March 16, 20xx, I caused defendant to be served with a three-day notice to perform covenant or

4 quit. She had another party on the 18th and didn't leave on the 19th, so I filed suit on the 20th.

5   7. I obtained a default Judgment for Possession on March 28, 20xx.

6   8. Defendant moved out on the second day of April.

7   9. The damages for the period I didn't receive rent were equal to the prorated daily reasonable rental

8 value of $20.00 per day, which for two days is $40.00. My court costs have been $80.00 for the filing fee, $30.00

9 process server's fees, $3.50 for issuance of the Writ of Possession, and $75.00 to have the sheriff evict, for a total

10 of $188.50

11   10. If sworn as a witness, I could testify competently to the facts stated herein.

12   I declare under penalty of perjury under the laws of the State of California that the foregoing is true and

13 correct.

14 Date: _April 15, 20xx_____   _Lorna D. Landlady_____
                                              Plaintiff in Pro Per

15

16

17

18

19

20

21

22

23

24

25

26

27

28

Sample Declaration: 30-, 60-, or 90-Day Notice—Page 1

1 | Name: LINDA D. LANDLADY
Address: 459 ROSE STREET
2 | BERKELEY, CA 94710
Phone: 510-555-1234

3 | Plaintiff in Pro Per

4

5

6

7 | SUPERIOR COURT OF CALIFORNIA, COUNTY OF Alameda—Limited Jurisdiction

8

9

10 | LINDA D. LANDLADY   ) Case No.   5-0258
Plaintiff,   )
11 |) DECLARATION IN SUPPORT OF DEFAULT
v.   ) JUDGMENT FOR DAMAGES AND COSTS
12 |)
THAD TENANT, et al.   )
13 | Defendant(s).   )
) (C.C.P. SECS. 585(d), 1169)
14

15 | I, the undersigned, declare:

16 | 1. I am the plaintiff in the above-entitled action and the owner of the premises at   950 9th Street

17 | _____, City of

18 | Albany   , County of   Alameda   , California.

19 | 2. On   February 1   ,   20xx   , defendant(s) rented the premises from me pursuant to

20 | a written/oral [cross out one] agreement under which the monthly rent was $ 400.00   payable in advance on the

21 | _____1st_____ day of each month.

22 | 3. The terms of the tenancy [check one]:

23 | ☒ were not changed; or

24 | ☐ were changed, effective _____, _____, in that monthly rent was validly and

25 | lawfully increased to $_____ by

26 | ☐ agreement of the parties and subsequent payment of such rent; or

27 | ☐ [month-to-month tenancy only] service on defendant(s) of a written notice of at least 30 days, setting forth the

28 | increase in rent.

Sample Declaration: 30-, 60-, or 90-Day Notice—Page 2

1   4. The reasonable rental value of the premises per day, that is, the current monthly rent divided by 30, is $ 13.33 .

2   5. Pursuant to the agreement, defendant(s) went into possession of the premises.

3   6. On _August 30_ , _20xx_ , I served defendant with a written 30-day/ 60-day

4 [cross out one] termination notice.

5   7. Defendant(s) was still in possession of the property after the period of the notice expired on

6 _September 30_ , _20xx_ , and stayed until _October 20_ , _20xx_ ,

7 when the sheriff evicted him/her/them pursuant to a clerk's Judgment for Possession and issuance of a Writ of Execution.

8   8. I sustained damages at the daily reasonable rental value of $_13.33_ for _21_ days between

9 _September 30_ , _20xx_ and _October 20_ , _20xx_ for a total of

10 $_279.93_ .

11   9. I have incurred filing, service, and writ fees in the total amount of $_188.50_ in this action.

12   10. If sworn as a witness, I could testify competently to the facts stated herein.

13   I declare under penalty of perjury under the laws of the State of California that the foregoing is true and correct.

14

15 Date: _October 31_ , _20xx_

16

                   Linda D. Landlady

17   Plaintiff in Pro Per

18

19

20

21

22

23

24

25

26

27

28

FORM

Blank copies of a Declaration in Support of Default Judgment for Rent, Damages, and Costs, and a Declaration in Support of Default Judgment Damages and Costs can be downloaded from the Nolo website. (See the appendix for the link to the forms in this book, and other information on using the forms.) The Judicial Council form UD-116 (Declaration for Default Judgment by Court) is also on the Nolo website.

In the event you want to use the optional Judicial Council Declaration for Default Judgment by Court, we have included a sample Judicial Council declaration form based on a hypothetical case in Los Angeles. (We have used the same scenario for all the samples in the book.) We chose this scenario because Los Angeles County represents one of the most complicated counties due to their local rules, multiple filing courthouses, and local rent control in the various cities in Los Angeles county.

Here are instructions for filling out the form.

Instructions for Completing Declaration for Default Judgment by Court (Judicial Council Statewide Optional Form)

First, enter the information (name, address, court location, case number, names of plaintiff and defendant) that you listed in the big boxes at the top of the complaint, Request for Entry of Default, and Writ of Possession forms.

Item 1: Check Box 1a. Check Box 1b(1) if you own the property and the facts of the rental are better known to you than anyone else. If, instead, a property manager or another agent is better informed than you and is, therefore, signing this declaration, check Box 1b(2) or 1b(3) as appropriate.

Item 2: List the complete address of the property.

Item 4a: This item asks for the same information you supplied in Items 6a and 6b in the complaint. Fill in the same information about whether the rental agreement was written or oral, the names(s) of the defendant(s) who signed it, the term of the tenancy, and the initial rent amount and due date.

Item 4b: If you have the original rental agreement, or attached it to the complaint (which we didn't recommend, because you may need the original at trial if the case is contested), check this box. If you attached a copy of the rental agreement to the complaint and are now going to attach the original to this declaration, check the box next to the words "to this declaration, labeled Exhibit 4b," and attach the original, labeling it "Exhibit 4b" at the bottom.

Item 4c: If you do not have an original rental agreement, and did not attach one to the complaint, you are supposed to check this box and the one next to the words "to this declaration, labeled Exhibit 4c," and attach your copy as "Exhibit 4c." However, if you do this, you are also required, according to this form, to include "a declaration and order to admit the copy."

In the absence of an original, many courts will require a declaration explaining why the original has not been submitted. (Technically speaking, under the rules of evidence copies of documents work as well as an original and can be used with a proper declaration or testimony laying the groundwork.) You can use Judicial Council MC-030 declaration form, and simply add your explanation. See below for the language you'll need to type in (a sample appears above also).

Complete this form now, or come back to it when you're done with the form you're working on at the moment (the declaration supporting your request for a default judgment).

FORM

A blank copy of the generic Declaration (Judicial Council Form MC-030) is available for down-loading on the Nolo website. (See the appendix for the link to the forms and other information on using them.)

Caption: Complete the caption with the same information as contained in prior declarations—your name, address, telephone number, representative capacity ("plaintiff in pro per"), court, and case number.

SUPERIOR COURT OF CALIFORNIA COUNTY OF LOS ANGELES	Reserved for Clerk's File Stamp

COURTHOUSE ADDRESS:

111 North Hill Street, Los Angeles, CA 90012

PLAINTIFF:

Lenny D. Landlord

DEFENDANT:

Terrence D. Tenant, et al.

DEFAULT JUDGMENT - UNLAWFUL DETAINER ☐ BY CLERK ☑ BY COURT	CASE NUMBER: A-123445-B

Upon review of the evidence in this action, the Court orders the following judgment:

Judgment is ordered for the PLAINTIFF (S):

Lenny D. Landlord

Against the DEFENDANT (S): Terrence D. Tenant, Tillie D. Tenant

Judgment is entered as follows:

☑ 1. $ 2492.60 _____ Rent and/or Damages.

☐ 2. $_____ Attorney Fees

☑ 3. $ 520 _____ Costs

☐ 4. $_____ Interest

☑ 5. $ 3012.60 _____ **TOTAL**

☑ 6. Forfeiture of the rental agreement/lease.

☑ 7. Judgment is pursuant to Code of Civil Procedure section 415.46 as to any and all unnamed occupants.

☑ 8. Possession of the Premises located at: 3815 Gower Canyon Avenue, Apt. 3, _____
Los Angeles, CA 90028 _____

☐ 9. Execution of the judgment stayed as follows: _____

☐ 10. **A WRIT OF EXECUTION/POSSESSION MAY ISSUE FORTHWITH BUT NO FINAL LOCK-OUT PRIOR TO:** _____.

Dated:_____

_____
Judicial Officer

John A. Clarke Executive Officer/Clerk

Dated: _____

By:_____
Deputy Clerk

DEFAULT JUDGMENT - UNLAWFUL DETAINER

LACIV 119 New 10-03
LASC Approved

Code Civ. Proc., §§ 585, 415.46

Body: Use the body of the declaration to state your reason for asking the court to accept your copy. Type the following:

"I, [*owner name*], declare:

1. I make this declaration of my own personal knowledge, and if called to testify, could testify competently thereto.

2. I am the plaintiff and custodian of records for the plaintiff, and I manage the premises that are the subject of this unlawful detainer action. Due and reasonable diligence has been made to locate the original lease. However, it cannot be located at this time. I request that this court accept the attached copy, which is a true and correct copy of the original lease.

3. This declaration is executed at [*city or county name*], California, as of the date indicated below."

Item 5: If the rental agreement has not changed since its inception (for example, you have not increased the rent, changed the rent due date, or changed any other term of the tenancy), skip this box and go to the second page. Otherwise, check the box and any box for Items 5a through 5f that apply.

If you have increased the rent more than once during the tenancy, you should check Box 5a and add a separate Attachment 5a listing a complete history of rent increase, including rent amounts and effective dates, *except for the most recent increase.* As to the most recent increase, check and fill out Item 5b, indicating the rent before and after the increase, and the effective date; you also should check Box 5b(1) (tenant paid the increased rent) or Box 5b(2) (tenant was served a notice of change of terms of tenancy) as appropriate.

In the rare case of an increase by written agreement, check Box 5b(3). If you have the original of such a document, check Box 5e and the box next to "to this declaration, labeled Exhibit 5e," and attach that agreement, labeled "Exhibit 5e." If you have only a copy, attach a separate statement under penalty of perjury and a proposed judge's order to admit the copy. (See similar example for rental agreement copies in instructions for Item 4c, above.)

Check Box 5f instead of 5e, check the words next to "to this declaration, labeled Exhibit 5f," and attach the copy labeled "Exhibit 5f."

On the second page, list, in capitals, the plaintiff and defendants' names and the case number.

Item 6a: Fill out Item 6a, referring to the type of notice served on the tenant, the same way you filled out Item 7a of the complaint.

Item 6b: If the notice served was a Three-Day Notice to Pay Rent or Quit, check this box to indicate the rent demanded in the notice (the same dollar figure as in Item 10 in the complaint) and the dates of the rental period (this information should be listed on the three-day notice to pay or quit).

Item 6c: If the rent demanded in a Three-Day Notice to Pay Rent or Quit is different from the monthly rent, explain why. For example, you might type in: "Monthly rent was $1,000.00, three-day notice demanded only $800 due to earlier partial payment on March 4, 20xx."

Item 6d: Check this box and the box next to the words "The original complaint."

Item 7a: List the name(s) of defendant(s) who were served a three-day, 30-day, or other notice and the date of service, in the same way you did in Item 9a in the complaint.

Item 7b: Check this box only if you used the optional procedure in Chapter 6 to have a Prejudgment Claim of Right to Possession served on unnamed occupants by a sheriff, marshal, or registered process server. Otherwise, leave this box blank.

Item 8: If the three-day notice you attached to the complaint included a filled out Proof of Service at the bottom, check the box next to the words, "the original complaint." If not, prepare a proof of service, using our sample three-day notice's Proof of Service as a guide, have the person who served the notice sign it, and attach that original as "Exhibit 8b."

Item 9: List the date the three-day, 30-day, or other notice expired. This should be the same date listed in Item 8b of your complaint.

UD-116

ATTORNEY OR PARTY WITHOUT ATTORNEY *(Name, state bar number, and address):* Lenny D. Landlord 12345 Angeleno Street Los Angeles, CA 90028 TELEPHONE NO.: 213-555-6789 FAX NO. *(Optional):* E-MAIL ADDRESS *(Optional):* LDLXX321@ispofchoice.com ATTORNEY FOR *(Name):* in Pro Per	FOR COURT USE ONLY

SUPERIOR COURT OF CALIFORNIA, COUNTY OF LOS ANGELES
STREET ADDRESS: 111 North Hill Street
MAILING ADDRESS:
CITY AND ZIP CODE: Los Angeles, California 90012
BRANCH NAME:

PLAINTIFF *(Name):* LENNY D. LANDLORD

DEFENDANT *(Name):* TERRENCE D. TENANT, et al.

DECLARATION FOR DEFAULT JUDGMENT BY COURT (Unlawful Detainer—Code Civil Proc., § 585(d))	CASE NUMBER: A-12345-B

1. My name is *(specify):* Lenny D. Landlord
    a. [x] I am the plaintiff in this action.
    b. I am
        (1) [x] an owner of the property   (3) [ ] an agent of the owner
        (2) [ ] a manager of the property   (4) [ ] other *(specify):*

2. *The property concerning this action is located at (street address, apartment number, city, and county):*
    3815 Gower Canyon Avenue, Apt. 3, Los Angeles, California 90028 (Los Angeles County)

3. Personal knowledge. I personally know the facts stated in this declaration and, if sworn as a witness, could testify competently thereto. I am personally familiar with the rental or lease agreement, defendant's payment record, the condition of the property, and defendant's conduct.

4. Agreement was [x] written   [ ] oral as follows:
    a. On or about *(date):* 1/2/20xx   defendant *(name each):* Terrence D. Tenant, Tillie D. Tenant
        (1) agreed to rent the property for a [x] month-to-month tenancy [ ] other tenancy *(specify):*
        (2) agreed to pay rent of $ 1,650.00   payable [x] monthly   [ ] other *(specify frequency):*
            with rent due on the [x] first of the month [ ] other day *(specify):*
    b. [x] Original agreement is attached *(specify):* [ ] to the original complaint.
        [ ] to the *Application for Immediate Writ of Possession.* [x] to this declaration, labeled Exhibit 4b.
    c. [ ] Copy of agreement with a declaration and order to admit the copy is attached *(specify):*
        [ ] to the *Application for Immediate Writ of Possession.* [ ] to this declaration, labeled Exhibit 4c.
5. [x] Agreement changed.
    a. [ ] More than one change in rent amount *(specify history of all rent changes and effective dates up to the last rent change)* on *Attachment* 5a (form MC-025).
    b. [x] Change in rent amount (specify last rent change). The rent was changed from $ 1,650.00 to $ 1,699.50,
        which became effective on *(date):* 1/2/20xx+1   and was made
        (1) [ ] by agreement of the parties and subsequent payment of such rent.
        (2) [x] by service on defendant of a notice of change in terms pursuant to Civil Code section 827 *(check item 5d).*
        (3) [ ] pursuant to a written agreement of the parties for change in terms *(check item 5e or 5f).*
    c. [ ] Change in rent due date. Rent was changed, payable in advance, due on *(specify day):*
    d. [x] A copy of the notice of change in terms is attached to this declaration, labeled Exhibit 5d.
    e. [ ] Original agreement for change in terms is attached *(specify):* [ ] to the original complaint.
        [ ] to the *Application for Immediate Writ of Possession.* [ ] to this declaration, labeled Exhibit 5e.
    f. [ ] Copy of agreement for change in terms with a declaration and order to admit the copy is attached *(specify):*
        [ ] to the *Application for Immediate Writ of Possession.* [ ] to this declaration, labeled Exhibit 5f.

Page 1 of 3

Form Approved for Optional Use Judicial Council of California UD-116 [Rev. July 1, 2003]	DECLARATION FOR DEFAULT JUDGMENT BY COURT (Unlawful Detainer—Code Civ. Proc., § 585(d))	Code of Civil Procedure, § 585(d) www.courts.ca.gov

UD-116

PLAINTIFF *(Name):* LENNY D. LANDLORD	CASE NUMBER:
DEFENDANT *(Name):* TERRENCE D. TENANT, et al.	A-12345-B

6. Notice to quit.

   a. [x] Defendant was served with a

     (1) [x] 3-day notice to pay rent or quit   (4) [   ] 3-day notice to quit

     (2) [   ] 3-day notice to perform covenants or quit   (5) [   ] 30-day notice to quit

     (3) [   ] Other *(specify):*   (6) [   ] 60-day notice to quit

   b. [x] The 3-day notice to pay rent or quit demanded rent due in the amount of *(specify):* $ 1,699.50 for the rental period beginning on *(date)* 4/1/20xx   and ending on *(date)* 4/30/20xx

   c. [x] The total rent demanded in the 3-day notice under item 6b is different from the agreed rent in item 4a(2) *(specify history of dates covered by the 3-day notice and any partial payments received to arrive at the balance)* on Attachment 6c (form MC-025).

   d. [x] The original or copy of the notice specified in item 6a is attached to *(specify):* [x] the original complaint.

       [   ] this declaration, labeled Exhibit 6d. *(The original or a copy of the notice MUST be attached to this declaration if not attached to the original complaint.)*

7. Service of notice.

   a. The notice was served on defendant *(name each):* Terrence D. Tenant, Tillie D. Tenant

     (1) [   ] personally *on (date):* 4/4/20xx

     (2) [x] by substituted service, including a copy mailed to the defendant, *on (date):* 4/4/20xx

     (3) [   ] by posting and mailing on *(date mailed):*

   b. [x] A prejudgment claim of right to possession was served on the occupants pursuant to Code of Civil Procedure section 415.46.

8. Proof of service of notice. The original or copy of the proof of service of the notice in item 6a is attached to *(specify):*

   a. [x] the original complaint.

   b. [   ] this declaration, labeled Exhibit 8b. *(The original or copy of the proof of service MUST be attached to this declaration if not attached to the original complaint.)*

9. Notice expired. On *(date):* 4/9/20xx   the notice in item 6 expired at the end of the day and defendant failed to comply with the requirements of the notice by that date. No money has been received and accepted after the notice expired.

10. The fair rental value of the property is $ 56.65   per day, calculated as follows:

   a. [   ] (rent per month) x (0.03288) *(12 months divided by 365 days)*

   b. [x] rent per month divided by 30

   c. [   ] other valuation *(specify):*

11. Possession. The defendant

   a. [x] vacated the premises *on (date):* 5/14/20xx

   b. [   ] continues to occupy the property on *(date of this declaration):*

12. [x] Holdover damages. Declarant has calculated the holdover damages as follows:

   a. Damages demanded in the complaint began on *(date):* 5/1/20xx

   b. Damages accrued through *(date specified in item 11):* 5/14/20xx

   c. Number of days that damages accrued *(count days using the dates in items 12a and 12b):* 14

   d. Total holdover damages *((daily rental value in item 10) x (number of days in item 12c)):* $ 793.10

13. [   ] Reasonable attorney fees are authorized in the lease or rental agreement pursuant to paragraph *(specify):* and reasonable attorney fees for plaintiff's attorney *(name):*   are $

14. [x] Court costs in this case, including the filing fee, are $ 520.00

UD-116 [Rev. July 1, 2003]

DECLARATION FOR DEFAULT JUDGMENT BY COURT
(Unlawful Detainer—Code Civ. Proc., § 585(d))

Page 2 of 3

UD-116

PLAINTIFF *(Name):* LENNY D. LANDLORD	CASE NUMBER:
DEFENDANT *(Name):* TERRENCE D. TENANT, et al.	A-12345-B

15. [x] Declarant requests a judgment on behalf of plaintiff for:

    a. [x] A money judgment as follows:

(1) [x] Past-due rent *(item 6b)*	$ 1,699.50
(2) [x] Holdover damages *(item 12d)*	$ 793.10
(3) [ ] Attorney fees *(item 13)**	$
(4) [x] Costs *(item 14)*	$ 520.00
(5) [ ] Other *(specify):*	$
(6) TOTAL JUDGMENT	$ 3,012.60

  * [ ] Attorney fees are to be paid by *(name)* only.

    b. [ ] Possession of the premises in item 2 *(check only if a clerk's judgment for possession was **not** entered).*

    c. [ ] Cancellation of the rental agreement. [x] Forfeiture of the lease.

I declare under penalty of perjury under the laws of the State of California that the foregoing is true and correct.

Date: May 20, 20xx

Lenny D. Landlord
_____
      (TYPE OR PRINT NAME)

▶ *Lenny D. Landlord*
_____
      (SIGNATURE OF DECLARANT)

Summary of Exhibits

16. [x] Exhibit 4b: Original rental agreement.

17. [ ] Exhibit 4c: Copy of rental agreement with declaration and order to admit the copy.

18. [x] Exhibit 5d: Copy of notice of change in terms.

19. [ ] Exhibit 5e: Original agreement for change of terms.

20. [ ] Exhibit 5f: Copy of agreement for change in terms with declaration and order to admit copy.

21. [ ] Exhibit 6d: Original or copy of the notice to quit under item 6a *(MUST be attached to this declaration if it is not attached to original complaint).*

22. [ ] Exhibit 8b: Original or copy of proof of service of notice in item 6a *(MUST be attached to this declaration if it is not attached to original complaint).*

23. [ ] Other exhibits *(specify number and describe):*

UD-116 [Rev. July 1, 2003]	Page 3 of 3

DECLARATION FOR DEFAULT JUDGMENT BY COURT
(Unlawful Detainer—Code Civ. Proc., § 585(d))

MC-025

SHORT TITLE:	CASE NUMBER:
Landlord v. Tenant	A-12345-B

ATTACHMENT *(Number):* 6c

(This Attachment may be used with any Judicial Council form.)

(1) The total rent demanded in the notice under item 6(b) was for the current rent as of 4/1/20xx in the amount of $1,699.50 for the month, per the notice of increase attached as as Exhibit 5d.

(2) The increase was lawfully in the amount permitted by the Rent Stabilization Ordinance of the City of Los Angeles, LA Municipal Code Chapter XV, enacted in 1979 and as amended.

(If the item that this Attachment concerns is made under penalty of perjury, all statements in this Attachment are made under penalty of perjury.)

Page 1 of 1

(Add pages as required)

Form Approved for Optional Use
Judicial Council of California
MC-025 [Rev. July 1, 2009]

ATTACHMENT
to Judicial Council Form

www.courtinfo.ca.gov

MC-030

ATTORNEY OR PARTY WITHOUT ATTORNEY *(Name, State Bar number, and address):*	FOR COURT USE ONLY
Lenny D. Landlord 12345 Angeleno Street Los Angeles, CA 90028 TELEPHONE NO.: 213-555-6789 FAX NO. *(Optional):* E-MAIL ADDRESS *(Optional):* ATTORNEY FOR *(Name):* in Pro Per	

SUPERIOR COURT OF CALIFORNIA, COUNTY OF LOS ANGELES
STREET ADDRESS: 111 N. Hill Street
MAILING ADDRESS:
CITY AND ZIP CODE: Los Angeles, CA 90012
BRANCH NAME:

PLAINTIFF/PETITIONER: Lenny D. Landlord

DEFENDANT/RESPONDENT: Terrence D. Tenant, et al.

DECLARATION	CASE NUMBER: A-12345-B

I, Lenny D. Landlord, declare:

1. I make this declaration of my own personal knowledge, and if called to testify, could testify competently thereto.

2. I am the plaintiff and custodian of records for the plaintiff, and I manage the premises that are the subject of this unlawful detainer action. Due and reasonable diligence has been made to locate the original lease. However, it cannot be located at this time. I request that this court accept the attached copy, which is a true and correct copy of the original lease.

3. This declaration is executed at [city or county name], California, as of the date indicated below.

I declare under penalty of perjury under the laws of the State of California that the foregoing is true and correct.

Date: May 20, 20xx

Lenny D. Landlord
_____
(TYPE OR PRINT NAME)

Lenny D. Landlord
_____
(SIGNATURE OF DECLARANT)

☐ Attorney for ☑ Plaintiff ☐ Petitioner ☐ Defendant
☐ Respondent ☐ Other *(Specify):*

Form Approved for Optional Use
Judicial Council of California
MC-030 [Rev. January 1, 2006]

DECLARATION

Page 1 of 1

Item 10: List the same daily fair rental value of the property that you listed in Complaint Item 13, and check Box b.

Item 11: Because you should have waited until after the tenant vacated to fill out this form, check Box 11a only, and list the date the tenant vacated.

Item 12: Check this box. In Item 12a, list the date you listed in Complaint Item 19. In Item 12b, again list the date the tenant vacated. In Item 12c, list the number of days between the date in Item 12a and 12b, *including* both those dates. (For example, if the day in 12a is January 10 and the day in 12b is January 15, the number of days is 6, not 5.) In Item 12d, multiply this number of days by the daily fair-rental-value damages amount in Item 10. This amount is called the "holdover damages" figure that goes in Item 15a(2) on the next page.

Item 13: Leave this item blank.

Item 14: Check this box and list your total court costs, consisting of filing fee, cost indicated on returned summons for service of process, fee for issuance of Writ of Possession, and sheriff's or marshal's eviction fee. This item goes in Item 15a(4), "Costs."

On the top of Page 3, again list names of plaintiff, defendant(s), and case number.

Item 15: Check Item 15a and list past due rent from Item 6b, "holdover damages" from Item 12d, and costs from Item 14. Add them for a "total judgment" amount. Leave Box 15b blank. If the eviction is based on rent nonpayment or another breach, check the box in Item 15c as applicable— either the one next to "Cancellation of the rental agreement" for a month-to-month rental agreement, or "Forfeiture of the lease" in the case of a fixed-term lease.

Finally, date and sign the document and check any of Items 16 through 23 to indicate what exhibits you've added.

Evictions based on violation of a lease provision or causing a nuisance. Such an eviction results in the tenant's "forfeiture" of the right to stay for a period for which he or she has already paid rent. In cases like this, judges are more reluctant to find in your favor, even in a default situation, so you have to be very specific and detailed in your testimony. You must explain how the tenant committed a "material" (serious) breach of the lease, illegally sublet, or committed a nuisance. Otherwise, a judge could rule that the eviction was unfounded, even though you got the tenant out with a Clerk's Judgment and Writ of Possession (a process described in "Getting a Default Judgment for Possession," above).

Preparing the Proposed Judgment

You should prepare a proposed judgment (using the Judicial Council's Judgment—Unlawful Detainer form) for the judge to sign. That way, you'll be able to simply hand the form to the judge to sign right after the hearing, instead of going home to prepare the judgment and going back to court to leave it for signature.

 FORM
A blank copy of the Judgment—Unlawful Detainer (Judicial Council form UD-110) is available for downloading from the Nolo website. (See the appendix for the link to the forms in this book, and other information on using the forms.)

The usual information goes in the big boxes at the top of this Judgment form. It's the same information you used on the form for a clerk's judgment for possession (described above).

In the box containing the words "JUDGMENT —UNLAWFUL DETAINER," put an X in the boxes next to the words "By Court" and "By Default."

Item 1: Put an X in Item 1 next to the words "BY DEFAULT," and also in Box 1e next to the words "Court Judgment." Then check Box 1e(1) if you will be attending a live default hearing, or Box 1e(2) if you will be submitting a written declaration.

UD-110

ATTORNEY OR PARTY WITHOUT ATTORNEY *(Name, state bar number, and address)*: LENNY D. LANDLORD 12345 Angeleno Street Los Angeles CA 90010 TELEPHONE NO.: 213-555-6789 FAX NO. *(Optional)*: 213-555-5678 E-MAIL ADDRESS *(Optional)*: ATTORNEY FOR *(Name)*: Plaintiff in Pro Per	FOR COURT USE ONLY

SUPERIOR COURT OF CALIFORNIA, COUNTY OF   Los Angeles
STREET ADDRESS: 110 North Hill Street
MAILING ADDRESS: Same
CITY AND ZIP CODE: Los Angeles, CA 90012
BRANCH NAME:

PLAINTIFF: LENNY D. LANDLORD

DEFENDANT: TERRENCE D. TENANT, TILLIE D. TENANT

JUDGMENT—UNLAWFUL DETAINER	CASE NUMBER:
[ ] By Clerk [X] By Default [ ] After Court Trial [X] By Court [ ] Possession Only [ ] Defendant Did Not Appear at Trial	A-12345-B

JUDGMENT

1. [X] **BY DEFAULT**
    a. Defendant was properly served with a copy of the summons and complaint.
    b. Defendant failed to answer the complaint or appear and defend the action within the time allowed by law.
    c. Defendant's default was entered by the clerk upon plaintiff's application.
    d. [ ] **Clerk's Judgment** (Code Civ. Proc., § 1169). For possession only of the premises described on page 2 (item 4).
    e. [X] **Court Judgment** (Code Civ. Proc., § 585(b)). The court considered
        (1) [ ] plaintiff's testimony and other evidence.
        (2) [X] plaintiff's or others' written declaration and evidence (Code Civ. Proc., § 585(d)).

2. [ ] **AFTER COURT TRIAL.** The jury was waived. The court considered the evidence.
    a. The case was tried on *(date and time)*:
       before *(name of judicial officer)*:

    b. Appearances by:
       [ ] Plaintiff *(name each)*:   [ ] Plaintiff's attorney *(name each)*:
                                                       (1)
                                                       (2)

       [ ] Continued on *Attachment* 2b (form MC-025).

       [ ] Defendant *(name each)*:   [ ] Defendant's attorney *(name each)*:
                                                         (1)
                                                       (2)

       [ ] Continued on *Attachment* 2b (form MC-025).

    c. [ ] Defendant did not appear at trial. Defendant was properly served with notice of trial.

    d. [ ] A statement of decision (Code Civ. Proc., § 632) [ ] was not [ ] was requested.

Page 1 of 2

PLAINTIFF: LENNY D. LANDLORD	CASE NUMBER:
DEFENDANT: TERRENCE D. TENANT, ET AL.	A-12345-B

JUDGMENT IS ENTERED AS FOLLOWS BY: [X] **THE COURT** [ ] **THE CLERK**

3. **Parties.** Judgment is

    a. [X] for plaintiff *(name each):* Lenny D. Landlord

       and against defendant *(name each):* Terrence D. Tenant, Tillie D. Tenant

       [ ] Continued on *Attachment* 3a (form MC-025).

    b. [ ] for defendant *(name each):*

4. [ ] Plaintiff [ ] Defendant is entitled to possession of the premises located at *(street address, apartment, city, and county):*

5. [ ] Judgment applies to all occupants of the premises including tenants, subtenants if any, and named claimants if any (Code Civ. Proc., §§ 715.010, 1169, and 1174.3).

6. **Amount and terms of judgment**

    a. [X] Defendant named in item 3a above must pay plaintiff on the complaint:
    b. [ ] Plaintiff is to receive nothing from defendant named in item 3b.

       [ ] Defendant named in item 3b is to recover costs: $

       [ ] and attorney fees: $

(1) [X] Past-due rent	$	list rent demanded in any three-day notice	
(2) [X] Holdover damages	$	list prorated damages	
(3) [ ] Attorney fees	$		
(4) [X] Costs	$	list court costs—filing, service, sheriff fees	
(5) [ ] Other *(specify):*	$		
(6) **TOTAL JUDGMENT**	$	Total	

    c. [ ] The rental agreement is canceled. [ ] The lease is forfeited.

7. [ ] **Conditional judgment.** Plaintiff has breached the agreement to provide habitable premises to defendant as stated in *Judgment—Unlawful Detainer Attachment* (form UD–110S), which is attached.

8. [ ] **Other** *(specify):*

    [ ] Continued on *Attachment* 8 (form MC-025).

Date: _____ [ ] _____

                                                                 JUDICIAL OFFICER

Date: _____ [ ] Clerk, by _____ , Deputy

(SEAL)	**CLERK'S CERTIFICATE** *(Optional)*
	I certify that this is a true copy of the original judgment on file in the court.
	Date:
	Clerk, by _____ , Deputy

UD-110 [New January 1, 2003]   **JUDGMENT—UNLAWFUL DETAINER**   Page 2 of 2

Item 2: Leave this part blank and proceed to Page 2 of the form. At the top of Page 2, fill in the names, in capitals, of the plaintiff (you), the first named defendant (followed by "ET AL." if there is more than one defendant), and the court case number. Also, put an X in the box preceding the words, "THE COURT," which itself follows the words "JUDGMENT IS ENTERED AS FOLLOWS BY."

Item 3: Put an X in Box 3a and type, in upper and lower case, the name(s) of the plaintiff(s) and the names of all defendants against whom you're obtaining this default judgment for the money owed you. Leave Box 3b blank.

Items 4 and 5: Leave these items blank, since you already have a judgment for possession of the property from the clerk.

Item 6: All the items here are exactly the same as in Item 15 of the statewide Declaration for Default Judgment by Court form. Check Box 6a and, in Item 6a(1), (2), and (4), check and list, as applicable, the rent, holdover damages, and costs, and add these for a "total judgment" amount in Item 6a(6). If the eviction is based on rent nonpayment or other breach, check, in Item 6c, either "The rental agreement is canceled" or "The lease is forfeited," as appropriate.

Items 7 and 8: Leave these blank.

Submitting Your Papers and/or Going to the Default Hearing

Make one copy of the proposed money judgment for your records, and one copy of the Request for Entry of Default for yourself plus one for each defendant. Mail a copy of the Request for Entry of Default to each tenant, and sign the proof of mailing on the back of the original. If you are submitting a declaration, also make a copy of it. You need to mail each defendant only a copy of the Request for Entry of Default, not a copy of any declaration or proposed judgment.

If you're submitting a declaration, give the original and copies of the Request for Entry of Default and the declaration to the court clerk, who should file the originals and rubber-stamp the copies and return them to you. Also give him or her the original and copy of the proposed judgment to hold on to for submission to the judge. After a few days, the judge should sign the original, and the clerk will file it and return your copy to you. (To avoid another trip to the courthouse, give the clerk a self-addressed, stamped envelope in which to mail your copy of the judgment.) Once you get the judgment, you will be ready to proceed to Chapter 9 to have the sheriff or marshal collect it.

If you are going to appear before a judge at a default hearing, file only the Request for Entry of Default and ask the court clerk to set a hearing date. In most counties, hearings are held on certain days and times during the week. The defendant is not allowed to participate in the hearing, and therefore is not given any notice of it—the defendant missed the chance to fight by not answering the complaint within the time allowed.

On the day of the default hearing, take the original and copy of the proposed judgment and go to court a few minutes early. When the clerk or judge calls your case, go forward and say to the judge something like, "Good morning, Your Honor, I'm Lenny D. Landlord appearing in pro per." The clerk will swear you in as your own witness. Some judges prefer that you take the witness stand, but others will allow you to present your case from the "counsel table" in front of the judge's bench.

You should be prepared to testify to the same kinds of facts that go into written declarations. (See above.) Lenny Landlord's testimony should go something like this:

"My name is Lenny D. Landlord. On January 2, 20xx, I rented my premises at 3815 Gower Canyon Ave., Apt. 3, to Terrence and Tillie Tenant, the defendants in this proceeding. They signed a rental agreement for a month-to-month tenancy. I have a copy of the rental agreement, which I wish to introduce into evidence as Exhibit No. 1. The rent agreed on was $1650 per month. On December 1, 20xx, I gave the defendants a 30-day notice that the rent would be increased to $1699.50 per month effective Jan. 2, 20xx +1. This amount of rent was paid in January, but on April 1 the defendants failed to pay the rent for April. On April 4, I served Terrence Tenant personally with a three-day notice to pay rent or quit and served Tillie Tenant by substituted service on the same day—leaving a copy with Terrence and mailing a copy to Tillie on the same day. I have a copy of the three-day notice which I wish to introduce into evidence as Exhibit No. 2. They didn't pay the rent and were still in possession on April 9, and I filed this lawsuit on April 10. They left the premises on May 14 under a clerk's judgment for possession only.

"The reasonable rental value for the premises is $56.65 per day.

"I am seeking a monetary judgment for $1,699.50 for rent, plus per diem damages for 14 days of $793.10, for a total of $2,492.60 plus court costs of $520."

If you need to call another witness, such as an agent who entered into the rental agreement on your behalf or a person who served the three-day notice, tell this to the judge and have that person testify.

The judge may ask you a question or two, but probably won't if you've been thorough. The judge will then announce the judgment that you should get possession of the property (in effect repeating the part of the judgment you got from the clerk) plus a specified amount of rent (damages), plus costs. Don't be afraid to ask the judge to specify the dollar amount of the court costs. (That way you'll have a judgment for them without having to file another form called a Memorandum of Costs.) Also, don't be afraid to politely differ with the judge ("Excuse me, Your Honor, but ...") as to the dollar amount of the rent/damages if you're sure you calculated the amount correctly—especially if the judge awarded only part of the rent for the first month the tenant didn't pay. You're entitled to the entire amount of unpaid rent that came due at the beginning of the month even if the tenant left before the month's end. However, if the judge declines to amend as you request, it's usually best to let it go.

Once the judge gives judgment in your favor, hand the judgment form with the correct amounts filled in to the courtroom clerk, and ask the clerk to file-stamp and return a copy to you. We discuss how to collect the money part of the judgment in Chapter 9.

Contested Cases

FORMS IN THIS CHAPTER

Chapter 8 includes instructions for and samples of the following forms:

- Stipulation for Entry of Judgment
- Answer—Unlawful Detainer
- Request/Counter-Request to Set Case for Trial—Unlawful Detainer
- Judgment—Unlawful Detainer, and
- Writ of Execution.

The Nolo website includes downloadable copies of these forms, plus the Judgment— Unlawful Detainer Attachment form described in this chapter, but for which a sample is not shown.

(See the appendix for the link to the forms in this book, and other information on using the forms.)

Read this chapter only if the tenant has filed a response to your unlawful detainer complaint. This chapter outlines how a contested unlawful detainer suit is resolved, either by settlement between the parties or at a trial. The purpose is to give you a solid idea of how a typical case is likely to proceed. We do not, and cannot, provide you with the full guidance necessary to handle all contested unlawful detainer cases to successful conclusions. But a detailed overview of the process is necessary whether you hire a lawyer or decide that your situation is simple enough that you can do it yourself.

SKIP THIS CHAPTER

If the tenant has not filed a response to your unlawful detainer complaint, and you have waited at least five days, you are entitled to seek a default judgment. That procedure is described in detail in Chapter 7.

What Is Involved in a Contested Eviction Case

Your tenant can complicate your life enormously simply by filing one or two pieces of paper with the court and mailing copies to you. If the tenant files a written response to your unlawful detainer complaint (whether it is in the form of a motion, a demurrer, or an answer—all described below), you will have to fill out some additional documents and probably appear in court one or more times. All of this will require that you be very much on your toes. As a general rule, judges will not evict a tenant unless every legal "t" and "i" has been scrupulously crossed and dotted.

In a contested case, some or all of the following may occur:

- If you or your process server erred in some way when serving the tenant, you might have to start from scratch by serving the tenant with a new notice to quit and/or a new summons and complaint.

- If the tenant convinces the judge that the complaint you filed is deficient in some way, you may have to redraft your complaint one or more times, without guidance from the judge.

- You might have to defend yourself against accusations like:

  - You illegally discriminated against the tenant (for example, you acted as you did because the tenant is gay, Latino, or has a disability).
  - The premises were legally uninhabitable.
  - Your eviction is in retaliation against the tenant for complaining to the health authorities or organizing other tenants.
  - Your eviction is in violation of the state or local rent control ordinance.

- You might have to disclose large amounts of business and sometimes personal information to the tenant, by answering written questions under oath (interrogatories), producing documents, and allowing the tenant to inspect the premises.

- You might have to appear before a judge (or jury) to argue your case.

- Even if you win, your tenant might be entitled to remain on the premises because of a hardship.

- Even if you win, if you have evicted your tenant for the wrong reasons, you could be setting yourself up for a lawsuit for wrongful eviction.

- If you lose, you're back to the drawing board and will owe the tenant court costs (and perhaps attorneys' fees, if the tenant was represented by an attorney), and maybe some damages as well.

Should You Hire an Attorney?

Clearly, you may be in for a good deal of trouble if your tenant contests your suit. Does this mean you should simply give up and hire a lawyer? At the very least, once you become aware of the tenant's response (and assuming you have not already filed for a default judgment), you should seriously consider locating and hiring an attorney experienced in landlord/tenant matters. Without knowing the particulars of a given contested case, we cannot predict whether you can safely handle it on your own.

Unless you are extremely experienced in these matters, you should always turn the case over to a lawyer if the tenant:

- is represented by a lawyer
- makes a motion or files a demurrer (these terms are explained below)
- demands a jury trial, or
- alleges any of the following defenses in his or her answer (discussed in "Preparing for Trial," below):
  - violation of a rent control ordinance or statute
  - discriminatory eviction
  - retaliatory eviction, or
- requests extensive pretrial disclosure of information that you feel would be harmful to disclose.

Understandably, you might be reluctant to turn the case over to a lawyer when you've taken it this far on your own. We're reluctant to recommend lawyers, too. The whole point of this book, after all, is to equip you to handle your unlawful detainer suit yourself. Unfortunately, we can't anticipate and prepare you to deal with every possible defense a tenant's lawyer may throw at you, or for that matter even predict what the tenant will raise in a motion. In short, once you find yourself facing a contested unlawful detainer suit, getting experienced help could be your best, and in the long run, most cost-efficient bet.

See "Attorneys and Eviction Services" in Chapter 1, for more information.

How to Settle a Case

You may negotiate a settlement with a tenant before or even during trial. Although it might not seem true in the heat of battle, it is our experience that because of the usually unpalatable prospect of a trial, it is very often in your economic interest to reach a settlement short of trial. That's why most unlawful detainer cases are settled without trials.

Why Settle?

Why is a reasonable—or sometimes even a somewhat unreasonable—settlement better than fighting it out in court? Aside from the possibility that your tenant might win the lawsuit (as well as a judgment against you for court costs and attorneys' fees), the time and trouble entailed in going to court often mean you are better off compromising. Often, landlords who plow forward to trial and ultimately "win" court judgments commonly suffer larger out-of-pocket losses than if they had compromised earlier. For example, tenants who refuse to pay the $1,000 rent on the first of the month will be able to stay anywhere from four to six weeks (or longer) before having to leave if they properly contest an unlawful detainer case. This means that if the tenants lose the case and are evicted after six weeks, the landlord loses $1,500 rent in the meantime, plus court costs approaching $500. If the case lasts longer, such as two months or more, the landlord loses even more money.

A landlord who hires a lawyer, will be out at least another thousand dollars, and probably a good deal more if a full-scale trial develops. Although these amounts might be added to the judgment against the tenant, the truth is that a great many such judgments are uncollectable. (See Chapter 9.)

Given this unhappy reality, the landlord usually comes out ahead of the game by accepting a reasonable compromise, even if the tenant gets an unfairly favorable result. Depending on the situation, this may mean that a tenant who has violated a lease or rental agreement provision is allowed to stay on if all past-due rent is paid. Or if the tenant is simply impossible to have around over the long term, the landlord may want to enter into a written settlement agreement under which the tenant agrees to leave within a few weeks or a couple of months in exchange for the forgiveness of some or all the rent that will have accrued through that time.

No matter what sort of deal you make, if it involves the tenant's moving out, it should be in writing, and should provide you with an immediate eviction remedy should the tenants refuse to keep their part of the bargain.

EXAMPLE: When Dmitri fails to pay his rent of $1,500 on May 1, Ivan serves him with a three-day notice. When that runs out without Dmitri paying the rent, Ivan sues Dmitri for an eviction order and the $1,500. Dmitri contests the suit with an answer that alleges Ivan breached the implied warranty of habitability by not getting rid of cockroaches. Ivan believes this is nonsense because he maintains the building very well, but does concede that the building is old and that tenants have had occasional problems with bugs and rodents. At trial, Ivan will attempt to prove that Dmitri's poor housekeeping caused the cockroaches and that Dmitri never complained about them before filing his answer. Both Ivan and Dmitri think they will win at trial, but each is sensible enough to know he might lose and that a trial will certainly take up a lot of time, money, and

energy. So they (or their lawyers) get together and hammer out a settlement agreement. Dmitri agrees to give Ivan a judgment for possession of the property, effective July 1, and Ivan agrees to drop his claim for back rent.

What Kind of Settlement Agreement Should You Make?

You and the tenant can settle the unlawful detainer lawsuit in one of two ways. You can agree to either of the following:

- **Unconditional judgment.** You'll file an unconditional entry of a judgment awarding you certain things, like possession of the property and rent, without your having to go back to court again (we'll call this the "unconditional judgment" option).
- **Deferred judgment.** You will be entitled to a judgment if the tenant fails to do certain things (such as leave or pay by a certain date), and a tenant who complies as promised will be entitled to a dismissal of the lawsuit. We'll refer to this second option as the "deferred judgment" option.

Differences Between an Unconditional and a Deferred Judgment

Here's the difference between these two approaches: With an unconditional entry of judgment, the tenant agrees that the landlord is entitled to file an unlawful detainer judgment that can be enforced on a certain date. With the deferred judgment option—an agreement that judgment will be entered if the tenant fails to comply as promised (and to dismiss the case if the tenant does comply)—the landlord does not initially have a judgment and must take additional steps to get one if he or she needs it.

How to Negotiate With a Tenant

Here are some thoughts on negotiating with a tenant you are trying to get out:

- Be courteous, but don't be weak. If you have a good case, let the tenant know you have the resources and evidence to fight and win if you can't reach a reasonable settlement.
- Know the probable eviction dates and procedure if you win at trial. Tenants may already have calculated the maximum time they can gain from going to trial and losing.
- Don't get too upset about how the tenant is using the system to get undeserved concessions out of you, and don't be so blinded by moral outrage that you reject workable compromises. At this point, you want to balance the costs of a settlement against the costs of fighting it out, and to choose the less expensive alternative. If this sometimes means that a rotten tenant gets a good deal, so be it. The alternative—your getting an even worse deal from California's court system—is even less desirable.
- Many courts have trained volunteer mediators and judges who help self-represented parties try to work out settlements on the eve of trial. Be open to this type of mediation, as it can be very helpful. Before trial, you can avail yourself of a local neighborhood mediation service, perhaps for a small fee. Look in your phone book yellow pages under "mediation," or do an Internet search using the name of the city or county in which the property is located, and the word "mediation."
- Keep your perspective and do not forget what you want to achieve—a business-like settlement. Often, an experienced mediator or judge will suggest possible settlements that are based on their experience. You should follow their leads. Often a business-like settlement consists of one you can live with, not necessarily one you like.

For advice on negotiating techniques, see *Getting to Yes: Negotiating Agreements Without Giving In*, by Fisher and Ury, of the Harvard Negotiation Project (Penguin).

Clearly, the unconditional entry of judgment favors the landlord, because if things go awry, the landlord won't have to go back to court. And an agreement that judgment will be entered only if the tenant fails to comply (a deferred judgment) favors the tenant, because if the tenant does not live up to the conditions, the landlord will have to revive the lawsuit that has been put on hold. Of course, tenants will also prefer the second route because they'll undoubtedly expect to perform as they promise (to move or pay), and would like to have the lawsuit dismissed, rather than suffer the consequences of having a judgment on file against them.

Be Careful About Designing an Agreement for the Deferred Judgment Option

A deferred judgment agreement gives the tenant extra time to move out while the landlord holds off on the eviction, but the tenant must satisfy certain additional conditions during that period in order to keep the eviction from going forward. For example, many times the landlord agrees to accept a payment plan for the back rent, coupled with a probation period on the current rent while the payment plan continues. This is a deferred judgment, because the landlord receives a judgment only if the tenant breaches the payment plan. Deferred judgments are common in large counties, particularly in rent control cities. Keep in mind that you're offering a substantial benefit to these tenants: the opportunity to avoid the negative mark of an eviction judgment to their credit records, which will haunt them for years. In exchange for your agreement to dismiss the lawsuit if the tenant performs, be sure that there is a fair trade-off, such as your getting an immediate, substantial payment of cash. If the tenant doesn't come through and you're forced to file for a judgment, you'll have just that—a mere judgment for money that can be hard to collect.

Preparing and Filing a Stipulation for Entry of Judgment

No matter which route you choose (an unconditional or a deferred judgment), you'll need to fill out a form called a Stipulation for Entry of Judgment. You'll fill it out differently, however, depending on your choice. Instructions for both ways of completing the form follow.

Completing the Stipulation for Entry of Judgment Form

Whether you and the tenant agree that you can file a judgment right now, or decide that you will file one only if the tenant fails to perform as promised, you'll need to complete and file a form. Here are instructions for each route. On the following pages is a filled-out sample Stipulation for Entry of Judgment using the Judicial Council form (UD-115).

 FORM

A blank copy of the Stipulation for Entry of Judgment (Judicial Council form UD-115) can be downloaded from the Nolo website. You'll also find on the Nolo website, a Judgment—Unlawful Detainer Attachment (Judicial Council Form UD 110S), which you might use as an attachment to this stipulation in certain situations (see Item 6c in the instructions, below). If you pursue an unconditional judgment or a deferred judgment, you will not need a separate Judgment Pursuant to Stipulation (the stipulation becomes the judgment when the judge signs it). (See the appendix for the link to the forms in this book, and other information on using the forms.)

Use a Checklist When Drafting Your Settlement

To guard against accidentally missing critical items, use a checklist for the elements the agreement needs to cover. Here are some suggested entries to your list:

- ☐ Possession (is the tenant moving out or staying? If moving, make sure to include the move-out date).
- ☐ Rent (specify whether you will waive the rent, or whether it will be paid, and if so, according to what schedule).
- ☐ Security deposit (specify whether you'll return it or keep it). Under Civ. Code § 1950.5, you ordinarily have to return the deposit unless you charge it for damage. However, you are also permitted to charge the deposit to remedy a breach of the lease (such as nonpayment). Your agreement should specify how you will charge or refund the deposit. Our model settlement agreement includes a paragraph with options and check boxes.
- ☐ Other conditions, such as making repairs to the apartment, cleaning the apartment by the tenant, any behavioral conduct (such as, do not disturb residents or manager). (See "'Masking' Court Records," below, for more information.)

- ☐ General release of claims (yes or no). (See Section 5 of the Settlement Agreement included in the forms for this book.)
- ☐ Dismissal on performance (for example, landlord will dismiss the case with prejudice after the tenant moves out, landlord will dismiss with prejudice after rent is paid, or landlord will dismiss without prejudice, reserving jurisdiction to enforce a complex agreement).
- ☐ Fees and costs (waived, paid, or included in the judgment only in the case of a default on a conditional entry of judgment).
- ☐ Enforcement (by way of an *ex parte* application or immediate judgment with enforcement and a stay of eviction). An "*ex parte* application" is a short form legal procedure that permits the court to enter a judgment or order on 25 hours' notice, without a formal hearing. The sample Settlement Agreement includes enforcement by an *ex parte* application in the Default section of the agreement.

UD–115

ATTORNEY OR PARTY WITHOUT ATTORNEY *(Name and state bar number, and address):*	FOR COURT USE ONLY
Lenny D. Landlord 12345 Angeleno Street Los Angles, CA 90028 TELEPHONE NO.: 213-555-6789 FAX NO. *(Optional):* E-MAIL ADDRESS *(Optional):* ATTORNEY FOR *(Name):* In pro per	

SUPERIOR COURT OF CALIFORNIA, COUNTY OF   LOS ANGELES
STREET ADDRESS: 111 North Hill St
MAILING ADDRESS:
CITY AND ZIP CODE: Los Angles, CA 90028
BRANCH NAME:

PLAINTIFF: Lenny D. Landlord
DEFENDANT: Terrence D. Tenant et al.

STIPULATION FOR ENTRY OF JUDGMENT (Unlawful Detainer)	CASE NUMBER: A-12345-B

1. IT IS STIPULATED by plaintiff *(name each):* Lenny D. Landlord   and

   defendant *(name each):* Terrence D. Tenant, Tillie D. Tenant

2. [**x**] Plaintiff [   ] Defendant *(specify name):* Lenny D. Landlord   is awarded

   a. [**x**] possession of the premises located at *(street address, apartment number, city, and county):*
       3815 Gower Canyon Ave., Apt. 3, Los Angeles, CA 90028 (Los Angeles County)

   b. [   ] cancellation of the rental agreement.   [   ] forfeiture of the lease.

   c. [**x**] past due rent $ 1,665.65

   d. [**x**] total holdover damages $ 731.10

   e. [   ] attorney fees $

   f. [**x**] costs $ 520.00

   g. [   ] deposit of $ [   ] See item 3.

   h. [**x**] other *(specify):*

   i. Total $ 2,916.75 to be paid by [   ] *(date):*   [   ] installment payments (see item 5)

3. [   ] Deposit. If not awarded under item 2g, then plaintiff must

   a. [   ] return deposit of $ to defendant by *(date):* July 1, 20xx

   b. [   ] give an itemized deposit statement to defendant within three weeks after defendant vacates the premises (Civ. Code, § 1950.5).

   c. [   ] mail the [   ] deposit [   ] itemized statement   to the defendant at *(mailing address):*

4. [**x**] A writ of possession will issue immediately, but there will be no lockout before *(date):*

5. [   ] AGREEMENT FOR INSTALLMENT PAYMENTS

   a. Defendant agrees to pay $ on the *(specify day)*   day of each month beginning

   on *(specify date)*   until paid In full.

   b. If any payment is more than *(specify)*   days late, the entire amount in item 2i will become immediately due and payable plus interest at the legal rate.

6. a. [   ] Judgment will be entered now.

   b. [   ] Judgment will be entered only upon default of payment of the amount in item 2i or the payment arrangement in item 5a. The case is calendared for dismissal on *(date and time)*   in department *(specify)*   unless plaintiff or defendant otherwise notifies the court.

   c. [   ] Judgment will be entered as stated in *Judgment—Unlawful Detainer Attachment* (form UD-110S), which is attached.

   d. [   ] Judgment will be entered as stated in item 7.

Page 1 of 2

STIPULATION FOR ENTRY OF JUDGMENT
(Unlawful Detainer)

Code of Civil Procedure, § 664.6

UD–115

PLAINTIFF: Lenny D. Landlord	CASE NUMBER:
DEFENDANT: Terrence D. Tenant, et al.	A-12345-B

7. [✖] Plaintiff and defendant further stipulate as follows *(specify):*

a. All amounts due under paragraph 2 will be waived by Plaintiff; provided Defendants vacate and surrender possession of the premises on or before June 30, 20xx, by delivering all keys and accessories to the Premises to Plaintiff, leaving the premises in reasonably clean, undamaged condition, ordinary wear and tear excepted, free and clear of all personal property and possessions.

b. Any property remaining in the premises following delivery of the keys and surrender of possession will be deemed to have been irrevocably abandoned by Defendants, and Plaintiff may dispose of or utilize said property as Plaintiff deems fit in Plaintiff's sole discretion.

8. a. **The parties named in item 1 understand that they have the right to (1) have an attorney present and (2) receive notice of and have a court hearing about any default in the terms of this stipulation.**

b. Date:

Lenny D. Landlord
_____
(TYPE OR PRINT NAME)

▶ *Lenny D. Landlord*
_____
(SIGNATURE OF PLAINTIFF OR ATTORNEY)

_____
(TYPE OR PRINT NAME)

▶ _____
(SIGNATURE OF PLAINTIFF OR ATTORNEY)

[ ] Continued on *Attachment* 8b (form MC-025).

c. Date:

Terrence D. Tenant
_____
(TYPE OR PRINT NAME)

▶ *Terrence D. Tenant*
_____
(SIGNATURE OF DEFENDANT OR ATTORNEY)

Tillie D. Tenant
_____
(TYPE OR PRINT NAME)

▶ *Tillie D. Tenant*
_____
(SIGNATURE OF DEFENDANT OR ATTORNEY)

_____
(TYPE OR PRINT NAME)

▶ _____
(SIGNATURE OF DEFENDANT OR ATTORNEY)

[ ] Continued on *Attachment* 8c (form MC-025).

9. IT IS SO ORDERED.

Date: _____

_____
JUDICIAL OFFICER

UD-115 [New January 1, 2003]

STIPULATION FOR ENTRY OF JUDGMENT
(Unlawful Detainer)

Page 2 of 2

"Masking" Court Records

Court records of eviction lawsuits are hidden, or "masked," during the first 60 days following the lawsuit's filing, but are accessible to specified persons (not including employers and potential landlords). After that, the records are unmasked only if the landlord has obtained a judgment against all defendants. Without a landlord's entry of judgment, the records remain masked. Also, if the judgment involves rent due from March 1, 2020, through September 30, 2021 (COVID debt), the judgment will remain masked. (Calif. C.C.P. §1161.2.)

FORM

A form for a deferred judgment agreement with a payment plan (Settlement Agreement) can be downloaded from the Nolo website. It covers the common issues encountered in settlement agreements, and includes sections for additional handwritten provisions, which you'll use depending on the negotiated terms. (See the appendix for the link to the forms in this book, and other information on using the forms.)

By now, you're familiar with the beginning parts of these forms. As with all Judicial Council forms, in the boxes at the top of the form list your name, address, and telephone number; the words "Plaintiff in Pro Per"; the court, county, court address, and branch, if applicable; and names of the plaintiff and defendants, as well as the case number.

Item 1: List your name and the names of the defendants who will be signing this stipulation.

Item 2: If the tenant will be vacating the property, put an X in the box next to the word "Plaintiff." Do not put an X in the box next to the word "Defendant," unless the tenant will be staying in possession of the premises, presumably after having come up to date on the rent that will accrue through the current month or other rental period, plus your court costs, paid immediately in cash or by cashier's or certified check or money order.

Item 2a: List the complete address of the property, including street address; unit number, if any; city; and county.

Item 2b: If the tenant will be vacating the property, put an X in the box next to either the words "cancellation of the rental agreement" or "forfeiture of the lease," as applicable.

Items 2c–2e: If the tenant will be paying past-due rent, and/or prorated daily damages, put Xs where appropriate and indicate the dollar amount(s) in these items.

Item 2f: If the tenant will also be paying your court costs, put an X in this box and indicate the amount.

Item 2g: If you are stating in Item 2 that you, the plaintiff, are awarded the things listed, and you agree that you will not have to return the tenant's security deposit, put an X in this box and indicate the dollar amount of the deposit. (Avoid agreeing to this, if possible, because it will leave you without any funds to claim or repair the premises, after the tenant has vacated.)

Item 2i: Add up the dollar amounts in Items 2c, 2d, 2f, and 2g.

Item 3: If you have declined to agree (as we suggest in the instructions for Item 2g, above) to apply the tenants' security deposit before they move out, then you should check Box 3a or 3b, indicating the deposit will be subject to proper deductions (for cleaning and damages) in the normal fashion. We recommend negotiating for a promise to return and/or itemizing the security deposit within three weeks after tenants vacate the premises, because that allows you a fund from which to deduct the costs of any necessary cleaning or repairs in excess of ordinary wear and tear, and allows you the time ordinarily allowed by law to do this. If, on the other hand, all you can negotiate for is to return a certain dollar amount of the deposit to the tenant by a certain date, then check Box 3a and indicate the dollar amount of the deposit and date. In either case, if Box 3a or 3b is checked, you should check the items in Box 3c to indicate the tenant's mailing address, to which you will be mailing the deposit and/or itemization.

Item 4: Check the box that gives you an immediate writ of possession. Chapter 7 covers this form (the name on the preprinted form is Writ of Execution). If the tenants will not be moving prior to a certain agreed date, you should still put an X in this box, and indicate that date. This allows you to agree that the tenants may stay in the premises until a certain date, and to have them evicted the next day if they fail to move. For example, if the tenant agrees to vacate by June 15, with that date specified in Item 4, you can have the clerk issue a Writ of Possession and give it to the sheriff on June 5, with appropriate instructions "to conduct final lockout and delivery of possession of premises to me on or after June 15, 20xx." This is important because, otherwise, there will be a delay of at least one week between the time you give the sheriff the Writ of Possession, and the time the tenant will have to leave.

Item 5: If you agree the tenant will pay a certain sum in monthly installments, this is the place to indicate that the tenant will pay a certain dollar amount each month, on a certain day of the month, until the amount listed in Item 2i has been paid. You can also specify that if any payment is more than a certain number of days later the entire amount listed in Item 2i becomes due.

Items 6a and 6b: Whether you check Box 6a or 6b is one of the most important aspects of this stipulation. Check Box 6a if you have been able to negotiate an unconditional judgment, hopefully one that says that you will be entitled to possession of the premises, whether by a certain date or immediately. If, on the other hand, you are merely entering into an agreement for judgment entered in the future, if the tenant fails to comply with certain conditions (such as failure to pay rent installments as promised in Item 5), then Box 6b should be checked. In that case, you will also have to fill out a date, time, and court department, approved by the judge, for the case

to be dismissed, in the event the tenant complies with all the provisions of this type of agreement.

Item 6c: Sometimes an actual judgment, which has certain conditions, can be entered. We've characterized this as a hybrid; you enter the judgment now, but it doesn't take effect until later, and only if the court finds that the conditions have been met. This type of judgment, however, is about as cumbersome to the landlord as is the agreement for entry of judgment in the future if certain conditions have not been met by the tenant. Judges do not like them and you can probably see why: It involves another trip to the courthouse. With this type of judgment, you'll need to set a future date for a court hearing, to determine whether the conditions have been met. If you want this kind of conditional judgment, check Box 6c, fill out another form called a Judgment—Unlawful Detainer Attachment (Form UD-110S), and attach it to the Stipulation for Entry of Judgment form. As mentioned above, we include a blank form of this type on the Nolo website, but because we do not recommend this path, we have not included instructions on completing it or a sample in this chapter.

Items 6d and 7: If you and the tenant agree on additional terms, which are not easily adapted to this form, you should check both these boxes, and indicate those terms in Item 7 on Page 2 of the form.

Item 8: In Items 8b and 8c, enter the date the stipulation is signed, together with the printed names and signatures of all plaintiffs and all defendants.

Once the form is filled out and signed by all parties, submit it to the judge, who should sign, date, and file it. If Box 6a is checked, this document will be the equivalent of an unconditional judgment. However, if Box 6b or 6c is checked, you might need to schedule further court hearings, or to file declarations under penalty of perjury, in order to proceed further. If Box 6b is checked and you end up back in court, you also will need to submit a separate judgment along with a written declaration under penalty of perjury, to the effect that the tenant has not complied with the agreement.

Appearing in Court

Regardless of which type of stipulation you are able to negotiate with the tenant, the law recognizes only two ways that stipulations can become binding. Either the terms must be recited in "open court" in front of a judge, or they must be in writing. In many ways, a written agreement is preferable, because it leaves no doubt as to what was agreed to. But most tenants will not seriously negotiate until they're at the courthouse, face to face with you, about to start trial in a few minutes if there's a failure to agree. If you're facing someone who won't even talk to you, it's often impossible to prepare a completed written stipulation beforehand.

You might, however, be able to begin negotiations and even come to a partial agreement with the tenant before going to court. If so, it's a good idea to at least fill in the boxes at the top of the form, including the names of the parties in Items 1, 2, and 8, and the address of the premises in Item 2. Finish as much of the remainder as you can, to reflect the extent of the settlement that's been agreed to. Bring an original and several copies to court with you on the day of trial. If you finalize your settlement at the courthouse and can complete the form neatly in ink as the terms are negotiated, you might be able to present it to the judge for signature and get it filed (some judges insist on typed forms). If the judge won't accept it, you must recite its terms in court, in front of a judge, while the proceedings are tape-recorded or a court reporter takes everything down.

Those of you who are dealing with tenants who won't negotiate prior to trial might find that the stomach-churning prospect of starting trial will convince a tenant to negotiate and settle. It won't hurt to be prepared—fill out parts of the stipulation form as directed above and hope for the

Stipulations for Entry of Judgment			
Type	**When judgment is entered in court**	**What happens if tenant doesn't move?**	**Filling out the form**
Unconditional Judgment	As soon as the judge signs the form, in Item 9 ("IT IS SO ORDERED"), the form becomes an unconditional judgment.	Landlord can ask sheriff to evict (see instructions to Item 4).	Check Box 6a.
Deferred Judgment	When the landlord establishes in court that the tenant hasn't complied with the agreement, the judge will sign the order.	The landlord will have to appear in court at a later date, or file a declaration under penalty of perjury, stating how the tenant has failed to live up to the agreement, and will have to submit a separate proposed judgment.	Check Box 6b.
Conditional Judgment	The judgment will be entered after a court hearing in which the landlord convinces the judge that the tenant did not comply.	The landlord initiates the hearing.	Check Box 6c, but this method is not recommended.

best. If you reach an agreement and the court will accept a neatly hand-filled form, great. If the court refuses your form, recite the terms in court, before a court reporter or in the presence of a tape recorder.

> ⚠ **CAUTION**
>
> **What it takes to settle a case.** Until the tenant(s) and the judge have accepted and signed a written Stipulation for Entry of Judgment, or you have the terms of the settlement "on the record," taken down by a court reporter or tape-recorded, do not tell the judge you have settled the case. Do not agree to "drop" the matter or take it "off calendar."

The Tenant's Written Response to an Unlawful Detainer Complaint

In the previous section, we discussed possible settlement negotiations between you and the tenant. Such negotiations usually occur after the tenant has filed a response to the complaint, because there's not much reason to negotiate if the tenant fails to respond and you get a default judgment. In this section, we discuss the types of written responses tenants may file with the court in response to your complaint, and how to deal with them.

Sooner or later, you will receive a copy of the tenant's written response to your unlawful detainer complaint. This response can take several forms. Let's discuss these in the order of their likelihood, assuming the tenant has a lawyer or is well-informed about responding to unlawful detainer complaints.

Tenant Motions as Responses to an Unlawful Detainer Complaint

A tenant can object to something in your summons or complaint (forms we cover in Chapter 6) by filing a response. Rather than answering the complaint allegations, the tenant's response simply asserts that the complaint isn't technically up to snuff.

It is common for tenants to bring these types of issues to the attention of the court (and thus obtain delay) in the form of a request called a motion.

A motion is a written request that a judge make a ruling on a particular issue, before any trial occurs. Once a motion (or motions) are filed with the court, the case will automatically be delayed by several weeks because the tenant doesn't have to respond to the substance of your complaint until the procedural questions raised in the motion (or motions) are cleared up.

For example, a tenant (or the tenant's attorney) could file a motion to "quash service of summons," in which they ask the judge to state that the summons wasn't properly served, and to require the landlord to serve it again, properly. The clerk will schedule a court hearing to consider the merits of the motion between one and two weeks after filing.

Or, a tenant might believe that a landlord's request for extra "statutory damages" (due to the tenant's malicious conduct) isn't backed up by enough allegations of ill will on the tenant's part. That tenant can make a motion to have the judge "strike" (consider as deleted) the request for statutory damages from the unlawful detainer complaint.

To have any motion heard by a judge, a tenant files a set of typewritten papers:

- **Notice of motion.** The first paper is a notice of motion, which notifies you of the date and time the motion will be heard and summarizes the basis ("grounds") for the motion.
- **A memorandum of points and authorities.** The second paper is a short legal essay called a memorandum of points and authorities, stating why the tenant should win the motion.
- **Declaration.** Motions sometimes also include a "declaration" in which the tenant states, under penalty of perjury, any relevant facts— for example, that the tenant wasn't properly served with the summons.

From the landlord's point of view, the worst thing about a tenant's motion is not only that the judge might grant it, but that it can delay the eviction for at least several weeks, during which the tenant will not be paying rent. This is true even if the tenant loses the motion. Motions generally can be heard no sooner than 26 days after the tenant files the motion papers and mails copies of them to the landlord. (C.C.P. §§ 1177 and 1005.) One exception is motions to quash, which under C.C.P. Section 1167.4(a) must be heard no later than seven days after filing.

At least nine court days before the hearing (or fewer if the court will hear the motion on shortened time), the landlord should file a written response arguing that the tenant's motion should be denied. The judge will read both sides' papers in advance and will allow limited discussion by each side at the hearing, perhaps asking a few questions. The judge then rules on the motion. If the motion is denied, the judge will require the tenant to file an answer to the complaint within five days.

Here is a brief discussion of the kinds of motions commonly filed in unlawful detainer cases.

Law and Motion

If you prepare and argue one of the motions described below, you will have entered the courthouse's toughest neighborhood. The Law and Motion Department (courtroom) represents the least friendly, most technical place a self-represented party—you—will encounter.

Complicated procedures and court rules govern motion practice. Before preparing your motion, look at the court's website for law and motion information. Many motion departments have schedules and rules that differ from those of the trial courts, including scheduled hearing dates, whether you must reserve a court day and time, and any tentative ruling practices (judges issue tentative rulings before the scheduled hearing, to give litigants a look at the judge's intended but not yet final decision). Some courts have created special housing departments, like the San Francisco Superior Court, which specialize in real estate and landlord-tenant matters.

Deadlines are firm. With the exception of motions for summary judgment or motions to quash service of the summons, all motions that require hearings must be filed at least 16 court days before the hearing. Too little notice will cause your motion to lose. Oppositions must be filed no later than nine court days before the hearing. Late filings may be ignored by the court. Replies to oppositions must be filed five court days before the hearing. (Technically, the law does not require the moving party to file a reply. However, many courts consider the lack of a reply to be a concession by the moving party.)

Tentative rulings are important. Courts that use tentative rulings do so in order to inform the parties of the court's probable ruling on the motion, save time for the court and parties at hearings, and give guidance on the court's thinking for discussion at the hearing. Courts wish to discourage party appearances, especially appearances that will not result in a change of decision. Nevertheless, both sides have the right to a hearing (as long as they follow the rules), and a judge cannot decide the motion without taking oral argument from the parties.

Most courts issue tentative rulings in writing, one or two court days before the hearing. You can read or hear the rulings on the court's website or by telephone. If the court issues a tentative ruling (and unless otherwise stated in the tentative ruling), if you want to appear and argue for or against the tentative ruling, you must telephone the other party (either the tenant's attorney or the tenant *in pro per*) by 4:00 p.m. the court day before the hearing and either inform the party directly or leave a message that you will appear at the hearing to argue.

The court will not permit you to speak at the hearing if you have not made the telephone call.

(See California Rules of Court, Rule 3.1308 for a more detailed explanation of the procedure.)

Some courts also require litigants to give the court notice, by telephone or in writing, that they will appear when they want to contest the tentative ruling. Some courts in limited circumstances request a summary of the legal argument you intend to make. However, if you have properly notified the opposing party and court, the court must hear your argument. (See California Rules of Court, Rule 3.1308(a)(2).)

If you appear at the hearing, courtroom etiquette applies:

- Always address the judge as "Your Honor," not "Judge."
- Listen to what the judge says and respond to direct questions. Judges ask questions about the points they consider important.
- Do not interrupt the judge or the other party—you will get your chance to speak.
- Wear full business attire, not casual clothing. For men, this requires a coat and tie. Do not wear a parka, raincoat, or other outer clothing in the courtroom.

Remote Appearances

The COVID-19 shelter-in-place orders and court closures led nearly all courts to adopt remote hearing procedures. Parties appear (particularly at motions) by video conference using computers, tablets, or even mobile smartphones. The technology required for remote appearances is so widely available that many courts prefer to hold hearings remotely. Effective January 1, 2022 until at least July 1, 2023 a new law gives parties (including self-represented litigants) throughout the state the option to appear remotely.

Parties may choose to appear remotely in any civil proceeding except in any of the following circumstances:

- The court requires a personal appearance.
- It does not have the technology to enable a remote appearance.

- The quality of the technology is not acceptable.

The court cannot require self-represented parties (that means you) to appear remotely, but you can choose to do so. If one side requests a remote session but the other wants to appear in person, each can usually appear as requested (remotely and in person). However, the court can order an in-person appearance for any reason. Because the law requires the courts to provide sufficient technology for remote appearances, if there is a technological problem (equipment shortage, poor video or audio quality, or simply poor Internet service), then an in-person appearance can be ordered on that basis alone. (C.C.P. §367.75.)

To choose remote appearances and specify the hearings that you want to attend remotely, you should file and serve a "Notice of Remote Appearance," Judicial Council Form RA-010. Copies are on the Judicial Council website.

Check your court's website for information on remotely conducted appearances. Finding what you need might require some poking around, but most departments publish their remote conferencing links and procedures.

- Remote hearings can be more efficient and professional than in-person hearings. However, you will effectively be on television and will have to keep in mind the limitations and pitfalls of being on a screen. The following recommendations all come from real-world experiences and disasters: You are always on camera during a video appearance, and everything you do can be seen by other persons in the conference—judges, clerks, lawyers, and litigants. Be mindful of how you look and what you do. No eating or drinking (beyond a sip of water), and no personal grooming.
- Dress appropriately, top and bottom, just as you would for an in-person appearance. Famous disasters have occurred when speakers stood up on camera unthinkingly to reveal inappropriate dress (and sometimes none at all).

- Be familiar with the platform you are using (Zoom, Google Meet, and so on), and avoid video filters, interesting electronic backgrounds, or electronic modifications to your appearance. One hapless lawyer appeared in court as a cat and the meme spread worldwide. No one remembers the lawyer or the issue, but *everyone* remembers the cat and the lawyer's helpless plight when he couldn't turn off the video filter.
- Avoid outside distractions and noise. Close doors and leave your pets in another room.
- Until your matter is called, keep your microphone muted.
- Unless you are appearing on your mobile phone, shut it off. Cell phone calls are as unwanted remotely as they are live in the courtroom.
- Be careful not to interrupt the judge. It can be tricky, because the technology often lags behind the real time event. You should allow a couple seconds after hearing the judge before speaking.

The Motion to Quash

Officially called a "motion to quash summons or service of summons," this motion alleges a defect in the summons or the way it was served. (If the defect is in the way it was served on one tenant, only that tenant may make this kind of motion.) If the judge agrees, the case is delayed until you have a new summons served on the tenant. Typical grounds for a tenant's motion to quash based on defective service include the following:

- The summons was served on one defendant but not the other.
- The wrong person was served.
- No one was served.
- The process server didn't personally serve the summons as claimed in the Proof of Service (and instead mailed it, laid it on the doorstep, or served it in some other unauthorized manner).
- You, the plaintiff, served the summons.

Grounds based on a defect in the summons itself include either of the following:

- The wrong court or judicial district is listed.
- The landlord used the wrong summons form (one for a nonunlawful detainer complaint).

You cannot use a motion to quash to test the allegations of the complaint. It tests only the personal jurisdiction over the defendant. (*Stancil v. Superior Court* (2021) 11 Cal.5th 381, 390-91.)

If the motion to quash is based on allegations that can logically be responded to by your process server, the server will have to appear at the hearing on the motion. Servers will need to testify as to when, where, and how they served the papers. For instance, if the tenant's motion to quash states that the summons and complaint were served solely by first-class mail (which is not permitted), you would need your process server to testify as to how the papers were, in fact, served. Before the hearing, you should file with the court clerk the Proof of Service (on the back of the original summons) that the process server filled out, and a declaration from the process server covering the details of the serve.

SEE AN EXPERT

If you encounter a motion to quash, you will need the assistance of an attorney. The exception is if you are able to interpret and contest the tenant's motion papers, know how to file and serve your response papers, and are prepared to argue the motion in a court hearing.

Motion to Strike

A motion to strike asks the judge to strike (delete) all or part of a complaint. For example, if your unlawful detainer complaint asks for additional statutory damages based on the tenant's "malice," but without alleging any specific facts that tend to show the tenant's malicious intent, the tenant may make a motion to strike the statutory damages request from the complaint. If the judge grants the motion, it doesn't mean that the judge or clerk goes through your complaint and crosses out the part objected to, but the judge will treat the case as if that had been done.

Motions to strike, like all noticed motions, are heard no sooner than 16 court days after the tenant files the motion, which means that, win or lose on the motion, you lose three weeks or more.

Other defects in the complaint that might subject it to a tenant's motion to strike include:

- a request for attorneys' fees, if you didn't allege a written rental agreement or lease that contains an attorneys' fees clause
- a request for prorated daily damages at the reasonable rental value, because the complaint lacks an allegation of the daily rental value
- a request for something not awardable in an unlawful detainer action (see motion to quash, above), or
- your failure to "verify" the complaint (sign it under penalty of perjury). This could result in a successful motion to strike the entire complaint.

How you should respond to a motion to strike depends on the part of your complaint objected to, but in most cases you can shorten the delay caused by the motion by simply filing and serving an "amended complaint" that corrects your errors. Telling you how and when to file an amended complaint depends on the severity of the defect and lies beyond the scope of this book.

However, you can amend the complaint once without special permission from the judge. (C.C.P. §472.) If the problem can be fixed simply, amending the complaint saves time and avoids a hearing. If you do amend the first time, you render the motion to strike moot and should be able to proceed with your unlawful detainer without waiting for a hearing.

If there is a hearing on the motion to strike, the judge will decide whether to strike the material the tenant objects to. Once the judge rules, the tenant has to file an answer within the time allowed by the judge, usually five days after service of a Notice of Entry of Order.

You may get a default judgment if the answer isn't filed by that time. (See Chapter 7.)

Demurrers

A "demurrer" is a written response to an unlawful detainer complaint that claims that the complaint (or the copy of the three-day, 30-day, or 60-day notice attached to it) is deficient in some way. When tenants file a demurrer, they are really saying, "Assuming only for the purpose of argument that everything the landlord says in the complaint is true, it still doesn't provide legal justification to order me evicted." Most demurrers allege that the complaint itself (including attachments) shows that the landlord has not complied with the strict requirements for preparation and service of the three-day, 30-day, or 60-day notice. For example, if the attached three-day notice doesn't demand that the tenant pay a specific dollar amount of rent or leave within three days, it's obvious from the complaint alone that the tenancy has not been properly terminated, and that the tenant therefore should win.

Typical objections directed to the attached three-day, 30-day, or 60-day notice by a demurrer include the following:

- not stating the premises' address, or stating an address different from that alleged elsewhere in the complaint
- stating an amount of rent as past due that is more than that alleged elsewhere in the complaint
- including in the termination notice charges other than rent, such as late fee charges
- alleging that the notice was served before the rent became past due, and
- failing to include some statement required by the local rent control ordinance.

Objections directed at the unlawful detainer complaint itself include:

- failure to check boxes containing essential allegations, such as compliance with rent control or just cause eviction ordinances, or
- allegation of contradictory statements.

Demurrers can often be more technical than motions to quash or strike. If a successful demurrer is based on a defect that can't be fixed by amendment, such as a defect in the notice attached to the complaint, you could wind up not only having the eviction delayed, but also with a judgment against you for court costs and attorneys' fees. It is for this reason (and because we simply can't predict the content of any particular demurrer) that we tell you to consult an attorney if you are faced with one.

The Tenant's Answer to Your Complaint

Sooner or later, if you adequately respond to any motions or demurrer filed by the tenant, the tenant will be required to respond to the substance of your complaint. This response is called the answer. It will finally let you know what aspects of your case the tenant plans to contest and what other arguments, if any, the tenant plans to advance as to why you should lose (called "affirmative defenses").

Like your unlawful detainer complaint, the tenant's answer is usually submitted on a standard fill-in-the-boxes form. (It can also be typed from scratch on 8½" × 11" paper with numbers in the left margin, but this is increasingly rare.) A typical answer is shown below.

Here is what you need to pay attention to in the tenant's answer.

The Tenant's Denial of Statements in the Complaint

The first part of the answer with which you must concern yourself is Item 2. Here, the defendant denies one or more of the allegations of your complaint. If Box 2a is checked, this means that the tenant denies everything you alleged.

At trial, you will have to testify to everything you alleged in the complaint: ownership, lease or rental agreement existence, rent amount, rent overdue, service of three-day notice, refusal to pay rent, and so on.

If Box 2b is checked, the space immediately below should indicate which, if any, of your allegations the tenant denies, either by specific reference to the numbered allegation paragraphs in your complaint or in a concise statement. At trial, you will be required to offer testimony or other evidence as to any of your allegations the tenant denies.

For example, in the sample answer, Terrence and Tillie Tenant deny the allegations of Paragraphs "6, 9, 10, 12, 13" of Lenny Landlord's complaint. This means Lenny has to go back and look at his complaint to see exactly what Terrence and Tillie are denying. He would find that the allegations denied are those concerning:

- the lease and lease terms
- the rental increase
- preparation and service of the three day notice, and
- damages and reasonable rental value.

In effect, a "standard" answer will require Lenny to prove all the important allegations of his case. Lenny will, at the very least, have to have the person who served the three-day notice testify in court that he or she in fact served it. Lenny, himself, will have to testify about the terms and identity of the lease agreement, when the defendants moved in, when the rent was increased, when he last received the rent, and how much the tenants owed when the notice was served.

The Tenant's Affirmative Defenses

SKIP AHEAD
If none of the boxes in Item 3 of the answer are checked, skip this discussion and go directly to "Other Things in the Answer," below.

In addition to responding to the landlord's statements in the complaint, tenants are entitled to use the answer to make some of their own. These statements (in Item 3 of the answer) are called "affirmative defenses." The tenant checks the boxes next to any applicable defenses and describes some of the relevant facts in Item 3w (on Page 4).

If the facts alleged in support of the affirmative defenses are too sparse or sketchy, you can (in theory) demurrer to the answer and demand a more complete statement of facts. However, you will also delay the proceedings by at least a month if you do so. Most landlords let the defective answer go, because the lost time outweighs any benefit to challenging the adequacy of the answer.

If the tenant proves an affirmative defense to the satisfaction of a judge, the tenant wins, even if everything you said in the unlawful detainer complaint is true. The duties imposed on you by law, the breach of which can give rise to these defenses, are discussed in detail in *The California Landlord's Law Book: Rights and Responsibilities*. Below, we discuss when you might need an attorney to help you handle a defense, and, if you decide to go it alone, how you will need to respond at trial.

SEE AN EXPERT

If you are still representing yourself, but upon inspecting the answer (Item 3) discover that an affirmative defense is being raised, now is the time to start looking for help. We are reluctant to advise a consultation with a lawyer solely because the tenant has raised an affirmative defense. However, even if you think the affirmative defense is untrue or just a bluff, please understand that by making such a response, the tenant is warning you that he or she has something in mind that may torpedo your case. If you proceed on your own and later are unable to handle the defense, all your hard work up to this point could go down the drain.

Here is a brief description of each affirmative defense that may be raised in the answer.

Item 3a: Breach of Warranty of Habitability

In suits based on nonpayment of rent, this defense asserts that the tenant should be excused from paying all the rent because of your failure to keep the place in good repair. (See *The California Landlord's Law Book: Rights & Responsibilities*, Chapter 11.) Technically, the habitability defense should not be raised in suits based on reasons other than nonpayment of rent. If a tenant does assert it improperly, you should object at trial.

Item 3b: Repair-and-Deduct Defense

Civil Code Section 1942 permits a tenant to spend up to one month's rent to make repairs to make the apartment or premises habitable after the landlord has failed to do so for at least 30 days. (See *The California Landlord's Law Book: Rights & Responsibilities*, Chapter 11.) Even if you think the tenant's deduction was improper, be prepared to prove a valid reason (under the repair-and-deduct statute) for the eviction.

Item 3c: Refusal of Rent

If you gave the tenant a Three-Day Notice to Pay Rent or Quit, you must accept rent offered during the three-day notice period. This defense is occasionally used when a tenant's offer of a check is rejected by the landlord during the three-day period for any reason including a requirement that payment be made by cash or money order—usually, after a few bounced checks. As long as you insisted on being paid by cash or money order well before the time that the tenant insists on using the check (and can document this), you should be able to beat this defense. (See *The California Landlord's Law Book: Rights & Responsibilities*, Chapter 3.) However, if the tenant has the rent money, a judge may make you take the money regardless, following a motion for relief from forfeiture (discussed below).

We recommend that you take and process a check tendered within the three-day period. If it clears, the tenant has satisfied the notice, and if it bounces you have written proof of nonpayment by the tenant (as long as you have a copy with "NSF" or the equivalent stamped on the check by the bank).

This point is often mistakenly raised by tenants when landlords properly refuse rent *after* the applicable notice period expired. Once the judge understands that the rent was offered only after the three-day period, and not before, you should prevail.

Item 3d: Waiver or Cancellation of Notice to Quit

If the landlord acted in a way that was somehow inconsistent with the three-, 30-, or 60-day notice, the notice may effectively be canceled. For example, if your three-day notice complained about the rent not being paid on the first of the month, but you'd accepted it on the fifth every month for the past year, you might have given up or "waived" the right to complain. Another example would be your acquiescing for several months to the tenant's breach of the no-pets lease clause and then serving the tenant with a Three-Day Notice to Perform Covenant or Quit that says the tenant must get rid of the pet or leave within three days. Item 3d might also be checked if the tenant claims you accepted or agreed to accept rent later than the notice deadline. (See Chapter 2 for a discussion of the consequences of accepting rent after serving a three-day notice, and Chapter 3 regarding acceptance of rent following service of a 30-day notice terminating a month-to-month tenancy.)

Item 3e: Retaliation

This alleges that your true reason for serving a notice—usually a 30- or 60-day notice terminating a month-to-month tenancy—was to retaliate for the tenant's exercise of a specified legal right. Tenants often claim retaliation when they have complained to local government authorities about housing conditions or have attempted to organize your other tenants. (See *The California Landlord's Law Book: Rights & Responsibilities*, Chapter 15.)

Retaliation cannot be raised legitimately as a defense to nonpayment of rent, but tenants invariably click the box in any type of eviction defense.

Item 3f: Discrimination

This defense refers to discrimination prohibited under state and federal law. (See *The California Landlord's Law Book: Rights & Responsibilities*, Chapter 9, for a discussion of this complex topic.)

Item 3g: Violation of Rent Control Ordinance

Many rent control ordinances not only limit the amount of rent you may charge, but also have "just cause eviction" provisions that limit your freedom to terminate a month-to-month tenancy. Your tenant can defend the lawsuit based on your failure to comply with any aspect of the ordinance, including:

- property registration requirements
- rent limits, or
- special requirements for three-day, 30-day, or 60-day eviction notices.

Cities that require registration of rents must limit the sanctions against landlords who are in "substantial compliance" with a rent control law, and who made only a good-faith mistake in calculating rent or registering property with the local rent control agency. (Civ. Code § 1947.7.) The statute appears to apply only to sanctions imposed by local rent control agencies, however. You should still expect to have your complaint dismissed if it is based on a three-day notice that demanded an amount of rent that was illegal under a rent control ordinance.

Item 3i: Acceptance of Rent

If you accepted rent for a period beyond the termination date in a termination notice, you might have revoked that notice. For example, if rent is due in advance on the first of each month, and you gave your tenant a 30-day notice on June 15, the tenancy terminates on July 15. By accepting a full month's rent on July 1, however, you accepted rent for the period through July 31, well beyond the termination date of the 15th, and you implicitly revoked the 30-day notice.

In many instances, this defense is identical to the "waiver and cancellation" defense (Item 3d, above), and the tenant can check either or both defenses.

Item 3j: Domestic Violence, Sexual Assault, stalking, trafficking, or elder or dependent adult abuse

If you terminated a tenancy with a 3 -30-, 60-, or 90-day notice, and the tenant or a household member has suffered domestic violence, abuse (sexual or otherwise) from a person identified in a court order or police report who is not a tenant of the unit, the tenant may plead this defense. (C.C.P. §1161.3.) If the tenant asserts this type of defense, be prepared to state the actual reason you terminated the tenancy.

Item 3v: Other Affirmative Defenses

Although Items 3a through 3u list the most common defenses, an imaginative tenant's attorney may use Item 3v to describe additional defenses. (Creative tenant attorneys are on the hunt for new affirmative defenses, and that is why we advise you to consult an attorney if the tenants have an attorney representing them.) As with the listed defenses, the facts specific to any defense checked here must be listed in Item 3w, below.

Item 3w: Specific Facts Relating to the Defenses

Under Item 3w on page 4 of the answer, the tenant is supposed to explain the affirmative defense boxes checked. No special language or format is necessary, and almost any brief, factual statement will do. These statements are supposed to give you an idea of what the defendant is going to try to prove at trial. At trial, the defendant may testify only to subjects that were mentioned in the answer.

Other Things in the Answer

Item 4 has spaces for miscellaneous "other statements." If the tenant has given up possession of the property before filing the answer (Item 4a), for instance, the case will be treated as a regular civil lawsuit. You and the tenant can then ask for things not allowed in an unlawful detainer action, but the case won't get to trial as fast as an unlawful detainer suit normally would. (Civ. Code § 1952.3.) An unlawful detainer suit is a special "summary" (expedited) procedure with shorter response times than regular suits, and more restrictions on the issues that may be raised.

In Item 4b, the tenant can state that the prorated daily "fair rental value" you alleged is too high (usually because of a habitability defense).

Failure to Provide Details on Where and When to Pay Rent

A landlord who has not complied with the requirement of Civ. Code §§ 1962 and 1962.5 to notify the tenant of the name and street address of the owner or manager responsible for collection of rent, how rent is to be paid, and who is available for services of notices may not evict for nonpayment of any rent that came due while the landlord was not in compliance.

This defense, designed to protect a tenant when a new owner takes over the property, has some potential for abuse. For example, a tenant who's paid the same landlord rent for months or even years, then stopped paying, might assert this defense if the landlord had failed to go through the motions of complying with the notice requirements, even when the tenant knew full well to whom, where, and how to pay the rent.

The best way to avoid this problem, of course, is to comply with the notice requirements listed in Chapter 2. If, however, you haven't complied with this requirement and such a tenant asserts this, you could argue either that the tenant failed to try to tender the rent, or that because the tenant previously paid rent to you, and knew full well to whom, where, and how to pay, the tenant is "estopped" from asserting this defense because the tenant wasn't "prejudiced." You can avoid this potential defense by complying fully with these notice requirements.

UD-105

ATTORNEY OR PARTY WITHOUT ATTORNEY NAME: Terrence D. Tenant, Tillie D. Tenant FIRM NAME: STREET ADDRESS: 8351 Gower Canyon Ave., Apt 3 CITY: Los Angles STATE: CA ZIP CODE: 90028 TELEPHONE NO.: 213-555-4321 FAX NO.: EMAIL ADDRESS: TDT2036@tsp.com ATTORNEY FOR *(name)*: In pro per	STATE BAR NUMBER:	*FOR COURT USE ONLY*

SUPERIOR COURT OF CALIFORNIA, COUNTY OF LOS ANGELES
STREET ADDRESS: 111 North Hill St
MAILING ADDRESS:
CITY AND ZIP CODE: Los Angles, CA 90028
BRANCH NAME:

PLAINTIFF: LENNY D. LANDLORD

DEFENDANT: TERRENCE D. TENANT, et al.

ANSWER—UNLAWFUL DETAINER	CASE NUMBER: A-12345-B

1. Defendant *(all defendants for whom this answer is filed must be named and must sign this answer unless their attorney signs)*:

   Terrence D. Tenant, Tillie D. Tenant

   answers the complaint as follows:

2. **DENIALS *(Check ONLY ONE of the next two boxes.)***

   a. ☐ **General Denial** *(Do not check this box if the complaint demands more than $1,000.)*
   Defendant generally denies each statement of the complaint and of the *Mandatory Cover Sheet and Supplemental Allegations—Unlawful Detainer* (form UD-101).

   b. ☒ **Specific Denials** *(Check this box and complete (1) and (2) below if complaint demands more than $1,000.)*
   Defendant admits that all of the statements of the complaint and of the *Mandatory Cover Sheet and Supplemental Allegations—Unlawful Detainer* (form UD-101) are true EXCEPT:

   (1) **Denial of Allegations in Complaint (Form UD-100 or Other Complaint for Unlawful Detainer)**

   (a) Defendant claims the following statements of the complaint are false *(state paragraph numbers from the complaint or explain below or, if more room needed, on form MC-025)*:

   ☐ Explanation is on form MC-025, titled as Attachment 2b(1)(a).

   6, 9, 10, 12, 13

   (b) Defendant has no information or belief that the following statements of the complaint are true, so defendant denies them *(state paragraph numbers from the complaint or explain below or, if more room needed, on form MC-025)*:

   ☐ Explanation is on form MC-025, titled as Attachment 2b(1)(b).

   4, 5, 7

   (2) **Denial of Allegations in *Mandatory Cover Sheet and Supplemental Allegations—Unlawful Detainer* (form UD-101)**

   (a) ☐ Defendant did not receive plaintiff's *Mandatory Cover Sheet and Supplemental Allegations* (form UD-101). *(If not checked, complete (b), (c), and (d), as appropriate.)*

   (b) ☐ Defendant claims the statements in the **Verification required for issuance of summons—residential**, item 3 of plaintiff's *Mandatory Cover Sheet and Supplemental Allegations* (form UD-101), are false.

   (c) Defendant claims the following statements on the *Mandatory Cover Sheet and Supplemental Allegations—Unlawful Detainer* (form UD-101) are false *(state paragraph numbers from form UD-101 or explain below or, if more room needed, on form MC-025)*: ☐ Explanation is on form MC-025, titled as Attachment 2b(2)(c).

Form Approved for Optional Use
Judicial Council of California
UD-105 [Rev. October 1, 2021]

ANSWER—UNLAWFUL DETAINER

Civil Code, § 1940 et seq.;
Code of Civil Procedure, §§ 425.12,
1161 et seq., 1179.01 et seq.
www.courts.ca.gov

UD-105

PLAINTIFF: LENNY D. LANDLORD	CASE NUMBER:
DEFENDANT: TERRENCE D. TENANT, et al.	A-12345-B

2. b. (2) (d) Defendant has no information or belief that the following statements on the *Mandatory Cover Sheet and Supplemental Allegations—Unlawful Detainer* (form UD-101) are true, so defendant denies them *(state paragraph numbers from form UD-101 or explain below or, if more room needed, on form MC-025):*

    ☐ Explanation is on form MC-025, titled as Attachment 2b(2)(d).

3. **DEFENSES AND OBJECTIONS** (*NOTE: For each box checked, you must state brief facts to support it in item 3w (on page 4) or, if more room is needed, on form MC-025. You can learn more about defenses and objections at www.courts.ca.gov/selfhelp-eviction.htm.*)

a. ☒ *(Nonpayment of rent only)* Plaintiff has breached the warranty to provide habitable premises.

b. ☐ *(Nonpayment of rent only)* Defendant made needed repairs and properly deducted the cost from the rent, and plaintiff did not give proper credit.

c. ☐ *(Nonpayment of rent only)* On *(date):* _____ before the notice to pay or quit expired, defendant offered the rent due but plaintiff would not accept it.

d. ☒ Plaintiff waived, changed, or canceled the notice to quit.

e. ☒ Plaintiff served defendant with the notice to quit or filed the complaint to retaliate against defendant.

f. ☒ By serving defendant with the notice to quit or filing the complaint, plaintiff is arbitrarily discriminating against the defendant in violation of the Constitution or the laws of the United States or California.

g. ☒ Plaintiff's demand for possession violates the local rent control or eviction control ordinance of *(city or county, title of ordinance, and date of passage):* Los Angeles Rent Stabilization Ordinance, enacted 1979, as amended
    (Also, briefly state in item 3w the facts showing violation of the ordinance.)

h. ☐ Plaintiff's demand for possession is subject to the Tenant Protection Act of 2019, Civil Code section 1946.2 or 1947.12, and is not in compliance with the act. *(Check all that apply and briefly state in item 3w the facts that support each.)*

    (1) ☐ Plaintiff failed to state a just cause for termination of tenancy in the written notice to terminate.

    (2) ☐ Plaintiff failed to provide an opportunity to cure any alleged violations of terms and conditions of the lease (other than payment of rent) as required under Civil Code section 1946.2(c).

    (3) ☐ Plaintiff failed to comply with the relocation assistance requirements of Civil Code section 1946.2(d).

    (4) ☐ Plaintiff has raised the rent more than the amount allowed under Civil Code section 1947.12, and the only unpaid rent is the unauthorized amount.

    (5) ☐ Plaintiff violated the Tenant Protection Act in another manner that defeats the complaint.

i. ☐ Plaintiff accepted rent from defendant to cover a period of time after the date the notice to quit expired.

j. ☐ Plaintiff seeks to evict defendant based on an act against defendant or a member of defendant's household that constitutes domestic violence, sexual assault, stalking, human trafficking, or abuse of an elder or a dependent adult. *(This defense requires one of the following: (1) **a temporary restraining order, protective order, or police report** that is not more than 180 days old; OR (2) **a signed statement from a qualified third party** (e.g., a doctor, domestic violence or sexual assault counselor, human trafficking caseworker, or psychologist) concerning the injuries or abuse resulting from these acts).)*

k. ☐ Plaintiff seeks to evict defendant based on defendant or another person calling the police or emergency assistance (e.g., ambulance) by or on behalf of a victim of abuse, a victim of crime, or an individual in an emergency when defendant or the other person believed that assistance was necessary.

l. ☒ Plaintiff's demand for possession of a residential property is in retaliation for nonpayment of rent or other financial obligations due between March 1, 2020, and September 30, 2021, even though alleged to be based on other reasons. (Civ. Code, § 1942.5(d); Gov. Code, § 12955.)

m. ☐ Plaintiff's demand for possession of a residential property is based on nonpayment of rent or other financial obligations due between March 1, 2020, and September 30, 2021, and *(check all that apply):*

    (1) ☐ Plaintiff did not serve the general notice or notices of rights under the COVID-19 Tenant Relief Act as required by Code of Civil Procedure section 1179.04.

    (2) ☐ Plaintiff did not serve the required 15-day notice. (Code Civ. Proc., § 1179.03(b) or (c).)

UD-105 [Rev. October 1, 2021]   **ANSWER—UNLAWFUL DETAINER**   Page 2 of 5

UD-105

PLAINTIFF: LENNY D. LANDLORD	CASE NUMBER:
DEFENDANT: TERRENCE D. TENANT, et al.	A-12345-B

3. m. (3) ☐ Plaintiff did not provide an unsigned declaration of COVID-19–related financial distress with the 15-day notice. (Code Civ. Proc., § 1179.03(d).)

(4) ☐ Plaintiff did not provide an unsigned declaration of COVID-19–related financial distress in the language in which the landlord was required to provide a translation of the rental agreement. (Code Civ. Proc., § 1179.03(d).)

(5) ☐ Plaintiff identified defendant as a "high-income tenant" in the 15-day notice, but plaintiff did not possess proof at the time the notice was served establishing that defendant met the definition of high-income tenant. (Code Civ. Proc., § 1179.02.5(b).)

(6) ☐ Defendant delivered to plaintiff one or more declarations of COVID-19–related financial distress and, if required as a "high-income tenant," documentation in support. (Code Civ. Proc., §§ 1179.03(f) and 1179.02.5.)

(Describe when and how delivered and check all other items below that apply):

(a) ☐ Plaintiff's demand for payment includes late fees on rent or other financial obligations due between March 1, 2020, and September 30, 2021.

(b) ☐ Plaintiff's demand for payment includes fees for services that were increased or not previously charged.

(c) ☐ Defendant, on or before September 30, 2021, paid or offered plaintiff payment of at least 25% of the total rental payments that were due between September 1, 2020, and September 30, 2021, and that were demanded in the termination notices for which defendant delivered the declarations described in (a). (Code Civ. Proc., § 1179.03(g)(2).)

(7) ☐ Defendant is currently filing or has already filed a declaration of COVID-19–related financial distress with the court. (Code Civ. Proc., § 1179.03(h).)

n. ☐ Plaintiff's demand for possession of a residential property is based on nonpayment of rent or other financial obligations due between October 1, 2021, and March 31, 2022, and (check all that apply):

(1) ☐ Plaintiff's notice to quit did not contain the required contact information for the pertinent governmental rental assistance program, or the other content required by Code of Civil Procedure section 1179.10(a).

(2) ☐ Plaintiff's notice to quit did not include a translation of the statutorily required notice. (Code Civ. Proc., § 1179.10(a)(2) and Civ. Code, § 1632.)

o. ☐ For a tenancy initially established before October 1, 2021, plaintiff's demand for possession of a residential property is based on nonpayment of rent or other financial obligations due between March 1, 2020, and March 31, 2022, **and** *(check all that apply):*

(1) ☐ Plaintiff did not complete an application for rental assistance to cover the rental debt demanded in the complaint before filing the complaint in this action.

(2) ☐ Plaintiff's application for rental assistance was not denied.

(3) ☐ Plaintiff's application for rental assistance was denied for a reason that does not support issuance of a summons or judgment in an unlawful detainer action *(check all that apply)*:

(a) ☐ Plaintiff did not fully or properly complete plaintiff's portion of the application. (Code Civ. Proc., § 1179.09(d)(2)(A).)

(b) ☐ Plaintiff did not apply to the correct rental assistance program. (Code Civ. Proc., § 1179.09(d)(2)(C).)

(4) ☐ Rental assistance has been approved and tenant is separately filing an application to prevent forfeiture (form UD-125).

p. ☐ Plaintiff's demand for possession of a residential property is based on nonpayment of rent or other financial obligations and *(check all that apply):*

(1) ☐ Plaintiff received or has a pending application for rental assistance from a governmental rental assistance program or some other source relating to the amount claimed in the notice to pay rent or quit. (Health & Saf. Code, §§ 50897.1(d)(2)(B) and 50897.3(e)(2).)

(2) ☐ Plaintiff received or has a pending application for rental assistance from a governmental rental assistance program or some other source for rent accruing since the notice to pay rent or quit. (Health & Saf. Code, §§ 50897.1(d)(2)(B) and 50897.3(e)(2).)

(3) ☐ Plaintiff's demand for possession is based only on late fees for defendant's failure to provide landlord payment within 15 days of receiving governmental rental assistance. (Health & Saf. Code, § 50897.1(e)(2)(B).)

ANSWER—UNLAWFUL DETAINER

UD-105

| PLAINTIFF: LENNY D. LANDLORD | CASE NUMBER: |
| DEFENDANT: TERRENCE D. TENANT, et al. | A-12345-B |

3. q. ☐ Plaintiff violated the COVID-19 Tenant Relief Act (Code Civ. Proc., § 1179.01 et seq.) or a local COVID-19–related ordinance regarding evictions in some other way *(briefly state facts describing this in item 3w)*.

   r. ☐ The property is covered by the federal CARES Act and the plaintiff did not provide 30 days' notice to vacate.
   (Property covered by the CARES Act means property where the landlord:
   • *is participating in a covered housing program as defined by the Violence Against Women Act;*
   • *is participating in the rural housing voucher program under section 542 of the Housing Act of 1949; or*
   • *has a federally backed mortgage loan or a federally backed multifamily mortgage loan.)*

   s. ☐ Plaintiff improperly applied payments made by defendant in a tenancy that was in existence between March 1, 2020, and September 30, 2021 (Code Civ. Proc., § 1179.04.5), as follows *(check all that apply)*:

   (1) ☐ Plaintiff applied a security deposit to rent, or other financial obligations due, without tenant's written agreement.

   (2) ☐ Plaintiff applied a monthly rental payment to rent or other financial obligations that were due between March 1, 2020, and September 30, 2021, other than to the prospective month's rent, without tenant's written agreement.

   t. ☒ Plaintiff refused to accept payment from a third party for rent due. (Civ. Code, § 1947.3; Gov. Code, § 12955.)

   u. ☐ Defendant has a disability and plaintiff refused to provide a reasonable accommodation that was requested.
   (Cal. Code Regs,. tit. 2, § 12176(c).)

   v. ☐ Other defenses and objections are stated in item 3w.

   w. *(Provide facts for each item checked above, either below or, if more room needed, on form MC-025)*:
   ☒ Description of facts or defenses are on form MC-025, titled as Attachment 3w.
   3(a): There are defects in the premises rendering them uninhabitable, including defective electrical plugs, inadequate heating, mold, and plumbing leaks. Defendants have also observed vermin and pests in the unit.

   3(l): Defendants obtained rent relief for part of the transition period and recovery period. Plaintiff had to wait to collect the COVID rents and wants to evict defendants.

   3(w): Plaintiff is not acting in good faith and has an ulterior motive. Plaintiff is guilty of unclean hands.

4. OTHER STATEMENTS
   a. ☐ Defendant vacated the premises on *(date)*:
   b. ☒ The fair rental value of the premises alleged in the complaint is excessive *(explain below or, if more room needed, on form MC-025)*:
   ☐ Explanation is on form MC-025, titled as Attachment 4b.
   See affirmative defense 3(a) with respect to defects in premises making them uninhabitable.

   c. ☐ Other *(specify below or, if more room needed, on form MC-025)*:
   ☐ Other statements are on form MC-025, titled as Attachment 4c.

5. DEFENDANT REQUESTS
   a. that plaintiff take nothing requested in the complaint.
   b. costs incurred in this proceeding.
   c. ☐ reasonable attorney fees.
   d. ☒ that plaintiff be ordered to (1) make repairs and correct the conditions that constitute a breach of the warranty to provide habitable premises and (2) reduce the monthly rent to a reasonable rental value until the conditions are corrected.

UD-105 [Rev. October 1, 2021]   **ANSWER—UNLAWFUL DETAINER**   Page 4 of 5

PLAINTIFF: LENNY D. LANDLORD	**UD-105**
DEFENDANT: TERRENCE D. TENANT, et al.	CASE NUMBER: A-12345-B

5. e. [✗] Other *(specify below or on form MC-025):*

      [ ] All other requests are stated on form MC-025, titled as Attachment 5e.

    Such other and further relief as the court deems just and proper.

6. Number of pages attached: _____

UNLAWFUL DETAINER ASSISTANT (Bus. & Prof. Code, §§ 6400–6415)

7. *(Must be completed in all cases.)* An **unlawful detainer assistant** [✗] did not   [ ] did   for compensation give advice or assistance with this form. *(If defendant has received **any** help or advice for pay from an unlawful detainer assistant, state):*

  a. Assistant's name: b. Telephone number:

  c. Street address, city, and zip code:

  d. County of registration: e. Registration number: f. Expiration date:

(Each defendant for whom this answer is filed must be named in item 1 and must sign this answer unless defendant's attorney signs.)

Terrence D. Tenant	▶ *Terrence D. Tenant*
(TYPE OR PRINT NAME)	(SIGNATURE OF DEFENDANT OR ATTORNEY)
Tillie D. Tenant	▶ *Tillie D. Tenant*
(TYPE OR PRINT NAME)	(SIGNATURE OF DEFENDANT OR ATTORNEY)
	▶
(TYPE OR PRINT NAME)	(SIGNATURE OF DEFENDANT OR ATTORNEY)

VERIFICATION

(Use a different verification form if the verification is by an attorney or for a corporation or partnership.)

I am the defendant in this proceeding and have read this answer. I declare under penalty of perjury under the laws of the State of California that the foregoing is true and correct.

Date: April 21, 20xx

Terrence D. Tenant	▶ *Terrence D. Tenant*
(TYPE OR PRINT NAME)	(SIGNATURE OF DEFENDANT)

Date: April 21, 20xx

Tillie D. Tenant	▶ *Tillie D. Tenant*
(TYPE OR PRINT NAME)	(SIGNATURE OF DEFENDANT)

Date:

	▶
(TYPE OR PRINT NAME)	(SIGNATURE OF DEFENDANT)

Defendant's Requests

In Item 5, the tenants say what they want. Item 5a allows the tenant to request attorneys' fees. This is proper only if the written rental agreement or lease has an attorneys' fees clause. Because of the restrictions on unlawful detainer suits, there is really nothing else the tenant can properly ask for here.

Finally, Item 5b allows the tenant to ask the court to order the landlord to make repairs and order the rent reduced, if the tenant claims breach of the warranty of habitability as a defense in Item 3a.

Responding to the Answer

If the answer raises affirmative defenses, you might consider initiating basic discovery against the tenant. Using discovery procedures is discussed later in this chapter. If the tenant has simply denied your allegations, not raised any affirmative defenses, and is not represented by an attorney, you are still on pretty firm ground as far as going ahead on your own is concerned. The next step is getting a trial date.

The Request to Set Case for Trial—Unlawful Detainer

Like almost everything else in the legal system, the trial on your now-contested unlawful detainer complaint will not happen automatically. You have to ask for it in a form known as a request to set case for trial. (The name on the preprinted form is Request/Counter-Request to Set Case for Trial—Unlawful Detainer.)

CAUTION

If the tenant has moved out. If the tenant moves out any time before the start of trial, possession is no longer "at issue," and the case stops and converts to an ordinary civil action for money. (Civ. Code § 1952.3.) You have the right to amend your complaint to state all the relief you seek, such as damages for breach of the lease, damage to the property, and possibly rerental costs. The complaint can be amended on a motion by the landlord. The court will set it for trial according to the schedule used by ordinary civil actions. It will take longer to get a judgment, but you can at least rent the unit beforehand.

In response to your amended complaint, the tenant can file a cross-complaint for affirmative claims, such as a breach of the implied warranty of habitability or violation of any rent control limitations.

FORM

A blank copy of the Request/Counter-Request to Set Case for Trial—Unlawful Detainer (Judicial Council UD-150) can be downloaded from the Nolo website. (See the appendix for the link to the forms in this book, and other information on using the forms.)

To complete this form, fill in the information in the boxes at the top of the form just as you did when preparing the complaint (your name and address, the court and its location, the names of the parties, the case number).

In the large box below the case identification queries, put an X next to the word "REQUEST," unless the tenant has already filed a request to set case for trial. (If the tenant has requested a jury trial, which happens often, you'll need to contact an attorney.) If the tenant has already filed this form, put an X in the box next to the words "COUNTER-REQUEST." Because you are the plaintiff (the one filing the motion), put an "X" in the "Plaintiff" box.

Item 1: Put an X in this box. If there is more than one defendant, and at least one of them has filed an answer, but at least one other defendant has not, you should obtain a default against all defendants who have not filed an answer. You'll be requesting only entry of a default, not a clerk's judgment for possession. (Later, after winning at trial against the defendants who have filed an answer, you can ask the judge to order that the judgment also be against those "defaulted" defendants.) (See Chapter 7 on filling out the Request for Entry of Default, but don't check the boxes relevant to obtaining a clerk's judgment for possession.)

Item 2: List the unit's address, including the county. If the tenant is still in possession of the property (that is, the tenant has not turned over the key or otherwise unequivocally demonstrated that he or she has turned over possession of the property to you), check Box (a). This should result in your having a trial within 20 days of filing your request to set case for trial. On the other hand, if the tenant has turned over possession of the property to you, and you still seek a money judgment, check Box (b). In this situation, as we have noted above, the court will likely set the case for trial much more slowly than if the tenant were still in possession of the property.

Item 3: Check the box next to the words "a nonjury trial." Do not request a jury trial. Jury trials are procedurally much more complex than trials before judges. It is easy to get in way over your head. Also, the party requesting a jury trial has to deposit jury fees with the court in advance (about $150 per day). All you want is a simple trial, lasting no more than a few hours at most, in front of a judge.

Item 4: The purpose of this item is to give the court a fair estimate of how long the trial will take. Unless the tenant has demanded a jury trial (in which case you should probably see an attorney), check Box (b) and indicate either one to four hours as an estimate for the trial length. Your estimated time for trial should be anywhere from one hour, for a simple case where the tenant has failed to assert any affirmative defenses, to four hours in cases involving fairly complicated issues like alleged rent control violations, discriminatory or retaliatory evictions, or breach of the warranty to provide habitable premises.

Item 5: Indicate any dates that you will not be available for trial. Remember that the court is required by law to set a trial date no later than 20 days from the date you file your request to set case for trial. If you list dates when you are unavailable (note that you must give a reason), the court may have to schedule trial for more than 20 days from the date you file the request. If you are content with this latter prospect, add the sentence, "Plaintiff waives the requirement under C.C.P. § 1170.5(a) for trial within 20 days of filing of this document."

Item 6: In this item, you simply indicate, as you did in the complaint and summons, that an unlawful detainer assistant "did not" assist you. Then, print your name and the date, and sign the document.

On the second page, in the box at the top, list your name after "PLAINTIFF" and the name of the first-named defendant, followed by "ET AL." if there is more than one defendant. Do this just as you did the top of the second and third pages of the complaint. Also list the case number.

This second page is a Proof of Service by Mail, which shows that a person other than you mailed copies of the form to the tenant who filed the answer. List the residence or business address of the person who will mail the form for you, in Item 2 of this side of the form. Also, put an X in Box 3a. In Boxes 3c(1) and (2), list the date the copy of your request to set case for trial will be mailed, and the name of the city in which it will be mailed. Just below the words "I declare under penalty of perjury … ," list the date that person will be signing the proof of service (after he or she mails it). Enter that person's name in the space at the left below the place for that date.

UD-150

ATTORNEY OR PARTY WITHOUT ATTORNEY *(Name, State Bar number, and address):*	FOR COURT USE ONLY
LENNY D. LANDLORD 12345 Angeleno Street Los Angeles, CA 90028 TELEPHONE NO.: 213-555-6789 FAX No. *(Optional):* 213-555-6789 E-MAIL ADDRESS *(Optional):* ATTORNEY FOR *(Name):* Plaintiff in Pro Per	

SUPERIOR COURT OF CALIFORNIA, COUNTY OF   LOS ANGELES
STREET ADDRESS: 110 N. Hill Street
MAILING ADDRESS: Same
CITY AND ZIP CODE: Los Angeles, Ca 90012
BRANCH NAME:

PLAINTIFF: Lenny D. Landlord

DEFENDANT: Terrence D. Tenant, Tillie D. Tenant

[X] **REQUEST** [ ] **COUNTER-REQUEST** **TO SET CASE FOR TRIAL—UNLAWFUL DETAINER** [X] **Plaintiff** [ ] **Defendant**	CASE NUMBER: A-12345-B

1. [X] **Plaintiff's request.** I represent to the court that all parties have been served with process and have appeared or have had a default or dismissal entered against them. I request that this case be set for trial.

2. **Trial preference.** The premises concerning this case are located at *(street address, apartment number, city, zip code, and county):*
3815 Gower Canyon Ave, Apt. 3, Los Angeles, CA 90028, Los Angeles County
   a. [X] To the best of my knowledge, the right to possession of the premises is still in issue. This case is entitled to legal preference under Code of Civil Procedure section 1179a.
   b. [ ] To the best of my knowledge, the right to possession of the premises is no longer in issue. No defendant or other person is in possession of the premises.

3. **Jury or nonjury trial.** I request [ ] a jury trial [X] a nonjury trial.

4. **Estimated length of trial.** I estimate that the trial will take *(check one):*
   a. [ ] days *(specify number):*   b. [X] hours *(specify if estimated trial is less than one day):* 1

5. **Trial date.** I am not available on the following dates *(specify dates and reasons for unavailability):*

UNLAWFUL DETAINER ASSISTANT (Bus. & Prof. Code, §§ 6400–6415)

6. *(Complete in all cases.)* An unlawful detainer assistant [X] did **not** [ ] did for compensation give advice or assistance with this form. *(If declarant has received **any** help or advice for pay from an unlawful detainer assistant, complete a–f.)*

   a. Assistant's name:
   b. Street address, city, and zip code:

   c. Telephone no.:
   d. County of registration:
   e. Registration no.:
   f. Expires on *(date):*

I declare under penalty of perjury under the laws of the State of California that the foregoing is true and correct.

Date: April 29, 20xx

Lenny D. Landlord
_____
(TYPE OR PRINT NAME)

▶ *Lenny D. Landlord*
_____
(SIGNATURE OF PARTY OR ATTORNEY FOR PARTY)

NOTICE
- An unlawful detainer case must be set for trial on a date not later than **20 days after the first request** to set the case for trial is made (Code Civ. Proc., § 1170.5(a)).
- If a jury is requested, $150 must be deposited with the court 5 days before trial (Code Civ. Proc., § 631).
- Court reporter and interpreter services vary. Check with the court for availability of services and fees charged.
- If you cannot pay the court fees and costs, you may apply for a fee waiver. Ask the court clerk for a fee waiver form.

Page 1 of 2

Form Adopted for Mandatory Use
Judicial Council of California
UD-150 [New January 1, 2005]

**REQUEST/COUNTER-REQUEST TO SET CASE
FOR TRIAL—UNLAWFUL DETAINER**

Code of Civil Procedure, §§ 631,
1170.5(a), 1179a
www.courtinfo.ca.gov

PLAINTIFF: LENNY D. LANDLORD	CASE NUMBER:
DEFENDANT: TERRENCE D. TENANT, ET AL.	A-12345-B

PROOF OF SERVICE BY MAIL

Instructions: *After having the parties served by mail with the* Request/Counter-Request to Set Case for Trial—Unlawful Detainer, *(form UD-150), have the person who mailed the form UD-150 complete this* Proof of Service by Mail. *An **unsigned** copy of the* Proof of Service by Mail *should be completed and served with form UD-150. Give the* Request/Counter-Request to Set Case for Trial —Unlawful Detainer *(form UD-150) and the completed* Proof of Service by Mail *to the clerk for filing. If you are representing yourself, someone else must mail these papers and sign the* Proof of Service by Mail.

1. I am over the age of 18 and **not a party to this case.** I am a resident of or employed in the county where the mailing took place.
2. My residence or business address is *(specify)*:

   100 A Street, Los Angeles, CA 90010

3. I served the *Request/Counter-Request to Set Case for Trial—Unlawful Detainer* (form UD-150) by enclosing a copy in an envelope addressed to each person whose name and address are shown below AND

   a. ☒ **depositing** the sealed envelope in the United States mail on the date and at the place shown in item 3c with the postage fully prepaid.

   b. ☐ **placing** the envelope for collection and mailing on the date and at the place shown in item 3c following ordinary business practices. I am readily familiar with this business's practice for collecting and processing correspondence for mailing. On the same day that correspondence is placed for collection and mailing, it is deposited in the ordinary course of business with the United States Postal Service in a sealed envelope with postage fully prepaid.

   c. (1) Date mailed: April 29, 20xx

   (2) Place mailed *(city and state)*: Los Angeles, CA

I declare under penalty of perjury under the laws of the State of California that the foregoing is true and correct:

Date: September 18, 20xx

Sam D. Server	▶ *Sam D. Server*
(TYPE OR PRINT NAME)	(SIGNATURE OF PERSON WHO MAILED *FORM UD-150*)

NAME AND ADDRESS OF EACH PERSON TO WHOM NOTICE WAS MAILED

	Name	Address *(number, street, city, and zip code)*
4.	Terrence D. Tenant	3815 Gower Canyon Ave, Apt. 3 Los Angeles, CA 90028
5.	Tillie D. Tenant	3815 Gower Canyon Ave, Apt. 3 Los Angeles, CA 90028
6.		
7.		
8.		
9.		

☐ List of names and addresses continued on a separate attachment or form MC-025, titled Attachment to Proof of Service by Mail.

UD-150 [New January 1, 2005] | **REQUEST/COUNTER-REQUEST TO SET CASE FOR TRIAL—UNLAWFUL DETAINER** | Page 2 of 2

Summary Judgments

Litigants in civil lawsuits can try to win their case short of going to trial: They file a motion for summary judgment (MSJ). The moving party argues that there are no disputes as to the facts in the case, and all of the law is indisputably in their favor. Of course, the opposing side tries to point to facts that are in dispute, and to the possibility that a correct application of the law will favor *their* side. Theoretically, landlords and tenants could file MSJs in an eviction case. (C.C.P. § 1170.7.)

However, these motions are rarely filed, even when each side has counsel; and the chances of winning are dim—the motions are about as successful as playing three card monte. The filing fee is a ridiculously high $500, and judges rarely grant these motions (even the sound ones) when tenants oppose them—which they can do effortlessly, by simply voicing their objections, without the need of a written response. (Rule 3.1351(b), California Rules of Court.) For all of these reasons, we do not recommend that you file a MSJ in your unlawful detainer case.

Finally, under the heading of "NAME AND ADDRESS OF EACH PERSON TO WHOM NOTICE WAS MAILED," put the names and addresses of each defendant who has filed an answer to the complaint. Use a separate set of boxes for each defendant, even if more than one defendant has filed the same answer. Also, use the mailing address the tenant (or the tenant's attorney) indicated in the upper left box in the answer. Do this even if the address is different from the tenant's residence address. (You do not have to list any defendants who have not answered, and against whom you will be taking a default.)

Make photocopies of the request to set case for trial and have a friend mail one to each tenant (or his or her attorney) at the mailing addresses in the boxes at the end of the form. Have the friend sign the Proof of Service by Mail, indicating that he or she mailed the copy, and take the original and one copy to the courthouse. The court clerk will file the original request to set case for trial and stamp the copy for your records.

The court will hold on to your request to set case for trial for up to five days to give the tenant a chance to file a counter-request to set. This gives the tenant the opportunity to also list unavailable dates and dispute any of the information you listed. Then the clerk will set the case for trial on a date no more than 20 days after the date you filed your memorandum, and will notify you by mail of the date, time, and place of the trial.

Pretrial Complications

Between the time you file a Request/Counter-Request to Set Case for Trial—Unlawful Detainer and the date set for trial, the tenant might file legal documents requiring action on your part. They can include the following.

Countermemo to Set/Jury Demand

Many tenants think it is in their interest to demand a jury trial. They are often right. Not only does this delay scheduling of the case, but (in certain areas) it sometimes guarantees an audience more receptive to the tenant's arguments and less skeptical than a case-worn judge.

The tenant can ask for a jury trial with a document called a "jury demand" or in a "counter-memorandum," a response to your Memorandum to set. There is normally nothing you can do to avoid a jury trial if the tenant demands it and pays the jury fees in advance.

SEE AN EXPERT

If a jury trial is demanded, seek legal representation. In a jury trial, a complex set of rules governs the evidence the jury may hear. It's very difficult for a nonlawyer to competently deal with these rules. In a trial before a judge without a jury, things are much simpler because judges, who know the rules themselves, disregard evidence that it is improper for them to consider.

Discovery Requests

One of the biggest surprises to many nonlawyers about the legal system is that in all civil cases, including eviction lawsuits, each side has the right to force the other side to disclose, before trial, any relevant information it has about the case. Discovery is most often initiated by lawyers, not by tenants representing themselves, and if your tenant is represented by a lawyer, you may want to be, too. This brief discussion of discovery techniques is just to give you an overview.

Depositions

In very rare instances, a tenant's lawyer will mail you a document that instructs you to show up at the lawyer's office or appear on a remote video conference for a deposition—to answer questions under oath about the case. A court reporter takes down the tenant's lawyer's questions and your responses to them. Any of your answers can be used against you later at trial. You must pay the court reporter a fairly hefty fee for a copy of the transcript, typically about $5 for each double-spaced page; if you win the lawsuit, you can recover this sum in the judgment as a court cost.

The rules on the types of questions one can ask are fairly complicated, because the form of the question must follow the rules of evidence. The basic rule concerning the answer is simply that the deponent (answering party) must answer any question that might lead the questioner to the discovery of relevant evidence. You may refuse to answer questions only when your objection is based on evidentiary privileges, such as attorney-client communications, physician-patient discussions, or financial privacy. Your refusal to answer a proper question or to attend a deposition after proper notification can be punished by a court-ordered fine, if the other side requests it, or, in extreme cases, by dismissal of your case.

Discovery cuts both ways, and you have the right to take the tenant's deposition as well. The cost will be a factor and you have to follow the rules as if you were a lawyer. Court reporters charge between $1,200 and $1,500 for a half day.

Interrogatories and Requests for Admissions

Another far more common way the tenant or you may obtain relevant information is to mail questions called "interrogatories." They can be typed or on a standard form provided by the Judicial Council (Judicial Council Form DISC-003). The responding party must answer all interrogatories within ten days if they're mailed or five days if they are delivered personally. As with depositions, the rules about the type of questions you have to answer are fairly technical, but if you use the Judicial Council form interrogatories, the questions have been officially framed. The responding party, you or the tenant, has to respond to all questions that might lead the other side to relevant information. Generally, with the form interrogatories, that includes all the checked standard questions. Complete answers to the best of your (or the tenant's) ability must be given.

Requests for Admissions seek to save time at trial by requesting an admission that either a document is genuine or a fact is true. Because admission or denial of a key statement can be used in court, one must carefully consider all the parts of the request before deciding whether it should be admitted as true. One does not admit the truth of a statement unless all the parts are true. If only some parts are true, the request must be denied.

A failure to answer (or to answer on time) can result in admitting that all the statements are true. One ignores a request for admission at one's peril, because silence is the same as admitting something is true. This can be extremely damaging, if not fatal, to your case if the fact is not true.

Inspection Demands and Requests for Production of Documents

A third discovery device is the Inspection Demand or Request for Production of Documents. This is a written request that you produce specified documents, books, or other records for inspection and copying by the other party, on a certain date and time. The party receiving the notice usually makes photocopies and mails them, rather than waiting for the other party or attorney to show up to inspect the records.

You must respond within five days with a statement that you will or will not produce the requested documents, and then produce the documents for actual inspection within ten days. Instead of producing originals for examination and copying you can often produce a full copy of the document. Again, the rules on the type of material that can be requested this way are technical, but generally any records that can lead to relevant information can be sought. You do not have to produce privileged documents, but the question of privilege is a technical matter best addressed by a lawyer.

SEE AN EXPERT

If the tenant seeks to have you produce sensitive or confidential business records that you do not believe are directly relevant to the proceeding, see a lawyer.

Discovery Initiated by the Landlord

You can also use discovery to obtain information relating to the tenant's defense of the case. While this is not necessary in a simple case, there are circumstances where you want more information or wish to nail down the tenant's story. For example, you might want the tenant claiming a bogus habitability defense to admit she didn't complain to you or anyone else about the condition of the property until after you insisted on receiving the rent.

You may use the Judicial Council form interrogatories (Judicial Council DISC-003) referenced just above to elicit information about the case. There are also forms for Requests for Admission (Judicial Council Form DISC-020) that you can use to cover facts and documents, such as admitting the genuineness of the lease or receipt of the three-day notice. These forms use checkboxes that save you from framing the questions yourself or arguing about the meaning of the question.

You can use any of the Judicial Council form interrogatories in the eviction. While the employment questions may offer you little use, the General Form Interrogatories can be very useful. In conjunction with the Request for Admissions, for example Form Interrogatory Number 17 delivers a large reward for checking a box, because it demands explanations for every denial of any request for admissions

Custom-drafted interrogatories, requests for admissions, and deposition notices require technical skills that are beyond the scope of this book to explain adequately.

Complications With "Discovery"

When parties to a lawsuit disagree about what should be produced at discovery, or when one party simply fails to respond to another party's discovery request, the party seeking the information can request that the judge order the other party to respond appropriately to the discovery request. One does this by filing a motion called a "motion to compel." In unlawful detainer cases, these motions can be made on only five days' notice, ten days where the moving papers are mailed. (C.C.P. § 1170.8.) These motions can also request that the loser pay the winner's attorneys' fees incurred in bringing the motion.

If you think you need to utilize discovery to find out more about the tenant's defense, or are facing a tenant's motion to compel (particularly where the tenant is represented by an attorney), you should consult an attorney.

Preparing for Trial

Preparing a case for trial and handling the trial itself are difficult subjects in a self-help law book, because you have to meet the standard of practice expected of a lawyer. Few eviction cases go to trial, but each case has its own unpredictable twists and turns that can greatly affect trial preparation and tactics. Simply put, there is no way for us to guide you step by step through this process. For this reason, we believe you will probably elect to bring a lawyer into the case, assuming you are still doing it yourself, to assist with the preparation and conduct of the trial.

Here we provide you with a basic overview of what needs to be done before and at the trial, so that you will know what to expect and better be able to assist your lawyer.

If the tenant filed an answer to your complaint, and the court has set the case for trial but you think the tenant has moved out and might not show up for trial, prepare for trial anyway. First, the tenant might not have actually moved out, and you're safer waiting to get a judgment before retaking possession (unless, of course, you've settled the case and the tenant has returned the keys). Second, unless you and the tenant have settled the case, you'll still want to get the money part of the judgment. Third, if you don't show up for trial—and the tenant does—the tenant will win and be entitled to move back in and to collect costs from you.

What You Have to Prove at Trial

What you must prove at trial obviously depends on the issues raised in your complaint and the tenant's answer. For example, the testimony in a case based on nonpayment of rent where the tenant's defense is that you failed to keep the premises habitable will be very different from that in a case based on termination of a month-to-month tenancy by 30-day notice, where the tenant denies receiving the notice.

All contested evictions are similar, however, in that you, the plaintiff, have to do the following two things in order to win.

First, you have to establish the basic elements of your case. This means you have to present hard evidence (usually through documents and live testimony) of the basic facts that would cause the judge to rule in your favor if the tenant didn't present a defense. If you don't produce evidence on every essential factual issue contested by the tenant in the answer, the tenant can win the case by pointing this out to the judge right after you "rest" your case. This is done by the tenant's making a "motion for judgment" after you have presented your evidence and closed your case.

Second, you have to provide an adequate response to any rebuttal or affirmative defense the tenant presents. For example, the tenant may say he didn't have to pay the rent because you didn't fix the leaky roof, overflowing toilet, or defective water heater. You should counter with whatever facts disprove the claim. Your evidence might be that you made the repairs promptly, kept the premises habitable, or the tenant didn't tell you about the defects before filing an answer in the case. (See *The California Landlord's Law Book: Rights & Responsibilities*, Chapter 11, on the landlord's duty to keep the property habitable.)

Elements of Your Case

If the tenant has denied everything in your complaint, you will have to prove your case. To give you an idea of what is required, below we set out the legal elements that you must prove for various types of evictions. If the tenant has admitted an element in the answer or a request for admissions, you can save a step and don't have to prove that element. The court will accept an admitted fact as a given. For example, if the tenant's answer admits that the tenant was served with a three-day notice on a certain date, you don't have to present testimony to prove it.

Okay, now find the symbol representing your type of eviction and review the elements that you will have to prove.

Eviction for Nonpayment of Rent

- You, your agent, or the person from whom you purchased the property (or the seller's agent) rented the property to the tenant pursuant to an oral or written agreement.
- The monthly rent was a certain amount.
- The tenant got behind in the rent, so that the tenant owed a certain amount.
- The tenant was properly served with a Three-Day Notice to Pay Rent or Quit.
- The notice demanded that the tenant pay the exact amount of rent due or leave within three days.
- The tenant neither paid the amount demanded in the notice nor left within three days (plus any extensions allowed if the third day fell on a weekend or holiday).
- The tenant is still in possession of the property.
- You have complied with any applicable rent control or just cause eviction ordinances and regulations.
- The daily amount listed in the complaint is the reasonable rental value.

Eviction for Termination of Month-to-Month Tenancy

- You, your agent, and so on, rented the property to the tenant.
- The tenancy is month to month, having either started out that way or having become month to month after a fixed-term lease expired.
- If a local rent control or eviction ordinance requires "just cause" for terminating a month-to-month tenancy, the reason you give for termination is true and you've complied with all aspects of the ordinance and any applicable regulations.

- The tenant was served with a written notice requiring that he or she leave and giving him or her at least 30 days to do so if his or her tenancy lasted less than a year, and at least 60 days if a year or more.
- The 30-day (or longer) period has expired and the tenant is still in possession of the property.
- The daily amount listed in the complaint is the reasonable rental value.

Eviction for Violation of Lease/Nuisance/Waste

- You, your agent, and so on, rented the property to the tenant.
- The lease or rental agreement contains a valid clause requiring the tenant to do something (for example, pay a security deposit installment by a certain date) or to refrain from doing something (like having pets or subletting the property), and the tenant has violated the clause, or the tenant seriously damaged the property, used it unlawfully, or created a legal nuisance.
- You have evidence concerning the facts of the violation, nuisance, or waste. This evidence can include witness testimony, photographs, video, and documents proving the tenant's fault.
- The tenant was served with a three-day notice demanding that the tenant vacate the property within that time, or, if the violation was correctable, that the tenant correct it within that time.
- The tenant neither vacated the property nor corrected the problem (if correctable) after the three days, plus any extensions.
- The tenant is still in possession of the property.
- You have complied with applicable rent control or just cause eviction ordinances or regulations.
- The daily amount listed in the complaint is the reasonable rental value.

Assessing and Countering the Tenant's Defenses

If the tenant raised any affirmative defenses in the answer, you must be ready to counter them at trial.

 SEE AN EXPERT

As we have emphasized, trying to assess and counter these defenses can be extremely difficult unless you are experienced in doing so. Even if you otherwise feel competent to conduct your own trial, assistance from a professional is never a bad idea. You should bring in a lawyer to advise or even represent you with this aspect of the case. (See "Should You Hire an Attorney?" above.)

Habitability Defense

Tenants often raise the "habitability defense" in evictions for nonpayment of rent. If the tenants' answer states that their rent payment was partly or entirely excused because you kept the property in poor repair, you should first read Chapter 11 in *The California Landlord's Law Book: Rights & Responsibilities*, on landlords' duties to keep rental property in good repair. If in fact you haven't properly maintained the property, the tenants might win the lawsuit. To win, the tenants must prove to the judge that you "breached" (violated) the implied "warranty" (obligation) to provide the tenant with "habitable" premises (safe, sanitary, in good repair) in exchange for the rent.

To establish that you breached the implied warranty of habitability, the tenant must prove all of the following:

- You failed to provide one or more of the minimum "tenantability" requirements, including waterproofing, a working toilet, adequate heating and electricity, and hot and cold running water. (See Civ. Code § 1941.1.)
- The defects were serious and substantial.
- The tenant or some other person (such as a health department inspector) notified you (or your manager) about the defect before you served the three-day notice to pay rent.

- You failed to make repairs within a reasonable time.

Once the tenant makes a showing described above, you must show a valid excuse for allowing the deficiency to continue or prove the assertion untrue.

If you can convince the judge that the problems the tenant is complaining about are either nonhabitability related (such as old interior paint, carpets, or drapes) or minor (cosmetic or insubstantial defects); or that the tenant didn't complain until after receiving the three-day notice, you will have knocked one or more holes in the tenant's habitability defense.

If the tenant produces evidence showing that you failed to make required repairs within 60 days after receiving written notice to do so from a health department or other official following an inspection of the property by that person, the burden shifts to you to show that you had an extremely good reason for not making the repair, such as that the tenant refused entry to make repairs. (See *The California Landlord's Law Book: Rights & Responsibilities*, Chapter 11.) (Civ. Code § 1942.3.)

If you have an uncorrected Notice of Violation older than 34 days, you should consider dismissing your case without prejudice before the trial date. Civil Code Section 1942.4 prohibits a landlord from demanding or collecting rent when a habitability violation exists, the applicable government housing inspector has issued a Notice of Violation, and the landlord has failed to correct the problem for at least 35 days.

If a landlord attempts to collect rent after the 35 days have passed, or brings an unlawful detainer, the tenant has a defense to the action, an affirmative action for relief, and will be entitled to recover damages, costs, and reasonable statutory attorneys' fees. (Civ. Code § 1942.4; C.C.P. § 1174.21; *The California Landlord's Law Book: Rights & Responsibilities*, Chapter 11.) Dismissing a case without prejudice allows you to file it again later. You may dismiss without prejudice any time

UD-110

ATTORNEY OR PARTY WITHOUT ATTORNEY *(Name, state bar number, and address):* ☐ list your name, address, and phone number TELEPHONE NO.: FAX NO. *(Optional):* E-MAIL ADDRESS *(Optional):* ATTORNEY FOR *(Name):* Plaintiff in Pro Per	FOR COURT USE ONLY

SUPERIOR COURT OF CALIFORNIA, COUNTY OF
STREET ADDRESS:
MAILING ADDRESS: ☐ court, county, address, and branch
CITY AND ZIP CODE:
BRANCH NAME:

PLAINTIFF:
   ☐ plaintiff's and defendants' names
DEFENDANT:

JUDGMENT—UNLAWFUL DETAINER	case number
☐ By Clerk ☐ By Default ☐ After Court Trial ☒ By Court ☐ Possession Only ☐ Defendant Did Not Appear at Trial	

JUDGMENT

1. ☐ **BY DEFAULT**
   a. Defendant was properly served with a copy of the summons and complaint.
   b. Defendant failed to answer the complaint or appear and defend the action within the time allowed by law.
   c. Defendant's default was entered by the clerk upon plaintiff's application.
   d. ☐ **Clerk's Judgment** (Code Civ. Proc., § 1169). For possession only of the premises described on page 2 (item 4).
   e. ☐ **Court Judgment** (Code Civ. Proc., § 585(b)). The court considered
      (1) ☐ plaintiff's testimony and other evidence.
      (2) ☐ plaintiff's or others' written declaration and evidence (Code Civ. Proc., § 585(d)).

2. ☐ **AFTER COURT TRIAL.** The jury was waived. The court considered the evidence.
   a. The case was tried on *(date and time):*

      before *(name of judicial officer):*   ☐ leave Items 1 and 2 blank everywhere

   b. Appearances by:
      ☐ Plaintiff *(name each):*   ☐ Plaintiff's attorney *(name each):*
                                                         (1)
                                                         (2)

      ☐ Continued on *Attachment* 2b (form MC-025).

      ☐ Defendant *(name each):*   ☐ Defendant's attorney *(name each):*
                                                         (1)
                                                         (2)

      ☐ Continued on *Attachment* 2b (form MC-025).

   c. ☐ Defendant did not appear at trial. Defendant was properly served with notice of trial.

   d. ☐ A statement of decision (Code Civ. Proc., § 632) ☐ was not ☐ was requested.

Form Approved for Optional Use Judicial Council of California UD-110 [New January 1, 2003]	**JUDGMENT—UNLAWFUL DETAINER**	Code of Civil Procedure, §§ 415.46, 585(d), 664.6, 1169

PLAINTIFF:		CASE NUMBER:
DEFENDANT:	plaintiff's and defendants' name(s)	case number

JUDGMENT IS ENTERED AS FOLLOWS BY: [X] THE COURT   [ ] THE CLERK

3. **Parties.** Judgment is

   a. [X] for plaintiff *(name each):* [plaintiff's name]

      and against defendant *(name each):* [defendants' name(s)]

      [ ] Continued on *Attachment* 3a (form MC-025).

   b. [ ] for defendant *(name each):*

4. [X] Plaintiff   [ ] Defendant   is entitled to possession of the premises located at *(street address, apartment, city, and county):*

   [list complete address of property]

5. [ ] Judgment applies to all occupants of the premises including tenants, subtenants if any, and named claimants if any (Code Civ. Proc., §§ 715.010, 1169, and 1174.3).

   [check only if you used Prejudgment Claim of Right to Possession procedure. See Ch. 6]

6. **Amount and terms of judgment**

   a. [X] Defendant named in item 3a above must pay plaintiff on the complaint:

   b. [ ] Plaintiff is to receive nothing from defendant named in item 3b.

      [ ] Defendant named in item 3b is to recover costs: $

      [ ] and attorney fees: $

(1) [ ] Past-due rent	$	list amounts of past-due rent demanded in 3-day notice and/or holdover (daily prorated) damages, and total court costs, and total them
(2) [ ] Holdover damages	$	
(3) [ ] Attorney fees	$	
(4) [ ] Costs	$	
(5) [ ] Other *(specify):*	$	
(6) **TOTAL JUDGMENT**	$	

   c. [ ] The rental agreement is canceled.   [ ] The lease is forfeited.

   [check as appropriate]

7. [ ] **Conditional judgment.** Plaintiff has breached the agreement to provide habitable premises to defendant as stated in *Judgment—Unlawful Detainer Attachment* (form UD–110S), which is attached.

8. [ ] **Other** *(specify):*

   [ ] Continued on *Attachment* 8 (form MC-025).

Date: _____ [ ] _____
                JUDICIAL OFFICER

Date: _____ [ ] Clerk, by _____, Deputy

(SEAL)

CLERK'S CERTIFICATE *(Optional)*

I certify that this is a true copy of the original judgment on file in the court.

Date:

Clerk, by _____, Deputy

ATTORNEY OR PARTY WITHOUT ATTORNEY *(Name, state bar number, and address):*

LENNY D. LANDLORD
1234 ANGELENO STREET
LOS ANGELES, CA 90028
TELEPHONE NO.: 213-555-6789   FAX NO. *(Optional):*
E-MAIL ADDRESS *(Optional):*
ATTORNEY FOR *(Name):* Plaintiff in Pro Per

FOR COURT USE ONLY

SUPERIOR COURT OF CALIFORNIA, COUNTY OF   LOS ANGELES
STREET ADDRESS: 110 N. Hill Street
MAILING ADDRESS: Same
CITY AND ZIP CODE: Los Angeles, CA 90012
BRANCH NAME: LOS ANGELES DIVISION

PLAINTIFF: LENNY D. LANDLORD

DEFENDANT: TERRENCE D. TENANT, TILLIE D. TENANT

UD-110

JUDGMENT—UNLAWFUL DETAINER	CASE NUMBER:

[X] By Clerk   [ ] By Default   [ ] After Court Trial
[ ] By Court   [ ] Possession Only   [ ] Defendant Did Not Appear at Trial

CASE NUMBER: A-12345-B

JUDGMENT

1. [ ] **BY DEFAULT**
   a. Defendant was properly served with a copy of the summons and complaint.
   b. Defendant failed to answer the complaint or appear and defend the action within the time allowed by law.
   c. Defendant's default was entered by the clerk upon plaintiff's application.
   d. [ ] **Clerk's Judgment** (Code Civ. Proc., § 1169). For possession only of the premises described on page 2 (item 4).
   e. [ ] **Court Judgment** (Code Civ. Proc., § 585(b)). The court considered
      (1) [ ] plaintiff's testimony and other evidence.
      (2) [ ] plaintiff's or others' written declaration and evidence (Code Civ. Proc., § 585(d)).

2. [X] **AFTER COURT TRIAL.** The jury was waived. The court considered the evidence.
   a. The case was tried on *(date and time):* May 25, 20xx at 9:00a.m.
      before *(name of judicial officer):* Julia Judge
   b. Appearances by:
      [X] Plaintiff *(name each):*   [ ] Plaintiff's attorney *(name each):*
          Lenny D. Landlord   (1)
                                             (2)

      [ ] Continued on *Attachment* 2b (form MC-025).

      [X] Defendant *(name each):*   [ ] Defendant's attorney *(name each):*
          Terrence D. Tenant, Tillie D. Tenant   (1)
                                             (2)

      [ ] Continued on *Attachment* 2b (form MC-025).

   c. [ ] Defendant did not appear at trial. Defendant was properly served with notice of trial.
   d. [ ] A statement of decision (Code Civ. Proc., § 632) [ ] was not [ ] was requested.

Form Approved for Optional Use
Judicial Council of California
UD-110 [New January 1, 2003]
JUDGMENT—UNLAWFUL DETAINER
Code of Civil Procedure, §§ 415.46, 585(d), 664.6, 1169

PLAINTIFF:	LENNY D. LANDLORD	CASE NUMBER:
DEFENDANT:	TERRENCE D. TENANT, ET AL.	A-12345-B

JUDGMENT IS ENTERED AS FOLLOWS BY: [X] THE COURT [ ] THE CLERK

3. **Parties.** Judgment is

   a. [X] for plaintiff (name each): Lenny D. Landlord

     and against defendant (name each): Terrence D. Tenant, Tillie D. Tenant

     [ ] Continued on Attachment 3a (form MC-025).

   b. [ ] for defendant (name each):

4. [X] Plaintiff [ ] Defendant is entitled to possession of the premises located at (street address, apartment, city, and county):

    3815 Gower Canyon Ave, Apt. 3, Los Angeles, California, 90028, Los Angeles County

5. [ ] Judgment applies to all occupants of the premises including tenants, subtenants if any, and named claimants if any (Code Civ. Proc., §§ 715.010, 1169, and 1174.3).

6. **Amount and terms of judgment**

   a. [X] Defendant named in item 3a above must pay plaintiff on the complaint:

(1)	[X]	Past-due rent	$ 1,699.50
(2)	[X]	Holdover damages	$ 1,416.25
(3)	[ ]	Attorney fees	$
(4)	[X]	Costs	$ 520.00
(5)	[ ]	Other (specify):	$
(6)	**TOTAL JUDGMENT**		$ 3,635.75

   b. [ ] Plaintiff is to receive nothing from defendant named in item 3b.

     [ ] Defendant named in item 3b is to recover costs: $

     [ ] and attorney fees: $.

   c. [ ] The rental agreement is canceled. [ ] The lease is forfeited.

7. [ ] **Conditional judgment.** Plaintiff has breached the agreement to provide habitable premises to defendant as stated in *Judgment—Unlawful Detainer Attachment* (form UD–110S), which is attached.

8. [ ] **Other** (specify):

    [X] Continued on Attachment 8 (form MC-025). Judgment granted pursuant to separate Order Granting Motion for Summary Judgment.

Date: _____ [ ] _____
                                       JUDICIAL OFFICER

Date: _____ [ ] Clerk, by _____, Deputy

(SEAL)	**CLERK'S CERTIFICATE** (Optional)
	I certify that this is a true copy of the original judgment on file in the court.
	Date:
	Clerk, by _____ , Deputy

before the commencement of trial. Once trial begins, you cannot dismiss without prejudice and can dismiss only with prejudice (the case cannot be revived). If your case has a fatal flaw, early dismissal without prejudice can be very prudent.

A dismissal without prejudice might not get you completely out from under the lawsuit. If the tenant alleged affirmative defenses, those could be brought as affirmative claims (in other words, the tenant could litigate them in this lawsuit). But a voluntary dismissal without prejudice before trial at least prevents the court from finding liability under Section 1942.4 (your failure to maintain habitable premises). The tenant does not automatically obtain attorneys' fees, and the tenant must start an entirely new proceeding for affirmative relief. The tenant may not bother to do so, because, as you know, lawsuits are a lot of work.

Other Defenses

Other defenses tenants often raise include:

- discrimination on the basis of race, sex, children, or another protected classification
- retaliation for the tenant's exercise of a legal right, such as complaining to the building inspector or organizing other tenants
- the landlord's breach of an express promise to make repairs, or other misconduct, or
- failure to comply with the requirements of a local rent control ordinance (see Chapter 4, and your "home" chapter—either Chapter 2, 3, 4, or 5—in this volume).

To avoid tenants' raising any of these defenses, be sure you comply with the law when it comes to discrimination, retaliation, repairs, and rent control. *The California Landlord's Law Book: Rights and Responsibilities*, includes extensive advice on how to comply with tenant rights in these areas.

Preparing the Judgment Form

When you go to trial you should have a judgment form ready for the judge to sign if you get a favorable ruling. Above are instructions for filling out a judgment after trial, on the statewide Judgment—Unlawful Detainer form (Judicial Council Form UD-110), together with a sample. Fill out the items in the heading and caption boxes, so as to include your name, address, and telephone number; the court's name and location; the names of the parties; and the case number, as you've done many times.

In the box containing the words "JUDGMENT—UNLAWFUL DETAINER," put an X in the boxes next to the words "By Court" and "After Court Trial." If no defendant appeared at trial, also put an X in the box next to the words "Defendant Did Not Appear at Trial."

Item 1: Leave this item blank.

Item 2: Put an X in this box. In 2a, list the date and time that trial occurred, together with the judge's name. In Item 2b, put an X next to the word "Plaintiff" and list your name. If any defendants showed up for trial, put an X next to "Defendant" and list the name of each defendant who appeared at trial. If any defendant appeared with an attorney, check the box next to "Defendant's attorney" and list his or her name on the right. If no defendant appeared at trial, put an X in Item 2c next to the words "Defendant did not appear at trial." Do not check Box 2d unless anyone requested that the judge give a "statement of decision" before the judge pronounced judgment. (This is extremely rare.)

Turn to Page 2 and list your and the defendants' names, and the case number, in the spaces at the top of Page 2.

Item 3: Put an X here and list your name and the names of all defendants.

Item 4: Put an X next to Plaintiff and list the complete rental property address.

Item 5: Do not put an X in this box unless you previously served a Prejudgment Claim of Right to Possession.

Preparing the Judgment When You've Partially Won—Or Lost

Customarily, the party who wins prepares the judgment. The instructions above are based on the assumption that you, the landlord, will win the case after trial—something that happens in the great majority of contested cases. But if the judge allows the tenant to stay and pay reduced rent because you breached the warranty of habitability, even though you're not a clear victor, you'll still need to fill out the judgment form. And if, heaven forbid, you lose outright, you may still be asked by the judge to prepare the judgment. In either event, here are a few pointers.

Partial victory for the tenant on the issue of breach of warranty of habitability. Suppose the tenant claimed he owed none of the $3,000 monthly rent because of a leaky roof, but the judge said he owed $1,500 and could stay if he pays that reduced amount within five days. Fill out the Judgment—Unlawful Detainer form as instructed above, but check Item 7 ("Conditional Judgment"). You'll have to fill out another form, Judgment—Unlawful Detainer form, Judgment— Unlawful Detainer Attachment (Judicial Council form UD—110S), and attach it to the judgment form. We include a blank form of this type on the Nolo website, but we hope you won't have to use it.

Total victory for the tenant. If the tenant prevails, check Item 3b, and in Item 4, check the box next to "defendant." Leave Item 6a blank, and check Item 6b ("plaintiff is to receive nothing from defendant ....").

Items 6 and 6a: Put an X in Box 6a. In nonpayment of rent cases, put an X in Box 6a(1) and list the past-due rent demanded in the three-day notice and in Item 10 and 17c of the complaint. In cases not involving failure to pay rent, such as a termination of month-to-month tenancy based on a 30-day or 60-day notice, do not check Box 6a(1) or fill in an amount. In all cases, put an X in Box 6a(2) "holdover damages" and list the amount obtained by multiplying the daily rental value (requested in Complaint Item 11) by the number of days between the date indicated in Complaint Item 17f and the date to and including the trial. Leave Box 6a(3) blank. Check Box 6a(4) and indicate the amount of court costs. Do not fill in anything in (5)—we don't think any sums other than those in (1) through (4) can be awarded in an unlawful detainer action. (For the same reason, leave Item 8 blank.) Finally, add up the amounts and put that total in Item 6a(6).

Item 6c: Put an X next to the "rental agreement is canceled" box if the tenancy was month to month. Put an X next to the "lease is forfeited" box if the tenant had a fixed-term lease and he or she breached it by nonpayment of rent or another violation of the rental agreement.

 FORM

A blank copy of the Judgment—Unlawful Detainer (Judicial Council form UD-110) can be downloaded from the Nolo website. A sample of this Judgment—Unlawful Detainer form is shown above. (See the appendix for the link to the forms in this book, and other information on using the forms.)

The Trial

As the plaintiff, you have the burden to prove to the judge (or jury if it's a jury trial) that you are entitled to the relief requested in your complaint. You present your case first.

Much of your case will consist of two types of evidence: your testimony, and documents that you offer to prove one or more of your points. In addition, you may want to bring in witnesses.

Once you have met your "burden of proof," it is the tenant's turn. To defeat your case the tenant must offer testimony and/or documents to:

- convince the judge (the jury, if it's a jury trial) that your proof on one or more issues was wrong or deficient, or
- prove that one of the tenant's affirmative defenses is valid.

Don't Send Your Manager to Court

If you handle your case yourself, without an attorney, don't make the mistake of sending your manager or another agent to court when your case is heard. Although a manager or an agent can appear in court to testify, the plaintiff (the property owner) who represents him- or herself must appear at trial to present the case. If the owner who self-represents does not appear at trial, and sends a manager or another agent instead, the judge may refuse to proceed further without a lawyer for you.

If you have an attorney, the attorney may appear on your behalf, although a judge has the authority to demand your presence.

After the tenant has put on his or her case, you will have an opportunity to rebut the tenant's case. After your rebuttal, both you and the tenant can summarize your cases. The case is then submitted to the judge or jury for its verdict. If you win, you will be entitled to evict the tenant (unless the tenant appeals the verdict and obtains a stay pending the appeal, successfully moves for a new trial, or obtains relief from forfeiture (paying your rent in the process).

Now let's take a minute to go into a little more detail on the procedures outlined above.

The Clerk Calls the Case

The trial begins when the clerk calls your case by name, usually by calling out the last name of the parties (for example, in the case of *Lenny D. Landlord v. Terrence and Tillie Tenant*, "*Landlord v. Tenant*"). As mentioned, since you're the plaintiff, you present your case first, when the judge asks you to begin.

Last-Minute Motions

Before you begin your case, the tenant may make a last-minute motion, perhaps for a continuance or postponement of the trial, or to disqualify the judge. A party to a lawsuit is allowed to disqualify one judge—sometimes even at the last minute—simply by filing a declaration under penalty of perjury that states a belief that the judge is prejudiced. (C.C.P. § 170.6.) Unlawful detainer defendants frequently use this procedure to disqualify judges seen to be unsympathetic to tenants or sometimes just to delay things. Landlords rarely use this procedure, even against somewhat pro-tenant judges, due to their desire to get the trial moving.

Except in dire circumstances (usually death of a party or close relative or illness requiring hospitalization), the presiding judge will not agree to postpone the trial. If the tenant disqualifies the judge, the case will be transferred to another judge or postponed if no other judge is available.

Another standard trial motion is one to "exclude witnesses." If you or the tenant so requests, witnesses (but not parties) will be required to leave the courtroom until it's their turn to testify. This prevents witnesses from patterning their testimony after other witnesses on their side they see testify. If you are your only witness and the tenant comes in with a string of friends to testify to what a slumlord you are, you can minimize the copycat risk by insisting that each be kept out while the others testify.

Remember, a motion to exclude witnesses works both ways. If you ask the judge to exclude the tenant's witnesses, your witnesses must also wait in the corridor.

Opening Statements

Both you and the tenant have a right to make an opening statement at the start of the trial. Chances are that the judge has heard many cases like yours and a long opening statement will be a fruitless exercise. Keep your statement brief, focusing on the critical points, such as the nuisance caused by the tenant. Say what you're going to prove, but don't start proving it, and above all, don't argue all the points.

Here's what an opening statement in a nonpayment of rent case might sound like:

"Your Honor, this is an unlawful detainer action based on nonpayment of rent. Mr. Tenant's answer admits the fact of the lease, and that the monthly rent is $1,550, due on the first of the month, but denies everything else. I will testify to my receipt of previous rents, so that the balance due the day the three-day notice was served was $1,550. I will also testify that I served the three-day notice to pay rent or quit on Mr. Tenant. Later when I called him he admitted having received it but he didn't pay the rent within three days after that, or move out."

Presenting Your Case

There are two ways you can offer testimony to prove the disputed elements of your case. The most common is to testify yourself.

As you may know from watching courtroom trials on television shows, whether the *Good Wife* or old *Perry Mason* episodes, parties to lawsuits usually testify in response to questions posed by their own lawyers. This is called "direct examination" (as opposed to "cross-examination," when the other side asks you questions). If you represent yourself, this is done by simply recounting the relevant facts.

> ### The Courtroom
>
> Unlawful detainer trials are conducted in courtrooms that look much like those on television. In addition to the judge, a clerk and bailiff are normally present. They sit at tables immediately in front of the judge's elevated bench, or slightly off to the side. The clerk's job is to keep the judge supplied with the necessary files and papers and to make sure that the proceedings flow smoothly. A clerk is not the same as a court reporter, who keeps a word-by-word record of the proceedings. In courtrooms where eviction cases are heard, a reporter is not present unless either party insists on (and pays for) one. The bailiff, usually a uniformed deputy sheriff or marshal, is present to keep order.
>
> Courtrooms are divided about two-thirds of the way toward the front by a sort of fence known as "the bar." The judge, court personnel, and lawyers use the area on one side of the bar, and the public, including parties and witnesses waiting to be called, sits on the other side. You're invited to cross the bar only when your case is called by the clerk, and any witnesses you have may do so only when you call them to testify. You then come forward and sit at the long table (the one closest to the empty jury box) known as the "counsel table," facing the judge.

Your testimony should be very much like that which you would give at a default hearing. (See Chapter 7.) If the tenant's answer admits certain of your allegations, such as the basic terms of the tenancy or service of the three-day or other termination notice, you can leave that part out, having noted in your opening remarks that it's not disputed.

After you've finished testifying, the tenant or tenant's lawyer may cross-examine you. The general rule is that you, like any other witness, can be cross-examined on anything relating to your testimony on direct examination. You should respond courteously, truthfully, and as briefly as possible. Contrary to popular myth, you don't have to give a "yes" or "no" answer to any question for which it would be inappropriate. You have a right to explain and expand on your answer in detail if you feel it's necessary. For example, the question, "Have you stopped pocketing security deposits?" is best answered by, "I have never 'pocketed' a deposit," rather than by "yes" or "no."

Don't appear hostile toward the person doing the cross-examining; it could hurt your case. If you have a lawyer, the lawyer has the right to object to any question that is abusive or irrelevant. If you are representing yourself and consider a question to be particularly awful, ask the judge if you have to answer it.

> EXAMPLE: After you've finished testifying, the tenant begins cross-examining you with, "Ms. Landlord, didn't you remember my telling you I couldn't pay the rent because I lost my job?" Even though the question may not be technically proper, you can answer yes or no according to your recollection. As a point of practice, this is a terrible question for the tenant, because the question admits nonpayment of rent. While you could legally object to the question as irrelevant, it is a gift to you as the landlord. Accept it gracefully.

If the case is tried by a judge without a jury, do not spend time objecting to questions unless they are outrageous. You can object to personally offensive or intrusive irrelevant questions, such as, "Aren't you rich?" but do not play lawyer even if you think the question objectionable. The judge will disregard improper questions out of habit and will take the lead on poor or irrelevant questioning. When a nonlawyer conducts a trial, the judge's largest fear is that the party will try to act like a lawyer on television.

Don't do it. While the judge should hold you to the same standards of practice that a lawyer must follow, the judge will give you some leeway as long as you are calm, businesslike, and do not try to play a role you cannot fill.

Another way to prove part or all of the disputed elements of your case is by questioning the tenant at the start. The law allows you to call the defendant as a witness before you or any of your own witnesses testify. (Evid. Code § 776.)

Handled properly, the tenant will testify truthfully, if reluctantly, so as to establish most or all of the basic elements of your lawsuit, even if the tenant denied these elements in the answer. Here's an example of such an exchange.

Landlord: *Mr. Tenant, you rented the premises at 123 State Street, Los Angeles, from me, didn't you?*

Tenant: *Yes.*

Landlord: *And that was in March 20xx, correct?*

Tenant: *Yes.*

Landlord: *I'd like to show you a copy of this document entitled "Rental Agreement," attached as Exhibit "A" to the complaint. This is your signature here at the bottom, isn't it?*

Tenant: *Well … ah.*

Landlord: *You paid the monthly rent of $1,550 until August 20xx, didn't you?*

Tenant: *Well, yeah, but in July I got laid off, and …*

Landlord: *And you didn't pay the $1,550 rent in August 20xx, did you?*

Tenant: *No.*

Landlord: *And I'd like to show you a copy of this document entitled "Three-Day Notice to Pay Rent or Quit" attached as Exhibit "B" to the complaint. Do you recognize this document?*

Tenant: *Yes. (Be forewarned, the tenant can just as easily answer "No" to this question. If the tenant starts to dispute your questions, end the questioning and take over directly as your own witness.)*

Landlord: *You told me on August 5 when I phoned you that you received my notice, didn't you?*

Tenant: *Yes.*

Landlord: *And you, in fact, did receive it, correct?*

Tenant: *Yes.*

Landlord: *And you're still living in the premises, aren't you?*

Tenant: *Yes.*

Landlord: *I have no further questions, Your Honor.*

You should also call other witnesses to testify about basic elements of your case that you were unable to cover, or that will likely be disputed by the tenant (such as service of a three-day notice served by a person other than yourself). After the clerk swears your witness in, the witness may answer only questions asked by you, unless the judge allows narrative testimony and the tenant doesn't object.

The Tenant's Case

After you and your witnesses have testified and been cross-examined, it's the tenant's turn to present evidence to contradict you on any of the elements of your case or to present defenses. He can testify himself and/or call other persons (even you) to testify.

After the tenant and any of his witnesses have testified, you or your lawyer may cross-examine them on any issue raised in their testimony.

Your Rebuttal

You now have a second chance to testify and to have any witnesses testify, to respond to denials or points raised by the tenant in his or her defense. This is called the "rebuttal" phase of the trial. The rules are the same as those for your earlier testimony, with one important difference: The only subjects you may go into on rebuttal are those addressed by the tenant or the tenant's witnesses. The purpose is to rebut what they said, not to raise new issues. For example, this is the time to testify that the problems the tenant complains about are fairly minor or that he never asked you to make repairs until after you served a three-day notice. Again, the tenant may cross-examine you and your witnesses.

Closing Arguments

After both sides have presented their testimony, each is allowed to make a brief closing argument to the judge. The plaintiff goes first. Your closing argument should contain three parts: First a summary how you proved your case, second a summary of the evidence that disproved the tenant's defenses, and third, the request for relief—a judgment for possession, the amount of the rent and rental damages, and costs.

The Judge's Decision

After the closing statements, the judge decides the case. Some judges do not announce their decisions in court, but rather take cases "under submission" or "under advisement." This may mean that the judge wants to think the matter over before deciding or simply doesn't want a debate in the courtroom with the losing party. If this happens, you will be notified of the result by mail.

If the judge announces a decision in your favor, you should produce your prepared judgment form for the judge to sign, fill in the dollar amount awarded, and hand it to the clerk. The judge might not award costs at first, instead requiring you to file a memorandum of costs.

The Writ of Execution and Having the Sheriff or Marshal Evict

To have the clerk issue a Writ of Execution after trial, simply hand the original writ form to the court clerk after the judge has signed the judgment and you have paid a writ issuance fee. (See Chapter 7 for instructions on how to fill out the writ form and what happens before and during the eviction.) The writ will be for both the money and possession parts of the judgment, but note that, as explained, Los Angeles and possibly other counties may require separate writs (follow the instructions in Chapter 7). A sample writ for both the possession and money parts of the judgment (following a summary judgment) is shown in Chapter 7. A writ to enforce a judgment obtained after trial is filled out the same way. Take the original and copies of the writ to the sheriff or marshal, along with appropriate instructions for evicting. (See Chapter 7.) We discuss collecting the money part of the judgment in the next chapter.

After the sheriff or marshal has evicted the tenant and turned possession of your property back over to you, you may find yourself stuck with property the tenant has left behind. You should not simply throw away or otherwise dispose of the property, nor should you refuse to return it because the tenant won't pay what he or she owes you. You do have the right to insist the tenant pay reasonable storage charges, and to hold on to the property if the tenant won't pay that. However, most of the time doing so isn't worth the trouble, and you'll be happier just to get rid of the stuff by turning it over to the tenant, no strings attached. If you wind up with property the tenant won't reclaim, you will have to hold onto it for at least 18 days, notify the tenant by mail to pick up the property, and auction it off if it's worth more than $700. (C.C.P. § 1174.) We discuss this at length in *The California Landlord's Law Book: Rights & Responsibilities*, Chapter 21.

Appeals

The losing party has a right of appeal, which must be filed with the clerk of the correct court within 30 or 60 days of the date of judgment, depending on the amount of the judgment. (See C.C.P. §§ 904.1, 904.2.) In a typical case, the loser appeals to the Superior Court Appellate Division.

Your argument on appeal can target only errors of law, not mistaken decisions on facts. In other words, as long as enough credible and relevant evidence was presented, you cannot reverse a judge who simply, in your view, got the facts wrong. Reversals occur only for getting the law wrong. For example, the tenant may argue that the trial court erred in refusing to hear evidence on the tenant's retaliation defense, because he was behind in the rent. This is a legal issue. But the tenant may not argue that the judge or jury was wrong in believing that you didn't retaliate against the tenant for calling the health department. This is an issue of fact.

Similarly, you could argue on appeal that the judge erred in ruling that your three-day notice was invalid because it didn't list all the tenants' names—an issue of law. But you couldn't argue that the judge shouldn't have believed the tenant who claimed never to have received the three-day notice—an issue of fact.

 SEE AN EXPERT
Appeals are very technical and time-consuming. You should contact a lawyer before undertaking an appeal.

Appeals by the Landlord

It seldom makes sense for a landlord to appeal a tenant's victory. Landlords who lose unlawful detainer cases generally do so because of rulings on factual issues, for example, the judge rules that the landlord didn't properly maintain the premises or had illegal retaliation in mind when giving the tenant a 30-day notice. As we saw above, an appeals court will not reconsider the factual findings made by the trial judge, and an appeal of this sort of ruling is a waste of time. When landlords do lose cases on legal issues that might be argued on appeal, it is usually for technical reasons, such as the three-day notice not being in the correct form. In these cases, it usually makes more sense for the landlord, instead of filing an appeal that will take months, to go back, correct the mistake, and start over. For example, the landlord would prepare and serve a new, proper three-day notice and begin a new unlawful detainer lawsuit.

Appeals by the Tenant

Most appeals of unlawful detainer judgments are by tenants, and many of these appeals seem designed to prolong the tenant's stay as long as possible.

Filing an appeal, however, does not automatically "stay" (delay) enforcement of your judgment for possession of the property and rent. A tenant who files an appeal can ask the court for a stay pending appeal if the tenant is willing to pay the rent during the period of the stay.

An appeal is initiated when the tenant files a Notice of Appeal in the trial court and pays the filing fee. This is a simple one-page document that says nothing more than that the tenant appeals the judgment. Pursuing an appeal becomes much more complicated with specific timeframes and rules. Judicial Council Forms App-001 and App-101 describe the procedure.

After tenants file the Notice of Appeal, they can move for a stay, which must be heard by the same judge who ruled against them. Trial judges routinely deny requests for stays and will grant them only if the tenant appears to be basing the appeal on a genuine legal issue, rather than simply stalling for time. If a tenant files a motion for a stay, you should receive written notice to appear in court to oppose the motion. In any event, a judge who grants a stay is required to condition the stay on the tenant's paying the monthly rent to the court. (C.C.P. § 1176(a).)

Whether or not a stay is granted, the appellant must prepare more documents. First, the appellant must designate the portions of the record for the clerk's transcript and pay the costs. Then the appellant must pay a court reporter to prepare a transcript of the trial proceedings, or file a narrative "proposed statement" of what occurred at trial. After that, the case is transferred to the appellate court, where the appellant files an opening "brief," which explains where the trial judge erred. At each stage, you will be notified by mail and required to file papers of your own in response.

Tenant's Possible "Relief from Forfeiture"

Under C.C.P. § 1179, a tenant found by a court to be in breach of the lease can avoid eviction by having a judge grant the tenant's "petition for relief from forfeiture." Simply, this means that if a tenant failed to pay rent, or otherwise violated the rental agreement (say, by having a dog in violation of a no-pets clause), the tenant could offer to pay all the back rent (or otherwise cure the violation), and pay the landlord's court costs, in exchange for being allowed to remain as a tenant—despite losing the case following a trial or even a default judgment. A judge has very wide discretion to grant or deny relief from forfeiture, and will be more inclined to do so if the tenant is facing serious hardship and the fault did not involve serious wrongdoing or harm to you or other tenants. This relief can be obtained before or during trial or immediately after judgment in your favor against the tenant—the judgment will be nullified if the tenant pays the rent or otherwise cures the violation.

This relief from forfeiture remedy does not apply to evictions based on a 30-day or 60-day termination notice, or on expiration of a fixed-term lease. It applies only where a tenant is said to have "forfeited" his or her remaining lease term by breaching the lease, most commonly by failing to pay rent.

In the past, tenant petitions for relief from forfeiture had been rare, because tenants not only had to pay the rent they were unable to pay earlier, but also had to prepare a rather complicated set of legal forms—none of them the fill-in-the-blanks variety you see in this book. However, a tenant representing him- or herself may make this type of request verbally, in court, if you are present—which you of course will be, in a trial of a contested case. In addition, the law also allows the judge to suggest granting relief from forfeiture, and then to grant his or her own suggestion! (This is called granting relief "on the court's own motion.")

This law provides several ways for tenants to try to stave off eviction: by filing a written petition for relief from forfeiture, after judgment has been entered against them by default or otherwise; or by simply asking the judge to allow them to remain in your property if they pay you the rent.

Should you receive legal papers called anything like a petition for relief from forfeiture, see a lawyer quickly—unless you don't mind the tenant's staying if the tenant brings the rent up to date and pays your court costs. If the tenant or the judge brings this subject up in court during a trial in a contested case, you might not have much time to deal with it, unless you ask the judge to let the case proceed to judgment or postpone the matter for a few days to allow you to contact an attorney.

Bear in mind, a judge does not generally raise the subject if the judge is planning to say, "No." If, on the judge's own motion, a judge asks you about relief from forfeiture, it usually means the judge is considering granting the request. Good trial preparation means you will have thought about this in advance and have a response for the judge, which includes reasonable conditions of acceptance or serious objections based on the tenant's conduct in the past.

Unfortunately, because the requested relief appeals to a judge's sense of fairness and equity, the judge has wide discretion and few rules. Your response has to consider the question objectively, ignoring your emotional investment in prosecuting the case. You will have to articulate solid reasons for your agreement or disagreement on what is "fair" or equitable.

Collecting Your Money Judgment

FORMS IN THIS CHAPTER

Chapter 9 includes instructions for and samples of the following forms:

- Application and Order for Appearance and Examination
- Writ of Execution
- Application for Earnings Withholding Order
- Confidential Statement of Judgment Debtor's Social Security Number, and
- Acknowledgment of Satisfaction of Judgment

The Nolo website includes downloadable copies of these forms, plus the Proof of Personal Service—Civil and the Questionnaire for Judgment-Debtor Examination discussed in this chapter (but for which samples are not shown). (See the appendix for the link to the forms in this book, and other information on using the forms.)

After you receive a judgment for possession that includes some amount of money (if only for court costs), you still have to collect it. Unless your ex-tenant voluntarily pays you (a highly unlikely event), you will have to take legal steps to be paid.

Your judgment for money represents little more than a sort of court-sanctioned hunting license, good for ten years (and renewable for subsequent ten-year periods), which allows you to use certain techniques to collect the debt. This chapter shows you a few of those techniques.

Collecting from cotenants. For convenience, we talk about judgments in this chapter as if they are against only one person. Many times, though, a landlord will get a money judgment against two or more people, usually cotenants under the same rental agreement. You have the right to pursue all the debtors or just the ones who have assets to seize until you collect the entire amount. This is because all the debtors are said to be "jointly and severally" liable to you.

> **EXAMPLE:** Because the two tenants you sued for nonpayment of rent, Larry and Moe, were cotenants under the same written lease, you obtained a judgment against both of them. Because Larry is unemployed, you garnished Moe's wages and eventually collected the entire amount from him. This is okay; that Moe wound up paying it all is something to be worked out between Larry and him.

Collection Strategy

Before you start trying to collect the money the tenant owes you, take a minute to assess your chances of success and devise a strategy for proceeding.

Your Chances of Collecting

Some assets are easier to grab than others. Generally, you should try to go after assets in this order:

- the tenant's security deposit
- the tenant's paycheck, then
- the tenant's bank or other deposit accounts.

In general, if you can't collect from the tenant's paycheck or bank account, you're probably out of luck for the time being. Most of the tenant's personal possessions are either exempt from being seized to pay a court judgment or not enough to bother with.

Even if the asset is valuable, the sale of personal property, including vehicles, will often net you less than the expenses you'll have to front the sheriff for storage and auction costs. In other words, you'll wind up losing money.

Finally, think twice (or do not bother trying) before attempting to collect from a tenant who is an active duty member of the armed forces. Under federal law, you'll have to proceed via an "Involuntary Allotment Application," which you will file with the Defense Finance and Accounting Service (DFAS). It could take many months before that agency reviews your garnishment request. For more information, as well as a link to a site that will tell you whether your tenant is indeed active, go to the DFAS website at www.dfas.mil/garnishment.

Using a Collection Agency

You might have better things to do—like running your rental business—than tracking down nonpaying tenants you've managed to evict. If you feel debt collection isn't worth the time it takes, or if your attempts at attaching wages or bank accounts are unsuccessful, you might consider turning the judgment over to a collection agency.

Generally, collection agencies take as their fee between 33% and 50% of what they collect. They do, however, typically pay fees for sheriffs or marshals, so you're not out money if you don't collect. The fee you pay a collection agency is not recoverable from the debtor. For example, if a collection agency collects a $1,000 judgment for you, pocketing $400, you get $600, but you have to give the judgment debtor full credit for the $1,000 that was collected.

Professional collection agencies would like to have you believe that only they have recourse to secret sources of information that will lead to the whereabouts or assets of a person who owes you money. This isn't true; anyone with a little ingenuity, energy, and a credit card can become a "skip tracer." (Skip tracing is the term used when you are trying to locate a current address and location for a debtor.) In fact, once you learn the tricks, you will most likely tackle the task with more dedication and commitment than any professional skip tracer.

As we explain below, you can start by going through databases of public records or purchasing a report from records bureau or service. Header information from credit reports can be useful as well because most people keep their account records up to date.

Using the Tenant's Security Deposit

As mentioned, your first option to collect the judgment lies in the security deposit the tenant put up when moving in. If there's anything of the deposit left over after making legitimate deductions for repairs and cleaning, you can apply it to the judgment. If the judgment is fully covered by the deposit, you're home free.

EXAMPLE 1: You collected a $1,800 security deposit from Maurice when he moved in in January. When he didn't pay his $1,100 rent in September, you moved quickly, got a judgment for possession, and had him evicted before the end of the month. Your court costs were $350. Maurice left a broken window that cost you $30 to repair and left the carpet very dirty, necessitating professional cleaning at a cost of $75. You got a judgment of $1,450 (unpaid rent plus costs). You're entitled to deduct $105 for repairs and cleaning from the deposit. This leaves $1,695 to apply to a judgment of $1,450, so you will be fully compensated. The money left over after that must be promptly returned to Maurice, using the procedures outlined in *The California Landlord's Law Book: Rights & Responsibilities*, Chapter 20.

EXAMPLE 2: In January, Francesca paid you a security deposit of $1,900, an amount equal to one month's rent. Because of her repeated loud parties, you gave Francesca a 30-day notice on April 5, terminating her tenancy effective May 5. Francesca refused to pay the rent for the five days in May and also refused to leave. You brought an unlawful detainer action, finally getting her evicted on May 30. You got a judgment for $1,583.33 prorated "damages" for the days she stayed after the 5th (25 days at $63.33 per day), plus $350 court costs, for a total of $1,933.33. After deductions for cleaning and damages ($200 for carpet cleaning and furniture repair), and the ten days' rent not reflected in the judgment (10 x $63.33 or $633.30), only $1,066.70 of Francesca's security deposit remains to apply toward the judgment. You can try to have the sheriff or marshal collect the remaining $833.33 of the judgment as explained in the rest of this chapter.

Remember that you must still send the tenant an itemized statement showing what you did with the security deposit, even if there's nothing left of it to return. If you use all or part of the security deposit to satisfy your judgment, you must include this fact in your accounting to the tenant. In the likely event the tenant leaves without giving you a forwarding address, you will be relieved of liability if you mail the statement to the address at the property you just evicted the tenant from. If the tenant left a forwarding address at the post office, the mail will be forwarded.

 RESOURCE
Useful guide for taking deductions from a tenant's security deposit. *The California Landlord's Law Book: Rights & Responsibilities*, explains the state-required procedures and includes forms for taking deductions, such as for repairs and cleaning, from a tenant's security deposit. The book also covers how to use part or all of the deposit to satisfy a court judgment.

Finding the Tenant

 SKIP AHEAD
Skip this section if you know where the ex-tenant works, lives, or banks.

If you can't find where your ex-tenant banks, works, or lives, you'll have to start the collection process by finding the tenant. This involves doing a little investigation before you prepare any more paperwork.

Internet

Ask any regular Internet surfer how to find a long-lost friend and you'll hear about several Internet sites that search for people. Admittedly, many of these records are out of date or incomplete, but they provide a starting place. Professional debt collectors use them all, with varying degrees of success. Here are several free Internet sites that might prove helpful as you search for your missing tenant:

- www.allonesearch.com—searches the data contained in over 400 search engines, databases, indexes, and directories
- www.555-1212.com—searches phone directories
- www.whowhere.com—searches for phone numbers, addresses, and websites
- www.infospace.com—searches white page directories, yellow page directories, and reverse directories
- www.switchboard.com—searches directory assistance listings for addresses, phone numbers, and email addresses
- www.bop.gov—searches the federal Bureau of Prisons to see if your missing debtor is an inmate in a federal penitentiary
- www.sos.ca.gov—searches corporation records of the California Secretary of State, and
- social media and search engines (such as Facebook, Google, Yahoo, and LinkedIn). If you conduct multiple searches, you may eventually get leads on a person's location.

If the free sites prove fruitless, you can try searching on one or more of the Internet sites that charge for their services:

- www.lexisnexis.com/risk—an employment screening company that searches driving records, criminal records, and credit reports, and
- www.ussearch.com—searches public records.

Telephone Directories

Searching phone directories might generate results, but bear in mind that directories do not include mobile phones, and many people no longer have landlines. Consequently, the following recommendations, which involve "old" technology, will yield diminishing returns. Still, it is worth trying.

If you haven't already done so, call directory assistance (area code plus 555-1212) for all areas the tenant might possibly live and ask if there is a listing. Or call 800-FREE-411 for similar information.

Directories of Unlisted Phone Numbers

It's possible the tenant now has an unlisted phone number. Calling it "unlisted" could be a misnomer, however. Unlisted numbers don't appear in the official phone company directories. But they often show up in directories of unlisted numbers, which are compiled surreptitiously and circulate among bill collectors. You might be able to gain access to one through an auto repossessor or other person who works in the collections industry. You can sometimes find phone numbers for or important information about a person by searching online. Simply type the person's name and city into a search engine (for example, "Tillie Tenant Los Angeles"). The more common the name, and the bigger the city, the less likely you'll get useful information.

Crisscross Directories

The idea behind crisscross directories is that if you know only certain information about the tenant, you can fill in the missing pieces. For example, if you know the street on which the tenant lives, you can locate the exact address. If you know the address, you can get the phone number. If you know just the phone number, you can find the address. Some crisscross directories include a person's occupation and business name. You can also obtain the names, addresses, and phone numbers of neighbors (or former neighbors); you can then ask them for information about the tenant.

Crisscross directories are available for most major metropolitan areas. You can find them in public libraries, title companies, or the county tax assessor's or recorder's office. Also, most Internet search services include a crisscross directory feature.

U.S. Postal Service and Post Office Boxes

The postal service will give you box holder and forwarding information under limited circumstances.

The post office usually won't give out an individual box holder's address unless you provide a statement that the name, address, and telephone number are needed to serve legal papers in a "pending proceeding." In this case, the pending proceeding consists of postjudgment enforcement proceedings. So, you'll need to tell them that you are trying to serve legal process. Use the Postal Service Form 5-2b, *Request for Change of Address or Boxholder Information Needed for Service of Legal Process*. A sample form is below and can be downloaded from the Nolo website.

If your tenant rented a post office box in the name of a business, the post office will release the street address and phone number of the box holder. Some post offices will give you this information over the phone, but often you must request it in writing. You do not have to explain why you want the information.

Tenants Who Leave Forwarding Addresses With the Post Office

In years past, if the tenant left a forwarding address with the Postal Service, you could find out what it is. We can't determine whether the Post Office still offers this service. But you can try: Send a first-class letter to the tenant's last known address, include your own return address on the envelope's top left corner, and write "Return Service Requested" in clear, legible script directly below your address. The Postal Service will send the letter back to you, at no charge, with a sticker indicating the ex-tenant's forwarding address.

(If the ex-tenant left no forwarding address, the Postal Service will stamp the letter with this information and return the letter to you.)

Exhibit 5-2b

Change of Address or Boxholder Request Format — Process Servers

Postmaster   Date_____

_____
City, State, ZIP Code

REQUEST FOR CHANGE OF ADDRESS OR BOXHOLDER INFORMATION NEEDED FOR SERVICE OF LEGAL PROCESS

Please furnish the new address or the name and street address (if a boxholder) for the following:

Name:_____
Address:_____

Note: Only one request may be made per completed form. The name and last known address are required for change of address information. The name, if known, and Post Office box address are required for boxholder information.

The following information is provided in accordance with 39 CFR 265.6(d)(5)(ii). There is no fee for providing boxholder or change of address information.

1. Capacity of requester (e.g., process server, attorney, party representing self):_____
2. Statute or regulation that empowers me to serve process (not required when requester is an attorney or a party acting pro se - except a corporation acting pro se must cite statute): _____
3. The names of all known parties to the litigation: _____
4. The court in which the case has been or will be heard:_____
5. The docket or other identifying number (a or b must be completed):
_____ a. Docket or other identifying number: _____
_____ b. Docket or other identifying number has not been issued.
6. The capacity in which this individual is to be served (e.g., defendant or witness) _____

WARNING

THE SUBMISSION OF FALSE INFORMATION TO OBTAIN AND USE CHANGE OF ADDRESS INFORMATION OR BOXHOLDER INFORMATION FOR ANY PURPOSE OTHER THAN THE SERVICE OF LEGAL PROCESS IN CONNECTION WITH ACTUAL OR PROSPECTIVE LITIGATION COULD RESULT IN CRIMINAL PENALTIES INCLUDING A FINE OF UP TO $10,000 OR IMPRISONMENT OF NOT MORE THAN 5 YEARS, OR BOTH (TITLE 18 U.S.C. SECTION 1001).

I certify that the above information is true and that the address information is needed and will be used solely for service of legal process in conjunction with actual or prospective litigation.

_____   _____
Signature   Printed Name

Address

_____
City, State, ZIP Code

_____

POST OFFICE USE ONLY

_____No change of address order on file.   NEW ADDRESS OR BOXHOLDER'S NAME
_____Moved, left no forwarding address.   AND STREET ADDRESS
_____No such address.
                                                                      _____
                                                                      _____

Credit Reports

A credit report includes a tenant's name, address, phone number, Social Security number, and date of birth, as well as credit history and possibly employment information. A credit bureau (also known as a credit reporting agency) might provide a copy of the tenant's credit report if you state that you need the information for a legitimate business purpose, such as collecting a debt. (Civ. Code § 1785.11(a)(3)(F).)

Credit bureaus typically provide credit reports to banks, credit card issuers, finance companies, mortgage lenders, landlords, and other businesses that subscribe to their credit reporting services. Credit bureaus often are unwilling to provide information to nonsubscribers; however, it can't hurt you to ask. Check your local phone book for the phone numbers of the "big three" bureaus—Experian, Equifax, or TransUnion. If you can't find a listing, check their Internet sites (www.experian.com, www.equifax.com, or www.transunion.com). Most of the information on the site is about ordering your own file or becoming a subscriber. But the bureaus constantly update their pages, and you can email their customer service departments with your inquiry.

If a bureau will provide you with a copy of the tenant's credit report, you will probably have to provide a copy of your judgment or other documents showing that you're entitled to the report. You will probably have to pay a fee of $50–$60.

Business Records

If the tenant owns a business that sells taxable goods (the sale of most goods in California is taxed), the statistics unit of the Board of Equalization (800-400-7115 or www.boe.ca.gov) will probably have information on the business.

If the tenant is one of the many of millions of Californians licensed by the Department of Consumer Affairs or another agency, location information may be easily available. Start with the Department of Consumer Affairs (800-952-5210 or www.dca.ca.gov). If another agency licenses the tenant, the Department of Consumer Affairs can provide a referral to the correct agency. Business addresses are usually listed in these records, and sometimes you'll get a home address.

If the tenant is a sole proprietor, California partnership, or member of a California partnership, you can search the fictitious name records at the clerk's office in the county in which the principal place of business is located. This lists the business's owners and their addresses.

If the tenant is a California corporation, or is the owner of a California corporation, a foreign corporation authorized to do business in California, a California limited liability company, a limited partnership, or a foreign general partnership authorized to do business in California, the business must register with the Secretary of State (www.sos.ca.gov). If you're trying to track down a tenant by finding the tenant's business, contact the Secretary of State. You can get information (for a fee) by phone (916-653-3365); the telephone menu will help you find the right office for corporation, LLC, or partnership information. You can also get this information online, at no cost, at http://kepler.sos.ca.gov.

Locating the Tenant's Assets

> **SKIP AHEAD**
> **If you already know where the tenant banks or works, skip to "Garnishing Wages and Bank Accounts," below.**

It doesn't make much sense to prepare papers and pay filing fees for papers to collect the money part of the judgment until you locate property of the tenant that can be legally taken ("levied on") by the sheriff or marshal to apply to the judgment. The first sources of funds you should try to locate are the tenant's bank accounts and paycheck.

Check the Tenant's Rental Application

If you used a good rental application, the tenant's bank accounts and employer should be listed on it. Of course, one or both may have changed since the application was prepared. If you keep copies of your tenant's rent checks (or you have the original of a bounced check), you might have more recent information. You might also be able to get that information from your bank, although you might be charged a search fee.

Go to Court: The Judgment Debtor Examination

Suppose you know your ex-tenant has money in a checking account, but you don't know which bank or branch. Or perhaps you know where she lives, but not where she works and has a paycheck to garnish. Wouldn't it be nice if you could get her to sit down and answer all your questions? Happily, you can, if you know where your former tenant lives or works. You do this by going to court to conduct a "judgment debtor's examination."

The judgment debtor's examination is a proceeding in which a person against whom an unpaid judgment is entered (a "judgment debtor") is ordered to show up in court at a certain date and time to answer, under oath, your questions about income and assets. The only requirements for using this procedure are that the debtor lives or works no more than 150 miles from the courthouse, and that you not have taken a debtor's examination in the past four months. There are exceptions to these requirements. If the debtor lives more than 150 miles from the courthouse, you may schedule an examination at a closer court. If you've conducted a debtor's exam within the last 120 days, you can submit an affidavit explaining why you need to hold another exam so soon. A tenant who fails to show or refuses to answer legitimate questions about his or her financial affairs can be fined or even (rarely) jailed for a few days.

Getting a Court Date

In order to have the court issue the Order of Examination (the court order that tells the tenant to come to court for the examination), fill out a form called Application and Order for Appearance and Examination. Once the judge has approved and signed it, the form serves as the order itself.

 FORM
A blank copy of the Application and Order for Appearance and Examination (Judicial Council form AT-138/EJ-125) can be downloaded from the Nolo website. A sample of this application and order form is shown below. (See the appendix for the link to the forms in this book, and other information on using the forms.)

Before you begin filling out the form, call the clerk of the court where you obtained a judgment. Find out in what courtroom or department debtor's examinations are held and ask the clerk to set a date and time for the debtor's examination. Many courts schedule debtor examinations on a particular day of the week. Some allow you to pick a convenient date yourself. Ask for a date at least four weeks away, to allow you some time to have the debtor served with the order. The debtor must be served personally at least ten days before the debtor's examination. Once you've obtained a date and time, fill out the form in the following manner.

Caption boxes: List your name, address, phone number, Plaintiff in Pro Per, court name and location, and case title and number in the boxes at the top of the form, in the same way as on the complaint and other court forms. Just below the spaces for the names of the parties, put Xs in the boxes next to "ENFORCEMENT OF JUDGMENT" and "Judgment Debtor."

The Order: The first portion of the form below the caption boxes is the "Order to Appear for Examination," the part addressed to the debtor. List the debtor's name in Item 1. In Item 2, put an X in Box a only. Below that, list the date and time for the examination, as well as the courtroom (or "department") number you got from the court

AT-138/EJ-125

ATTORNEY OR PARTY WITHOUT ATTORNEY:	STATE BAR NO.:	FOR COURT USE ONLY

NAME: Lenny D. Landlord

FIRM NAME:

STREET ADDRESS: 12345 Angeleno Street

CITY: Los Angeles   STATE: CA   ZIP CODE: 90028

TELEPHONE NO.: 213-555-6789   FAX NO.:

E-MAIL ADDRESS:

ATTORNEY FOR (name): in Pro Per

The Court Clerk will fill in this information (in LA)

SUPERIOR COURT OF CALIFORNIA, COUNTY OF LOS ANGELES

STREET ADDRESS: 111 N. Hill Street

MAILING ADDRESS:

CITY AND ZIP CODE: Los Angeles, CA 90012

BRANCH NAME:

PLAINTIFF LENNY D. LANDLORD, et al.

DEFENDANT TERRENCE D. TENANT, et al.

APPLICATION AND ORDER FOR APPEARANCE AND EXAMINATION	CASE NUMBER:
[X] ENFORCEMENT OF JUDGMENT [ ] ATTACHMENT (Third Person)	A-12345-B
[X] Judgment Debtor [ ] Third Person	

ORDER TO APPEAR FOR EXAMINATION

1. TO (name): Terrence D. Tenant, Tillie D. Tenant
2. YOU ARE ORDERED TO APPEAR personally before this court, or before a referee appointed by the court, to
   a. [X] furnish information to aid in enforcement of a money judgment against you.
   b. [ ] answer concerning property of the judgment debtor in your possession or control or concerning a debt you owe the judgment debtor.
   c. [ ] answer concerning property of the defendant in your possession or control or concerning a debt you owe the defendant that is subject to attachment.

Date:	Time:	Dept. or Div.:	Rm.:
Address of court [ ] is shown above [ ] is:			

3. This order may be served by a sheriff, marshal, registered process server, **or** the following specially appointed person (name):

Date:

_____
JUDGE

This order must be served not less than 10 days before the date set for the examination.
IMPORTANT NOTICES ON REVERSE

APPLICATION FOR ORDER TO APPEAR FOR EXAMINATION

4. [X] Original judgment creditor   [ ] Assignee of record   [ ] Plaintiff who has a right to attach order
   applies for an order requiring (name): Terrence D. Tenant and Tillie D. Tenant
   to appear and furnish information to aid in enforcement of the money judgment or to answer concerning property or debt.

5. The person to be examined is
   a. [X] the judgment debtor.
   b. [ ] a third person (1) who has possession or control of property belonging to the judgment debtor or the defendant or (2) who owes the judgment debtor or the defendant more than $250. An affidavit supporting this application under Code of Civil Procedure section 491.110 or 708.120 is attached.

6. The person to be examined resides or has a place of business in this county or within 150 miles of the place of examination.

7. [ ] This court is **not** the court in which the money judgment is entered or (attachment only) the court that issued the writ of attachment. An affidavit supporting an application under Code of Civil Procedure section 491.150 or 708.160 is attached.

8. [ ] The judgment debtor has been examined within the past 120 days. An affidavit showing good cause for another examination is attached.

I declare under penalty of perjury under the laws of the State of California that the foregoing is true and correct.

Date: April 1, 20xx

Lenny D. Landlord	►	*Lenny D. Landlord*
(TYPE OR PRINT NAME)		(SIGNATURE OF DECLARANT)

(Continued on reverse)   Page 1 of 2

Form Adopted for Mandatory Use Judicial Council of California AT-138/EJ-125 [Rev. January 1, 2017]	**APPLICATION AND ORDER FOR APPEARANCE AND EXAMINATION** (Attachment—Enforcement of Judgment)	Code of Civil Procedure, §§ 491.110, 708.110, 708.120, 708.170 www.courts.ca.gov

clerk. If the address of the court is the same as that in the caption box (it usually is), check the box next to the words "shown above." If for some reason the court at which the examination is to take place has an address different from that on the caption, list that address instead.

Leave Item 3 blank unless you want someone besides the sheriff or a registered process server to serve the order on the ex-tenant. If you want someone else to serve the order (this must be an adult who isn't a party in the case), put that person's name in Item 3. Leave the date and signature blank; the judge will complete them.

The Application: The second part of the form, below the order, is the application for issuance of the order. In Item 4, put an X in the box next to the words "the Judgment creditor" (you), and fill in the ex-tenant's name in the blank. In Item 5, put an X in the first box, before the words "judgment debtor" (tenant) only. Fill in the date and your name and sign the application.

Make at least three copies of the form, being sure to copy both pages. (Page 2 contains important warnings to the debtor about failure to appear as ordered, and the order is void without this information.) Take the original and the copies to the court clerk, who will have the original signed by the judge and file it. You can either pick up the file-stamped copies later or give the clerk a self-addressed, stamped envelope to mail the copies to you. One of these copies must be personally served on the debtor.

Having a Copy Served on the Debtor

You must make arrangements to have the order of examination served on the debtor. Unlike most other legal documents, an order of examination must be served personally by a sheriff, marshal, or registered private process server unless you listed someone else's name in Item 3 of the order. As a general rule, private process servers are faster and more aggressive—but also more expensive—than using a sheriff or marshal. Give the process server the debtor's home or business address as well as

the best time to attempt service. Make sure the process server understands that service must be completed at least ten days before the date of the examination.

About two weeks before the hearing, call the process server to see if the order of examination has been served. If it has, make sure the process server has filed a proof of personal service with the court (or given you the filled-out form for you to file in court yourself). The process server should use the Judicial Council form Proof of Personal Service—Civil (Form POS-020) when serving the order of examination.

 FORM
A blank copy of the Proof of Personal Service—Civil (Judicial Council Form POS-020) can be downloaded from the Nolo website. (See the appendix for the link to the forms in this book, and other information on using the forms.)

The proof of personal service should be filed at least five days before the date of the examination. Some courts cancel the debtor's examination if you don't file the proof of personal service on time; check with your court if you're running late. If the process server has been unable to serve the paper at least ten days before the hearing, you'll have to call the court clerk to ask that the examination be taken "off calendar" and to get a new date at least two to three weeks off. Unless the court will let you change the date, you'll have to prepare and submit a new application form, with the new date, and try again.

What to Ask at the Examination

Our form Questionnaire for Judgment-Debtor Examination gives some sample questions to ask the debtor, including details about:

- the debtor's employer and pay (and that of any spouse)
- cash, savings, or checking accounts
- vehicles

- housing costs, such as rent or mortgage payments, and
- assets, such as stocks, jewelry, or other property.

Go through these questions carefully before the hearing and ask only those that apply. Use a photocopy of the form to list the answers to the questions. Don't feel intimidated by the length of this questionnaire; many questions will not apply.

FORM

A blank copy of the Questionnaire for Judgment-Debtor Examination can be downloaded from the Nolo website. (See the appendix for the link to the forms in this book, and other information on using the forms.)

On the day of the examination, appear in court prepared to meet the debtor. If the debtor doesn't show, the judge may reschedule the examination or issue a "bench warrant" for his or her arrest. To have a bench warrant issued, you will have to complete a form and return it to the court with a fee of $35 to have the sheriff or marshal serve it.

When your case is called, you and the debtor should come forward. The debtor will be ordered to take an oath and answer your questions about income or assets. The two of you will probably be directed to a spare room or some part of the courthouse, perhaps just the benches down the hall (or seats right in the courtroom if it isn't being used for something else). Should the debtor refuse to give you straight answers, say that you're going back to the courtroom to ask the judge to order him or her to answer. If the debtor refuses to come back to the courtroom for this, or simply wanders off, you can ask the judge to order the bailiff to bring him or her back—or issue an arrest warrant if he or she skips out altogether.

CAUTION

Be sure to ask: "Do you have any money with you today?" If the answer is "no," you have the right to insist that the debtor show you an empty wallet to make sure. If the debtor has money, you can ask the judge to order that it be turned over to you on the spot. The judge has the power to order the debtor to do this, but may allow the debtor to keep some of it for essentials. Ask also if the debtor is carrying a checkbook and knows the balance in the account. You might be able to get the judge to order the debtor to write you a check—which you should cash at the debtor's bank immediately after the hearing. If you put it in your account, chances are the debtor's account will be closed before the check can be presented for collection. You can even ask the judge to order the debtor to turn over to you any jewelry, cell phone, laptop computer, or other goods the tenant unthinkingly brings to the exam.

Once you've found out where the former tenant banks or works, you're ready to go after a bank account or paycheck. See the discussion just below.

Garnishing Wages and Bank Accounts

This section describes your next step: how to prepare the proper documents to give to the sheriff or marshal. These are:

- a Writ of Execution, and
- written instructions to the sheriff or marshal (or, if you're going after wages, an Application for Earnings Withholding Order).

Once you start emptying a tenant's bank account or garnishing wages, you might have to wait only a few weeks before the money from the marshal or sheriff comes in the mail.

Preparing the Writ of Execution

The Writ of Execution for the money part of the judgment allows the sheriff or marshal to take all the money out of the tenant's bank savings or checking account (up to the amount of the judgment, of course) or to order an employer to take up to 25% out of the tenant's paycheck.

EJ-130

ATTORNEY OR PARTY WITHOUT ATTORNEY: STATE BAR NO.:	FOR COURT USE ONLY

NAME: Lenny D. Landlord

FIRM NAME:

STREET ADDRESS: 12345 Angeleno Street

CITY: Los Angeles STATE: CA ZIP CODE: 90028

TELEPHONE NO.: 213-555-6789 FAX NO.:

EMAIL ADDRESS: LDLXXX@ispofchoice.com

ATTORNEY FOR *(name)*: in pro per

[ ] ATTORNEY FOR [X] ORIGINAL JUDGMENT CREDITOR [ ] ASSIGNEE OF RECORD

SUPERIOR COURT OF CALIFORNIA, COUNTY OF LOS ANGELES

STREET ADDRESS: 111 N. Hill Street

MAILING ADDRESS:

CITY AND ZIP CODE: Los Angeles, CA 90012

BRANCH NAME:

PLAINTIFF/PETITIONER: Lenny D. Landlord	CASE NUMBER:
DEFENDANT/RESPONDENT: Terrence D. Tenant, et al.	A-12345-B

WRIT OF	[X] EXECUTION (Money Judgment)		[X] Limited Civil Case (including Small Claims)
	[ ] POSSESSION OF	[ ] Personal Property	
		[ ] Real Property	[ ] Unlimited Civil Case (including Family and Probate)
	[ ] SALE		

1. **To the Sheriff or Marshal of the County of:** Los Angeles

   You are directed to enforce the judgment described below with daily interest and your costs as provided by law.

2. **To any registered process server:** You are authorized to serve this writ only in accordance with CCP 699.080 or CCP 715.040.

3. (Name): Lenny D. Landlord

   is the [X] original judgment creditor [ ] assignee of record whose address is shown on this form above the court's name.

4. **Judgment debtor** *(name, type of legal entity if not a natural person, and last known address):*

   Terrance D. Tenant
   3815 Gower Canyon Ave., Apt. 3
   Los Angeles, CA 90028

   [X] Additional judgment debtors on next page

5. **Judgment entered on** *(date):* 5/28/20xx
   (See type of judgment in item 22.)

6. [ ] Judgment renewed on *(dates):*

7. **Notice of sale** under this writ:
   a. [X] has not been requested.
   b. [ ] has been requested *(see next page).*

8. [ ] Joint debtor information on next page.

   [SEAL]

9. [ ] Writ of Possession/Writ of Sale information on next page.

10. [ ] This writ is issued on a sister-state judgment.

—— For items 11–17, see form MC-012 and form MC-013-INFO.

11. Total judgment *(as entered or renewed)*	$	3,012.60
12. Costs after judgment (CCP 685.090)	$	0.00
13. Subtotal *(add 11 and 12)*	$	3,012.60
14. Credits to principal *(after credit to interest)*	$	0.00
15. Principal remaining due *(subtract 14 from 13)*	$	3,012.60
16. Accrued interest remaining due per CCP 685.050(b) *(not on GC 6103.5 fees)*	$	0.00
17. Fee for issuance of writ *(per GC 70626(a)(I))*	$	25.00
18. **Total amount due** *(add 15, 16, and 17)*	$	3,037.60

19. **Levying officer:**
   a. Add daily interest from date of writ *(at the legal rate on 15) (not on GC 6103.5 fees)* . . . . $ 0.83
   b. Pay directly to court costs included in 11 and 17 (GC 6103.5, 68637; CCP 699.520(j)) . . . . $ 0.00

20. [ ] The amounts called for in items 11–19 are different for each debtor. These amounts are stated for each debtor on Attachment 20.

Date: _____ Clerk, by _____, Deputy

NOTICE TO PERSON SERVED: SEE PAGE 3 FOR IMPORTANT INFORMATION.

Page 1 of 3

Form Approved for Optional Use Judicial Council of California EJ-130 [Rev. September 1, 2020]	**WRIT OF EXECUTION**	Code of Civil Procedure, §§ 699.520, 712.010, 715.010 Government Code, § 6103.5 www.courts.ca.gov

EJ-130

| Plaintiff/Petitioner: Lenny D. Landlord | CASE NUMBER: |
| Defendant/Respondent: Terrence D. Tenant, et al. | A-12345-B |

21. [x] Additional judgment debtor(s) *(name, type of legal entity if not a natural person, and last known address):*

Tillie D. Tenant
3815 Gower Canyon Ave., Apt. 3
Los Angeles, CA 90028

22. The judgment is for *(check one):*

    a. [ ] wages owed.
    b. [ ] child support or spousal support.
    c. [x] other.

23. [ ] Notice of sale has been requested by *(name and address):*

24. [ ] Joint debtor was declared bound by the judgment (CCP 989-994)

    a. *on (date):*
    b. name, type of legal entity if not a natural person, and
       last known address of joint debtor:

    a. *on (date):*
    b. name, type of legal entity if not a natural person, and
       last known address of joint debtor:

    c. [ ] Additional costs against certain joint debtors are itemized: [ ] below [ ] on Attachment 24c.

25. [ ] (Writ of Possession or Writ of Sale) **Judgment** was entered for the following:

    a. [ ] Possession of real property: The complaint was filed on *(date):* April 10, 20xx
       (Check (1) or (2). Check (3) if applicable. Complete (4) if (2) or (3) have been checked.)

      (1) [ ] The *Prejudgment Claim of Right to Possession* was served in compliance with CCP 415.46. The judgment includes all tenants, subtenants, named claimants, and other occupants of the premises.

      (2) [ ] The *Prejudgment Claim of Right to Possession* was NOT served in compliance with CCP 415.46.

      (3) [ ] The unlawful detainer resulted from a foreclosure sale of a rental housing unit. (An occupant not named in the judgment may file a *Claim of Right to Possession* at any time up to and including the time the levying officer returns to effect eviction, regardless of whether a *Prejudgment Claim of Right to Possession* was served.) *(See CCP 415.46 and 1174.3(a)(2).)*

      (4) If the unlawful detainer resulted from a foreclosure (item 25a(3)), or if the *Prejudgment Claim of Right to Possession* was not served in compliance with CCP 415.46 (item 25a(2)), answer the following:

        (a) The daily rental value on the date the complaint was filed was $

        (b) The court will hear objections to enforcement of the judgment under CCP 1174.3 on the following dates *(specify):*

Item 25 continued on next page

EJ-130 [Rev. September 1, 2020]   **WRIT OF EXECUTION**   Page 2 of 3

EJ-130

Plaintiff/Petitioner: Lenny D. Landlord	CASE NUMBER:
Defendant/Respondent: Terrence D. Tenant, et al.	A-12345-B

25. b. ☐ Possession of personal property.

☐ If delivery cannot be had, then for the value *(itemize in 25e)* specified in the judgment or supplemental order.

c. ☐ Sale of personal property.

d. ☐ Sale of real property.

e. The property is described ☐ below ☐ on Attachment 25e.

NOTICE TO PERSON SERVED

WRIT OF EXECUTION OR SALE. Your rights and duties are indicated on the accompanying *Notice of Levy* (form EJ-150).

WRIT OF POSSESSION OF PERSONAL PROPERTY. If the levying officer is not able to take custody of the property, the levying officer will demand that you turn over the property. If custody is not obtained following demand, the judgment may be enforced as a money judgment for the value of the property specified in the judgment or in a supplemental order.

WRIT OF POSSESSION OF REAL PROPERTY. If the premises are not vacated within five days after the date of service on the occupant or, if service is by posting, within five days after service on you, the levying officer will remove the occupants from the real property and place the judgment creditor in possession of the property. Except for a mobile home, personal property remaining on the premises will be sold or otherwise disposed of in accordance with CCP 1174 unless you or the owner of the property pays the judgment creditor the reasonable cost of storage and takes possession of the personal property not later than 15 days after the time the judgment creditor takes possession of the premises.

EXCEPTION IF RENTAL HOUSING UNIT WAS FORECLOSED. If the residential property that you are renting was sold in a foreclosure, you have additional time before you must vacate the premises. If you have a lease for a fixed term, such as for a year, you may remain in the property until the term is up. If you have a periodic lease or tenancy, such as from month-to-month, you may remain in the property for 90 days after receiving a notice to quit. A blank form *Claim of Right to Possession and Notice of Hearing* (form CP10) accompanies this writ. You may claim your right to remain on the property by filling it out and giving it to the sheriff or levying officer.

EXCEPTION IF YOU WERE NOT SERVED WITH A FORM CALLED PREJUDGMENT CLAIM OF RIGHT TO POSSESSION. If you were not named in the judgment for possession and you occupied the premises on the date on which the unlawful detainer case was filed, you may object to the enforcement of the judgment against you. You must complete the form *Claim of Right to Possession and Notice of Hearing* (form CP10) and give it to the sheriff or levying officer. A blank form accompanies this writ. You have this right whether or not the property you are renting was sold in a foreclosure.

EJ-130 [Rev. September 1, 2020] **WRIT OF EXECUTION** Page 3 of 3

Once issued by the court, the Writ of Execution remains valid for 180 days.

You prepare the Writ of Execution for a money judgment in the same manner as the writ of possession of the premises (see Chapter 7), with the following exceptions.

Check the "EXECUTION (Money Judgment)" box, rather than the "POSSESSION OF" and "Real Property" boxes in the top part of the form.

Be sure to check the box next to "Limited Civil Case." In Item 1, fill in the county in which the levy will take place, regardless of what county the judgment was entered in.

Leave all of Item 9 blank.

In Item 11, list the total judgment that was awarded as rent, damages, and costs.

Item 12 is filled in as zero ("0.00"), since it refers to certain costs incurred to collect a judgment. You must file special papers to be entitled to receive postjudgment costs.

In Item 13, fill in the same amount that you listed for Item 11.

In Item 14, credit should be given for any payments made by the tenant toward the judgment. Be sure to apply any amount of the security deposit left over after deducting for cleaning, damages, and any rent not reflected in the judgment.

After subtracting any partial payments and other credits, fill in the balance in Item 15.

Fill in "0.00" in Item 16. Again, you must file special papers with the court before you're entitled to receive postjudgment interest.

In item 17, enter $25, the fee for issuance of this Writ of Execution (the fee for the issuance of the first writ, for possession, should be included in the judge's award of costs).

Add the amounts in Items 15–17 together, putting the sum in Item 18.

Finally, calculate the daily interest on the judgment at the rate of 10%. (This can add up, since it may take a long time to collect the judgment.) Multiply the amount in Item 15 by 0.10

to get the yearly interest, then divide this amount by 365 to get the daily interest amount. List this amount in Item 19a. List 0.00 in Item 19b. Item 19b tells the sheriff or marshal to collect for the county any court fees that were waived for the plaintiff on account of indigency. Because you are a rental property owner, you almost certainly cannot claim you're indigent, so this figure should be zero.

The second page of the Writ of Execution does not need to be filled out for a money judgment, the way you did when filing a Writ of Execution for possession in Chapter 7. The exception would be when there is more than one judgment debtor. In this case, you would fill in the name and address of the first debtor in Item 4 and check the box "Additional judgment debtors on next page"; then, you would complete Item 21 (Additional judgment debtor) on the second page of the writ.

A sample money judgment Writ of Execution is shown above. This form may look familiar (see the Chapter 7 discussion of taking a default judgment).

 FORM

A blank copy of the Writ of Execution (Judicial Council form EJ-130) can be downloaded from the Nolo website. (See the appendix for the link to the forms in this book, and other information on using the forms.)

When you have filled out your writ, make four copies (remember to copy the second page) and ask the court clerk to open the file, check the judgment, and issue the Writ of Execution. After collecting the $25 writ issuance fee from you, the clerk will stamp the original writ with the date and a court seal, stamp the copies with the date (but not the court seal), and hand you back both the original and copies. The original and three copies are given to the sheriff or marshal. Keep one copy for your records.

Bank Accounts

Once you have a Writ of Execution, the law allows you to collect funds in deposit accounts in a bank, savings and loan, or credit union. But before you waste the fees you'll have to pay the sheriff or marshal for this, call your ex-tenant's bank and find out if there's money in the account.

Although banks are forbidden to tell you specifically how much money an individual has in a checking account, virtually all banks will respond to a telephone request as to whether a particular check is good. For example, if you call the bank and ask whether your "$100 check from Skelly Jones, Account No. 123-45678, is good," a bank employee will normally answer "Yes" or "No." Some banks give this type of information over an automated telephone answering system.

To get cash in a bank account, start by calling the sheriff or marshal in the county in which the account is located. Make sure that the office serves bank levies; in a few counties, you must hire a registered process server. Give the original and three copies of the Writ of Execution to the sheriff, marshal, or registered process server, along with the necessary fee (about $75 as of this writing, but call ahead to get the exact amount) and a letter or filled-out "instructions" form. Most sheriff's or marshal's departments have their own form, which they like you to use. If you use a simple letter, it should look like the one below ("Sample Instructions to Sheriff for Writ of Execution").

After the sheriff, marshal, or process server serves the necessary papers on the bank, the bank will hold the money for ten days, then pay it over to the county sheriff or marshal. After a few more weeks, the sheriff or marshal will forward the money to you, provided the tenant hasn't filed a Claim of Exemption. (See "If the Debtor Files a Claim of Exemption," below.)

Sample Instructions to Sheriff for Writ of Execution

September 15, 20xx

Lenny Landlord
12345 Angeleno Street
Los Angeles, CA 90010

Los Angeles County Sheriff
111 N. Hill Street
Los Angeles, California 90012

Re: Lenny Landlord v. Terrence D. Tenant and
    Tillie D. Tenant
    Los Angeles County Superior Court No.
    A-12345-B

Enclosed are the original and three copies of a Writ of Execution issued by the municipal court, and a check in the amount of $40. Please levy on all monies of the judgment debtors Terrence D. Tenant and Tillie D. Tenant at the West Los Angeles branch of First National Bank, 123 First Street, Los Angeles, California.

Sincerely,

Lenny D. Landlord

Lenny D. Landlord

Wages

The law allows you to have the sheriff or marshal order the judgment debtor's employer to withhold up to 25% of wages each pay period to satisfy a judgment. (If the person has a very low income, the amount you can recover can be considerably less than 25%.) Also, you might have to wait in line if other creditors got to the employer first. So if you know where your ex-tenant works (and the tenant doesn't quit or declare bankruptcy when you start garnishing his or her paycheck), you might be able to collect the entire judgment, though it might take a while before all the money dribbles in.

WG-001

ATTORNEY OR PARTY WITHOUT ATTORNEY *(Name, State Bar number, and address)*:	LEVYING OFFICER *(Name and Address)*:
Lenny D. Landlord 12345 Angeleno Street Los Angeles, CA 90028 TELEPHONE NO.: **(213) 555-6789** FAX NO.: E-MAIL ADDRESS: ATTORNEY FOR *(Name)*: **Plaintiff in Pro Per**	

SUPERIOR COURT OF CALIFORNIA, COUNTY OF LOS ANGELES
STREET ADDRESS: 110 N. Hill Street
MAILING ADDRESS:
CITY AND ZIP CODE: Los Angeles, CA 90012
BRANCH NAME:

PLAINTIFF/PETITIONER: **LENNY D. LANDLORD** DEFENDANT/RESPONDENT: **TERRENCE D. TENANT, TILLIE D. TENANT**	COURT CASE NUMBER: A-12345-B
APPLICATION FOR EARNINGS WITHHOLDING ORDER **(Wage Garnishment)**	LEVYING OFFICER FILE NUMBER:

TO THE SHERIFF OR ANY MARSHAL OR CONSTABLE OF THE COUNTY OF: Los Angeles
OR ANY REGISTERED PROCESS SERVER

1. The judgment creditor *(name):* Lenny D. Landlord   requests
   issuance of an Earnings Withholding Order directing the employer to withhold the earnings of the judgment debtor (employee).

Name and address of employer	Name and address of employee
Ernie Employer 123 Business Lane Los Angeles, CA	Terrence D. Tenant 3815 Gower Canyon Ave., Apt. 3 Los Angeles, CA 90010

2. The amounts withheld are to be paid to   Social Security no. [X] on form WG-035 [ ] unknown
   a. [X] The attorney (or party without an attorney)   b. [ ] Other *(name, address, and telephone)*:
       named at the top of this page.

3. a. Judgment was entered on *(date):* May 29, 20xx
   b. Collect the amount directed by the Writ of Execution unless a lesser amount is specified here: $ _____

4. *Check any that apply:*
   a. [ ] The Writ of Execution was issued to collect delinquent amounts payable for the **support** of a child, former spouse, or spouse of the employee.
   b. [ ] The Writ of Execution was issued to collect a judgment based entirely on a claim for elder or dependent adult financial abuse.
   c. [ ] The Writ of Execution was issued to collect a judgment based in part on a claim for elder or dependent adult financial abuse. The amount that arises from the claim for elder or dependent adult financial abuse is *(state amount):* $ _____

5. [ ] Special instructions *(specify):*

6. *Check a or b:*
   a. [X] I have not previously obtained an order directing this employer to withhold the earnings of this employee.
      —OR—
   b. [ ] I have previously obtained such an order, but that order *(check one):*
      [ ] was terminated by a court order, but I am entitled to apply for another Earnings Withholding Order under the provisions of Code of Civil Procedure section 706.105(h).
      [ ] was ineffective.

Lenny D. Landlord   *Lenny D. Landlord*
_____   _____
(TYPE OR PRINT NAME)   (SIGNATURE OF ATTORNEY OR PARTY WITHOUT ATTORNEY)

I declare under penalty of perjury under the laws of the State of California that the foregoing is true and correct.
Date: June 10, 20xx

Lenny D. Landlord   *Lenny D. Landlord*
_____   _____
(TYPE OR PRINT NAME)   (SIGNATURE OF DECLARANT)   Page 1 of 1

Form Adopted for Mandatory Use
Judicial Council of California
WG-001 [Rev. January 1, 2012]

APPLICATION FOR EARNINGS WITHHOLDING ORDER
(Wage Garnishment)

Code Civ. Procedure, § 706.121
www.courts.ca.gov

CONFIDENTIAL

WG-035

ATTORNEY OR PARTY WITHOUT ATTORNEY *(Name, State Bar number, and address)*:	DATE RECEIVED BY COURT *(Do not file in public court file.)*
Lenny D. Landlord 12345 Angeleno Street Los Angeles, CA 90010 TELEPHONE NO.: FAX NO.: E-MAIL ADDRESS: ATTORNEY FOR *(Name)*: Plaintiff in Pro Per	

SUPERIOR COURT OF CALIFORNIA, COUNTY OF LOS ANGELES STREET ADDRESS: 110 North Hill St. MAILING ADDRESS: CITY AND ZIP CODE: Los Angeles, CA 90012 BRANCH NAME: CENTRAL DISTRICT/DOWNTOWN BRANCH	
PLAINTIFF/PETITIONER: LENNY D. LANDLORD DEFENDANT/RESPONDENT: TERRENCE D. TENANT, TILLIE D. TENANT	COURT CASE NUMBER: A-12345-B
CONFIDENTIAL STATEMENT OF JUDGMENT DEBTOR'S **SOCIAL SECURITY NUMBER** **(Supplement to Wage Garnishment Forms** **WG-001, WG-002, WG-004, WG-005, WG-009, WG-012, and WG-030)**	LEVYING OFFICER FILE NUMBER:

(Do not attach to forms.)

This separate *Confidential Statement of Judgment Debtor's Social Security Number* contains the Social Security number of the judgment debtor for whom an earnings withholding order is being sought or has issued in the case referenced above. **This supplement must be kept separate from any applications or orders filed in this case, and should not be a public record.**

INFORMATION ON JUDGMENT DEBTOR:

1. Name: Terrence D. Tenant

2. Social Security Number: 555-12-3456

TO COURT CLERK
THIS STATEMENT IS **CONFIDENTIAL**.
DO NOT FILE THIS CONFIDENTIAL STATEMENT IN A PUBLIC COURT FILE.

Form Adopted for Mandatory Use
Judicial Council of California
WG-035 [New January 1, 2012]

CONFIDENTIAL STATEMENT OF JUDGMENT DEBTOR'S
SOCIAL SECURITY NUMBER
Wage Garnishment

www.courts.ca.gov

Like double-checking on bank accounts, it's a good idea to check to see if the debtor is still employed before paying fees to the sheriff or marshal. You can easily check on whether a tenant is employed at a particular business. Call the personnel department and simply state that you'd like to "verify the employment of Emmett Employee." If the tenant no longer works there, ask to speak to his former supervisor or someone in that person's department, who may have been contacted by a more recent employer following through on a reference. Also, people who once worked together sometimes keep in touch for years afterwards. You'll get the most information if you assume a polite, friendly approach. If you're asked why you need the information, you can truthfully say that you're the ex-tenant's former landlord and that you need his new address so you can send him an accounting of his security deposit.

To initiate a wage garnishment, start by completing an Application for Earnings Withholding Order.

FORM

A blank copy of the Application for Earnings Withholding Order (Judicial Council form WG-001) can be downloaded from the Nolo website. (See the appendix for the link to the forms in this book, and other information on using the forms.)

List your name and the usual information about the court name and address, the names of the parties, and the case number in the boxes at the top of the form. In the box at the upper right-hand corner, list the name and address of the office of the sheriff or marshal. Be sure also to enter the name of the county where the debtor is employed below these boxes, just before Item 1.

List your name in Item 1, and the names and addresses of the debtor and his employer in the boxes below that. You must provide the employer's street address; a mailing address isn't enough. Below the box at the right for the employee/debtor's name and address are two boxes to indicate whether or not you know that person's Social Security number (SSN). Hopefully, you have this SSN from the now-former tenant's rental application. If so, check the box next to the words "on form WG-035 (Confidential Statement of Judgment Debtor's Social Security Number)." You'll need to fill out the usual case caption and case number at the top of the form, and then list the debtor's name and Social Security number in Items 1 and 2.

FORM

A blank copy of the Confidential Statement of Judgment Debtor's Social Security Number can be downloaded from the Nolo website. (See the appendix for the link to the forms in this book, and other information on using the forms.)

Put an X in Box 2a to indicate that the funds are to be paid to you. In Item 3a, list the date the judgment was entered. Leave Item 3b blank unless for some reason you aren't owed the full amount listed in the Writ of Execution. Check Item 6a if this is your first wage garnishment. Or check the appropriate boxes in Item 6b to reflect previous wage garnishment attempts you have made. Finally, type or print your name and sign twice at the bottom, listing the date as well.

Call the sheriff or marshal for the county in which the judgment debtor works and find out if they serve wage garnishments, or whether you must use a registered process server. Also, find out the fee for a wage garnishment. Forward the original and three copies of the Writ of Execution, a check for the required fee, a letter of instructions, and the completed Application for Earnings Withholding Order.

The original goes to the sheriff or marshal of the county in which the employer is located or to a registered process server, if required by county policies. Send along the original and three copies of the Writ of Execution and the appropriate fee. The fee varies from county to county, so call the marshal or sheriff's civil division to find out the amount.

Sample Instructions to Marshal for Application for Earnings Withholding Order

October 10, 20xx

Lenny Landlord
12345 Angeleno Street
Los Angeles, CA 90010

Office of the Marshal
Los Angeles Division, Los Angeles County
110 N. Hill Street
Los Angeles, CA 90012

Re: Landlord v. Tenant
     Los Angeles Superior Court Case No.
     A-12345-B

Enclosed is an Application for Earnings Withholding Order, an original and three copies of a Writ of Execution from the Superior Court for the Los Angeles Division, and a check for $XX.00. Please levy on the wages of Terrence D. Tenant, who is employed at Ernie Employer, 123 Business Lane, Los Angeles, California.

Sincerely,

Lenny D. Landlord

Lenny D. Landlord

The debtor's wages should be levied on until you are paid in full unless one of the following applies:

- The debtor successfully claims an exemption (see below).
- Someone else already has effected a wage garnishment.
- Your garnishment is subordinate to a support order (for example, for child support), which was received during your garnishment period.
- The debtor stops working at that place of employment.
- The debtor declares bankruptcy. (See Chapter 10 for your options if the tenant declares bankruptcy.)

Seizing Other Property

Although it's not likely to be worth the time and trouble, you may want to try to seize property of the debtor if you haven't gotten the whole judgment paid yet.

Motor Vehicles

To find out whether it is worth the time and trouble to have the tenant's vehicle seized and sold at an auction to pay off the judgment, first find out its market value. Check the *Kelley Blue Book* (www.kbb.com), Edmunds (edmunds.com), or Craigslist for the price of similar vehicles. If the value isn't around $5,000 (depending on circumstances too detailed to discuss here), forget it. Even if the vehicle is paid off, the owner/debtor is legally entitled to the first $3,050 of the proceeds. Sheriff's storage and sales charges, which you'll have to pay for up front, will run at least $700, and likely more.

If the "legal owner" of the vehicle is the bank or finance company that loaned the money to buy the vehicle, the situation is even worse. If you have the car sold, the legal owner (who normally has the right to repossess if payments aren't made) is entitled to be paid what it is owed out of the proceeds of the sale. This amount is called the "payoff figure"; it may well equal, or even exceed, the sale value of the vehicle. If it does, a levy and sale of a debtor's vehicle will net you no money and you'll be out substantial costs. Here are a few examples.

> EXAMPLE 1: You have a judgment against your former tenant Skip, the owner of a three-year-old Chevrolet with a book value of $5,000. The DMV informs you, in its response to your Vehicle Registration Information Request, that the legal owner is General Motors Acceptance Corp. in San Jose. You call GMAC, giving the owner's name, license plate number, and V.I.N. (serial) number (if you have it), and ask for a payoff figure. They tell you it's $3,500.

This means that even if the vehicle is sold for $4,500 at a sheriff's auction, GMAC will get the first $3,500. Because Skip is entitled to the $3,050 exemption, the remaining $1,000 will go to him, and you'll get nothing. Moreover, you'll be out the $700 you fronted to the sheriff for service, storage, and sales costs.

EXAMPLE 2: The legal owner of Darlene's four-year-old Honda is Household Finance. Household Finance tells you the payoff figure is $3,000. The book value of the vehicle is $7,000, but at a sheriff's auction it might not net more than $5,000, leaving only $2,000 after the legal owner is paid off. Subtract the $3,050 exemption that goes to Darlene, and that leaves you with zero. You would get nothing and be out the costs of storage and sale.

As the above examples show, levying on a vehicle can actually cost you money. Most owners of new autos owe more on them than they could sell them for at an auction. By the time the loan is paid off, the auction value of the vehicle is fairly low, and might not be enough over $3,050 to be profitable for you. As a general rule, you should forget about having the debtor's vehicle seized and sold unless its auction value is at least $5,000 above what the debtor still owes on it.

If you decide it's worthwhile, give the original and at least two copies of the Writ of Execution to the sheriff or marshal, along with your letter or other written instructions (see the sample below) requesting a levy on defendant's automobile. Be sure to give the description and license number of the vehicle and say where and when it can be found on a street or another public place (the sheriff cannot go into a private garage or warehouse). You will also need to give the sheriff or marshal a check for the total amount of the fees and deposit for towing and storage; check to find out how much this will be. Be patient, because the whole process could easily take several months.

First, it may take up to several weeks for the sheriff or marshal to arrange for a tow truck to be present when the vehicle is available and not locked in a garage. Second, once it's picked up, it will take at least a month to auction it off (unless the debtor redeems the vehicle by paying off the judgment, which sometimes happens). Finally, once the sheriff's department gets the money from the auction, they will hold it for about another month after paying off the towing and storage charges and any loan.

Instructions to Sheriff for Levying on a Vehicle

Cruz Creditor
123 Market Street
Monterey, California

November 1, 20xx

Monterey County Sheriff
P.O. Box 809
Salinas, CA 93902

Re: Creditor v. Debtor
Monterey County Superior Court
Case No. 2468-C

As instructed yesterday by a member of your office staff, I am enclosing a deposit check for $700 and an original and three copies of a Writ of Execution in the above-entitled case.

Please levy on the automobile of judgment debtor Dale Debtor; the vehicle is a 2018 Toyota Prius, license number 1SAM123. It is normally parked in front of the debtor's residence address of 12345 East Main Street, Salinas, California. Please call me at 408-555-5678 if you have any questions.

Sincerely,
Cruz Creditor
Cruz Creditor

Identifying the Legal Owner of a Vehicle

You might be able to identify the legal owner of your ex-tenant's vehicle by filing a Vehicle Registration Information Request with the DMV. But before the DMV releases that information, it allows the ex-tenant the opportunity to object to having the information released. Because most debtors won't let the DMV release information to you, a debtor's examination might be a better bet. (See above.)

Other Personal Property

As mentioned, most of your tenant's personal property is probably protected from creditors. Here is a list of statutorily exempt property that was current when this book went to press (these limits change every three years, with the last change occurring on September 1, 2021). (All references are to the California Code of Civil Procedure.) Exempt property includes:

- motor vehicles, up to a net equity (market value less payoff) of $3,325 (§ 704.010)
- household items, including furniture, appliances, and clothing that are "ordinarily and reasonably necessary" (§ 704.020)
- materials to be used for repair or maintenance of a residence, up to a net equity of $3,500 (§ 704.030)
- jewelry, heirlooms, and artworks, up to a net value of $8,725 (§ 704.040)
- health aids (§ 704.050)
- tools used in a trade or business, up to a net value of $8,725 for each spouse in business (§ 704.060)
- all paid earnings except earnings subject to earnings withholding order or support order (§ 704.070)

- bank deposits from the Social Security Administration to $3,500 ($5,250 for husband and wife); unlimited if SS funds are not commingled with other funds; bank deposits of other public benefits to $1,750 ($2,600 for husband and wife) (§ 704.080)
- jail or prison inmate's trust account, up to $1,750 (§ 704.090)
- matured life insurance benefits needed for support; unmatured life insurance policy cash surrender value completely exempt; loan value exempt to $13,975 (§ 704.100)
- retirement benefits paid by a public entity (§ 704.110)
- all vacation credits payable to a public employee (§ 704.113)
- private retirement benefits, including IRAs and Keoghs (§ 704.115)
- unemployment, disability, and strike benefits (§ 704.120)
- health or disability insurance benefits (§ 704.130)
- personal injury or wrongful death damages (§§ 704.140, 704.150) to the extent of necessary support
- workers' compensation benefits (§ 704.160)
- welfare benefits and aid from charitable organizations (§ 704.170)
- relocation benefits paid by government entity (§ 704.180)
- student financial aid (§ 704.190)
- burial plots (§ 704.200)
- bank account and cash traceable to an exempt asset (§ 703.080), and
- business licenses, except liquor licenses (§§ 695.060, 708.630).

You can learn the current exemption amounts by going to the Judicial Council website at www.courts.ca.gov. Using the "browse by number" feature, search for Form EJ 156.

Real Estate

Don't overlook the possibility that the ex-tenant owns or might purchase real estate. Putting a lien on real estate is simple and inexpensive, and it will likely get you results if the debtor wants to sell or refinance the property. The way to do this is to have the court clerk issue an Abstract of Judgment (Judicial Council Form EJ-001), and record it with the recorder for the county in which the debtor owns real estate. This establishes a "judgment lien" on the property, which will have to be paid off before it's sold or refinanced.

If the Debtor Files a Claim of Exemption

A debtor can use several legal maneuvers to delay or even stop the collection process. The most common is the filing, with the sheriff or marshal, of a simple form known as a Claim of Exemption. In it, a debtor claims that the bank account, paycheck, or property being subjected to garnishment is legally exempt from execution to satisfy a judgment; or that the debtor needs the wages to support him- or herself and his or her family.

For example, an ex-tenant whose bank account is attached might claim that the funds in the account consist entirely of funds that are exempt by law, such as welfare or Social Security payments. Another exemption commonly claimed is that the debtor has insufficient funds to provide for "ordinary necessities" of life. A judgment debtor may not claim this type of exemption if the debt was itself incurred to pay for necessities of life—like rent. What this means in practice is that it's improper for your ex-tenant to claim a hardship exemption to avoid paying a judgment for rent. However, if the tenant attempts to claim this exemption anyway (easy to do on the standard fill-in-the-blanks exemption forms), you have the burden of pointing out to a judge that the debtor can't claim a "necessities of life" exemption if the money you're seeking was for nonpayment of rent. If you do nothing, the tenant will be able to claim the exemption and get back any seized property or prevent a wage garnishment.

If the sheriff or marshal notifies you that the debtor has filed a Claim of Exemption, you will have to respond with a few forms of your own. If you do nothing in the face of a Claim of Exemption filed by a debtor, the sheriff or marshal will automatically treat the wages or bank account attached as legally exempt. Your response depends on what the tenant's Claim of Exemption states. A good general discussion of exemption law is contained in *Solve Your Money Troubles,* by Attorneys Cara O'Neill and Amy Loftsgordon (Nolo).

Once the Judgment Is Paid Off

You might be pleasantly surprised to find that through deposit credits, wage garnishments, bank account seizures, or a combination of these, your judgment is in fact paid off entirely, including interest and costs. This could take a long time, but after that, the judgment is said to be "satisfied" (even if you aren't). When this happens, you are legally required to fill out a form called an Acknowledgment of Satisfaction of Judgment and file it with the court, so that the court records no longer reflect an unpaid judgment against your ex-tenant. A sample filled-out form is shown below. Most of the items are self explanatory. Here are a few tips on completing the form:

- Fill in the caption boxes and case number at top, and check the box Judgment Creditor.
- Note the court address and plaintiff and defendant names.
- Indicate whether the judgment has been paid in full (and, if not, provide details in Item 1).
- Provide your full name and address in Item 2.
- Put N/A under Item 3 (assignee of record).
- Provide the judgment debtor (tenant) name(s) in Item 4.
- Note the date the judgment was entered (Item 5).
- Date and sign your name.

EJ-100

ATTORNEY OR PARTY WITHOUT ATTORNEY *(Name, address, and State Bar number):*
After recording, return to:

LENNY D. LANDLORD
1234 ANGELENO STREET
LOS ANGELES, CA 90010

TEL NO.: 213-555-6789   FAX NO. (optional):

E-MAIL ADDRESS *(Optional)*:

[ ] ATTORNEY FOR   [X] JUDGMENT CREDITOR   [ ] ASSIGNEE OF RECORD

SUPERIOR COURT OF CALIFORNIA, COUNTY OF LOS ANGELES

STREET ADDRESS: 110 N. Grand Hill St.

MAILING ADDRESS: same

CITY AND ZIP CODE: Los Angeles, CA 90012

BRANCH NAME:

FOR RECORDER'S OR SECRETARY OF STATE'S USE ONLY

PLAINTIFF: LENNY D. LANDLORD
DEFENDANT: TERRENCE D. TENANT, ET.AL.

CASE NUMBER:

ACKNOWLEDGMENT OF SATISFACTION OF JUDGMENT

[X] FULL   [ ] PARTIAL   [ ] MATURED INSTALLMENT

FOR COURT USE ONLY

1. Satisfaction of the judgment is acknowledged as follows:
   a. [X] Full satisfaction
      (1) [X] Judgment is satisfied in full.
      (2) [ ] The judgment creditor has accepted payment or performance other than that specified in the judgment in full satisfaction of the judgment.
   b. [ ] Partial satisfaction
      The amount received in partial satisfaction of the judgment is $
   c. [ ] Matured installment
      All matured installments under the installment judgment have been satisfied as of *(date):*

2. Full name and address of judgment creditor:*

   Lenny D. Landlord, 1234 Angeleno St, Los Angeles, CA 90010

3. Full name and address of assignee of record, if any:

   N/A

4. Full name and address of judgment debtor being fully or partially released:*

   Terrence D. Tenant, Tillie D. Tenant

5. a. Judgment entered on *(date):* May 28, 20xx
   b. [ ] Renewal entered on *(date):*

6. [ ] An [ ] abstract of judgment [ ] certified copy of the judgment has been recorded as follows *(complete all information for each county where recorded):*

COUNTY	DATE OF RECORDING	INSTRUMENT NUMBER

7. [ ] A notice of judgment lien has been filed in the office of the Secretary of State as file number *(specify):*

NOTICE TO JUDGMENT DEBTOR: If this is an acknowledgment of full satisfaction of judgment, it will have to be recorded in each county shown in item 6 above, if any, in order to release the judgment lien, and will have to be filed in the office of the Secretary of State to terminate any judgment lien on personal property.

Date: October 20, 20xx

▶ *Lenny D. Landlord*

(SIGNATURE OF JUDGMENT CREDITOR OR ASSIGNEE OF CREDITOR OR ATTORNEY**)

*The names of the judgment creditor and judgment debtor must be stated as shown in any Abstract of Judgment which was recorded and is being released by this satisfaction. ** A separate notary acknowledgment must be attached for each signature.

Form Approved for Optional Use
Judicial Council of California
EJ-100 [Rev. July 1, 2014]

ACKNOWLEDGMENT OF SATISFACTION OF JUDGMENT

Page 1 of 1
Code of Civil Procedure, §§ 724.060, 724.120, 724.250

If you previously had an Abstract of Judgment recorded with the County Recorder (so as to obtain a lien on any realty in the county owned by the judgment debtor), the form must be notarized before you file it with the court and a certified copy of the Acknowledgment of Satisfaction of Judgment (or a notarized duplicate original) recorded with the Recorder's office.

FORM

A blank copy of the Acknowledgment of Satisfaction of Judgment (Judicial Council Form EJ-100) can be downloaded from the Nolo website. (See the appendix for the link to the forms in this book, and other information on using the forms.)

When a Tenant Files for Bankruptcy

FORMS IN THIS CHAPTER

Chapter 10 includes samples of the following forms:

- Notice of Motion for Relief From Automatic Stay
- Motion for Relief From Automatic Stay
- Declaration in Support of Motion for Relief From Automatic Stay
- Order Granting Relief From Automatic Stay, and
- Proof of Service by Mail.

The Nolo website includes downloadable copies of the Proof of Service by Mail form and a blank sheet of pleading paper for use in preparing the various forms described in this chapter. (See the appendix for the link to the forms in this book, and other information on using the forms.)

When tenants file for bankruptcy, almost all ongoing legal proceedings against them—including an eviction lawsuit—must cease until the bankruptcy court says otherwise. (11 U.S.C. § 362.) The bankruptcy law imposes an "automatic stay" that freezes any collection efforts or litigation in place while the process sorts itself out. Any creditor who violates the stay—that is, attempts to collect from the person who declared bankruptcy (the "debtor") or pursues a legal proceeding, such as eviction—can, and probably will, be fined by the bankruptcy court.

The bankruptcy court will agree to remove or lift the automatic stay for a creditor or landlord who can show legal grounds to lift the stay. In the case of a residential tenancy, the judge will look to how much time remains on the lease, as explained below.

An unexpired fixed-term lease has value because either the debtor can stay in the unit by paying the rent, or another person might pay to take over the lease. On the other hand, month-to-month tenancies and final eviction judgments have no value in terms of bankruptcy. because the debtor's leasehold interest (the tenants' right to remain in the property and pay rent) has no remaining life. A month-to-month tenancy can terminate on only one month's notice, and an unlawful detainer judgment terminates the leasehold entirely. Getting the court to lift the stay takes time, and while the motion for relief from the stay is fairly "standard," it requires specific documents and facts.

 SEE A LAWYER

Bankruptcy procedures were made with lawyers in mind—the exact opposite of small claims court. Bankruptcy law and procedure is highly technical, so you should get advice from a qualified attorney on how to proceed to maximize your creditor's rights in bankruptcy. Many creditors represent themselves in consumer bankruptcies, but the learning curve can be formidable.

Kinds of Bankruptcy

A tenant can file for different kinds of bankruptcy. The most common are Chapter 7, which erases many debts completely, and Chapter 13, which lets debtors repay a portion of their debts over three to five years. Most tenants who file bankruptcy just to delay an eviction file Chapter 7 bankruptcies, and most of this chapter's discussion assumes your tenant has filed a Chapter 7. Also possible, though very rare for residential tenants, are Chapter 11 bankruptcies (repayment plans generally used only by individuals with too much debt for a Chapter 13); or Chapter 12 bankruptcies (repayment plans for family farmers or fishermen). The word "chapter" refers to a particular chapter of the Bankruptcy Code, Title 11 of the U.S. Code, the federal laws that govern bankruptcy.

When a Tenant Can File for Bankruptcy

A tenant can file for bankruptcy at any time— before the tenancy begins, during the tenancy, after you've served a three-day notice, after you've filed an eviction lawsuit, or even after you've won and obtained a judgment for possession. However, tenants who wait until the last possible moment to file—sometimes just a day before the sheriff shows up—lose. In many cases, if the property has been posted, the sheriff can evict even if a bankruptcy was filed after posting. (C.C.P. § 715.050; *Eden Place, LLC v. Perl* (In re Perl) (9th Cir. 2016) 811 F.3d 1120.)

The Judge's Use of the Automatic Stay

As explained, if a tenant has filed for either Chapter 7 or Chapter 13 bankruptcy and is behind in the rent, becomes unable to pay the rent, or violates another term of the tenancy that would justify a termination, a landlord cannot deliver a termination notice or proceed with an eviction after the bankruptcy has been filed without permission of the bankruptcy court. In most cases, the judge will lift the stay relatively quickly and the landlord can proceed with a termination and eviction. If a tenant is using illegal drugs or endangering the property, the landlord can take steps to significantly shorten the automatic stay period, as explained below in "Exceptions to the Automatic Stay: Drugs or Damage to Property."

Prebankruptcy Actions

The automatic stay does not apply, however, where the landlord obtained a judgment for possession before the tenant filed for bankruptcy. (*Eden Place, LLC v. Perl* (*In re Perl*) (9th Cir. 2016) 811 F.3d 1120; *Lee v. Baca*, 73 Cal.App.4th 1116 (1999).)

However, in narrow (and fairly rare) circumstances that apply only to evictions based on rent nonpayment or other curable monetary violations, a tenant who has a term lease (not month to month) can try to stop the eviction after the landlord has a judgment prior to the bankruptcy filing. (See 11 U.S.C. §362(l) and Bankruptcy Official Form 101A.) A tenant has only 30 days after filing for bankruptcy to try this, and must complete all three of the following steps:

1. The tenant must file a paper with the court certifying that state law allows the tenant to avoid eviction by paying the unpaid rent, even after the landlord has won a judgment for possession. In California, that statute is C.C.P. § 1179 and is entirely discretionary.

The certification must be served on the landlord.

If you face this type of request for relief (and you want to continue with the eviction), you can argue in defense that California's anti-hardship law does not apply here, because there is no right to relief, only a judicial possibility. In other words, because Section 1179 depends upon the discretion of the individual judge in each case., the tenant does not have an automatic right to cure the default. Therefore, the tenant cannot certify its eligibility for state law relief under bankruptcy law. See, for example, *In re Davis*, 2021 WL 247781, a Florida bankruptcy case, that draws the distinction between a right to cure and discretionary relief from hardship.

2. The tenant must deposit with the clerk of the bankruptcy court any rent that will become due 30 days from the date the petition was filed.

3. The tenant then has 30 days to pay back all rent arrears owed and file another certification to that effect with the bankruptcy court (and serve the landlord with this certification).

At any point during the 30-day period, the landlord can file an objection to the tenant's certification. The court will hold a hearing within ten days. If the landlord convinces the judge that the tenant's certifications are not true, the court will lift the stay and the landlord can proceed to recover possession of the property. Some judges also make the tenant pay the landlord's fees and costs, as a condition to granting the motion; and a judge could even require the tenant to pay additional sums, if they are needed to make the landlord whole. Keep in mind that the court has discretion on whether to grant or deny the tenant's request—the mere filing of the motion does not guarantee its success.

Exceptions to the Automatic Stay: Drugs or Damage to Property

Landlords sometimes need to evict a tenant who is using illegal drugs or endangering the property. If the tenant files for bankruptcy before the landlord wins a judgment for possession, the landlord can proceed with the eviction without asking the bankruptcy judge to lift the stay—but not immediately. The landlord must still meet certain requirements. Here are the specifics:

- **When the landlord has begun an eviction case but doesn't have a judgment.** Landlords must prepare a certification, or sworn statement, that they have begun an unlawful detainer case based on the tenant's endangerment of the property or use of illegal drugs (or such use by the tenant's guests).
- **When the landlord hasn't yet filed an eviction lawsuit.** Landlords must prepare a certification, or sworn statement, that the activity described above has happened within the past 30 days.

The landlord must file the certification with the bankruptcy court and serve the tenant as one would serve any legal notice. If the tenant does not file an objection within 15 days of being served, the landlord can proceed with the eviction without asking the court for relief from the stay.

A tenant who objects must file with the court, and serve on the landlord a certification challenging the truth of the landlord's certification. The bankruptcy court will hold a hearing within ten days, at which the tenant must convince the court that the situation the landlord describes did not exist or has been remedied. If the court rules for the landlord, the landlord may proceed with the eviction without asking that the stay be lifted; but if the tenant wins, the landlord may not proceed.

Finding the Right Bankruptcy Court

To file a motion in bankruptcy court to have the automatic stay lifted, you must first find out which bankruptcy court the tenant filed in. Look for the court's address and phone number on any bankruptcy paper you receive from the court, the tenant, or the tenant's bankruptcy lawyer. If you can't find the information, just look for the district name. Then type the court's name into your browser—for example, United States Bankruptcy Court Central District of California. (California has four districts: Northern, Southern, Central, and Eastern.) The list of results will include a website with that name. From there, using the "Federal Court Finder," (www.uscourts. gov/federal-court-finder/search), you can access detailed information about the court (its hours, address, contact information, and so on).

Once you know the location of the court, you'll want to review the court's local rules and forms posted on the court's website.

In the local court rules, read the section entitled "Motion Practice," "Notice," or something similar. It will tell you how the court wants motions to be filed. It's very important to follow all local court rules scrupulously; if you don't, your papers could get thrown out.

Also look for local forms and pleadings. For example, the U.S. Bankruptcy Court for the Central District of California has a mandatory Notice of Motion and Motion for Relief From Automatic Stay that you can complete and file. In fact, the Central District of California, which covers Los Angeles County, has made this easier than any of the other California districts. The Central District website contains much more information for self-represented parties as well.

Each court's website contains instructions, forms, and advice. You can download the local rules and forms. If you have difficulty finding what you need, try calling the court clerk and asking for assistance.

Preparing the Papers

Before your court date, you must prepare these documents:

- Relief From Stay Cover Sheet
- Notice of Motion for Relief From Automatic Stay and Proof of Service
- Motion for Relief From Automatic Stay
- Declaration in Support of Motion for Relief From Automatic Stay, and
- Order Granting Relief From Automatic Stay.

For the banktruptcy courts in the Central and Southern Districts of California, the court has local forms that replace the pleadings you would otherwise have to prepare. For the Northern and Eastern Districts, you will have to prepare the documents from scratch except the cover sheets, which are available as forms.

Samples are shown below for all these forms except the Relief From Stay Cover Sheet, a preprinted form that you should download from the court's website. You will need to use pleading paper (8½" × 11" paper with the numbers down the left side) for all forms. All papers need to be double-spaced, with numbers 1-28 next to the left margin. Courts want to see 28 lines of text to a page, no smaller than 12-point font.

We *strongly* recommend using a legal pleading word processing template — it will make your drafting easier. You can make copies of the blank sheet (if you have a penchant for suffering), use the one included on the Nolo website, or modify the legal pleading template in MS *Word* (see the appendix for details on using the forms in this book).

Have the following papers in front of you when you get ready to start preparing your own documents; they contain much of the information you need:

- the tenant's bankruptcy papers that were sent to you
- the papers you filed in court for the eviction, and
- any papers the tenant filed in court to oppose the eviction.

Fill out the top of the forms accurately. Be sure the caption on the top of all the papers accurately states the bankruptcy district, the case name as indicated on the tenant's bankruptcy papers, the bankruptcy case number, and the type of bankruptcy (Chapter 7 or 13) the tenant is filing, as well as the court date, time, place of hearing, and other information the bankruptcy court clerk has given to you. The clerk will fill in the item "R.S. No." when you file each form.

Tell the truth. The facts you state in the Motion for Relief From Automatic Stay and the Declaration in Support of Motion for Relief From Automatic Stay must be true. Remember that you are signing these documents under penalty of perjury and that it is a federal crime to lie.

The declaration is not about fairness or whether the tenant might be taking advantage of the system. After all, in bankruptcy every unsecured creditor loses something. Relief from stay aims to cut your losses, not make any gains.

Relief from stay under the law depends on checking boxes in the statute by proving certain facts. Overall, you have to establish either that the lease is not property of the bankruptcy estate (you have a judgment), the debtor has no equity in the property (the tenant breached and the lease was terminated), or in rare cases, the lease is not necessary for an effective reorganization (there is nothing for the trustee to assume, sell, or assign).

The facts that will interest the court are:

- the provisions of the lease and the *term* (month to month, other periodic tenancy, or fixed term)
- the date and type of default (nonpayment of rent or breach of lease)
- the stage of proceedings in state court, particularly if there is a judgment declaring a forfeiture of the lease and awarding possession
- current status (writ of possession issued and posted, trial pending), and
- that the lease is neither property of the bankruptcy estate (due to forfeiture) and is not needed for an effective reorganization (there is nothing for a trustee to assume or assign).

Be sure to include, if true, that the tenant has not paid or offered any rent for any month after filing bankruptcy. This matters, because to prevent eviction in a Chapter 13, the tenant has to pay all the rent as it comes due and keep the lease current.

Below are two sets of sample forms for guidance. The first form uses the mandatory Central District Filing forms and needs a supplemental declaration (you can use the declaration in the second set).

The second set of sample forms gives you the generic version of a motion where no mandatory court form exists. You can also use the generic declaration as a model for the supplemental declaration for the Central District.

Setting the Date

Once you have prepared your papers and you're ready to move forward with your filing, find a date for the hearing. You should first check the individual courtroom assignments for standing orders or information on setting motions.

Every bankruptcy case has been assigned to a single department. It should be listed on the papers you received from the tenant.

Most courts have preset motion days. Otherwise, you can call the courtroom clerk or courtroom deputy and ask how to "calendar" (set a date for) a court hearing on a motion for relief from the automatic stay. The court might reserve the date or just tell you what date to pick, depending on the individual judge's preferences.

Filing the Papers

File the original documents, including a Proof of Service by Mail (see the next section), with the bankruptcy court. Be sure to attach relevant eviction documents to the Declaration in Support of Motion for Relief From Automatic Stay, including copies of the complaint you filed in the eviction lawsuit; the tenant's answer, if any; and any judgment. Label each attachment (on the bottom of the form) as "Exhibit A," "Exhibit B," and so on.

A few courts allow nonattorneys to use the court's online filing system (ask the clerk whether your court is one of them). If online filing is available, you might have to register as a filer at https://pacer.psc.uscourts.gov/pscof/regWizard.jsf. Also, check the court's website—courts are developing new online capabilities in response to social distancing needs.

Other options include filing in person at the court (best option), using a qualified filing service, or mailing the documents to the bankruptcy court. If you are filing in person and live a great distance from the bankruptcy court, you might want to take along extra copies of pleading paper and a laptop so you can fix the papers on the spot and reprint them at a library or FedEx. Also, take your checkbook. You must pay a $188 filing fee, and the clerk who makes copies will charge you 50 cents or more a page.

When you make copies of your motion papers, make a set for yourself, the tenant, and anyone else who must receive copies (see the next section), plus an extra few copies for the court clerk.

Mailing the Motion Papers and Preparing a Proof of Service

Someone over age 18 who isn't a party to the eviction case must mail copies of your motion papers to tenants who have filed bankruptcy; their bankruptcy attorney, if any; the "trustee" (a person appointed by the bankruptcy court to oversee the bankruptcy); and all the creditors listed on the debtor's bankruptcy papers. The trustee's and creditors' names and addresses should be listed on the tenant's bankruptcy papers; you can also get this information from the court clerk or by using Pacer.

If the tenant has numerous creditors and you have online Pacer access, here's a handy tip: You can speed up the process by printing out the names and addresses of the creditors on inexpensive mailing labels. You'll find a list formatted just for that purpose on the tenant's case page.

The person who mails the motion papers must complete and sign a Proof of Service by Mail, which you will attach to the original Notice of Motion for Relief From Automatic Stay that you file with the court.

FORM

A sample copy of the Proof of Service by Mail shown above, and the form can be downloaded from the Nolo website. (See the appendix for the link to the forms in this book and information on using the forms.)

CAUTION

Prepare your forms carefully. Your documents should look something like the samples shown above. However, it is crucial that you adapt the documents according to your own particular circumstances, based on the facts you know to be true.

Preparing for the Hearing

If the debtor files and sends you an opposition paper, study it before the hearing. Go through your records and jot down some notes in response to each argument the debtor raises. For instance, you might want to get statements from appraisers stating that the tenant's rent is not below market rate, to show that the lease is not a valuable asset, if that issue was raised by the debtor or trustee. Or, you might want to make copies of your monthly mortgage payment bills to show that you are suffering a hardship because the tenant is delaying eviction with bankruptcy.

If You Want to Hire an Attorney

If you don't want to represent yourself in filing a motion for relief from the automatic stay, you need to hire an attorney. But be careful—not just any attorney will do. You will want to hire an attorney with experience representing creditors in bankruptcy. If you know other landlords who have used bankruptcy attorneys, call for a referral. (See "Attorneys and Eviction Services" in Chapter 1 for advice on finding and hiring an attorney.)

Call one and ask if the lawyer handles motions for relief from automatic stays for landlords. You don't want someone for whom your case will be the first. One quick way to determine experience is to ask if the lawyer is a registered e-filer with the bankruptcy court. Attorneys who practice in federal courts, including bankruptcy, must register for electronic filing, and are not likely to register unless they expect to be in court often enough to warrant it.

If the lawyer is registered and handles motions for relief from automatic stays for landlords, explain that a tenant filed bankruptcy to delay your eviction and that you'd like to hire the lawyer to file a motion for relief from the automatic stay. Ask what the fee is, assuming one court appearance. Anything much above $1,500 is excessive. If the attorney bills by the hour, ask for an estimate of how many hours the job should take—and get it in writing before you agree.

1 LENNY D. LANDLORD
   12345 Angeleno Street
2 Los Angeles, CA 90010
   Tel: 213-555-1234
3

4 Creditor and Moving Party in Pro Se

5

6

7

8   UNITED STATES BANKRUPTCY COURT
             CENTRAL DISTRICT OF CALIFORNIA
9

10 In re:) Case No. 292-12345-ABCDE
)
11 TERRENCE D. TENANT,   ) CHAPTER 7
    TILLIE D. TENANT   )
) R.S. No. _____
12   )
)
13   Debtors.   ) Hearing Date: 9/15/xx
    _____) Time: 10:00 AM

14

15   NOTICE OF MOTION FOR RELIEF FROM AUTOMATIC STAY

16 TO TERRENCE D. TENANT AND TILLIE D. TENANT, DEBTORS,
    AND TO THEIR ATTORNEY OF RECORD:

17   PLEASE TAKE NOTICE that on September 15, 20xx, at 10:00 AM, in the above-entitled Court, at 312

18 North Spring Street, Los Angeles, California, Creditor LENNY D. LANDLORD will move for relief from the

19 automatic stay herein, with regard to obtaining a judgment in state court that includes possession of the

20 real property at 6789 Angel Street, Apartment 10, Los Angeles, California. The grounds for the motion are

21 set forth in the accompanying motion and declaration.

22   You, and the trustee in this case, are advised that no written response is required to oppose this

23 motion, and that no oral testimony will normally be permitted in opposition to the motion. You and/or

24 your attorney, or other party including the trustee, however, must appear to oppose the motion or the

25 relief requested may be granted. Applicable law is 11 U.S.C. § 362, Bankruptcy Rules 4001 and 9014, and <u>In</u>

26 <u>re Smith</u> (C.D. Cal. 1989) 105 B.R. 50, or C.C.P. § 715.050.

27 Date: August 30, 20xx   *Lenny D. Landlord*
                                              _____
28   Lenny D. Landlord
                                              Creditor in Pro Per

---

1 LENNY D. LANDLORD
12345 Angeleno Street
2 Los Angeles, CA 90010
Tel: 213-555-1234
3

4 Creditor and Moving Party in Pro Per

5

6

7

8

9   UNITED STATES BANKRUPTCY COURT
                         CENTRAL DISTRICT OF CALIFORNIA

In re:	) Case No. 292-12345-ABCDE
10	)
TERRENCE D. TENANT,	) CHAPTER 7
11 TILLIE D. TENANT	)
	) R.S. No. _____
12	)
Debtors.	) Hearing Date: 9/15/xx
13	) Time: 10:00 AM

14

15   <u>MOTION FOR RELIEF FROM AUTOMATIC STAY</u>

16   Creditor LENNY D. LANDLORD moves this Court for an Order granting relief from the automatic stay, on

17 the following grounds:

18   On August 15, 20xx, Debtors filed a petition under Chapter 7 of the U.S. Bankruptcy Code.

19   Debtors occupy the real property at 6789 Angel Street, Apartment 10, Los Angeles, California, pursuant

20 to a tenancy from month to month. Debtors failed to pay the rent of $900 for the period of August 1, 20xx,

21 to August 31, 20xx, and have paid no rent for any period subsequent. As a result, on August 5, 20xx, Creditor

22 served Debtors with a three-day notice to pay rent or quit, to which Debtors failed to respond. Creditor filed an

23 unlawful detainer action entitled Landlord v. Tenant, Case No. A-12345-B, in the Superior Court of California for

24 the County of Los Angeles, on August 9, 20xx. Creditor obtained against Debtors a judgment for possession of

25 the premises on August 15, 20xx.

26   Creditor is informed and believes that Debtors filed the petition in bankruptcy solely to avoid execution

27 of any judgment for possession of real property in the state court proceeding, and without intending to seek

28 the fresh start provided under Title 11 of the U.S. Code. In addition, as evidence of bad faith in their bankruptcy

1

2

3

4

5

6

7

8

9

10

11

12

13

14

15

16

17

18

19

20

21

22

23

24

25

26

27

28

filing, Debtors filed only a "skeleton petition" and listed this Creditor as the only substantial creditor in the case. Creditor attaches his declaration under penalty of perjury, which includes true copies of all litigation documents in the state court unlawful detainer proceeding.

Date: _August 30, 20xx_   *Lenny D. Landlord*
                                      Lenny D. Landlord
                                      Creditor in Pro Per

1

LENNY D. LANDLORD
12345 Angeleno Street

2

Los Angeles, CA 90010
Tel: 213-555-1234

3

4

Creditor and Moving Party in Pro Per

5

6

7

8

UNITED STATES BANKRUPTCY COURT
CENTRAL DISTRICT OF CALIFORNIA

9

10

In re:) Case No. 292-12345-ABCDE
)

11

TERRENCE D. TENANT,   ) CHAPTER 7
TILLIE D. TENANT,   )

12

) R.S. No. _____
)

13

Debtors.   ) Hearing Date: 9/15/xx
_____   ) Time: 10:00 AM

14

DECLARATION IN SUPPORT OF MOTION FOR RELIEF FROM AUTOMATIC STAY

15

16

I, LENNY D. LANDLORD, declare:

17

I am over the age of 18 years. I am the moving party in the above-entitled action. If called as a witness,

18

I could testify competently to the following:

19

On August 9, 20xx, I caused to be filed in the Superior Court of the State of California, for the County

20

of Los Angeles, Los Angeles Judicial District, a verified complaint in unlawful detainer, a copy of which is

21

attached hereto as Exhibit "A." The case number is A-12345-B. All the allegations stated therein are true to

22

my knowledge.

23

I obtained a judgment for possession of the real property at 6789 Angel Street, Apartment 10, Los

24

Angeles, California, in the state-court action against Debtors, on August 15, 20xx.

25

As is indicated in the unlawful detainer complaint, the tenancy is a residential month-to-month

26

tenancy. I am the owner of the premises. In my opinion, the rent that Debtors agreed to pay as alleged in

27

the unlawful detainer complaint is the reasonable rental value of the premises.

28

Debtors remain in possession of the premises. I will suffer irreparable harm if the automatic stay is not

1 vacated as to enforcement of any judgment for possession of the real property, because each day I incur

2 additional costs as the result of Debtors' nonpayment of rent and their failure to vacate the premises, in

3 that I must make mortgage payments on the property while I am unable to rent it to prospective tenants,

4 other than Debtors, who would pay rent that I could use to defray the mortgage.

5   I am informed and believe that the tenancy is not a sellable asset of the bankruptcy estate, so that

6 continued possession of the real property by Debtors is not necessary to freeze their assets for sale to

7 benefit their creditors or to effect any reorganization by Debtors.

8   I declare under penalty of perjury under the laws of the United States that the foregoing is true and

9 correct.

10

11 Date: _August 30, 20xx_   _Lenny D. Landlord_

                                 Lenny D. Landlord

12   Creditor in Pro Per

13

14

15

16

17

18

19

20

21

22

23

24

25

26

27

28

1   LENNY D. LANDLORD
     12345 Angeleno Street
2   Los Angeles, CA 90010
     Tel: 213-555-1234
3

     Creditor and Moving Party in Pro Per
4

5

6

7

8   UNITED STATES BANKRUPTCY COURT
                    CENTRAL DISTRICT OF CALIFORNIA
9

10   In re:) Case No. 292-12345-ABCDE
)
11   TERRENCE D. TENANT,   ) CHAPTER 7
     TILLIE D. TENANT   )
12   ) R.S. No. _____
)
13   Debtors.   ) Hearing Date: 9/15/xx
   _____) Time: 10:00 AM
14

15   ORDER GRANTING RELIEF FROM AUTOMATIC STAY

16   The motion of Creditor LENNY D. LANDLORD for relief from the automatic stay under 11 U.S.C.

17 § 362 came on for hearing in the above-entitled Court on September 15, 20xx, at 10:00 AM; the Creditor

18 appearing in pro per. The Court having taken the matter under submission following argument:

19   It is hereby ordered that Creditor LENNY D. LANDLORD have relief from the automatic stay provided

20 by Debtors' filing of the petition in this case, in that Creditor may proceed with the prosecution of the

21 state court unlawful detainer action of Landlord v. Tenant, et al., Case No. A-12345-B, in the Superior Court

22 of California for the County of Los Angeles, Los Angeles Division, and that Creditor may execute on any

23 judgment for possession or restitution of the premises at 6789 Angel Street, Apartment 10, Los Angeles,

24 California, notwithstanding the pendency of the within-entitled action.

25   Date: _____ , 20_____

26   _____
                            United States Bankruptcy Judge

27

28

PROOF OF SERVICE BY MAIL

My address is _____ 123 Main Street _____

_____ Los Angeles _____, California.

On _August 30_ , 20_xx_ , I served the within: _Notice of Motion for Relief From Automatic Stay,_

Declaration in Support of Motion for Relief From Automatic Stay, and Proposed Order Granting Relief

From Automatic Stay _____

_____

by depositing true copies thereof, enclosed in separate, sealed envelopes, with the postage thereon fully

prepaid, in the United States Postal Service mail in _Los Angeles_ _____ County, addressed as follows:

_____ Terrence D. Tenant _____

_____ Tillie D. Tenant _____

_____ 6789 Angel Street, Apt. 10 _____

_____ Los Angeles, CA 90010 _____

_____ (Debtors) _____

_____

_____ Thomas T. Trustee _____

_____ 12345 Business Boulevard _____

_____ Los Angeles, CA 90010 _____

_____ (Trustee) _____

_____

_____ Lana L. Lawyer _____

_____ 246 Litigation Lane _____

_____ Los Angeles, CA 90010 _____

_____ (Debtors' Attorney) _____

I am, and was at the time herein-mentioned mailing took place, a resident of or employed in the County

where the mailing occurred, over the age of eighteen years old, and not a party to the within cause.

I declare under penalty of perjury under the laws of California and of the United States of America that

the foregoing is true and correct.

Date: _August 30_ , _20xx_

Samuel D. Server _____

Signature   Samuel D. Server

The Bankruptcy Court Hearing

The day before the hearing, check online for a preliminary decision issued by the judge. If you find one, you'll either learn the direction the judge is leaning or find out that you don't have to show up.

On the day of the hearing, arrive at the bankruptcy courtroom about a half-hour early. If there are several courtrooms, and you don't know where your motion will be heard, check the calendar that is usually posted outside each courtroom. Typically, bankruptcy courts hear many cases, and many different types of motions, on a given day and time. If a calendar is not posted, or if you can't find your case on the list, check with the court clerk.

Once you find the correct courtroom, pay attention to the cases that are called before yours —even if the motions are not similar to yours— to get a feel for how the judge conducts hearings.

When your case is called, walk up to the podium, state your name, and say that you are appearing "in pro se, or without an attorney." If the tenants and their attorney show up, they should identify themselves, too. Because you are the party making the motion, the judge may ask you questions or ask you to speak first. Very briefly summarize the points you made in your papers and be sure you can back up your assertions. For example, you may want to say:

- The bankruptcy was filed only after you filed the unlawful detainer lawsuit in court or just before the eviction was to take place.
- The tenancy is from month to month.
- The tenancy is not a valuable asset of the bankruptcy estate because the rent you're charging is not significantly less than the fair-market rental.
- The tenant filed only a "skeleton petition," without detailed schedules of assets and liabilities.
- The tenant listed only a few creditors, including you.

- The tenant hasn't paid any rent that came due after the tenant filed bankruptcy.

Whether or not the tenant shows up (many don't), the hearing will probably be very brief. The judge may ask you some questions, but hearings are not like trials. The facts supporting your motion should have been included in your declaration.

The judge will probably decide on the spot whether to grant the motion. If the judge grants your motion, ask the judge to use the proposed Order Granting Relief From Automatic Stay. If the judge won't sign your order, ask if you should prepare one with different language, or whether the judge will prepare one and, if so, when that will be ready.

Once the judge signs the order, give a copy of it to the court clerk or the sheriff or marshal performing the eviction. They might require a certified copy of the order. If so, you will have to pay the bankruptcy court clerk's office a small fee for a certified copy. You're now ready to proceed with your eviction.

Chapter 13 Considerations with a Term Lease

The relief from stay motion in this book assumes that you have a month-to-month lease with a judgment for possession. Although it rarely happens, you might have a term lease (such as for a year) and a tenant who wants to pay and stay, particularly in a Chapter 13 case.

In that situation, the tenant may have the right to stay, but only if the tenant abides completely by the lease terms, repays any arrearages within a "reasonable time" (usually 30 days), and pays the rent in full and on time while the case proceeds.

If your tenant has filed a Chapter 13 bankruptcy with the aim of keeping the lease, you should consult an experienced creditors' rights attorney.

Evicting Tenants in Rental Property Purchased at Foreclosure

If you have purchased occupied rental property at a foreclosure sale, you have likely inherited the tenants too. If you want to do an eviction based simply on your having foreclosed (as opposed to your tenant's later failing to pay rent), you have extremely few options. Also, you cannot use the forms described in this book. That's because according to the Judicial Council itself, the forms cannot be used when an eviction is carried out under C.C.P. § 1161a. That's the section used for evictions following foreclosure. You'll need to see a lawyer.

Here's an explanation of the legal battlefield you have entered as a landlord of foreclosed property. Formerly, before the 2008 mortgage crisis and the COVID pandemic, if the tenant's lease predated the mortgage later foreclosed upon, the foreclosure nullified the lease under common law. Because most leases last no longer than a year, nearly every mortgage predated any given lease. The old law gave the occupants (they were no longer tenants) 60 days' written notice to vacate, or 30 days if a former mortgagor lived with the tenant. (C.C.P. §§ 1161a, 1161b.) This was true whether the lease was for a fixed term or just month to month.

These harsh results for tenants on leases signed after the mortgage was recorded changed dramatically in 2009 (leases signed before the mortgage was recorded continue to survive under common law). Under current state law (C.C.P. § 1161b(b)), when a loan is foreclosed upon, even postmortgage leases now survive a foreclosure—meaning the tenant can stay at least until the end of the lease. Month-to-month tenants lacking just cause eviction protection receive 90 days' notice before having to move out This notice period is even longer than the normal 30-day or 60-day notice required to terminate a month-to-month tenancy.

If you purchased the property at a foreclosure sale and intend to live on the property, you don't have to honor a lease that was signed postmortgage, but can give 90 days' notice as long as just cause does not apply. Foreclosure sales do not, in themselves, constitute just cause under the TPA or local rent control ordinances. And remember that leases signed premortgage remain in effect, regardless of your desire to move right in.

There are some important qualifications for tenants with leases who insist you honor them, and for month-to-month tenants to be entitled to the full 90 days' notice. The tenants must be "bona fide" tenants, which will be true if all of the following are true:

- The tenant isn't the spouse, child, or parent of the former owner.
- The leasing transaction between the tenant and the former owner was conducted in an "arm's length" transaction.
- The rent isn't "substantially below" fair market value.

This ability of a new owner to oust a tenant on 90 days' notice applies only where the individual wanting to live in the property is the purchaser *at the foreclosure sale*, not where the bank becomes the owner and then later sells to an individual. If you are a buyer at such a later sale, you must honor the lease because the bank was required to do so, and you bought the property subject to that lease.

The new law also means that a new owner, whether a bank or an individual who bought it from a bank as an investor, can insist that the tenant comply with the lease or rental agreement the tenant entered into with the old owner. This means that on the first rent due date after the property changes hands, the tenant must pay the same rent to you, the new owner. If the tenant doesn't pay, you can give that tenant a Three-Day Notice to Pay Rent or Quit if necessary (assuming you have given all the change of ownership notices required by law).

In sum, for postmortgage leases, when you purchase the property at a foreclosure sale, you become the new landlord of any bona fide tenants in the property and must honor the lease. You can terminate that fixed-term lease with a 90-day notice only if you intend to live there as your *primary* residence. In the case of a month-to-month tenancy, you must give 90 days' notice of termination of tenancy.

These changes in the laws concerning tenants in foreclosed properties also affect unnamed occupants. In general, unnamed occupants can assert rights during your eviction lawsuit that might cause you to have to begin all over again (see "Service on Unknown Occupants (Optional)" in Chapter 6). To avoid this eventuality, you should prepare the Prejudgment Claim of Right to Possession form, and your process server should serve it on any unnamed occupants the server learns of. These occupants have ten days to respond. But unnamed occupants whose landlord (the prior owner) lost the property to foreclosure can file the claim *at any time* prior to judgment.

Tenants often learn of the foreclosure after the sale occurs, not before, and have little opportunity to protect themselves in the dust-up between lenders, investors, and the debtors. Individual purchasers at the sale may know nothing of the occupants when they bid on the property. The new relationship begins with a series of feints and probes between the new owner and the occupants.

Consequently, the Judicial Council prejudgment form states prominently at the top that unnamed occupants whose landlord lost the property to foreclosure may file the form at any time. The upshot is that in a foreclosure situation, serving the prejudgment claim form is crucial to identify and deal with every possible occupant of the property as soon as possible.

Month-to-month tenants who live in cities with just cause eviction protection, including many cities with rent control as well as San Diego, Glendale, and Maywood, and tenants covered by the TPA or renting under the Section 8 federal subsidy program, are also protected from terminations at the hands of acquiring banks or new owners. These tenants can rely on the laws' list of allowable reasons for termination (or the just cause list in the Section 8 lease addendum). Because a change of ownership, without more, does not justify a termination under the lists of allowable reasons to evict, the fact that the change occurred through foreclosure will not justify a termination.

However, all of the just cause lists presently include an owner's wish to move into a unit (or move in a qualified family member) as a just cause; for Section 8 tenancies, an owner's desire to use the unit for personal or family use is a just cause only after the initial term of the tenancy. So a new owner who wants to do an "owner move-in" eviction on month-to-month tenants may do so, as long as the owner complies with the ordinance or state law procedures.

Also, like any new owner, you must advise your tenants in writing, per Civ. Code § 1962, of the name and street address (not P.O. box address) of the person (you or a manager) authorized to accept rent payments. Effective January 1, 2013, you cannot base any rent nonpayment eviction (topic of Chapter 2) on any rent that accrued prior to your giving the tenant notice in this regard.

 SEE AN EXPERT

Some foreclosure situations require a lawyer's help. If you have any questions about evicting a tenant in a property purchased at foreclosure, be sure to get help from an experienced attorney. And you will definitely need to see a lawyer if you bought property at a foreclosure sale and need to evict the former owner, who has not moved out; in this case, you must use a special unlawful detainer complaint, unlike the forms contained in this book.

How to Use the Downloadable Forms on the Nolo Website

The forms in this book are available at

www.nolo.com/back-of-book/LBEV.html

To use the files, your computer must have specific software programs installed. Here is a list of types of files provided by this book, as well as the software programs you'll need to access them.

RTF. You can open, edit, print, and save these form files with most word processing programs, such as Microsoft *Word*, Windows *WordPad*, and recent versions of *WordPerfect*.

PDF. You can view these files with Adobe *Reader*, free software from www.adobe.com. Judicial Council PDFs are fillable using your computer, and can also be printed and completed by hand.

See below for advice on using Judicial Council forms.

Editing RTFs

Here are some general instructions about editing RTF forms in your word processing program. Refer to the book's instructions and sample agreements for help about what should go in each blank.

- **Underlines.** Underlines indicate where to enter information. After filling in the needed text, delete the underline. In most word processing programs, you can do this by highlighting the underlined portion and typing CTRL-U.
- **Bracketed and italicized text.** Bracketed and italicized text indicates instructions. Be sure to remove all instructional text before you finalize your document.
- **Optional text.** Optional text gives you the choice to include or exclude text. Delete any optional text you don't want to use. Renumber numbered items, if necessary.
- **Alternative text.** Alternative text gives you the choice between two or more text options. Delete those options you don't want to use. Renumber numbered items, if necessary.
- **Signature lines.** Signature lines should appear on a page with at least some text from the document itself.

Every word processing program uses different commands to open, format, save, and print documents, so refer to your software's help documents for help using your program. Nolo cannot provide technical support for questions about how to use your computer or your software.

(!) **CAUTION**
In accordance with U.S. copyright laws, the forms provided by this book are for your personal use only.

Using Judicial Council and Government Forms

The Nolo website includes government forms in Adobe *Acrobat* PDF format. These form files were created by the government (usually the Judicial Council), not by Nolo.

To use them, you need Adobe *Reader* installed on your computer. If you don't already have this software, you can download it for free at www.adobe.com.

In addition to being available on the Nolo website, the Judicial Council forms are available at www. courts.ca.gov/forms.htm. To find a specific Judicial Council form on the courts website, just search for the name of the form and the form number. The Judicial Council forms will have the words Judicial Council of California in the bottom left-hand corner of the form with the revision date and a form number; the form number also appears in the upper right; for example, the Judgment—Unlawful Detainer is Judicial Council Form UC-110.

Special Requirements for Motions and Declarations

The sample motions and declarations in this book are all printed on "pleading paper" (8.5" × 11" paper with numbered lines and a vertical line on the left). The purpose of the numbers is to allow judges or lawyers to easily refer to portions of a document (for example, you might want to refer to "Line 12 of Plaintiff's motion"). The RTF form files in this book use a legal template that includes these features. When you print your document, the line and numbers will show. Most recent versions of Microsoft *Word* support this pleading paper template.

If Your Word Processor Doesn't Support the Pleading Paper Format

If your word processor doesn't support the pleading paper format—that is, when you print out your document, the lines are not numbered on the left—you'll need to manually insert pages of lined pleading paper into your printer and print your motions and declarations on them. A blank sheet of pleading paper has been included in the forms listed below as PLEADING.pdf.

As you might expect, there are rules (California Rule of Court 2.100–2.119) regarding what should be typed on which lines. While you may find these ridiculously picky, ignore them at your peril. Officious clerks have been known to reject papers that don't comply.

To read these and other relevant rules, go to the Judicial Council website at www.courts.ca.gov/rules. Choose Title Two of the Rules.

List of Forms Available on the Nolo Website

Use the tables below to find the file name for each form.

The following files are included as RTF files and are available for download at www.nolo.com/back-of-book/LBEV.html

Form Title	File Name	Discussed in Chapter
Three-Day Notice to Pay Rent or Quit	3-DayNoticeRent.rtf	2
30-Day Notice of Termination of Tenancy	30-DayNotice.rtf	3
60-Day Notice of Termination of Tenancy	60-DayNotice.rtf	3
90-Day Notice of Termination of Tenancy	90-DayNotice.rtf	3
Three-Day Notice to Perform Covenant or Quit	3-DayNoticeCovenant.rtf	4
Three-Day Notice to Quit	3-DayNoticeQuit.rtf	4
Verification of Partnership by Plaintiff	Partnership.rtf	6
Declaration in Support of Default Judgment for Rent, Damages, and Costs	DeclarationRDC.rtf	7
Declaration in Support of Default Judgment for Damages and Costs (Violation of Lease)	DeclarationDC.rtf	7
Settlement Agreement	Settlement.rtf	8
Questionnaire for Judgment-Debtor Examination	Questionnaire.rtf	9
Proof of Service by Mail	ProofofService.rtf	10

The following files are in Adobe *Acrobat* PDF format and are available for download at:
www.nolo.com/back-of-book/LBEV.html
These are all Judicial Council forms except for three Los Angeles County forms noted below.

Form Title	File Name	Discussed in Chapter
Summons—Unlawful Detainer—Eviction	sum130.pdf	6
Proof of Service of Summons	pos010.pdf	6
Complaint—Unlawful Detainer	ud100.pdf	6
Civil Case Cover Sheet	cm010.pdf	6
Plaintiff's Mandatory Cover Sheet and Supplemental Allegations—Unlawful Detainer	ud101.pdf	6
Civil Case Cover Sheet Addendum and Statement of Location (L.A. form)	LACIV109.pdf	6
Attachment to Judicial Council Form	mc-025.pdf	6
Application and Order to Serve Summons by Posting for Unlawful Detainer (L.A. form)	LACIV107.pdf	6
Prejudgment Claim of Right to Possession	cp105.pdf	6
Blank Pleading Paper	PLEADING.pdf	6
Request for Entry of Default	civ100.pdf	7
Request for Dismissal	CIV110.pdf	7
Writ of Execution	ej130.pdf	7, 8, 9
Declaration	MC030.pdf	7
Application for Issuance of Writ of Execution, Possession or Sale (L.A. form)	LACIV096.pdf	7
Declaration for Default Judgment by Court	ud116.pdf	7
Judgment—Unlawful Detainer	ud110.pdf	7, 8
Notice of Remote Appearance	ra010.pdf	8
Stipulation for Entry of Judgment	ud115.pdf	8
Answer—Unlawful Detainer	ud105.pdf	8
Request/Counter-Request to Set Case for Trial—Unlawful Detainer	ud150.pdf	8
Judgment—Unlawful Detainer Attachment	ud110s.pdf	8
Form 5-2b, Request for Change of Address or Boxholder Information Needed for Service of Legal Process	USPSAddressChange.pdf	9
Application and Order for Appearance and Examination	ej125.pdf	9
Application for Earnings Withholding Order (Wage Garnishment)	wg001.pdf	9
Confidential Statement of Judgment Debtor's Social Security Number	wg035.pdf	9
Acknowledgment of Satisfaction of Judgment	ej100.pdf	9
Proof of Personal Service—Civil	pos020.pdf	10

Index

M